WITHDRAWN BY THE
UNIVERSITY OF MICHIGAN

Radical democracy

Manchester University Press

REAPPRAISING THE POLITICAL

Simon Tormey and Jon Simons · series editors

The times we live in are troubling, and as always theory struggles to keep pace with events in its efforts to analyse and assess society, culture and politics. Many of the 'contemporary' political theories emerged and developed in the twentieth century or earlier, but how well do they work at the start of the twenty-first century?

Reappraising the Political realigns political theory with its contemporary context. The series is interdisciplinary in approach, seeking new inspiration from both traditional sister disciplines, and from more recent neighbours such as literary theory and cultural studies. It encompasses an international range, recognising both the diffusion and adaptation of Western political thought
in the rest of the world, and the impact of global processes and non-Western ideas on Western politics.

edited by Lars Tønder and Lasse Thomassen

RADICAL DEMOCRACY

Politics between abundance
and lack

Manchester University Press
Manchester and New York

distributed exclusively in the USA by Palgrave

Copyright © Manchester University Press 2005

While copyright in the volume as a whole is vested in Manchester University Press, copyright in individual chapters belongs to their respective authors, and no chapter may be reproduced wholly or in part without the express permission in writing of both author and publisher.

Published by Manchester University Press
Oxford Road, Manchester M13 9NR, UK
and Room 400, 175 Fifth Avenue, New York, NY 10010, USA
www.manchesteruniversitypress.co.uk

Distributed exclusively in the USA by
Palgrave, 175 Fifth Avenue, New York, NY 10010, USA

Distributed exclusively in Canada by
UBC Press, University of British Columbia, 2029 West Mall, Vancouver, BC, Canada V6T 1Z2

British Library Cataloguing-in-Publication Data
A catalogue record for this book is available from the British Library

Library of Congress Cataloging-in-Publication Data applied for

ISBN 0 7190 7044 9 *hardback*
EAN 978 0 7190 7044 0

First published 2005

13 12 11 10 09 08 07 06 05   10 9 8 7 6 5 4 3 2 1

Typeset in Minion by Action Publishing Technology Ltd, Gloucester
Printed in Great Britain
by CPI, Bath

Contents

Contributors	page vii
Acknowledgements	ix
Introduction: rethinking radical democracy between abundance and lack LARS TØNDER AND LASSE THOMASSEN	1

I RADICAL DEMOCRACY: ABUNDANCE AND/OR LACK?

1 The absence at the heart of presence: radical democracy and the 'ontology of lack' OLIVER MARCHART	17
2 Two routes from Hegel NATHAN WIDDER	32
3 Deleuze and democratic politics PAUL PATTON	50
4 The wild patience of radical democracy: beyond Žižek's lack ROMAND COLES	68
5 Theorising hegemony: between deconstruction and psychoanalysis ALETTA J. NORVAL	86
6 In/exclusions: towards a radical democratic approach to exclusion LASSE THOMASSEN	103

II THE POLITICS OF RADICAL DEMOCRACY

7 For an agonistic public sphere CHANTAL MOUFFE	123
8 In parliament with things JANE BENNETT	133
9 The radical democratic possibilities of popular culture JON SIMONS	149
10 Radical and plural democracy: in defence of right/left and public reason TORBEN BECH DYRBERG	167
11 Negativity and democratic politics: radical democracy beyond reoccupation and conformism YANNIS STAVRAKAKIS	185
12 Inessential commonality: immanence, transcendence, abundance LARS TØNDER	203
13 True democracy: Marx, political subjectivity and anarchic meta-politics SIMON CRITCHLEY	219

Contents

III AFTERWORDS

14 Immanence, abundance, democracy   WILLIAM E. CONNOLLY   239

15 The future of radical democracy   ERNESTO LACLAU   256

Index   263

Contributors

JANE BENNETT is Professor of Political Science at Johns Hopkins University and a founding member of the journal *theory & event*. Her recent publications include *The Enchantment of Modern Life* (Princeton, 2001), 'The Force of Things: Steps Toward an Ecology of Matter' (*Political Theory*, June 2004) and 'The Agency of Assemblages' (*Public Culture*, 2005). She is currently working on a book that explores the ecological implications of different conceptions of materiality in contemporary political thought.

ROMAND COLES is Associate Professor of Political Science at Duke University. He is the author of numerous articles in journals such as *Political Theory, Polity, American Political Science Review*, and *Modern Theology*. His books are *Self/Power/Other: Political Theory and Dialogical Ethics* (1992), *Rethinking Generosity: Critical Theory and the Politics of Caritas* (1997) and *Moving Democracy* (2005).

WILLIAM E. CONNOLLY is Krieger-Eisenhower Professor of Politics at Johns Hopkins University, and is the former editor of the journal *Political Theory*. His book *The Terms of Political Discourse* won the Benjamin Lippert Award in 1999, an award given for an outstanding achievement still significant 15 years after its publication. His recent books include *Identity\Difference: Democratic Negotiations of Political Paradox* (2nd edition, 2002), *The Ethos of Pluralization* (1995), *Why I am not a Secularist* (1999) and *Neuropolitics: Thinking, Culture, Speed* (2002). His latest book is *Pluralism* (2005).

SIMON CRITCHLEY is Professor of Philosophy at the New School for Social Research, New York and at the University of Essex. Among his numerous books and other publications are *The Ethics of Deconstruction* (2nd Edition, 1999), *Very Little ... Almost Nothing* (2nd Edition, 2004), *Ethics–politics–subjectivity: Derrida, Levinas and Contemporary French Thought* (1999), *On Humour* (2002), and *Things Merely Are* (2005). He is currently writing a book on political ethics.

TORBEN BECH DYRBERG is Lecturer in the Department of Social Sciences at Roskilde University, Denmark. His research interests cover theories of power, democracy and political identification, and his publications include *The Circular Structure of Power* (1997) as well as articles and edited books on post-structuralist political and social theory, nationalist, racist and populist trends in politics today, and the right/left distinction.

ERNESTO LACLAU is Professor of political theory at the University of Essex and visiting professor at the Department of Political Science, Northwestern University. He is the co-author, with Chantal Mouffe, of *Hegemony and Socialist Strategy* (1985) and, with Judith Butler and Slavoj Žižek, of *Contingency, Hegemony, Universality* (2000), and the author of, among others, *New Reflections on the Revolution of Our Time* (1990), *Emancipation(s)* (1996) and *On Populist Reason* (2005).

OLIVER MARCHART is Lecturer in Cultural and Media Theory at the University of Basel and in Political Theory at the University of Vienna. His latest books include, in German, *Techno-Colonialism. Theory and Imaginary Cartography of Culture and the Media* (2004) and *Beginning Anew: Hannah Arendt, the World and the Revolution* (2005), and the co-edited *Laclau: A Critical Reader* (2004).

CHANTAL MOUFFE is Professor of Political Theory at the Centre for the Study of Democracy at the University of Westminster. She is the author of, among other

Contributors

works, *Hegemony and Socialist Strategy* (with Ernesto Laclau), *The Return of the Political* (1993), *The Democratic Paradox* (2000) and *On the Political* (2005). Her current research interests include the emergence of right-wing populism in Europe and the critique of liberal and consensual approaches to democracy.

ALETTA J. NORVAL is Reader in the Department of Government, University of Essex, where she teaches political theory and is the Director of the PhD Programme in Ideology and Discourse Analysis. She has published widely on discourse analysis (including a co-edited volume, *Discourse Theory and Political Analysis*), South Africa (including *Deconstruction Apartheid Discourse*), and contemporary critical and post-structuralist political theory. Her current research focuses on issues in democratic theory.

PAUL PATTON is Professor of Philosophy at the University of New South Wales, Australia. His research focuses on issues in social and political philosophy, including colonialism and the rights of indigenous peoples. He has translated work by Deleuze, Baudrillard Nancy and Foucault, and has written widely on post-structuralist and post-modernist thought. His most recent publications include *Deleuze and the Political* (2000) and, as editor, *Deleuze: A Critical Reader* (1996), with D. Ivison and W. Sanders, *Political Theory and the Rights of Indigenous People* (2002) and, with J. Protevi, *Between Deleuze and Derrida* (2003).

JON SIMONS is Senior Lecturer in Critical Theory at the Postgraduate School of Critical Theory and Cultural Studies, University of Nottingham. He is the author of, among others, *Foucault and the Political* (1995) and numerous essays on political, feminist and cultural theory. He is currently preparing a new book, *Politics and Aesthetics: Style, Emotion and Mediation* (Edinburgh University Press and New York University Press).

YANNIS STAVRAKAKIS is Visiting Fellow in the Department of Government, University of Essex. His research interests include politics and psychoanalysis (Freud and Lacan), Green political thought and Greek political culture. His publications include *Lacan and the Political* (1999), the co-edited volumes *Discourse Theory and Political Analysis* (2000) and *Lacan and Science* (2002) and a variety of articles in English, Greek, German, Spanish, Portuguese, Serbo-Croatian, Russian and Japanese.

LASSE THOMASSEN is Teaching Fellow in Political Theory in the Department of Government at the University of Essex. His work and publications focus on Habermas, deconstruction and radical democracy. He is currently working on two book projects: *The Derrida–Habermas Reader* to be published with Edinburgh University Press and *Habermas and Radical Democracy* to be published with Routledge.

LARS TØNDER is a political theorist, trained at the University of Copenhagen (BA, MA) and at the University of Essex (MA). He is writing his PhD dissertation at Johns Hopkins University, USA, where he is also teaching political theory, political economy and American politics. He has published articles, book reviews and papers on post-structuralist theory and theories of democracy and community.

NATHAN WIDDER is Lecturer in political theory at the University of Exeter. His research engages in issues of identity, power, meaning and knowledge, combining strands of contemporary Continental philosophy with strategic engagements with ancient, early Christian and medieval philosophies. He has published articles in *Continental Philosophy Review*, *Contemporary Political Theory*, *European Journal of Political Theory* and *Theory & Event*. He is the author of *Genealogies of Difference* (University of Illinois Press, 2002) and is currently working on a book on time and politics.

Acknowledgements

In the process of preparing this volume, we have acquired a number of debts. First of all, we would like to extend our thanks to all the contributors without whom this volume would not have been possible, and to Jane Bennett, William E. Connolly, Yannis Stavrakakis, Aletta J. Norval and Jon Simons in particular for their continued support and inputs that helped keep us on track. The book started as a co-written paper at the 'Reclaiming Radicalism: Theorizing Contemporary Politics Workshop' at the 2002 Midwest Modern Language Association Conference in Minneapolis, USA, November 2002, and a workshop and two panels at the ISSEI conference in Aberystwyth, Wales, July 2002, and at the PSA Annual Conference, Leicester, England, April 2003 respectively. We would like to thank the participants at these occasions for the feedback they provided us. We would also like to thank Manchester University Press's external reader for comments on the manuscript. Finally, we would like to thank Documenta 11 for permission to reprint, with minor changes, Chantal Mouffe, 'For an agonistic public sphere', in Okwui Enwezor *et al.* (eds), *Documenta11_Platform1: Democracy Unrealized* (Ostfildern-Ruit, Germany: Hatje Cantz, 2002), pp. 87–96 (03–7757–9082–9).

Introduction • Lars Tønder and Lasse Thomassen

Rethinking radical democracy between abundance and lack

CONTRARY to predictions at the time, the fall of the Berlin Wall did not signal the end of history, nor did it indicate a new period of peace and prosperity. Instead, recent years have seen new challenges to democracy, for instance cultural and economic globalisation undermining the nation-state as the unit of democratic government, the emergence of nationalist and xenophobic discourses, and, since the terrorist attacks on 11 September 2001, the curtailment of civil liberties. Faced with these challenges, political theorists have become increasingly dissatisfied with existing models of democracy, which have difficulties capturing the stakes of these new challenges. Moreover, a significant number of theorists have turned their attention to radical democracy, making it one of the most promising areas of contemporary democratic theory.

Inspired by so-called 'post-structuralist' theories of language and power[1], theorists of radical democracy have distinguished themselves from Marxism, liberalism and communitarianism on a number of issues. One example is the rejection by radical democrats of the possibility of founding democracy on a pre-established universality, such as human rights, principles of rational discourse or the teleology of history. Another example is their insistence that social identities are always incomplete and subject to contestation and subversion. However, contrary to popular interpretations of radical democracy, these arguments do not entail an outright rejection of either universality or identity. Rather, radical democrats have reworked the assumptions structuring classical democratic theory, many of which are ontological in nature, outlining a new approach to universality, identity and democracy.

Behind this new approach lies the claim, common to radical democratic thought as a whole, that there is always some difference escaping subsumption to identity or to any simple dichotomy between identity and difference. In the following, we refer to this difference as a 'radical difference', and argue, in agreement with the existing literature on radical democracy, that it entails a view of universality and identity as 'a process or condition irreducible to any of its determinate modes of appearance'.[2] However, we also argue that the existing literature has failed to appreciate the way in which the conceptualisation of radical difference has led to significantly different versions of radical democracy – what we refer to as the ontological imaginary of abundance and the ontological imaginary of lack respectively. These two imaginaries share the idea of a radical difference and the critique of conventional conceptualisations of universality and identity; yet they also differ in the manner in which they approach these questions. For instance, they disagree on whether political analysis should start from the level of signification or from networks of embodied matter. And they disagree on the kind of politics that follows from the idea of radical difference: whereas theorists of lack emphasise the need to build hegemonic constellations, theorists of abundance emphasise never-receding pluralisation.[3]

The purpose of this volume is to examine these disagreements in the context of philosophical considerations as well as concrete concerns about politics and ethics. In what follows, we outline the main features of this context. While radical democracy is not the name of a new political programme, it is nonetheless possible to situate it in relation to, first, Marxism and, then, contemporary liberal and communitarian theories of democracy.

The Marxist legacy: a radical difference

The inspiration that radical democratic theory draws from Karl Marx stems from the way in which Marx discloses the shortcomings of modern democratic theory. The shortcomings concern the very *raison d'être* of democracy. What matters, Marx famously argued, is not the ability of the state to protect individual property, but whether society serves the true purpose of human existence, namely the free and equal development of a self-determining community. Moreover, given Marx's critique of the capitalist mode of production, this argument suggests that the liberal state is too disconnected from the embedded life of citizens, thus setting the stage for a radical democracy based on principles of economic equality and social justice. As Marx and Engels argued: 'In place of the old bourgeois society, with its classes and antagonisms, we shall have an association, in which the free development of each is the condition for the free development of all.'[4]

Nevertheless, this convergence between Marx's thought and contemporary radical democracy has not stopped the latter from being critical of not only Marx but also twentieth-century Marxism. Accordingly, radical democrats declare themselves to be 'post-Marxists' or 'post-structuralists' – that is, they object to the Marxist tendency, often expressed in the name of scientific laws or historical necessities, to turn politics into an epiphenomenon of economic structures. Theorists of radical democracy object to three things in particular.[5] First, they criticise Marxism for its economic determinism, which not only forecloses human agency, but also eliminates the autonomy of political organisation. The proletariat does not have a privileged status as the agent of

Introduction

social change; instead, radical democrats look to other constituencies, such as the new social movements. Second, they criticise Marxism for its essentialism, disputing the possibility of defining human existence with reference to necessary laws about the centrality of labour. And, finally, they criticise Marxism for eradicating historical and philosophical heterogeneity – in short, all that which cannot be subsumed to Marx's conceptual categories – claiming that this risks aligning Marxism with the paradigms of thought that it sought to overcome.

All of these objections hinge on what we earlier called radical difference, that is, a difference that goes beyond the dualism of identity and difference. One way to explain this is with reference to the class-analysis defining most of the Marxist tradition. On the one hand, the class-analysis identifies the capitalist class as those who, as owners of the means of production, seek to maximise surplus value. On the other hand, the same analysis identifies the proletarian class as those who, as a result of the exploitation that comes with the maximisation of surplus value, seek to overturn capitalism. On the face of it, this reveals two clearly demarcated identities, both of which justify themselves with reference to objective but mutually exclusive interests. However, radical democrats argue, the line between the two identities is in fact blurred: although the proletarian and the capitalist appear to be mutually exclusive, they both rely on a difference between what they are and what they are not (that is, the proletarian is *not* capitalist, and the capitalist is *not* proletarian). What is more, this difference is not simply yet another difference, in the sense that it would be possible to subsume it – through a dialectical resolution – under an all-inclusive identity such as a future communist society. Rather, it is a radical difference that – without itself being stable – constitutes the difference between the two identities. This destabilises the identities of both the capitalist and the proletarian, and indicates the futility of searching for an ontological centre that could guarantee the completeness of any social identity. Moreover, radical democrats conclude, it points to the primacy of difference over identity, asking us to accept what is the slogan of radical democracy, namely, that *difference constitutes identity*.[6]

This conclusion has wide-ranging implications for democratic theory. First and foremost, it means that the political is ubiquitous; that is, that the blurring of social identities makes political struggles and conflicts prevalent. In addition, it means that the idea of democracy is inherently open-ended, and that – to paraphrase Jacques Derrida – it is always 'to come', subject to new amendments and untimely contestations.[7] Both of these consequences make radical democracy easy to identify in the context of contemporary democratic theory.

Radical democracy and contemporary democratic theory

While most textbooks define contemporary democratic theory as a debate between liberals and communitarians,[8] the emergence of radical democratic theory as a mature field of study makes it not only possible, but also necessary to add radical democracy as a third element to this debate. In this context, radical democracy resuscitates Marx's critique of modern democratic thought, revealing the shortcomings of both liberalism and communitarianism.

With regard to liberalism, radical democrats do not reject liberal democratic values such as liberty and equality, but argue that we must deepen and radicalise these values. Moreover, radical democrats argue that liberals misconstrue liberty and equality by turning them into abstract rights beyond dispute. The problem with doing so, radical democrats assert, is that it makes difference dependent on a prior commitment to liberal democracy, thereby excluding those political constituencies that challenge liberal interpretations of liberty and equality. In contrast, theorists of radical democracy argue that the foundations of democracy are political 'all the way down', and that this warrants deep contestation of both social identities and political formations in the name of liberty and equality.

Likewise, while radical democrats agree with communitarianism about the context-dependence of democracy, they nonetheless refuse to ground democracy on the identity of a community. Doing so, radical democrats argue, not only overlooks the plural, fluid and criss-crossing character of identity, but also risks stifling the pursuit of democratic pluralism. Rather than simply allowing for different communities to co-exist side-by-side, radical democrats continue, one must put into question the very notion of a community with stable limits. This turns democratic pluralism into a field of contestation, thus making it possible to recognise the existence of differences that escape subsumption to any identity. As Lars Tønder and Simon Critchley argue in their contributions to the volume, radical democracy emphasises identification as an ongoing process rather than fully constituted identities. Like deliberative models of democracy, and against aggregative and communitarian models, radical democrats hold that the political process is constitutive of identities and interests. However, they also object to the deliberative model's assumption that procedures can be rational and can produce rational decisions.

As described above, for radical democrats, democracy is a never-ending process, always to come, and not simply an end-goal or the promise of a perfect democratic society. Yet, the politicisation of its foundations does not undermine democracy *per se*, radical democrats insist, for it entails the pluralisation of perspectives, identities and values, thereby energising democratic practice in a way that other models of democracy are unable to do. Moreover, radical democrats add, the pluralisation that contestation and openness facilitate hinges on the cultivation of agonistic respect; that is, the simultaneous welcoming of radical difference and the questioning of the violence that this welcoming may entail. As the contributions to the volume suggest, this cultivation can take many forms. For instance, in her contribution, Chantal Mouffe argues that an

Introduction

agonistic public sphere may revitalise democracy in a way that deliberative and Third Way approaches are unable to. And in his contribution, Romand Coles looks at alternative ways to organise and influence decision-making procedures and thereby combining the cultivation of agonistic respect with the invigoration of democracy. For both Mouffe and Coles, as for radical democrats generally, politics cannot be reduced to the rational or procedural, but contains an irreducible element of passion.

Even so, although we find a shared commitment to the virtues of contestation and incompleteness, there are also important disagreements among radical democrats, some of which concern the very agenda of radical democracy. In the following, we argue that these disagreements stem from different views of the specific nature of radical difference, reflecting two ontological imaginaries of lack and abundance.

Radical democracy and the ontology of lack

Theorists working within the ontological imaginary of lack conceive of radical difference in terms of a non-symbolisable lack operating at the heart of any subject or system of signification. This idea is most explicitly developed in the psychoanalysis of Jacques Lacan whose thought is the focus of several other theorists of lack, such as Ernesto Laclau and Yannis Stavrakakis.[9]

Lacan's most fundamental claim is that identity is simultaneously constituted and decentred by a constitutive lack. The subject, who is only a subject in language, is constituted through identification with a signifier in language, for instance 'white' or 'male'. However, while this serves to fill the lack and thus constitute the identity of the subject, the filling of the lack is always incomplete and temporary. Identification always fails, the Lacanian argument goes, because it comes up against the limit of signification, which cannot itself be signified within language. Moreover, the limit of signification is not something lying beyond the realm of language, but a lack inherent to language itself. So, while the identity of the subject is constituted through the endless process of filling the lack, the lack itself arises from the failure of this process, thus securing that the identity of the subject remains decentred.

As a consequence of the link between identity and signification, theorists of lack take signification as their starting point for political analysis. The critical aim of political analysis is to show that there is a lack – that is, a radical difference – at the heart of any identity or signification. What is more, theorists of lack argue that, like identity and systems of signification, any political regime is organised around and simultaneously subverted by a constitutive lack. Democracy is a special kind of regime, however, because it institutionalises the continuous reoccupation of the lack in political practices such as periodical elections.[10] Radical democracy, as conceived from the ontological imaginary of lack, radicalises this idea, first, by extending it to every aspect of society and, second, by acknowledging that at the heart of democracy there is no universal principle or stable identity, but only an ineradicable lack. Accordingly, radical democrats inspired by this view of radical difference criticise discourses that seek to cover up the constitutive lack, such as nationalist discourses that construct an essence of the national community, thereby suppressing the inherent contingency and historicity of its identity.

Yet, theorists of lack not only see radical democracy as a source for continual critique; they also seek to articulate hegemonic alternatives, even if these are ultimately destabilised by the lack at the heart of them. Hegemony – the articulation of different constituencies into a whole – describes the formation of political projects such as radical democracy.[11] Although radical democracy foregrounds lack and openness, theorists of lack also argue that this is only possible through some – always partial and temporary – hegemonic closure. In this sense, no democratic project or institution can claim to be beyond contestation, and theorists of lack conclude that the radical democratic challenge consists in finding ways to institute contestation, even if this, paradoxically, always involves some closure.

Radical democracy and the ontology of abundance

There is little doubt that the ontology of lack has become a significant pillar in contemporary radical democratic theory. However, an equally important strand of radical democratic theory is what we call the ontology of abundance, which emphasises networks of materiality, flows of energy, processes of becoming and experimenting modes of affirmation. Moreover, the ontology of abundance points to a second vision of radical democracy, which, inspired by the work of Gilles Deleuze,[12] has become increasingly important to theorists such as Jane Bennett, William E. Connolly, Paul Patton and Nathan Widder.

Deleuze's most important contribution to the theory of radical democracy lies in his insistence on approaching difference in such a way that it involves no necessary connection with notions of failure and lack. The problem with these notions, Deleuze argues, is that they are too constrained by what they negate. For example, in the case of lack, Deleuze suggests that Lacanians are caught by a spectre of structuralism, which does not appreciate the complexity and depth of social life, but instead reduces the experience of difference to a question of failure.[13] Deleuze seeks to avoid this reductionism with the idea of 'the rhizome'. The rhizome adds two new dimensions to the conceptualisation of radical difference. On the one hand, it enables us to see how radical difference operates within contingently defined networks that are capable of synthesising existing differences into something radically new and different. On the other hand, the idea of a rhizome also enables us to make sense of the many outcomes

Introduction

of this synthesis – some of which may be hegemonic in nature – making it appear as if the creation of new differences is governed by the need to fill a pre-existing lack. However, Deleuze stresses that the appearance of a lack is merely secondary to radical difference, which, existing below the threshold of lack and hegemony, keeps propelling new things into being. In his words, the appearance of new things 'presupposes a swarm of differences, a pluralism of free, wild or untamed differences ... one which is determined as an abstract and potential multiplicity'.[14]

So rather than interpreting radical difference in terms of a structural failure, theorists of abundance point to its potentiality when it comes to the empowerment of alternative modes of life. This sets the stage for a radical politics that differs from the one inspired by the ontology of lack in three ways. First, theorists of abundance interpret ethical injunctions and moral commands in light of a sensibility of enchantment, which not only discriminates between those who resent and those who affirm the incompleteness of social life, but also seeks to cultivate an ethics of joy.[15] Second, they outline a critique of existing hegemonies, especially capitalism, and commit themselves to economic reforms based on equality and collectivism, nurturing those components of contemporary societies that are ripe for transformation. Finally, theorists of abundance link the commitment to alternative life-forms to a strategy of pluralisation, which emphasises the virtues of agonistic respect and critical responsiveness.[16] That is, they experiment with those minority groups that, although operating below the radar of existing social codes, may contribute to the deepening of democratic government.

Radical democracy between abundance and lack

The preceding discussion shows how radical democracy stands at a critical junction between two different ontological imaginaries – abundance and lack – each of which conceptualises difference in distinctive ways. One way of summarising the stakes of this discussion is to say that, whereas the ontology of lack conceptualises radical difference in terms of a non-symbolisable lack, the ontology of abundance approaches radical difference as an abstract multiplicity from which contingently defined networks emerge, adding both depth and stature to the flows of experience. As we have seen, two different versions of radical democracy follow from this: one that emphasises the hegemonic nature of politics, and another that cultivates a strategy of pluralisation.

Nevertheless, the discussion about radical democracy should not stop at this point, because the distinction between abundance and lack may itself be contestable. First of all, one may ask what status we should assign to the distinction itself. A modest interpretation would be to see the abundance/lack distinction as a heuristic tool that makes explicit the ontological assumptions of different theories of radical democracy. This interpretation may explain why some theorists of radical democracy insist that their own ontological imaginary accounts for the perspective of their counterpart. Yet, as the contributions to the volume show, there *are* real differences between the two groups of theorists. This not only indicates a correlation between, on the one hand, one's allegiance to a particular ontological imaginary and, on the other hand, one's stance on specific theoretical and political issues, but also the impossibility of reducing radical democracy to a single ontological imaginary. Equally important, one may ask whether there are alternative and, perhaps, more important lines of division within the field of radical democratic thought. An example is the distinction between immanence and transcendence, which has been another focal point in recent discussions of radical democracy.[17] These discussions refer to two different trajectories in contemporary French philosophy: one that agrees with Spinoza's writings on the oneness of Nature, holding that there is nothing outside the field of being (that is, of what is); and another that follows the tradition of negative theology, maintaining that the field of being is never sufficient to itself. Both of these trajectories inform the discussion of radical democracy – indeed, the distinction plays a significant role in Connolly and Laclau's contributions to this volume – and yet they do not simply replicate the distinction between those who subscribe to an ontological imaginary of lack and those subscribing to an imaginary of abundance. Rather, they intersect at various points (for instance, in connection with the issues of time and becoming) and contribute to the ongoing contestation of ontological imaginaries. For this reason, we believe that it is important to consider the relationship between the immanence–transcendence distinction and the one between abundance and lack. Moreover, we conclude that, although the distinction between abundance and lack is more than a heuristic tool, the distinction itself represents a line of division likely to change *pari passu* with further discussions of radical democracy.

In one way or the other, the chapters in this volume all grapple with the abundance/lack distinction and its philosophical and political implications for radical democracy. The chapters in Part I discuss the intellectual implications of the distinction between abundance and lack for the study of radical democracy. In chapter 1, Oliver Marchart sets the stage for a consideration of the advantages and disadvantages of different political ontologies and of the relationship between ontology and politics. Marchart traces the ontology of lack back to Heidegger's ontology and to Kojève's reading of Hegel. This provides the background for the political appropriation of the notion of lack by Alain Badiou, Slavoj Žižek, Ernesto Laclau and Chantal Mouffe, and Claude Lefort. Marchart argues that it is not only necessary to differentiate between different theories of lack, but also to avoid a politics that seeks to bring into being, in a pure form, either lack, abundance or difference.

Introduction

In chapter 2, Nathan Widder continues to unravel the intellectual luggage of radical democracy, showing how the writings of Hegel are looming over contemporary discussions of this particular model of democracy. At issue here are different interpretations of the relationship between identity and difference, a question central to Hegel's work. Through a discussion of different interpretations of desire, Widder argues that theorists of lack – primarily Lacan and his followers – remain caught within the dualism between identity and difference, where the latter is merely conceived as the negation of the former. Instead, taking side with the ontology of abundance, Widder finds in the Deleuzean notion of disjunctive synthesis a way out of this cul-de-sac. Disjunctive synthesis, Widder argues, provides a way to think about identity and difference in non-dualistic terms, something he suggests has important implications for how radical democrats approach micro-politics and relations of power.

Widder's argument forms the backdrop of the contribution by Paul Patton (chapter 3). Taking issue with recent criticisms of the Deleuzean oeuvre, Patton argues that, while Deleuze may not provide us with a blueprint for a future radical democratic society, he is nonetheless deeply committed to democratic principles in the broad sense of equality and freedom of expression. Moreover, at issue here is the role of political thought: for Patton its role is to bring into question the present organisation of society, rather than to provide rational grounds for democracy or to legislate on which institutions are just. Seen in this light, Deleuze is not only a theorist of abundance, Patton argues, but also a political thinker who offers a compelling starting point for thinking about radical democracy, one that does not reject the core values of democracy, even if he is critical of democracy in its present forms.

While both Widder and Patton are committed to an ontology of abundance, Romand Coles warns in chapter 4 against what he calls 'squinting' – that is, a kind of theoretical vision that is fixed and unreflective. This, Coles argues, goes for the ontology of abundance as well as the ontology of lack. Thus, Coles criticises the work of Slavoj Žižek for a dogmatic fixation on lack, which, he argues, leads to a decisionistic theory of the Act – what Coles calls a 'Big Bang' theory of democratic agency. The problem with this theory of agency, according to Coles, is that it overlooks how democratic practices are always a multifaceted and never-ending engagement with otherness (rather than a once and for all assertion of universality). This is the background against which Coles develops his own alternative of grass root politics, which combines a reworked version of the ontology of abundance with the kind of negativity often associated with the ontology of lack.

Taking this argument one step further, in chapter 5, Aletta Norval engages the work of Ernesto Laclau, whose theory of hegemony has been important for the theorisation of radical democracy in general and the ontology of lack in particular. However, Norval nuances this picture in her examination of the dual sources of inspiration of Laclau's theory of hegemony: Jacques Lacan and Jacques Derrida. Norval considers the former a theorist of lack and the latter a theorist of abundance, and she argues that, while there is nothing wrong with eclecticism *per se*, these two different sources of inspiration create (productive) tensions in Laclau's work that deserve further consideration.

Finally, in chapter 6, Lasse Thomassen, too, engages the work of Laclau. Thomassen argues that by stressing the deconstructive strand of Laclau's work and, in particular, the notion of heterogeneity, Laclau appears to be both a theorist of lack and a theorist of abundance; although, for Laclau, the latter is related to representation, as opposed to the Deleuzian notion of abundance, which rejects the primacy of representation. Moreover, taking heterogeneity rather than the notion of antagonism from Laclau's theory of hegemony as the leading thread, Thomassen argues that it is possible to conceive of a radical democratic approach to exclusion that does not reduce exclusion to an antagonistic relation.

Although some of the contributions in Part I also address questions of concrete politics, the chapters in Part II do so more overtly. More specifically, the chapters in the second part ask how, given the current state of affairs, we can move in the direction of radical democracy. In chapter 7, Chantal Mouffe shows how contemporary approaches to the public sphere, ranging from Rawlsian and Habermasian deliberative approaches to Third Way approaches, stifle the public sphere, because they prevent division and strife from becoming the very drive of our democratic imaginary. As an alternative, Mouffe suggests an agonistic conception of the public sphere, in which dissensus forms an inherent part. This, Mouffe argues, contributes to the revitalisation of democracy, in particular in the struggle against right-wing populism.

Coming from the perspective of abundance, Jane Bennett continues this revitalisation of democracy in chapter 8, probing the place of the nonhuman in radical democratic thought. Inspired by Bruno Latour, Bennett argues that decentring the traditional anthropocentric perspective on politics requires us to rethink democratic institutions in a way that does not reduce the non-human to something that only has value in relation to 'we, humans'. This, she writes, should not only lead us to take seriously the non-human, but also to reconsider the way in which we, humans, think of ourselves as democratic agents.

In chapter 9, Jon Simons argues that the distinction between abundance and lack is mirrored within cultural studies as a distinction between cultural populists and cultural pessimists. In both cases, he writes, we need to strike the right balance. Thus, from the cultural populists, he takes the idea of popular culture as a resource for radical politics, reminding us to combine this with attention to the role of critique and hegemony, especially the necessity of building counter-hegemonies to the present liberalist and capitalist hegemony.

In the following chapter, Torben Dyrberg continues the discussion of

Introduction

counter-hegemonies, taking the rise of right-wing populism in Europe as his starting point. More specifically, Dyrberg argues that the problem of right-wing populism is that, despite its name, it has substituted the spatial metaphor of inside/outside for the right/left dimension orienting democratic politics since the French Revolution. Dyrberg finds this substitution problematic insofar as it undermines the values of liberty and equality that are not only inherent to the right/left dimension, but also critical to the idea – most eloquently captured by Claude Lefort – that modern democracy is organised around an empty place of power, which any democratic party can occupy.

Likewise, emphasising the idea of democracy as the institutionalisation of the empty place of power, Yannis Stavrakakis probes a radical democratic strategy that avoids both totalitarianism and consumerist conformism. In this light, he argues that the work of Alain Badiou and Slavoj Žižek, both inspired by Lacan and a notion of lack, are flawed insofar as they rely on what Coles in chapter 3 called a 'Big Bang' theory of democratic agency. Even so, Stavrakakis does not reject the ontology of lack, but instead suggests that, if conceived in the right way, it captures the essence of radical democracy, which is never-ending contestation (what we might think of as a permanent democratic revolution).

In chapter 12, Lars Tønder challenges the idea that the ontology of lack provides the best ground for the pursuit of radical democracy. Tønder uses the ontology of abundance to explore the space in between the metaphysical doctrines of immanence and transcendence. He argues that this exploration points to the notion of what he calls 'inessential commonality'. Finally, he argues that it cultivates a communal experience of becoming, encouraging radical democrats to experiment with new modes of economic organisation, such as democratisation of money-lending and alternative forms of self-employment.

Like the rest of the contributions to this part of the book, Simon Critchley asks how we can best move in the direction of radical democracy, given the state of the world today (chapter 13). His answer is that we need to go back to Marx. While rejecting Marx's ontology, Critchley finds in Marx's earlier work a notion of the political, close to that in Laclau's theory of hegemony. This leads him to ask if there is a political subject in the present capable of taking up the task of radical democratic transformation. The answer is neither Marx's proletariat, nor Hardt and Negri's multitude, but those who are not counted as partaking in the demos in the present, for instance refugees.

In two afterwords to the volume, William Connolly and Ernesto Laclau discuss the state of and challenges for radical democratic theory today. They both argue that it is necessary to view the distinction between abundance and lack in relation to other divisions dividing the field, first of all that between immanence and transcendence. Connolly takes a close look at the philosophy of William James, and argues that the way we negotiate between immanence and transcendence has important consequences for ethical and political strategies. Laclau argues that lack and abundance are two sides of the same coin, and it is only possible to think of lack and abundance if one resists the pure forms of immanence and transcendence.

Notes

1. 'Post-structuralism' refers to a variety of approaches in contemporary political theory and continental philosophy inspired by thinkers such as Jacques Derrida, Gilles Deleuze, Michel Foucault and Jacques Lacan.
2. J. Butler, E. Laclau and S. Žižek, *Contingency, Hegemony, Universality: Contemporary Dialogues on the Left* (London: Verso, 2000), p. 3. See also C. Mouffe (ed.), *Dimensions of Radical Democracy: Pluralism, Citizenship, Community* (London: Verso, 1992); and D. Trend (ed.), *Radical Democracy: Identity, Citizenship and the State* (London: Routledge, 1996).
3. Nathan Widder provides an earlier version of this argument in 'What's lacking in the lack: a comment on the virtual', *Angelaki*, 5:3 (2000), 117–38. See also the exchange between Slavoj Žižek and William E. Connolly in *Theory and Event*, 6:1 (2002), and Lars Tønder's introduction to this exchange in the same volume.
4. K. Marx and F. Engels, *Manifesto of the Communist Party*, in R. C. Tucker (ed.), *The Marx-Engels Reader*, 2nd edition (New York: W. W. Norton & Co, 1978), p. 491.
5. See Maurice Blanchot's seminal article 'Marx's three voices', in *Friendship*, trans. E. Rottenberg (Stanford, CA: Stanford University Press, 1997), for a catalogue of these objections, many of which are taken up in Jon Simon's and Simon Critchley's contributions to this volume.
6. See W. E. Connolly, *Identity\Difference: Democratic Negotiations of Political Paradox*, 2nd edition (Minneapolis, MN: University of Minnesota Press, 2002), p. 64, for what has become a classical statement of this slogan.
7. J. Derrida, *Specters of Marx: The State of the Debt, the Work of Mourning, and the New International*, trans. P. Kamuf (London: Routledge, 1994), especially at pp. 64f.
8. See, for instance, D. Held, *Models of Democracy*, 2nd edition (Cambridge: Polity Press, 1996); and S. Mulhall and A. Swift, *Liberals and Communitarians*, 2nd edition (Oxford: Blackwell, 1992).
9. See Y. Stavrakakis, *Lacan and the Political* (London: Routledge, 1999).
10. See C. Lefort, *Democracy and Political Theory*, trans. D. Macey (Oxford: Blackwell, 1988). See also Torben Dyrberg's and Yannis Stavrakakis' contributions in this volume.
11. E. Laclau and C. Mouffe, *Hegemony and Socialist Strategy: Towards a Radical Democratic Politics*, 2nd edition (London: Verso, 2001).
12. See P. Patton, *Deleuze and the Political* (London: Routledge, 2000).
13. See G. Deleuze and F. Guattari, *Anti-Oedipus: Capitalism and Schizophrenia*, trans. R. Hurley, M. Seem and H. R. Lane (Minneapolis, MN: University of Minnesota Press, 1983), pp. 82f.
14. G. Deleuze, *Difference and Repetition*, trans. P. Patton (New York: Columbia University Press, 1994), p. 50.
15. J. Bennett, *The Enchantment of Modern Life: Attachments, Crossings, and Ethics* (Princeton, NJ: Princeton University Press, 2001), pp. 131–59.
16. W. E. Connolly, *Why I Am Not a Secularist* (Minneapolis, MN: University of Minnesota Press, 1999), pp. 62–70.

Introduction

17 See G. Agamben, *Potentialities: Collected Essays in Philosophy*, trans. D. Heller-Roazen (Stanford, CA: Stanford University Press, 1999), pp. 238f; E. Laclau, 'Can immanence explain social struggles?', *Diacritics*, 31:4 (2001), 3–10; and D. W. Smith, 'Deleuze and Derrida, immanence and transcendence: two directions in recent French thought', in P. Patton and J. Protevi, *Between Deleuze and Derrida* (London: Continuum, 2003).

RADICAL DEMOCRACY: ABUNDANCE AND/OR LACK?

1 • Oliver Marchart

The absence at the heart of presence: radical democracy and the 'ontology of lack'

SHORTLY after the publication of Deleuze and Guattari's *Anti-Oedipus*, which was, of course, an outright attack against the Lacanian 'ontology of lack' and a manifesto for the primacy of desire over lack and, hence, for an 'ontology of abundance', Deleuze was summoned to Lacan's apartment. There Lacan told him that he absolutely needed someone like Deleuze, since all of his disciples, with the exception of Jacques-Alain Miller, were hopeless. As a matter of fact, Lacan did not see in *Anti-Oedipus* a refutation of his own theories, but he was fully convinced that everything Deleuze and Guattari said had been said by himself already.[1] If this were the case, if the Lacanian 'ontology of lack' and the Deleuzian 'ontology of abundance' were one and the same thing, there would be no point in proceeding with this chapter. Instead, I will claim that, while the theoretical concepts of lack and of abundance are not necessarily incompatible at the ontological level, the actual political conclusions derived from these ontologies differ significantly. In order to prepare the ground for this argument, I will first outline – in the shortest possible way – the philosophical history as well as some theoretical implications of the 'ontology of lack'. In a second step, I will then try to show how the ontology of lack has been transformed into political theory proper, particularly into democratic theory. Finally, I will show what the ontology of lack shares with 'rival' ontologies currently circulating, in particular the ontology of abundance and the ontology of difference, and what kinds of politics, if any, may be derived from them.[2]

An incomplete history of 'lack' (Kojève, Sartre, Lacan)

Before engaging with the concept of lack, let us first clarify what is to be understood by 'ontology'. What ontology traditionally designated was the science of being in general. This means that what is investigated from an ontological point of view is not this or that sub-species of beings, but being-*qua*-being. While this sort of ontological reflection can be traced back to Aristotelian metaphysics, the term 'ontology' appears for the first time at the beginning of the seventeenth century. With Christian Wolff ontology is eventually designated as 'metaphysica generalis', thereby assuming the status of a *prima philosophia vis-à-vis* the other metaphysical disciplines of the time (such as cosmology, psychology and theology). Simultaneously, ontology as a discipline was increasingly displaced by modern *epistemology* – a process that started with Descartes and culminated in the work of Berkeley, Kant and their heirs. Briefly, the shift from ontology to epistemology can be described as a shift from questions regarding *being*-qua-*being* to questions regarding *being*-qua-*understanding*. In other words, modern philosophy increasingly turns into a quest for the grounds and conditions of understanding, bypassing all questions concerning the nature of being *eo ipso*. Only in the early twentieth century, but certainly prepared by Hegel, Schelling and Nietzsche, we can witness what one may call a 'return to ontology' and corresponding devaluation of epistemological concerns. So with Heidegger, who was extremely scornful of all epistemologists – in fact he claimed that there was not a single great philosopher who actually *was* an epistemologist – the situation turned around once more. In Heidegger's celebrated 1929 reading of Kant,[3] the latter's philosophy is, in characteristic opposition to everything that had ever before been thought about Kant, interpreted not as a critical epistemology but as an *ontology* – a direct assault on the Neo-Kantianism of Heidegger's times. Similarly, the introduction of Hegel and Heidegger into French philosophy in the 1930s, to which I will turn in a moment, was to a significant degree directed against the dominance of Cartesian rationalism, which in France had assumed the role of a quasi-official state philosophy.[4]

However, ontology did not re-emerge *in full glory*, as a return to the pre-critical, 'pre-modern' stable ground of being. By the time of its return, the category of being had turned into something intrinsically precarious, something *haunted* by the spectre of its own absent ground. For this reason, today's ontology must not be understood in terms of, to use Derrida's words, traditional *onto-theology*, in which the role of being was to provide us with a stable ground, rather it must be conceived of as *hauntology*, where being is always out-of-joint, never fully present.[5] Again, this move was prepared to a significant extent by Heidegger's work. He pointed out that metaphysical thought – whenever the traditional difference between the general (that is, ontological) realm of being-*qua*-being and the particular (that is, ontic) realm of beings was established – has always taken this ontological difference for granted and never inquired into the difference *as difference*. Hence, being (or *beying*) in the most radical Heideggerian sense does not reside on the ontological level, nor does it reside on the ontic plane. Rather it is the play which simultaneously unites *and* separates the ontic and the ontological, thus introducing an irresolvable difference into being that amounts to a constitutive deferral of every stable ground of being – a move later taken up by Derrida with his concept of *différance*, as we will see in the third part of this chapter. But, while this aspect of Heidegger's work turned out to be formative for ontologies of difference, what was of greater importance as one of the sources for subsequent theorisations of a constitutive *lack-in-being* was the early Heidegger's notion of *finitude*. According to Heidegger's *Being and Time*, the *Dasein* of man is intrinsically temporal because it is *finite*: the being of *Dasein* is being-towards-death.[6] Although death cannot be experienced directly (we can only witness the death of others, but not our own), it still makes itself felt within our life as an absence, which has a very real presence. Finite being is thus held out in a *Nothing* that is not at all neutral or indifferent. For if Nothing, as Heidegger puts it, 'were only something indifferently negative, how could we understand, for example, horror and terror before the Nothing and nihilation'.[7]

It was during the perhaps single most important academic event of the twentieth century that the Heideggerian notion of finitude was folded back into Hegelian dialectics, thus producing an 'anthropological' theory of negativity, lack and desire that should prove to be the starting point for subsequent ontologies of lack. Alexandre Kojève's seminar on Hegel's *Phenomenology of Spirit*, held at the *École pratique des hautes etudes* between 1933 and 1939 and visited by, among others, Bataille, Queneau, Aron, Breton, Merleau-Ponty, Hyppolite, Éric Weil and Lacan (even Hannah Arendt paid the seminar an occasional visit), was silently devoted to the *Heideggerianisation* of Hegel.[8] Hegel is celebrated by Kojève for having introduced into ontology the fundamental category of negativity, yet by assimilating that category to the Heideggerian notion of finitude, Kojève proposes an 'existential' or 'anthropological' version of Hegelian dialectics, whose field of application is now entirely restricted to the realm of human affairs, thus excluding the realm of nature. As a result, Kojève can define negation as the constructive act by which man, under the sign of his/her own finitude (or death), freely creates history. To define negativity in terms of a free and creative form of human *action* allows Kojève to simultaneously abandon the more contemplative approach of Heidegger and radicalise the Hegelian idea of historicity. In Hegel's dialectics between lord and bondsman, Kojève detects a fundamental antagonism at the heart of history. Lord and bondsman are bound together by their negatory struggle for recognition. Initially, the lord is not the one who is more powerful but the one who is prepared to accept his finitude and risk his life in the struggle for recognition – thus forcing the bondsman to recognise him as lord. However, *forced* recognition can never be *full* recognition. Full recognition can only be achieved if it is *mutual*, which would imply the ultimate 'sublation' (*Aufhebung*) or dissolution of negativity and lack, and the final resolution of struggle. But, if the struggle for recognition functions as the engine of history, then the achievement of a state of universal and reciprocal recognition of all individuals would be tantamount to the *end* of history. As is well known, Kojève was more than happy to draw that conclusion.

However, to presume such final sublation and reconciliation of historical struggle does not fit easily with the Heideggerian trend of Kojève's argument. In

Heidegger, 'finitude' should in no way be confused with the 'end' of our life, because our 'death' can never be reached *as such*. No wonder that subsequent ontologies of lack would insist on the irresolvability of negation. Jean-Paul Sartre was one of the first who in this respect would take up and radicalise the Kojèvian model. It is in Sartre's *Being and Nothingness* that the traditional ontological question regarding *being*-qua-*being* is most explicitly reworked into a theory of *being*-qua-*lack-of-being*.[9] Like Kojève, Sartre starts from a clear-cut separation between the subjective realm of consciousness or *being-for-itself* (*être-pour-soi*) and the objective realm of natural *being-in-itself* (*être-en-soi*). While the latter is a sphere of pure positivity and plenitude, the former, that is conscious human being, is permeated by nothing: it always is what it isn't, and it isn't what it is. Since consciousness necessarily means consciousness *of something, it is always incomplete and in need of an outside object*. Now, insofar as being-for-itself is characterised by such irresolvable *lack-of-being* (*manque-à-être*), the conscious subject can never entirely overlap with the realm of objective being, nor can it ever overlap with itself. This lack of self-identity lies at the very core of subjectivity and, according to Sartre, has to be fully accepted (an imaginary future totality towards which consciousness may project itself is unreachable; the *for-itself* will never become *in-itself-for-itself*, no ground of being will ever be attained). In this way, lack-of-being turns into a source of human freedom; not least because the *for-itself*, equipped with the power of negation, is able to disengage from the realm of causal and determinate being. As in Kojève, the moment of active negation is the moment of freedom, and freedom in turn becomes synonymous with lack. So again, lack and negativity have to be understood, not as nihilistic, but as *productive* categories.

With respect to the ontological trajectory outlined so far, it is now possible to describe the work of Jacques Lacan as a specific articulation of Freud's thought with Kojèvian dialectics and the Sartrean concept of lack-of-being. As for Sartre, for Lacan the irresolvable lack-of-being constitutes the ontological ground of the subject's *desire* for being. It is on the premise of the subject's lack-of-being – and 'subject' in Lacan is just the very name for that lack – that the dialectics of desire is set in motion. This dialectics is itself deeply indebted to the Kojèvian dialectics of recognition. For Kojève, man's desire (*Begierde* in Hegel) is always another desire: it is the desire for recognition by the other and, hence, for the *desire of a desire* (that is, the desire *of the other*) around which the struggle for recognition turns. In short, the engine of history is fuelled by nothing else than desire for an other desire. However, for Kojève, this other desire is a purely negative term, since the desire one desires does not really 'exist', at least not in the way objects of the natural world can be said to exist, nor does it have any specific content. Desire is therefore defined by Kojève as the '"manifest" presence of the *absence* of a reality'.[10] Lacan, on his part, radicalises these insight by speaking about desire as being *le désir de l'Autre*, the symbolic desire of the

Other.[11] Here, the 'Other' designates the symbolic order – language or the social – as the instance by which the subject (and the subject's desire) is addressed. Depending on the context, this Lacanian phrase can be read in a variety of ways: it can mean that man's desire is desire *for* the Other (starting with the (m)other), or, that man desires what the Other desires, or, that man always desires something other (always something else). In any case, man's desire is not to be found within the subject – which is lack – but originates from the outside world of language and society. The subject remains *excentric vis-à-vis* itself. On the *imaginary* level, desire is positivised within an *object* promising to fill up the subject's lack-of-being. This *objet petit a* serves as a positive incarnation of what is absent. And, since the subject of desire is pure lack, what is absent can only be *pure* presence: *jouissance*, a pre-symbolic, real enjoyment that was lost when the subject entered into the symbolic order. With his formula of fantasy – designating the attempt at re-establishing an imaginary fullness – Lacan places the divided subject of the symbolic order (the subject of lack) in a relation to the *objet petit a* as an element that necessarily escapes the grasp of the subject and still serves as the (absent) *cause* of his/her desire for being.

The ontology of lack as political ontology (Badiou, Žižek Laclau and Mouffe, Lefort)

After this, no doubt, all too schematic, rudimentary and incomplete history of the concept of lack – but what could be a 'complete' history of lack? – we are in a better position to establish what we mean by an 'ontology of lack'. I have tried to show how the phenomenon of lack in most cases is endowed with a *productive negativity*. Hence, the 'lack' or 'hole' within the heart of being should not be misinterpreted as a neutral or indifferent form of emptiness; rather it is an instance that exerts a constructive power of negation, which is constitutive with respect to being. We can therefore define 'lack', on the most general level, as the name for an *absence constitutive of and operative within presence*. In other words, it is the very *absence of the ground of being* which, at the moment of philosophy's 'return to ontology', becomes the only ground available. The instance of ground does not disappear entirely but, paradoxically, turns the ground into a ground haunted by its very own absence: an entirely *unstable* ground. Being is thus founded, literally, on nothing – but this in turn becomes the very condition of possibility for a being which is necessarily *not-all*, a being struck by constitutive incompletion. Conversely, the 'lack' of ground does not necessarily *transcend* the realm of being, thus assuming a transcendent being of its own – which would only bring us back to the transcendent ground of negative (onto-)theology. Rather than transcending the realm of being, it undermines the realm of being from *within*. This is even the case where ontology eventually experiences, as in Lacan, the *linguistic turn* in form of (post-)structuralism and where 'being' comes to be understood in terms of structure and signification. So, if we insist on the *immanent* character of absence with respect to presence, then lack can only be experienced in the cracks and fissures *within* being, or, in the breakdown of signification and the unconscious slips and failures of the Other (the Symbolic).[12]

Now, how was the 'ontology of lack' made productive within political thought? First of all, one has to stress that the Kojèvian/Lacanian model already presents us with a *social* or *political* ontology. The antagonism between lord and bondsman, together with the concept of the Other as an essentially *intersubjective* agency, brings ontology and dialectics down to the worldly ground of the social and the political. This project has been continued and extended by what might be called our contemporary political ontologies. I will now discuss, again in the most rudimentary and incomplete fashion, four of the currently most influential political ontologies associated with a notion of lack. Let us start with Alain Badiou, and then move to Slavoj Žižek, Ernesto Laclau and Chantal Mouffe, and Claude Lefort.

While the early Badiou was influenced by Sartre, the later Badiou – through the influence of Althusser – increasingly adopted a sort of Lacanianism in the broad sense. Still, Sartre does play an important but not explicit role even in Badiou's later work – a fact that can be inferred already from the quasi-Sartrean title of Badiou's *magnum opus*: *Being and the Event*. As a contemporary candidate for ontology in the strict sense, that is, the science of being-*qua*-being, Badiou only accepts mathematics. His equation 'ontology=mathematics' thus delimits the possible space for all philosophy, which in turn is concerned, in Heideggerian terms, with the field of the *ontic* rather than the ontological. In actual fact, philosophy for Badiou is concerned with only four fields that serve as 'conditions' or 'generic procedures' of philosophy: art, love, science and politics. The *event*, on the other hand, is 'what-is-not-being-*qua*-being'. It is a remainder which cannot be absorbed by the state (or structure) of a given situation by which the situation is counted as *One* (as *this* situation). It has to be theorised as the *dysfunction* of and a *supplement* to the regime of the One. However, it only becomes an event if it is *named* as such by an intervening subject – otherwise it passes by. As in Lacan, this subject is entirely devoid of substance: 'The contemporary Subject is empty, divided, a-substantial, irreflexive.'[13] For Badiou, the subject is only the retroactive outcome of the very intervention of naming and of declaring fidelity to the event. In Badiou's own case, for instance, one can think of his quasi-Maoist group – the *Organisation politique* of which he is a member – that still remains faithful, of course under changing conditions, to the double event of the Cultural Revolution and 'the events' of 1968. So, with explicit reference to Lacan's psychoanalytic maxim 'do not give up on your desire', Badiou formulates his own maxim of an ethic of the Real: *Continuer! – Keep going*, that is, *be faithful to what you have encountered!*

The absence at the heart of presence

Apart from this quasi-Lacanian notion of the subject, one can detect another figure of lack in Badiou. The place from where the event occurs is the place of the *void* of a given situation. What we have earlier called the 'absent ground' of being is conceptualised by Badiou in terms of the figure of the *void*. Every situation is founded upon something it excludes: the void. In Badiou's words, this 'means that at the heart of every situation, as the foundation of its being, there is a "situated" void, around which is organized the plenitude (or the stable multiples) of the situation in question'.[14] The grounding void must be named together with the event. For instance, the event that Karl Marx signifies for political theory consists in his naming of the proletariat as the foundational yet disavowed void of bourgeois society ('For the proletariat – being entirely dispossessed, and absent from the political stage – is that around which is organized the complacent plenitude established by the rule of those who possess'[15]). So we can eventually define emancipatory politics, within the Badiouian model, as the procedure which, via an intervention, gives consistency to the *event*.[16]

With the work of Slavoj Žižek we encounter an even more rigorously Lacanian theory of politics, ideology and emancipation. In order to approach what could provide the ontological basis for a Lacanian theory of radical democracy, I want to point out an aspect of Lacan's claim that *desire is always the desire of the Other*, which so far has not received sufficient attention. What the claim implies is that not only the subject, but also the Other itself, is defined by a constitutive lack (and, hence, is not in possession of the subject's object of desire). So, from a democratic point of view the subject has to realise that desire is the desire of the Other, and that not only the subject *lacks* being, but the Other too desires and therefore *lacks* the fullness of being. At the moment this is realised the subject traverses the ideological fantasy of completion. As Žižek puts it: The 'lack in the Other gives the subject – so to speak – a breathing space, it enables him to avoid the total alienation in the signifier not by filling out his lack but by allowing him to identify himself, his own lack, with the lack in the Other'.[17] In this case we are confronted with symbolic, not with imaginary identification. Herein we can now easily detect the 'ontological' underpinnings of Žižek's theory of democracy and ideology, which is precisely based on the difference between symbolic and imaginary or phantasmatic identification. Within the framework of democratic politics what we identify with is precisely the *lack in the Other*, the fact that society is necessarily incomplete and, as we will see in a moment, blocked by a fundamental antagonism. Žižek illustrates this point with a nice interpretation of the pictures that circulated in the media after Ceausescu's fall. What some of these pictures showed was the Romanian flag with a huge hole in the centre: the place where the red star, the former ideological symbol around which the entire social life was organised, had been cut out by the insurgents.[18] What was left was precisely a representation of the unrepresentable lack in the Other. According to Žižek, it is the duty of critical intellectuals, and of emancipatory politics in general, to try to keep this empty place open, and to defend it against any ideology promising once and for all to fill up this place. Democracy then is nothing else than the – impossible, but necessary – attempt to institutionalise lack. In *ideology*, conversely, fantasy (the desiring subject put in a relation to the *objet petit a*) functions as a protective shield concealing the inconsistency of the Other. The ultimate role of this shield or phantasmatic scene is to promise full enjoyment, social harmony, and the end of all class struggle and all political disturbances. Yet again, the moment of *emancipation* – both in analysis and in politics – is only reached when the subject identifies not with this or that imaginary object supposed to fill up his/her lack, but when s/he 'identifies' with *lack* itself: with the constitutive impossibility of social fullness.[19]

On this account, Žižek's political theory is deeply indebted to the work of Ernesto Laclau and Chantal Mouffe. In their by now classic study *Hegemony and Socialist Strategy*, where Laclau and Mouffe developed a post-Marxist theory of hegemony and radical democracy, they argued that the premise of 'society' as a self-defined totality had to be abandoned. Nevertheless, the impossibility of society as a closed ensemble does not imply the impossibility of *any* form of social meaning. On the contrary, it constitutes the very condition of possibility for a *partial* fixation of social meaning: 'If the social does not manage to fix itself in the intelligible and instituted forms of a *society*, the social only exists, however, as an effort to construct that impossible object.'[20] The name for such effort is *politics*. Political articulation or construction is therefore only possible 'insofar as "society" is impossible'.[21] But why is it impossible? Of course, from a Lacanian perspective the impossibility of society – the fact that society is not a closed ensemble – is reminiscent of Lacan's claim that the big Other is constitutively *non-all*. Yet in Laclau and Mouffe, one can find an intrinsically *political* reflection on the impossibility of the (full) Other. What we find encapsulated in their concept of *antagonism* is a political logic that accounts for the partial construction of social meaning with respect to an entirely *negatory* instance: if a hegemonic project seeks to establish a more or less stable identity (for instance, a temporary alliance) a certain number of differential demands will have to be brought in some form of equivalence (what Laclau and Mouffe call 'chains of equivalence').[22] But, what is it that they have in common? Laclau and Mouffe's point is that what brings these differences into an equivalential relation is not this or that positive content they share, but the entirely negative instance against which the chain of equivalence is constructed. Antagonisms, as the operators of equivalence, 'annul all positivity of the object and give a real existence to negativity as such. This impossibility of the real – negativity – has attained a form of presence.'[23] While Slavoj Žižek took up Laclau and Mouffe's notion of antagonism, integrating it into his own political ontology, he also pointed out that one has to take into consideration a concept strictly correlative to the notion of antagonism: the notion of the subject. Žižek: 'the Lacanian notion of the subject aims precisely at the experience of "pure" antagonism as self-hindering, self-blockage, this internal limit preventing the symbolic field from realizing its full identity'.[24] The model of politics developed in *Hegemony and Socialist Strategy*, where only the structuralist concept of *subject-positions* was to be found, had to be supplemented with the Lacanian notion of the subject-as-lack (a criticism basically accepted by Laclau and integrated into his later work):

> The limit of the social as it is defined by Laclau and Mouffe, this paradoxical limit which means that 'Society doesn't exist', isn't just something that subverts each subject-position, each defined identity of the subject; on the contrary, it is at the same time what sustains the subject in its most radical dimension: 'the subject' in the Lacanian sense is the name for this internal limit, this internal impossibility of the Other, of the 'substance'.[25]

For Laclau and Mouffe, a project of radical democracy must be premised upon the overall acceptance of the impossibility of society. On the 'ontic' level of institutional arrangements – the 'democratic dispositive' – their point is supported by the work of Claude Lefort, which actually serves as frequent point of reference for Laclau and Mouffe as well as for Žižek. The role of 'lack' within the symbolic dispositive of democracy is played by what Lefort famously calls the *empty place of power*. With the French revolution, the symbolic locus of power, formerly occupied by the Monarch, became empty. From then on, no single political actor could legitimately claim to occupy it permanently. Instead, the constant struggle for the *temporary* occupation of that place turned into the very core of democratic politics. Yet while this struggle is irresolvable, it also serves as the main sources of social cohesion. Through their antagonism – in which the organisation, the *raison d'être* and the goals of society are under debate – the antagonists affirm themselves as members of the *same* community. Conflict establishes a common bond. Society can be instituted only as far as there exists a founding antagonism internal to society. Far from destroying society as a whole, division in fact implicates a dimension of totality. And totality is implicated precisely by the figure of an absence that emerges from the incapacity of any social actor to master the meaning of society as a whole. Society must thus be understood as the effect of an absence or negativity residing exactly in the irresolvable antagonism *between* competing attempts at mastering the meaning of the social. In addition to this fundamental conflict, the evacuation of the place of power resulted, according to Lefort, in the experience of a fundamental indeterminacy as to the very basis of power, law and knowledge. As a consequence, democracy 'is instituted and sustained by the *dissolution of the markers of certainty*'.[26] Or, to put it differently, democracy is a regime that is grounded on the very absence of any stable ontological ground.

Unstable ontologies: lack, abundance, difference

So far I have tried to outline the way in which a modern ontology of lack unfolded historically from Alexandre Kojève's articulation of Heidegger with Hegel to the political theory of Alain Badiou, Slavoj Žižek, Ernesto Laclau, Chantal Mouffe and Claude Lefort. In this part of the chapter, I would like to locate the ontology of lack within the broader landscape of current post-structural theorising. This is all the more necessary as the notion of lack has come under severe criticism, in particular from the Deleuzian camp favouring what Lars Tønder and Lasse Thomassen call an ontology of abundance. For Gilles Deleuze and his followers, desire is not at all premised upon a primordial lack-of-being, and where we encounter lack the latter will be secondary with respect to the positivity of desire: '[l]ack refers to a positivity of desire and not desire to a positivity of lack'.[27] Here, the phenomenon of *positivity* or *superabundance* of being is claimed to be ontological prior to the phenomenon of lack and negativity. Obviously, to the extent that this Deleuzian move simply constitutes a reversal of terms, it will not be possible to decide, on the level of argumentation, which phenomenon is prior: lack or abundance. One will simply have to take sides between two apparently incompatible paradigms.

The picture becomes even more complicated if one takes into account a third option, which is not reducible to either paradigm of lack or abundance: the ontology of *difference* initiated by Heidegger and developed in deconstruction. Derrida claims to have found an ontological category prior to either or lack and abundance, presence or absence. The play of *différance*, for Derrida, 'is always play of absence and presence, but if it is to be thought radically, play must be conceived of before the alternative of presence and absence'.[28] Such deconstructive notion of difference is already prefigured in the work of Heidegger where there is no ultimate ground of being, rather being is grounded on a movement of *simultaneous* excess (*Überschwung*) and withdrawal (*Entzug*) of ground – a movement that constitutes the most fundamental play of being also called by Heidegger the play of the (ontological) difference-*as-difference*.

While the ontologies of lack, abundance and difference may seem at first sight incompatible, a closer look will reveal that on the *ontological level* they are not necessarily so. Rather, they are all what I would propose to call *unstable ontologies*,[29] entirely located within the post-foundational horizon. In the case of the ontology of lack, as we said, all presence is defined by a constitutive absence, so that no firm ground will ever be attained. In the case of deconstruction, 'difference' may be defined as the constant *deferral* of *full* presence, so that no stable ground of being is attainable either. In other words, the work of *différance* is not the work of negation, nor is it another name for lack, it is the constant play between presence and absence which simply renders impossible the attainment of either full presence (totality) or full absence (radical lack).

The absence at the heart of presence

And thirdly, 'abundance' could be defined as the immanent *overflow* of presence *from* presence (what Deleuze calls *immanation*). Being, to put it paradoxically, is *too present* to be fully present, which again leads to a constitutive *instability* of being (and this *hyper*-plenitude still distinguishes Deleuze's modern ontology from the closed or crystal-clear universe of stability to be found in Plotin, Spinoza and Leibniz). The field of being remains groundless no matter whether we turn to an ontology of lack, an ontology of difference or an ontology of abundance. Therefore, it should not come as a surprise that in fact one rarely encounters a *pure* version of one or the other theory. Although a much more elaborated and refined study would be required to show how these ontologies intersect within the work of theorists usually located exclusively in one or the other camp, may it suffice at this point to give only a couple of examples in order to illustrate that claim. Let us just remember that Deleuze's theory provides *both* a theory of abundance and a theory of difference; that Heidegger's work can be read under any of these perspectives (lack, difference and abundance); that the same could be said about Lacan's work if one thinks of the three registers of the Real, the Symbolic and the Imaginary as necessarily intertwined approaches to lack, difference and plenitude; that Laclau and Mouffe's theory certainly is predominantly deconstructive but still integrates a Lacanian notion of lack and even an element of abundance.[30]

Therefore, if, in the last instance, the ontologies of lack, abundance and difference may not be entirely incompatible on the ontological level, where do all the quarrels between the different 'schools' stem from? I submit that there are indeed incompatibilities but they are to be located on the *ontic* rather than the ontological level. By this I mean that from a general ontology a highly diverse range of political conclusions can be drawn, precisely because there is no relation of continuity between the ontological (the realm of being-qua-being, even where it is developed as a *political* ontology) and the ontic (the realm of concrete politics). As the cases of, for instance, Badiou, Laclau and Žižek demonstrate, it is possible to derive from an ontology of lack a Maoist (Badiou), a radical democratic (Laclau) and a 'sometimes Leninist, sometimes radical democratic' (Žižek) political stance. So from a general ontology of instability no *particular* political theory follows, let alone an intrinsically democratic theory: there is no direct link between lack, abundance or difference and a specific political project or form of government. However, if we look at ontology from the other side – that is from the *ontic* level – then it seems that, on the contrary, *every democratic theory* will necessarily have to be premised upon an *unstable ontology*, that is, an ontology of either lack, abundance or difference. So while the passage from an unstable ontology to democratic politics is a *non sequitur*, the passage from a democratic politics to an unstable ontology is a *necessity*. Hence, radical democracy has to be based on the post-foundational assumption that a stable ground will never be within reach for any democratic politics. To engage in democratic politics therefore means abstaining from any attempt at hypostatising lack, abundance or difference into a new ground. Such *stabilisation* of unstable ontologies could have catastrophic effects. A politics in which lack is turned into a new ground, for instance by conflating finitude with death, could easily turn in some sort of fascist celebration of death along the maxim of *viva la muerte!* A politics in which abundance is turned into a seemingly stable ground would be equally in danger of leading to a fascist version of vitalism, biologism and voluntarism. And a politics in which difference is made into a stable ground would be prone to become a politics of separatism and of apartheid.

Hence, we must conclude that in the field of politics there are not guarantees, there are only dangers. So even where lack, abundance and difference come to be accepted by emancipatory political projects, there is no guarantee that these projects will necessarily be radical democratic. Again, I can only point out the specific dangers inherent to unstable ontologies – where they are short-circuited with *ontic* emancipatory politics – in the most schematic way. The main danger consists in *abolishing politics* for the very *sake of politics*. This danger, a danger amounting to a disavowal of the political, is often encountered when emancipatory projects seek to enact the ontological conditions of lack, abundance and difference in a literal or unmediated way within the field of the ontic. In this case, an immediate politics of lack will be in danger of turning into a Jacobine form of terrorism based on the paradox that, in order for the empty place of power to be kept empty, it has to be defended at all costs, even at the price of the democratic forces themselves permanently occupying it. This is the classic case in which the defence of democracy is enacted by way of the very abolition of democracy. The political is defended by getting rid of politics. Something similar can be said about an emancipatory politics seeking to enact the ontological condition of difference in an all too immediate ontic way. Such politics is in danger of abolishing the political for the sake of the ethical or unconditional. Yet politics does not take place within the realm of the unconditional. An *unconditional* respect for the other cannot be the premise for an emancipatory or democratic politics, because then we would have to respect even those whose aim it is to *destroy* democracy (so here we encounter precisely the obverse side of the paradox of Jacobinism: if the latter tries to defend the empty place of power at all costs, a politics of *ethicism* would be completely defenceless, leaving the place of power open for everybody to occupy).[31]

And finally, does the immediate application of an ontology of abundance to the realm of emancipatory politics not frequently lead to a rather simple-minded form of anarchism that is not necessarily democratic either? Of course, precisely because the passage from the ontological to the ontic does not produce *necessary* effects, it is indeed possible to develop out of a Nietzschean/Deleuzian ontology a democratic politics of agonistic respect, as the work of William Connolly proves. Yet in less sophisticated cases, the celebratory and often pseudo-revolutionary rhetorics of 'deterritorialisation', 'flows of desire', 'lines of flights' and so on, go hand in hand with the deliberate denial of the importance of political organisation and democratic institutions. Again the political is abolished, this time for the sake of the pseudo-politics of spontaneism. It is not difficult to imagine the criticism such 'revolutionary' pseudo-politics may encounter from the Lacanian side. When Lacan addressed the students of May '68, to which he had great sympathies, he told them: 'As revolutionaries, what you long for is a master, You'll get one ...'[32] There are certainly different ways to interpret Lacan's dictum, but confronted with the current fad of 'vulgar Deleuzianism' (and Negriism), in many ways reminiscent of the Situationist promotion of the 'politics' of desire so characteristic for the movement of '68, it is hard not to think of the following: at the very moment when you think you have once and for all thrown out the Master through the front-door, he will return through the backdoor. The call for the reign of anarchic spontaneity (theoretically encapsulated in the psychotic or 'schizoid' foreclosure of the Name-of-the-Father recommended by Deleuze and Guattari) turns out to be a secret call for a Master. For what is expelled from the Symbolic returns in the Real. Isn't this precisely the danger Lacan alluded to with his prediction *'You'll get one ...'*? It is here, on the level of the ontic *conclusions* drawn from an unstable ontology, where the differences between a politics oriented towards an ontology of lack and a politics oriented towards an ontology of abundance can be most dramatic.

Notes

1 See E. Roudinesco, *Jacques Lacan* (New York: Columbia University Press, 1997), p. 347.
2 In so doing, I to some degree depart from the proposal of the editors of this volume for whom the ontologies of lack and of abundance share a democratic commitment to what they call *radical difference*. While I entirely agree that the category difference does play an important role both within the Lacanian and the Deleuzian framework, I would nevertheless feel uncomfortable to simply subsume it under the categories of lack and abundance. Wouldn't this merely make deconstruction a sub-label of Lacanianism and Deleuzianism? In the following I prefer to locate the ontology of lack, as well as radical democratic theories premised upon that ontology, not so much in opposition to the ontology of abundance, but, rather, within the triangle of theories premised upon lack, abundance and difference.
3 M. Heidegger, *Kant and the Problem of Metaphysics* (Bloomington, IN: Indiana University Press, 1962).
4 On the reception of Hegel in France, see M. S. Roth, *Knowing and History: Appropriations of Hegel in Twentieth-Century France* (Ithaca, NY: Cornell University Press, 1988). On French Heideggerianism, see D. Janicaud, *Heidegger en France*, 2 vols. (Paris: A. Michel, 2001).
5 In Derrida's words: 'To haunt does not mean to be present, and it is necessary to introduce haunting into the very construction of a concept. Of every concept.

Beginning with the concepts of being and time. That is what we would be calling here a hauntology.' J. Derrida, *Specters of Marx: The State of the Debt, the Work of Mourning, and the New International*, trans. P. Kamuf (London. Routledge, 1994), p. 161.
6 M. Heidegger, *Being and Time*, trans. J. Stambaugh (Albany, NY: State University of New York Press, 1953).
7 M. Heidegger, *Basic Concepts*, trans. G. E. Aylesworth (Bloomington, IN: Indiana University Press, 1998), p. 45.
8 A. Kojève, *Introduction to the Reading of Hegel* (New York: Basic Books, 1969). Kojève's seminar was only rivalled by Heidegger's own seminar of the late 1920s – with students such as Arendt, Löwith, Jonas and Marcuse.
9 J.-P. Sartre, *Being and Nothingness* (London: Philosophical Library, 1956).
10 The whole quote, which is crucial, reads as follows: 'The Desire for Recognition which provokes the Fight is the desire for a desire – that is, for something that does not *exist* really (since Desire is the "manifest" presence of the *absence* of a reality): to want to be "recognized" is to want to be accepted as a positive "value" – that is, precisely speaking, to cause oneself to be "desired". To want to risk one's *life*, which is the *whole* reality of a living being, in favor of something that does not *exist* and cannot exist as inert or merely living real *things* exist – this, then, is indeed to *negate* the given which one is oneself, this is to be *free* or *independent* of it. Now, to negate oneself, in this full sense, and nevertheless to preserve oneself in existence, is indeed to *create* oneself as new and therefore to exist as created by oneself – that is, as free or autonomous.' Kojève, *Introduction*, pp. 225f.
11 Lacan criticises Hegel (and whenever he says Hegel he means Kojève) for not integrating the Symbolic into the framework of the dialectics of recognition, thus remaining within the impasse of the Imaginary. While Lacan also uses the Kojèvian dialectics as a model for the dialectics of the Imaginary (where the other is written with a small *a*), Lacan's capitalisation of the Kojèvian Imaginary other into the Other (of the Symbolic) can be perceived to be already a way out of that impasse.
12 For reasons of space I cannot engage into the debate around immanentism, or the relation between transcendence and immanence, yet the theories discussed so far adhere to neither a full-blown immanentism nor to a pure concept of transcendence. At least it is necessary to underline that, if the constitutive absence we call 'lack' is in any way transcendent, then only in the sense of an entirely *immanent* transcendence.
13 A. Badiou, *L'être et l'événement* (Paris: Éditions du Seuil, 1988), p. 9.
14 A. Badiou, *Ethics: An Essay on the Understanding of Evil*, trans. P. Hallward (London: Verso, 2001), p. 68. It should be noted, however, that Badiou makes a clear distinction between such an, as it were, *ontic* (Badiou would say logical) void and the ontological void of being (that is void as the 'name of being' to be found in set theory as the 'empty set'). See his *Manifesto for Philosophy*, trans. N. Madarasz (Albany NY: State University of New York Press, 1999), p. 124; and *L'être et l'événement*, pp. 65–72.
15 Badiou, *Ethics*, p. 69.
16 See A. Badiou: *Peut-on penser la politique?* (Paris: Seuil, 1985), p. 77. For a more in-depth survey of Badiou's political philosophy, including his disavowed Heideggerianism, see O. Marchart, 'Nothing but a truth: Alain Badiou's "philosophy of politics" and the Left Heideggerians', *Polygraph*, 16 (2004).
17 S. Žižek, *The Sublime Object of Ideology* (London: Verso, 1989), p. 122.
18 S. Žižek, *Tarrying with the Negative* (Durham: Duke University Press, 1993), pp. 1f.
19 Respectively with the *symptom*, which is presented by ideology as the scapegoat whose ultimate fault it is that fullness cannot be reached. For Žižek, the classical example for

The absence at the heart of presence

such a symptom is the figure of 'the Jew' in anti-Semitic discourse, cf. Žižek, *The Sublime Object of Ideology*, p. 127.
20 E. Laclau and C. Mouffe, *Hegemony and Socialist Strategy: Towards a Radical Democratic Politics* (London: Verso, 1988), p. 112.
21 *Ibid.*, p. 114.
22 Again, as the Laclau and Mouffe stress, the ontological instance of negativity is entirely *internal* to the field of the positively given (the ontic field of beings): 'The limit of the social must be given within the social itself as something subverting it, destroying its ambition to constitute full presence. Society never manages fully to be society, because everything in it is penetrated by its limits, which prevent it from constituting itself as an objective reality.' *Ibid.*, p. 127. See also O. Marchart: 'Politics and the ontological difference. on the "strictly philosophical" in Ernesto Laclau's work', in S. Critchley and O. Marchart (eds), *Laclau: A Critical Reader* (London: Routledge, 2004).
23 Laclau and Mouffe, *Hegemony and Socialist* Strategy, pp. 128f.
24 S. Žižek, 'Beyond discourse analysis', in E. Laclau, *New Reflections on the Revolution of Our Time* (London: Verso, 1990), p. 253.
25 *Ibid.*, pp. 253f.
26 C. Lefort, *Democracy and Political Theory* (Minneapolis, MN: University of Minnesota Press, 1988), p. 19 (emphases in original). See also O. Marchart, 'Division and democracy: on Claude Lefort's post-foundational political philosophy', *Filozofski Vestnik/Acta Philosophica*, 21:2 (2000), pp. 51–82.
27 Quoted in P. Patton, *Deleuze and the Political* (London: Routledge, 2000), p. 70.
28 J. Derrida, *Writing and Difference*, trans. A. Bass (Chicago: The University of Chicago Press, 1978), p. 292.
29 From a different perspective Stephen K. White speaks about 'weak ontology' and even a 'weak ontological turn' in recent political thought. In the camp of 'weak ontologists', he includes George Kateb, Charles Taylor, Judith Butler, and William Connolly. S. K. White, *Sustaining Affirmation: The Strengths of Weak Ontology in Political Theory* (Princeton, NJ: Princeton University Press, 2000).
30 In *Hegemony and Socialist Strategy* (p. 113), they claim that every partial fixation of meaning 'is constituted within an intertextuality that overflows it', and that the 'partial character of this fixation proceeds from the openness of the social, a result, in its turn, of the constant overflowing of every discourse by the infinitude of the field of discursivity'.
31 A similar critique of the deconstructivist short-circuit between the ontological and the ontic has been made by Ernesto Laclau à propos Derrida's *Specters of Marx*' in *Emancipation(s)* (London: Verso, 1996), chapter 5.
32 Roudinesco, *Jacques Lacan*, p. 342.

2 • *Nathan Widder*

Two routes from Hegel

Two syntheses of difference

THERE may still be places where post-structuralist concerns about difference, language and representation are considered nihilistic threats to the very possibility of political theory and practice. Nevertheless, the work of radical democratic theorists since the 1980s has demonstrated that their critiques of universalism and foundationalism are not only eminently political and ethical in their own right, but also capable of shifting political theory away from standard paradigms that seem increasingly anachronistic in a complex and globalised age. Theorists of radical democracy have developed novel and complex understandings of the constituted and contestable character of political and social meanings and the structure of the human self or subject, politicising dimensions of social life that do not fit well into the traditional public/private divide. Unsurprisingly, these same theorists have differed over their underlying ontological commitments, but, as this volume attests, these differences have not often been outlined explicitly.

Whilst I agree that within contemporary radical democracy debates one can discern two general strands of thought, corresponding very much to what have been named 'ontologies of abundance' and 'ontologies of lack', I am unsure that 'abundance' and 'lack' are the best terms with which to approach the disagreements between them. It seems to me that each ontology articulates a conception of difference that can be understood *both* as abundance and as lack. Consequently, framing the debate between the two ontologies on these terms suggests that their difference primarily amounts to privileging either the aspect of 'abundance' or that of 'lack'.[1] My concern is that the fundamental difference between the two ontological imaginaries is not one of degree but of type, and that, beyond general similarities in their respective articulations of an abundant/lacking difference, the two ontologies specify these terms differently, articulating two irreducible conceptions of difference. Ultimately, I contend, these divergent understandings of difference reflect different ontological commitments towards identity, its relationship to difference and its importance in theorising politics and subjectivity.[2]

In their introduction, Lars Tønder and Lasse Thomassen suggest that the disagreements between the two ontological imaginaries stem from their shared view that 'social identities are always incomplete and subject to contestation and subversion'.[3] I hope to show in this chapter that the disagreements amongst radical democratic theories actually start here, with one ontology (that of 'lack') maintaining that social identities, although contingent and necessarily incomplete, are indispensable for any conceptualisation of politics, power and pluralism, and the other (that of 'abundance') refusing to grant this central status to identity. Without dispensing with the division itself, or even fully with the terminology of abundance vs. lack, I will argue that the crucial differences between these two ontologies concern what each affirms as the form of constitutive synthesis – that is, how each understands differences to be woven together to constitute meaningful subjectivity or selfhood, thereby defining the possibilities and necessities for political thought and practice – and what is the status of identity in relation to difference in each synthesis. These claims, of course, issue from my own 'ontological imaginary' and may not be shared by others in this debate.

Certainly the various radical democratic ontologies converge in a renewed exploration of difference, but one that escapes 'subsumption to identity or to any simple dichotomy between identity and difference'.[4] The difference in question therefore differs from both a Platonic/Augustinian conception, in which difference has being only in relation to a transcendent identity that measures it, and the difference of Hegelian dialectics, which first negates but ultimately constitutes and secures identity by internally mediating any identity with what it is not. Against these conceptions, this radical democratic Other embodies neither identity nor a conception of difference premised upon the priority of identity. In relation to the traditional dualism of identity and difference, therefore, it has an undefined and enigmatic status, and, in relation to a representational understanding of meaning, it remains opaque. In general terms, therefore, it suggests both abundance and lack: abundance, insofar as it 'exceeds' any dialectical or representative schema of difference; lack, insofar as it shows the incompleteness of such structures of differences. Crucially, however, this opaque Otherness is not in any simple way outside socially constituted meaning or subjectivity. It cannot be understood as a prediscusive reality that would appear clearly if only we could penetrate the lens of discourse through which we approach the world, for this would enframe it within a binary opposition of inside and outside that it problematises. Thus, even if it seems to be outside or prior to discourse, this different difference is constituted *within* discourse as that which – at least according to the logic of representation – lies beyond it.

Beyond this common general affirmation of a difference that breaks with representational frameworks, however, there is significant divergence between the two ontological imaginaries in terms of what this abundant/lacking difference is and how it functions. For those ontologies that hold socially constituted identities, even in their contingent and ever-fluctuating nature, to be indispensable to subjectivity, meaning and therefore politics, this difference tends to be considered an interruption of meaning and subjectivity that makes them inherently unstable (in this sense it is appropriate to note an emphasis on 'lack'). In other words, it is understood as a limit concept, a meaningless remainder constituting any structure of meaning by its erasure, but also internally subverting this structure by postponing indefinitely the final establishment of 'an ontological centre that could guarantee the completeness of any social identity'.[5] Representation and identity are not dispensed with but rather displaced, as identity is seen to secure itself not only in relation to an opposite, but also through the exclusion of another difference that is neither identity nor its opposite. In this sense, a dialectical synthesis of the traditional dualism of identity and difference is still crucial to this ontological imaginary, although it is problematised by the articulation of a difference that cannot be synthesised. Judith Butler summarises the political stakes of this position when she writes:

> None of the above is meant to suggest that identity is to be denied, overcome, erased. None of us can fully answer to the demand to 'get over yourself!' The demand to overcome radically the constitutive constraints by which cultural viability is achieved would be its own form of violence. But when that very viability is itself the consequence of a repudiation, a subordination, or an exploitative relation, the negotiation becomes increasingly complex. What this analysis does suggest is that an economy of difference is in order in which the matrices, the crossroads at which various identifications are formed and displaced, force a reworking of that logic of non-contradiction by which one identification is always and only purchased at the expense of another ... Thus every insistence on identity must at some point lead to a taking stock of the constitutive exclusions that reconsolidate hegemonic power differentials, exclusions that each articulation was forced to make in order to proceed.[6]

Identity and representation, for Butler, thus rest upon constitutive exclusions that establish the conditions of possibility and impossibility for any identity to consolidate itself dialectically in relation to differences that can be represented as what it is not. This constitutive exclusion of Otherness makes any dialectical synthesis of identity in relation to difference more complex and creates the political necessity of continual negotiations of its boundaries. But identity, built on exclusion, continues to serve as a necessary marker, because the denial of constitutive exclusion would suggest a metaphysical pipedream of inclusiveness and wholeness: 'The ideal of transforming all excluded identifications into inclusive features ... would mark the return to a Hegelian synthesis which has no exterior and that, in appropriating all difference as exemplary features of itself, becomes a figure for imperialism, a figure that installs itself by way of a romantic, insidious, and all-consuming humanism.'[7]

Conversely, for those ontologies that are not 'identity-centred' in this way, this difference underpins another conception of meaning, subjectivity and politics that breaks with dialectical and identity-based structures as such. Here, Otherness no longer has the status of that which is excluded, because *constitutive* exclusion is denied (and, in this sense, it is easy to see how these ontologies can be said to emphasise 'abundance' over 'lack'). Deleuze and Guattari express this rejection when they argue that lack is never originary, as does Foucault when he criticises juridico-discursive models of power – under which he includes psychoanalytic models that make the prohibitions of Law constitutive of desire – for treating power as the same on all levels, micro as well as macro.[8] The denial of constitutive exclusion does not mean this ontology affirms inclusion, because what is constituted in this ontological imaginary is not an identity, inclusive or otherwise. Instead of treating meaning and subjectivity as dependent on the fixing of an ontological centre through a constitutive exclusion that both enables and subverts the dialectical construction of identity through difference, this ontological imaginary sees meaning and subjectivity arising from a perpetual differenciation or de-centring synthesis. The commitment to this alternative understanding of synthesis, which might be called 'disjunctive' as opposed to dialectical, announces a new kind of politics – or, more accurately, a micropolitics – that presses individuals and collectives to overcome the assumption that some form of identity is necessary for their subjectivity.

Given these divergent commitments, it is unsurprising that each ontology appears, from the perspective of the other, to be mired in fundamental errors. For the first ontology, the rejection by the second of the constitutive exclusion needed to fix any identity leaves it open to criticisms of either being unable to explain the formation of meaning and subjectivity altogether or relying on an ontological anchor that is untouched by discursive difference, thereby suggesting a leap outside the discourse in which we are necessarily constructed. Reflecting the reasoning underlying the first line of criticism (the inability to explain the formation of subjectivity), Ernesto Laclau and Chantal Mouffe maintain that, with the lack of any transcendental signified to centre a discursive system of differences, movements to establish partial and always precarious fixings remain necessary: 'The impossibility of an ultimate fixity of meaning implies that there have to be partial fixations – otherwise, the very flow of differences would be impossible. Even in order to differ, to subvert meaning, there has to be *a* meaning ... Any discourse is constituted as an attempt to dominate the field of discursivity, to arrest the flow of differences, to construct a centre.'[9] The role of hegemonic articulations is precisely to create the equivalences and corollary exclusions necessary for identity and fixity. Even as the theory of hegemony has developed, focusing initially on the antagonistic relation to an Other that can be represented only as a pure threat to identity and moving later to the exclusion of heterogeneity necessary for this antagonistic frontier to be established,[10] the link between fixing identity in a synthetic relation and the possibility of meaning remains. As Laclau states, 'A discourse in which meaning cannot possibly be fixed is nothing else but the discourse of the psychotic.'[11] Butler regularly employs the second line of criticism (the reliance on a prediscursive ontological anchor) against Foucault and Deleuze, arguing that their attempts to think outside representational discourse consistently invoke a metaphysical plenitude of bodies, pleasures or desire prior to discourse and power.[12]

Conversely, for the second ontology, the first, despite its deconstruction of the binary oppositions of representational discourse, remains mistakenly committed to their necessity, thus falling back upon the paradigm of identity. For the second ontology, it is not enough to articulate a difference exceeding the binary of identity and difference and showing it to be lacking. Classical metaphysical expositions of identity and difference themselves acknowledge such an Other, even while conceiving it on their own terms, either elevating it to divine status (consider Plato's Good and Augustine's God) or reducing it to the status of abyss, chaos or materiality lying 'beneath' the Concept. By continuing to oppose partial fixity to free flowing chaos, the first ontology of radical democracy would seem to reinvoke what Deleuze calls the metaphysical 'summary law of all or nothing', which poses the simple alternative of 'either an undifferentiated ground, a groundlessness, formless nonbeing, or an abyss without differences and without properties, *or* a supremely individuated Being and an intensely personalised Form. Without this Being or this Form, you will have only chaos.'[13] For a thinker like Deleuze, who considers opposition to be an abstract conceptualisation of difference, the first ontology's view of the alterity in question remains abstract and one-sided.

Given that the different varieties of post-structuralist theory have as their starting point a reflection on how to move beyond the synthesis of identity of Hegelian dialectics, I will develop these claims about the two ontologies by analysing the routes taken by Lacan and Deleuze in relation to Hegel's thought, using Irigaray's critique of phallogocentric treatments of the feminine as a bridge from the former to the latter. Proceeding in this way, I hope to demonstrate both the close proximity of the two radical democratic ontological imaginaries and the way these imaginaries, despite their nearness, remain separated. In the final section, I will explore some micropolitical implications of the second ontology. I do not intend to argue here for the simple superiority of one ontology over the other; although I certainly prefer one of them, their incongruous ontological (and ethico-political) commitments suggest it is inappropriate to rank them on a single scale. I do, however, aim to show that the positive multiplicity theorised by Deleuze and others, who can be grouped under the second ontology, is neither some incoherent or illegitimate leap into metaphysical plenitude nor a regression to a pre-Kantian assertion of external reality, as some critics claim; rather, it is consistent with an internal critique of dialectical thought that not only inverts it, but unhinges it from identity. Answering this frequent criticism, I feel, has some value in advancing the debate between the various theories of radical democracy.

Lacan and unrecuperable desire; Irigaray on the curvature of the feminine

As Kojève explains,[14] two levels comprise Hegelian desire. Natural desire seeks to negate the otherness of an object in order to possess or consume it. Human desire, however, negates this negation, though it also preserves and sublates both natural desire and the other it would consume. Human desire desires not to negate some other, but to negate itself, becoming an object of desire for another. This level of desire, which expresses itself the demand for recognition by a worthy other, drives the dialectic in *The Phenomenology of Spirit* to its conclusion in the moral society of reciprocal recognition. Hegel's promise is that such reciprocity can be actualised, securing the identity of each counterpart in an Identity of identity and difference.

In contrast, Lacanian desire exceeds this negativity. It goes beyond the satisfaction of (material) need and the demand for love (recognition from the Other), although it is also generated by their interplay. Demand reconfigures every satisfaction of need as proof of love and thereby 'cancels out ... the particularity of anything which might be granted'.[15] Yet this cancelled particularity returns as a residue 'beyond demand',[16] as no particular gift can demonstrate unconditional love.

> In a reversal which is not a simple negation of negation, the force of pure loss arises from the relic of an obliteration. In place of the unconditional aspect of demand, desire substitutes the 'absolute' condition: in effect this condition releases that part of the proof of love which is resistant to the satisfaction of a need. Thus desire is neither the appetite for satisfaction, nor the demand for love, but the difference resulting from the subtraction of the first from the second, the very phenomenon of their splitting.[17]

Desire is thus an indispensable but unsatisfiable element in the formation of a subject's identity. It indicates an enigmatic and alienated something that 'constitutes an *Urverdrängung* (primal repression) because it cannot, by definition, be articulated in demand'.[18] The failure of the dialectical reconciliation of identity through difference thereby signals a 'beyond' that differs from identity and dialectical difference.

How this excess is implicated in subjectivity indicates two forms of slippage, one dialectical and one extra-dialectical, which characterise any identity. A subject initially gets a sense of itself through an image conveyed from without,[19] so that unity always comes paradoxically from a passage through an outside. Nevertheless, the subject only truly comes into being through the trauma of the Phallic Law of the Father, which must be repressed. Trauma implies an original unity that has been fractured – the castration complex thus retroactively gives sense to the mirror stage, even while the latter prepares the way for the former – but it is an imaginary unity that never existed. The subject comes into being necessarily carrying a sense of loss, but since what is felt to be missing is not part of a prior unity, it is unrecoverable. The subject's desire to restore its unity thus becomes a desire for an impossible lost object – a desire beyond demand. Always incomplete, the subject seeks precariously to establish its identity in relation to an existing other, confirming its split nature even as it seeks to 'repair' itself; yet no actual other is ever sufficient to fill the void created by the lost Other. Furthermore, as subjectivity is also a product of language – it arises with 'the deviation of man's needs by the fact that he speaks'[20] – the two forms of displacement are also located here. On the one hand, signs gain their meaning in relation to other signs, opening them to metaphoric and metonymic shifts within language. But linguistic signs also metaphorically substitute for referents in order to function in the latter's absence; and these referents, lacking any pregiven unity since unity is a product of language, are in themselves nameless. There are instabilities internal to language, insofar as signs refer outside of themselves to other signs, but there is a more fundamental instability arising from the split/substitution that founds language in relation to a nameless excess.

The Lacanian subject and sign, therefore, present two sorts of relation: a dialectical relation that precariously establishes meaning and subjectivity and another relation to an enigmatic Other implied in the foundational split and the imaginary unity, which makes full resolution of identity and meaning impossible. While the former establishes the terrain of possible identifications – establishing, for example, the dichotomy of masculine and feminine around the being or having of the Phallus, thereby providing positions actual men and women can assume[21] – the latter precludes any identification consolidating itself as a firm identity. Two points concerning this second difference must be noted. First, although this Other has a constitutive role in meaning, this role is effectively negative: on the one hand, meaning becomes possible only through the traumatic split, and everything that *is*, that has sufficient unity to *be*, is so only by being marked by the Phallus as split, traumatised and castrated; on the other hand, however, only to the degree that this trauma is repressed can partially stable identifications come into being. Second, this Other is in no way singular: one can disaggregate several kinds of namelessness that are excluded from discourse by remaining unmarked by the Phallic Law. These include the Phallus itself, which threatens and splits, but which therefore has a unity different from the split unity of all that can be represented, giving it a mysterious, transcendent and divine status; the lost object of enjoyment (*jouissance*), the *objet a*, which the Phallic Law prohibits and which the subject must repress, accepting other enjoyments instead; and the feminine, which is defined through the Phallic Law as lacking a phallus, being unmarked by it, or being marked only as not being so marked, and which thereby becomes both an object of desire and a mysterious truth. A central role of analysis, for Lacan, is to perform this disaggregation, to separate the imaginary abundance of the object of desire from the symbolic excess that points to transcendence, and thereby 'to dissociate the *a* and the O [the symbolic Other], by reducing the former to what belongs to the imaginary and the latter to what belongs to the symbolic'.[22]

Nevertheless, an irresolvable dual status remains for the feminine, insofar as it resides along the two axes of difference. On the one hand, the feminine is located within language as the opposite or complement to the masculine, but this oppositional identity is always inadequate to it – hence the mystery of women. On the other hand, the feminine is designated, again within language, as the nameless lost object. At once on the margins of language and seemingly outside it, the feminine both completes the masculine and subverts their relation. This allows the mystery of the feminine to be closely associated with the divine and leads to the mystery of feminine enjoyment, which men clumsily locate as being 'vaginal' or 'not clitoral', but which cannot be articulated even by the women who enjoy it.[23] It is also the basis for Lacan's declaration that 'The woman' does not exist.[24]

Lacan goes beyond Freud on the question of feminine desire, but not very far. Freud denies that there can be two libidos, insisting that it is appropriate, even if it is strictly speaking incorrect, to call the one libido masculine. Freud proceeds through this theory of a single libido to resolve the mystery of femininity, but in a way that domesticates the very question of sexual difference he says has plagued men throughout the ages: women are defined through representational or oppositional terms of more or less – more passive, having less developed superegos and so forth – but if this were *all* that differentiated male and female sexuality, there would have been no mystery of femininity in the first place.[25] Lacan, in contrast, maintains that, if feminine desire exists, it remains unrepresentable: hence, no women patients or analysts have ever been able to say what it is.[26] And so, it at best 'exists' as that which *is not*, for what exists can only exist within language. Any attempt to retrieve this feminine desire, Lacan argues, violates the basic principles of psychoanalysis by positing the feminine as a truth prior to language and subjectivity, presupposing exactly the sexual difference that requires explanation.

Nevertheless, this insistence rests solely on a precommitment to a subject-centred and identity-based understanding of language, whereby any attempt to articulate another form of meaningful relation must be seen as an illegitimate attempt to go outside discourse and invoke a non-linguistic essence. Thus language, subjectivity and identity must inevitably fail to secure themselves, but we cannot theorise other possibilities because, for Lacan, all we have are the subjectivity and identity of this language. But for Irigaray, a feminist psychoanalyst highly critical of the Lacanian position, this attitude is unsurprising, given how its thinking rests upon sameness. The problem, as she conceives it, is not that this economy of sameness cannot acknowledge an Otherness irreconcilable *within its terms*, but that it nevertheless conceives this irreconcilability *on its own terms* as something that cannot be spoken, understood or recognised. The purported necessity of this subject-centred language and its identity-based conception of difference are, for Irigaray, the result of abstractions of a masculinist logic that parallel the abstractions Marx locates in the capitalist logic of commodity exchange. It is precisely because of the abstract nature of these relations of identity and difference that another economy of relations is conceivable.

Commodities are exchanged only through an abstraction that establishes an equivalence among qualitatively distinct goods, allowing each good to have value in relation to another commodity held as a fixed value. Buyers and sellers on the market can reciprocally recognise and mirror one another as subjects, but only through the detour of commodities that are simultaneously treated as objects and endowed with a value transcending the commodities themselves and enslaving the men who exchange them. The commodity thus inhabits two positions, one involving an abstract (but representative) value in a dialectic of exchange and the other involving an enigmatic value that marks the commodity and makes it stand for the promise to satisfy an impossible, insatiable desire. Unsurprisingly, for Irigaray, these forms of difference and the production of a mysterious and transcendent Other have their structural counterparts in the phallic economy Lacan declares to be indispensable.

> Thus, starting with the simplest relation of equivalence between commodities, starting with the possible exchange of women, the entire enigma of the money form – of the phallic function – is implied. That is, the appropriation–disappropriation by man, for man, of nature and its productive forces, insofar as a certain mirror now divides and travesties both nature and labour. Man endows the commodities he produces with a narcissism that blurs the seriousness of utility, of use. Desire, as soon as there is exchange, 'perverts' need. But that perversion will be attributed to commodities and to their alleged relations. Whereas they can have no relationships except from the perspective of speculating third parties.[27]

If this economy of sameness rests on an abstraction, what is it an abstraction from? Just as Marx held that commodity exchange effaces not only the real qualities of goods, but also the real relations that constitute them; Irigaray answers that what is abstracted away is the feminine, but the feminine is not a substance but a relation. The character of this relation might be understood in terms of mirroring. The philosophy of subjectivity and identity, Irigaray says, depends upon 'recourse, explicitly or more often implicitly, to the *flat mirror*'.[28] An image that passes between two flat mirrors remains the same, and even though there is something that is not mirrored, such as the back side of each mirror, this is of little concern insofar as the movement of the image is concerned: the tains of the mirrors make the mirroring possible, but even granting this point the reflection continues to be one of identity. But everything changes if the mirrors are curved.[29] The image that returns spins out of control, becoming amorphous and liquid. No point relates in a clear one-to-one way with its reflection, yet all points are related nonetheless. Masculine logics, Irigaray maintains, abstract the curvature from the mirrors, reconfiguring the difference that actually structures, by means of decentring, the contours of relations of difference, and making it reappear as the constitutive remainder of a dialectical relation of identity. The result is a feminine conceived in terms of lack, absence or failure. In contrast, the removal of these abstractions brings to light a feminine relation that, by structuring relations through decentring, invokes a nearness, but not 'a "near" not (re)captured in the spatio-temporal economy of philosophical tradition'.[30]

Insofar as identity – even if always failing – remains central to Lacan, and more generally to the exponents of the ontological imaginary of 'lack', these theorists would seem to remain caught up in the classical abstractions Irigaray describes. Yet this is unsurprising given the route from Hegel taken by Lacan, which traces the limits of the dialectic of identity and difference, not to deny its necessity altogether, but to show that its synthesis is conditioned by an unrecuperable Other. Deleuze's route, however, has much in common with Irigaray, at least on the issue of abstraction. It is precisely because any dialectical structure abstracts away a more concrete relation of differences that it misunderstands the difference, exceeding its terms and the way it structures meaning and subjectivity. For Deleuze, explicating the fundamental instability of identity in order to affirm the necessity of its partial and always incomplete stabilisation fails to fully grasp the significance of a difference that differs from identity and difference.

Deleuze and the disjunctive synthesis

One of Deleuze's earliest publications is the 1954 review of Jean Hyppolite's *Logic and Existence*. Opposing anthropological interpretations such as Kojève, Hyppolite argues that for Hegel the full mediation of differences does not occur through the agency of human desire, but instead requires an Absolute Spirit that links the phenomenology, logic and philosophy of nature. The significance of Hyppolite's reading, Deleuze contends, is that it places Hegel's thought on the trajectory of an ontology of sense.[31] Such an ontology, for Deleuze, aspires to overcome metaphysical dichotomies such as essence/appearance, form/content, universal/particular and so forth, and thereby to surmount the transcendent barriers, such as God and the thing-in-itself, that metaphysical philosophy has placed as limits to thought. It therefore demands a synthesis of differences capable of bridging these aporias, demonstrating the internal passage from one side of any of these divides to the other and thereby securing an immanent ontology by overcoming the need to anchor differences in a transcendent positivity. Ultimately, however, Hegel's dialectic fails in this task, as Hyppolite himself notes a remaining unmediatable gap between the phenomenology and the logic. Deleuze concludes his review by suggesting that dialectical contradiction is too abstract and restricted a conception of difference – 'only the phenomenal and anthropological aspect of difference'[32] – to provide the synthesis of differences necessary to achieve immanence.[33]

The idea that dialectical contradiction is abstract is central to Deleuze's later thought. Despite Hegel's contention that contradiction or opposition – which specifies the identity of a thing by defining it against what it 'is not', but also establishes an internal relation between these opposites – is the greatest difference from any identity, Deleuze maintains that it is merely the maximum form of difference compatible with identity.[34] But what does it mean to say that contradiction is abstract and therefore 'less than difference and not more'?[35] For Hegel, abstraction means not general and conceptual as opposed to particular and material, but rather isolated and one-sided. The thing-in-itself, for example, is abstract because any thing in its concreteness refers outside itself, making its identity as an isolated thing merely a moment in a more comprehensive synthetic relation. Deleuze's understanding is similar: the dialectical synthesis of identity and difference, he argues, remains abstract because it refers beyond itself to differences that remain excluded or unsynthesised. On the one hand, the dialectical conception of difference as opposition remains abstract, even as it develops its movement of internal negation and sublation, because it is synthesising abstractions: 'Dialectic thrives on oppositions because it is unaware of far more subtle and subterranean differential mechanisms: topological displacements, typological variations.'[36] On the other hand, however, the inclusion of these fugitive differences within a synthetic structure, precisely because they are incompatible with identity, necessarily breaks with any dialectical synthesis. A truly concrete synthesis of differences, for Deleuze, must be a synthesis of not identity but *disjunction*.[37] As such, it cannot be a synthesis based on a constitutive exclusion.

In this disjunctive synthesis, Otherness functions as a conduit: a thing gains its meaning or sense only through its relations to others, but these relations pass through a knot of Otherness that links them in heterogeneity, discontinuity and strife. Otherness, or 'difference in itself', is a second order of difference – a 'differenciator'[38] – that relates differences internally such that they resonate and communicate with one another, but never simply correspond to or oppose one another. It creates a structural dissymmetry within any being by relating its constitutive differences *through their difference* rather than through identity.

> In accordance with Heidegger's ontological intuition, difference must be articulation and connection in itself; it must relate different to different without any mediation whatsoever by the identical, the similar, the analogous or the opposed. There must be a differenciation of difference, an in-itself which is like a *differenciator* ... by virtue of which the different is gathered all at once rather than represented on condition of a prior resemblance, identity, analogy or opposition.[39]

As with the first ontology, this Otherness is enigmatic. It is characterised, Deleuze says, by never being where it appears to be. Its place cannot be delineated, since 'this would be to assign it a fixed place and an identity repugnant to its whole nature',[40] and so it remains an 'empty square' or a 'dark precursor' that is unlocalisable and *untimely*. The discontinuity established by this Otherness is thus both spatial and temporal. Spatial because, like the curvature of Irigaray's mirrors, it warps the very terrain on which relations are established and therefore cannot be located on that terrain itself. Temporal because, insofar as these constitutive, heterogeneous differences remain irreducible to harmony or identity, because they relate through this untimely differenciator, they are necessarily *out of sync* with one another.

The terms of this spatial and temporal disjuncture allow Deleuze to proffer a novel rereading of psychoanalysis, and particularly the story of the formation of the psyche through Oedipal trauma and phantasy, providing a useful point of comparison with the Lacanian reading of self-formation examined earlier.[41] The event that establishes the Oedipal trauma may or may not be a real event from childhood. By defining sexual difference in heterosexual and genital terms and establishing the castration threat, it separates and connects two orders, one infantile and pre-genital and the other adult and genital, each having divergent body images and both real and imaginary objects of desire, memories of the past and expectations of the future. The expression of this event is the mysterious Phallic signifier, which seems to give meaning and structure to the psyche, but is never entirely comprehensible. Because it establishes the separate series through a radical or traumatic break, it cannot be localised within either series, although it traverses both. But, importantly, the Phallus does not establish an identity between the two series, because it has no identity itself. It is only a marker for a 'something is there' or a 'something happens', making it something vague and unfathomable in both series. It is therefore univocal across the series, but its univocity is that of an enigma.[42] Both series continue within the post-Oedipal unconscious and relate to one another through this 'something is there', which acts as a differenciator. It structures a phantasy that circulates between consciousness and the unconscious, composed of 'the resonance of the two independent and temporally disjointed series'.[43] Despite their discontinuity, infantile and adult series might appear to succeed each other in time. But in fact, Deleuze says, there is no continuity of the subject across the event of trauma – 'the two series ... are not distributed within the same subject'[44] – and the series coexist simultaneously in the unconscious. Moreover, the traumatic event, again, need not be a real event and, as such, it does not mark a chronological moment when the self becomes cracked, but rather indicates a crack that is a fundamental structure: the self is always already cracked, always structured through discontinuity.

The condition of the self, for Deleuze, is thus caught up in at least two lines of time referring to different subjectivities. The 'I' is a multiplicity of subjects living different temporalities within the same, not-so-unified being. These diverging subjects and times are brought together by way of their repetition and resonance with one another. The adults one knew in childhood, Deleuze says, resonate in the unconscious with the adult subjects one is among other adults and children.[45] Moreover, the communication of the series is established by a crack that can never be fully defined for any of these subjectivities, but that serves as their enigmatic link. Certainly this subjective multiplicity can be effaced, giving rise to the appearance of a single subject living a single line of successive events. The 'something happens' may come to appear as an original or early event, defined as a repressed but recoverable 'this has happened', and thereby losing its mysterious status. One may consequently come to think that one's later loves repeat a repressed original love for one's mother, forgetting that the different loves do not even refer to the same subject or that the love of one's mother may be only part of an adult subjectivity projected on to childhood. Yet all this, for Deleuze, this is not the result of desire demanding, in Lacanian fashion, a unified subjectivity and a complete identity, and thereby repressing an impossible remainder that it can signify only as a lack. Instead, he maintains, it is the product of the positive resonance of the different series, which produces the 'optical "effect"'[46] of identity and of stability as the differenciator, structuring the communication between the series, which projects a place for itself in the process of hiding itself.

> In short, there is no ultimate term – our loves do not refer back to the mother; it is simply that the mother occupies a certain place in relation to the virtual object [the differenciator] in the series which constitutes our present, a place which is necessarily filled by another character in the series which constitutes the present of another subjectivity ... The parental characters are not the ultimate terms of individual subjecthood but the middle terms of an intersubjectivity, forms of communication and disguise from one series to another for different subjects, to the extent that these forms are determined by the displacement of the virtual object.[47]

This last point is crucial to Deleuze's route away from Hegel. Identity is not the result of partial and temporary fixations of flowing differences; rather, it is an illusion or simulation engendered by these flows in their interaction and repetition: 'We should say of this identity and this resemblance that they are "simulated": they are products of systems which relate different to different by means of difference ... there is no longer error but *illusion*: inevitable illusion which is the source of error, but may nevertheless be distinguished from it.'[48] Just as where two flows of water meet, quasi-stable patterns of bubbles and folds appear on the surface, for Deleuze the disjointed differences of psychic life generate illusions of identity and continuity. The error is to take the illusions and superficial patterns to be more substantial then they actually are. Once this is done, it is certainly possible to establish, in dialectical fashion, internal relations among these simulacra, showing how their differences and distances from one another can reciprocally define each other. Further, as with any dialectical schema, one can deconstruct its claims to totality and indicate a remainder that it excludes. But this critical operation, like the dialectics it deconstructs, operates on a terrain that has already ironed out its curvatures, thus 'missing ... the original, intensive depth which is the matrix of the entire space.'[49] Moreover, the Otherness it affirms remains all too close to the metaphysical Others – the divine on one side, the abyss on the other – that it purports to move beyond. While it is still possible to achieve immanence by refusing to grant this excess a positive and transcendent status, maintaining instead that it is an outside always produced from within, the result is an abstract ontology that fails to grasp the dissymmetries and disjunctions that concretely structure meaning and sense.

A micropolitics 'beneath' identity

Deleuze is not especially interested in a politics that exposes the necessary failure of any identity or identification, nor with emphasising the need 'to articulate hegemonic alternatives, even if these are ultimately destabilised by the lack at the heart of them'.[50] This is not because exclusions do not occur, nor because identity has no political efficacy. On the contrary, despite their illusionary nature, identity and the oppositional differences that consolidate it do structure a certain level of political and social life. But this layer and its exclusions are not constitutive. Rather, they are only the most visible and terminal surface thrown up from the processes of disjunctive syntheses. A politics focused on this level, for Deleuze, necessarily misses an underlying complex where other political possibilities reside.

Relating to the way the disjunctive synthesis occurs 'below' any abstract dialectical synthesis, Deleuze considers three levels at which an alternative vision of politics may be pitched.[51] The first is a 'molar' level of practices and institutions. This is a level of rigid and dichotomous segments, such as school, family and workplace, through which subjects pass and assume various identities, such as student, husband and worker. A politics directed against these segments might seek to modify or reform them, perhaps even radically, but these are hardly simple procedures. On the one hand, it is not a matter of simply making rigid segments more flexible, 'believing that a little suppleness is enough to make things "better"';[52] on the other hand, 'the segments which run through us and through which we pass are ... marked by a rigidity which reassures us ... Even if we had the power to blow it up, could we succeed in doing so without destroying ourselves, since it is so much a part of the conditions of life, including our organism and our very reason?'[53] Caution is imperative, but despite the importance of these segments, they remain part of the most superficial level of politics.

The segments of the first level depend upon the standards that 'code' them with a set of normal identities that consolidate themselves in relation to other identities defined as deviant, evil or ill. Since these identities are neither pre-given nor exhaustive, they are products of power, and so they indicate a 'molecular' level of power relations that must be analysed and negotiated. Here reside political possibilities to expose the contingency of any identity and its relation to difference and to show how the same power that constructs 'normal' identities also produces the 'marginal' identities that seem to oppose the norm and are policed in the name of the norm. There is also the potential to reconfigure relations of identity by inverting the relation between the norm and the marginal or affirming new and different kinds of identities. Yet there is also a danger that this identity-oriented politics will degenerate into a 'micro-fascism' that, affirming the necessity of opposition to secure identity, reinforces a friend/enemy complex that is so common today. At the very least, this politics will foreclose other possibilities by treating the constitution of identity as a necessity for politics to exist at all. It will affirm the constructed nature of identity, but not its *simulated* status.

A third kind of politics is therefore necessary, which is about neither reforming the institutions and practices in which identities reside nor negotiating the contingency of every identity. Because identity and opposition are abstractions, they refer back to another molecular level of differenciation and disjunction. This is a level of strife and the interplay of differences that are always out of sync with one another, where the notion of constitutive exclusion is too blunt and abstract to fully capture its dynamic. Here emerges a domain of micropolitics, which is concerned literally with 'doing something different' by exploring how individuals and collectives can overcome the logics of identity and difference that seem to exhaust their meaning and sense. With respect to this idea, Deleuze and Guattari speak of making oneself a body without organs ('BwO')[54] by disaggregating the various relations that organise oneself into the segmented and stratified identities one assumes, exposing the concrete assemblage of heterogeneous differences lying underneath. The BwO is an experiment in the opportunities for mutation that this complex but seemingly sedimented structure provides.

> This is how it should be done: Lodge yourself on a stratum, experiment with the opportunities it offers, find an advantageous place on it, find potential movements of deterritorialization, possible lines of flight, experience them, produce flow conjunctions here and there, try out continuums of intensities segment by segment, have a small plot of new land at all times. It is through a meticulous relation with the strata that one succeeds in freeing lines of flight, causing conjugated flows to pass and escape and bringing forth continuous intensities for the BwO.[55]

This kind of experimentation might not be considered political from within standard political theory, but it is eminently political in its power to surmount the categories of standard politics. Yet it also differs from the kind of negotiation called for by an ontology stressing the contingent exclusions that underpin any identity. In striving beyond the crude oppositions that structure so much of the most visible layers of political and social life toward more subtle and complex relations to Otherness, this politics seeks to overcome the categories of identity that have been treated as necessities, but are in fact fictions.

There are certainly no guarantees at this level of politics, as Deleuze and Guattari know well. Experimental BwOs can be botched, ultimately becoming isolated and empty or self-destructive 'black holes' or they may give rise to their own kind of fascism.[56] But despite the dangers, the experimentalism of this micropolitics is indispensable to a radical democratic politics that seeks not only to provide opportunities for new identities to exist, but also to struggle against the dangers inherent in the closures that can accompany even the most self-reflective identity-based thinking. When Foucault outlines the ethical lessons of Deleuze and Guattari's *Anti-Oedipus*, he suggests a different role for groups and collectives, whereby they become not guarantors of identity but 'a constant generator of de-individualization'.[57] This short statement suggests much about the politics that can follow from an ontology that sees meaning and selfhood structured by differenciation. The role of collective politics, when treated here as a micropolitics, is to navigate the impasses imposed upon us by the very identities and binary differences that seem to give us meaning and sense but are also inadequate.

Notes

1 The view I am contesting here seems to be the one taken by Lars Tønder at the 2003 Political Studies Association conference in Leicester, England, during the discussion period of a panel organised on the topic of radical democracy.

2 I have previously outlined these points with respect to the different ontologies of radical democracy in N. Widder, 'What's lacking in the lack: a comment on the virtual', *Angelaki*, 5:3 (2000), 117–38.
3 L. Thomassen and L. Tønder, 'Introduction: rethinking radical democracy between abundance and lack' (this volume), p. 1.
4 *Ibid.*
5 *Ibid.*, p. 3.
6 J. Butler, *Bodies that Matter: On the Discursive Limits of 'Sex'* (London: Routledge, 1993), pp. 117f.
7 *Ibid.*, p. 116.
8 G. Deleuze and F. Guattari, *Anti-Oedipus: Capitalism and Schizophrenia*, trans. R. Hurley, M. Seem and H. R. Lane (Minneapolis, MN: University of Minnesota Press, 1983), p. 28; M. Foucault, *The History of Sexuality, Volume One: An Introduction*, trans. R. Hurley (New York: Vintage Books, 1990), pp. 82–5.
9 E. Laclau and C. Mouffe, *Hegemony and Socialist Strategy: Towards a Radical Democratic Politics* (London: Verso, 1985), p. 112. While there are certainly differences between Laclau and Mouffe's thinking, I take them to be in basic agreement about the necessity of constitutive exclusions.
10 On this development of the theory of hegemony, see Lasse Thomassen's chapter 6 'In/exclusions: towards a radical democratic approach to exclusion' in this volume.
11 E. Laclau, *New Reflections on the Revolution of our Time* (London: Verso, 1990), p. 90.
12 See the critical readings of Foucault and Deleuze in J. Butler, *Subjects of Desire: Hegelian Reflections in Twentieth-Century France* (New York: Columbia University Press, 1987), pp. 186–238; and the critique of Foucault's reading of Herculine Barbin in J. Butler, *Gender Trouble: Feminism and the Subversion of Identity* (London: Routledge, 1990), pp. 93–106.
13 G. Deleuze, *The Logic of Sense*, trans. M. Lester with C. Stivale (New York: Columbia University Press, 1990), pp. 306, 106.
14 A. Kojève, *An Introduction to the Reading of Hegel*, trans. J. H. Nichols, Jr (New York: Basic Books, 1969), esp. 'In Place of an Introduction'.
15 J. Lacan, 'The meaning of the phallus', in J. Mitchell and J. Rose (eds), *Feminine Sexuality: Jacques Lacan and the école freudienne*, trans. J. Rose (London: Macmillan, 1982), pp. 74–85, 80f.
16 *Ibid.*, p. 81.
17 *Ibid.*
18 *Ibid.*, p. 80.
19 See J. Lacan, *Ecrits: A Selection*, trans. A. Sheridan (London: Tavistock and Routledge, 1989), pp. 1–7.
20 Lacan, 'The meaning of the phallus', p. 80.
21 *Ibid.*, pp. 83–5.
22 J. Lacan, 'God and the *jouissance* of T̶h̶e̶ woman: a love letter', in *Feminine Sexuality*, pp. 137–61, 153f.
23 *Ibid.*, pp. 145–7.
24 *Ibid.*, pp. 143f.
25 S. Freud, 'Lecture XXXIII: the psychology of women', in *New Introductory Lectures on Psycho-Analysis*, trans. W. J. H. Sprott (London: The Hogarth Press, 1962), pp. 144–74.
26 Lacan, 'God and the *jouissance* of T̶h̶e̶ woman', pp. 143–5.
27 L. Irigaray, *This Sex Which is Not One*, trans. C. Porter with C. Burke (Ithaca, NY: Cornell University Press, 1985), p. 177.

28 *Ibid.*, p. 154.
29 *Ibid.*, pp. 154f.
30 *Ibid.*, pp. 153f.
31 G. Deleuze, 'Review of Jean Hyppolite', in J. Hyppolite, *Logic and Existence*, trans. L. Lawlor and A. Sen (Albany, NY: State University of New York Press, 1997), p. 191: 'Philosophy must be ontology, it cannot be anything else; but there is no ontology of essence, there is only an ontology of sense.'
32 *Ibid.*, p. 195.
33 For an elaboration of Hyppolite's work, Deleuze's review, and how both of these works set the direction for Deleuze's later thought in relation to Hegel and the development of an ontology of immanence, see N. Widder, 'Thought after dialectics: Deleuze's ontology of sense', *The Southern Journal of Philosophy*, 41:3 (2003), 451–76.
34 G. Deleuze, *Difference and Repetition*, trans. P. Patton (London: Athlone Press, 1994), pp. 49f.
35 Deleuze, 'Review of Jean Hyppolite', p. 195.
36 G. Deleuze, *Nietzsche and Philosophy*, trans. H. Tomlinson (London: Athlone Press, 1983), p. 157.
37 Deleuze introduces the term 'disjunctive synthesis' in *Logic of Sense* (*passim*).
38 Deleuze makes use of the distinction in French between the verbs *différencier*, to make or become different, and *différentier*, which is restricted to the mathematical operation. The English translation correspondingly employs the terms 'differenciate' and 'differentiate'. Differenciation, Deleuze argues, requires a differenciator that escapes the orders of identity and which differenciates itself in such a way that it gives rise to the quasi-stabilities that can be organised by higher orders of identity. See P. Patton, 'Translator's Preface', in Deleuze, *Difference and Repetition*, p. xi.
39 Deleuze, *Difference and Repetition*, p. 117.
40 *Ibid.*, p. 105.
41 See particularly Deleuze, *The Logic of Sense*, pp. 186–233.
42 The thesis of univocity is developed primarily in Deleuze, *Difference and Repetition*, esp. at pp. 354. For elaboration, see N. Widder, 'The rights of simulacra: Deleuze and the univocity of Being', *Continental Philosophy Review*, 34:4 (2001), 437–53.
43 Deleuze, *Logic of Sense*, p. 226.
44 Deleuze, *Difference and Repetition*, p. 124.
45 *Ibid.*
46 *Ibid.*, p. xix.
47 *Ibid.*, pp. 105f.
48 *Ibid.*, p. 126.
49 *Ibid.*, p. 50.
50 L. Thomassen and L. Tønder, 'Introduction: rethinking radical democracy between abundance and lack', p. 6 (in this volume).
51 See in particular G. Deleuze and C. Parnet, *Dialogues*, trans. H. Tomlinson and B. Habberjam (New York: Columbia University Press, 1987), pp. 124–47; and G. Deleuze and F. Guattari, *A Thousand Plateaus: Capitalism and Schizophrenia*, trans. B. Massumi (Minneapolis, MN: University of Minnesota Press, 1987), pp. 208–31.
52 Deleuze and Guattari, *A Thousand Plateaus*, p. 215.
53 Deleuze and Parnet, *Dialogues*, p. 138.
54 See Deleuze and Guattari, *A Thousand Plateaus*, pp. 149–66.
55 *Ibid.*, p. 161.
56 *Ibid.*, pp. 149, 163.
57 M. Foucault, 'Preface', in G. Deleuze and F. Guattari, *Anti-Oedipus*, p. xiv.

3 • *Paul Patton*

Deleuze and democratic politics[1]

Introduction

MUCH of the excitement and difficulty of reading Deleuze as a political thinker derives from the fact that he does not speak the familiar languages of politics or political theory. He does not address standard problems of liberal political philosophy, such as the elaboration of principles of justice or freedom or the definition of democracy. His work with Guattari is more closely aligned to the Marxist political tradition, but shows little sympathy for class analysis or the classical forms of revolutionary politics. Even when it addresses standard problems within the Marxist tradition, it does so using novel concepts: exploitation reconceived in terms of apparatuses of capture, capitalism reconceived as an axiomatic system in which nation-states function as models of realisation, and so on. The aim of *Anti-Oedipus* and *A Thousand Plateaus* is to provide a descriptive ontology of assemblages, lines and processes of various kinds. They provide a language in which to describe social and political phenomena as apparatuses of capture or nomadic war machines, processes of axiomatisation or becoming. They provide a theory or series of theories that privilege movement, creativity and transformation in the assemblages that determine who we are. Their goal is to assist the emergence of new forms of affective, linguistic, social, economic and political life.

Although the authors do not spell out the underlying principles of evaluation, this ontology is normative in the sense that it accords axiological as well as ontological priority to processes of deterritorialisation, becoming and metamorphosis. The primacy of rhizomatic over arborescent, molecular over molar, difference over identity is reiterated throughout *A Thousand Plateaus*. For example, it appears in the idea that lines of flight or deterritorialisation constitute assemblages. In contrast to Foucault's suggestion that power is the primary dimension of assemblages, they insist that lines of flight are the 'cutting edges of creation and deterritorialisation' within a given assemblage and that these precede phenomena of resistance and reterritorialisation.[2] In contrast to Marx's historical materialism, they suggest that societies are defined less by their conflicts and contradictions than by the lines of flight running through them. In the sense that lines of flight and processes of metamorphosis and deterritorialisation take precedence over the forms of reproduction, capture and reterritorialisation, Deleuze and Guattari are philosophers of abundance rather than lack. For them, the non-coincident nature of things and the permanent instability of all forms of identity result from the fact that chaotic processes of flux, becoming or 'absolute deterritorialisation' lie at the heart of being. Ultimately, they suggest, absolute deterritorialisation is 'the deeper movement ... identical to the earth itself'.[3]

Despite or rather because of this reluctance to employ traditional concepts or to pursue traditional problems, Deleuze affirms the status of both *Anti-Oedipus* and *A Thousand Plateaus* as works of political philosophy. But what kind of political philosophy is this and what purpose does it serve? Of the four functions that John Rawls identifies for political philosophy, Deleuze and Guattari's political philosophy addresses only the one that he refers to as the 'realistically utopian' task of 'probing the limits of practical political possibility'. The others include the attempt to resolve deeply disputed questions by searching for a common philosophical and moral ground between the protagonists; the task of orientation that seeks to show how reasonable and rational ends can 'cohere within a well-articulated conception of a just and reasonable society'; and the task of reconciliation which seeks to show the limits of what can be achieved within a democratic society characterised by the fact of 'profound and irreconcilable differences'.[4] Deleuze and Guattari do not address the normative functions of resolution, orientation or reconciliation and their conception of the political vocation of philosophy as helping to bring about 'new earths and new peoples' suggests more extravagant ambitions than those acknowledged in Rawls' realistic utopianism. On their view:

> Philosophy takes the relative deterritorialisation of capital to the absolute; it makes it pass over the plane of immanence as movement of the infinite and suppresses it as internal limit, *turns it back against itself so as to summon forth a new earth, a new people* ... Actually, *utopia is what links* philosophy with its own epoch, with European capitalism, but also already with the Greek city. In each case it is with utopia that philosophy becomes political and takes the criticism of its own time to its highest point.[5]

Success in this kind of political philosophy is not measured by the test of reflective equilibrium or by the capacity to maintain a well-ordered society but by the capacity of its concepts to engage with and assist movements of deterritorialisation or becoming in the present, in the hope of contributing to the invention of new forms of individual and collective life. Examples of such becomings include a becoming-revolutionary that is not reducible to the historical reality of past or future revolutions, and 'a becoming-democratic that is not the same as any actual constitutional State'.[6] As these examples suggest, Deleuzian political philosophy is not so utopian that it is completely disconnected from the normative and conceptual horizons of the present. It incorporates both a recognisably Marxist critique of capitalist society and a post-Marxist critique of revolutionary vanguard politics and the philosophy of history that sustained them. It criticises the workings of actually existing democracies in the name of the egalitarian principles that underpin those democracies. For this reason, I will argue, there is no fundamental incompatibility between Deleuze's political thought and democratic politics.

Other commentators take a different view. Arguing from a position of sympathy towards the *Autonomia* tendency within Italian Marxism, Nicholas Thoburn sees Deleuze and Guattari's minoritarian politics as an alternative to Laclau and Mouffe's neo-Gramscian post-Marxism. Whereas Laclau and Mouffe represent a movement 'from the politics of *production* to the politics of *democracy* and civil society', Deleuze and Guattari represent an 'intensification' of Marx's critical engagement with the entire field of capitalist social relations.[7] For Thoburn, Deleuzian Marxism implies more than just a broader conception of politics: 'Inasmuch as it is a critique and problematization of the forms of identity and practice composed in the capitalist socius, this politics is an explicit *challenge* to social democratic politics.' As such, he suggests, Deleuze's position is 'not dissimilar' to the explicitly anti-democratic politics which some tendencies within Marxism attribute to Marx.[8]

Arguing from a position of sympathy towards liberal democratic politics, Philippe Mengue also claims that there is a fundamental antipathy towards democracy in Deleuze's political thought: democracy is devalued not just for its empirical failings but 'for reasons of principle'.[9] Mengue argues that this hostility is paradoxical because Deleuze's ontological intuitions ought to have made him more sympathetic to liberalism in both its economic and political incarnations. He accuses him of blindness towards the affinities between his own social theory and the economic liberalism of Hayek, and charges him with failure to acknowledge the truly revolutionary social and economic changes for which liberal democracy was responsible in France during the post-War period.[10] In agreement at least with the substance of Thoburn's diagnosis, he attributes this hostility towards democracy to an uncritical acceptance of Marxist doxa, common among French intellectuals at the time. Ultimately, he suggests, notwithstanding their abandonment of the language of class struggle, Deleuze and Guattari's account of the relationship between modern forms of state and capital relies on the thesis of economic determinism. They reproduce their own version of the classical Marxist denunciation of liberal democracy as little more than a concession or alibi, which only serves to maintain the system of exploitation and repression.[11]

Deleuze and democratic politics

To whatever extent this is an accurate reading of Deleuze and Guattari's account of the relationship between state and capital, it does not address the issue of their commitment to the normative principles of democratic government. Similar problems arise in relation to the interpretation of Marx and many have argued that his critique of capitalist society ultimately relies on principles of equality, which fall within the democratic tradition of political thought.[12] For these theorists, there is no inconsistency in criticising existing forms of liberal democratic government for their complicity with capitalism, while remaining committed to liberal and democratic principles. From Luxembourg to Derrida, Laclau and Mouffe and beyond, many have argued for an understanding of the communist ideal as an extended application of democratic principles to include economic and social as well as political life.[13] For this reason, I leave aside the question of Deleuze's relation to Marx and that part of his criticism of existing democratic states that is bound up with the analysis of their role within global capitalism, in order to concentrate on the deeper question of his relation to democratic principles. Thoburn and Mengue's claims of anti-democratic bias in Deleuze's political thought are unconvincing, but they nevertheless raise important questions which help to clarify his approach to politics and his relation to democracy: What is meant by 'democracy' in this context? What evidence is there for the claim that Deleuze's philosophy excludes or condemns democratic politics? I explore these questions below primarily with reference to Philippe Mengue, since he presents the more extensive engagement with Deleuze and Guattari's political philosophy.

What is democracy?

'Democracy' has both wide and narrow senses. In the broad sense, it refers to a form of society characterised by the absence of class or caste privilege and by the implementation of the egalitarian principle of the equal worth of individuals, such that no person's life, beliefs or values are inherently worth more than those of anyone else. Within a democratic polity, each citizen is entitled to their own conception of the good and to express their own ideas on matters of public policy. Such a political society is an association of equals in which there is neither justification for the exclusion of individuals or groups from the widest possible system of basic civil and political liberties, nor any justification for the arbitrary exclusion of particular individuals or groups from the benefits of social and political cooperation. In the narrow sense, 'democracy' refers to a form of government in which the governed exercise control over governments and their policies, typically through regular and fair elections. Contemporary liberal democracies purport to be democratic in this sense. They ensure equal rights to effective participation in political processes, but also set limits to what majorities can decide by protecting basic civil and political rights and ensuring the maintenance of a rule of law. These two senses of democracy are related and the connections between them run in both directions. However, it is the conception of individuals as of equal moral worth that is fundamental. While this implies a form of government in which individuals have an equal voice on matters of public concern, it leaves open a range of possible institutional forms of democratic government.

There is no doubt that Deleuze is not a theorist of democracy in the narrow sense of the term. Neither the institutions nor the values associated with democratic government feature prominently in his work and, on the few occasions in which they are mentioned, this is primarily in the context of pointing to the shortcomings of existing liberal democratic governments. However, it does not follow from this that Deleuze is hostile to democratic government, or that his political philosophy implies a rejection of democracy in either the broad or the narrow sense. In fact there is no shortage of evidence to suggest that, in his political practice as well as in his theoretical views, he is committed to democracy in both senses of the term.

Mengue argues that Deleuze's apparent failure to embrace democratic politics is all the more surprising in view of the affinities between his ethico-ontological principles and the political domain understood as a field in which conflicting opinions are pitted against one another and resolved according to the principle of majority rule. Because it takes place between conflicting opinions and conflicting political orientations, democracy involves a rhizomatic politics rather than a politics of demonstration or deduction. As such, democratic politics is inherently experimental and creative in a way that accords with the Deleuzian ethic of deterritorialisation. Because democratic politics is played out in the space in between the orientations or opinions of particular individuals or groups, it is a politics of pure immanence, a politics without foundation: 'We are in the middle in all senses, horizontally, between equals, with equal and unprivileged capacities for opinion and choice, and vertically, by virtue of the absence of transcendent values.'[14] Although in later writings Deleuze puts forward a critical concept of opinion (this will be discussed below), the suggestion that the Deleuzian theory of micropolitics and molecular assemblages has a particular affinity with the mobile and fluctuating character of public opinion is indeed to be found in *A Thousand Plateaus*.[15] The issue here, however, is the relation between such micropolitics and democracy.

Mengue objects that Deleuzian micropolitics is not properly a theory of politics because it does not seek to theorise or render legitimate the institutions required to constitute a properly political society, such as the necessary space for debate and free political action. In other words, it is only in so far as there are political institutions, which subject the exercise of power to the rule of law and the consent of the governed, that the concerns of the micro-revolutionary can be transformed into political reality. Without these, micropolitics remains no more than the attempt to impose private opinions on others by force. It is undoubtedly true that the space of democratic politics requires more than the unregulated play of conflicting opinions. Without at least some regulation of the constitutional form and procedures within which the play of opinions is resolved, the result would be a populist and unstable form of democracy. Constitutional principles of right are necessary to protect individuals and minorities against majority opinions. In Rawlsian terms, the normative framework of democratic politics is provided by the principles of equality and justice that ultimately rest upon the considered moral convictions of those who make up the relevant political community. This is not to say that such principles must be derived from a higher source of authority than the value judgments of the people concerned, or that they are immune to change, but it is to introduce some vertical differentiation into the field in which conflicting opinions and political orientations are played out.

Mengue's objection points to the need for an explicit account of such principles of right in democratic states. If, as he suggests, the goal of political association is to determine a collective will as the basis for laws and public policy, then there is indeed a properly political or 'doxological' plane of immanence, which is the space of public debate with a view to collective decision on matters of public policy. What are produced on this plane are not concepts, percepts or affects but 'solidarity and consensus regarding what is to be done here and now'.[16] The formation of such consensus or 'right opinion' can be understood as the outcome of a specific and rhizomatic play of opinions, expert advice, interests and values such that it 'operates a veritable deterritorialisation of opinion'.[17] We might add that such collective decision-making also involves the reterritorialisation of opinion on the idea of the public good, including the idea that decisions have to be made and that it is appropriate they respect the wishes of the majority of those concerned. Mengue is undoubtedly correct to point to the importance of a specifically political reason of this kind for democratic politics. He is also right to point out that it may be characterised in Deleuzian terms, even though Deleuze himself does not provide any such theory of political reason as a specific form of thought irreducible to philosophy, science or art. But does this neglect of political reason in Deleuze's thought justify the charge that he provides an aesthetics or ethics but not properly a theory of politics?[18] Does the neglect of the public political sphere in the elaboration of Deleuzian micropolitics justify the stronger charge of anti-democratic bias?

At most, it might support the claim that, in the absence of an explicit embrace of democratic institutions and processes, micropolitics deprives itself of the institutions necessary to realise its egalitarian ambitions. This amounts to claiming that the Deleuzian theory of micropolitics is only a partial account of the process of political decision making. However, incompleteness is not antipathy and there is no reason to suppose that Deleuzian theory proposes an alternative rather than a supplement to democratic political theory. William Connolly presents a compelling case for the latter view of the relationship between Deleuzian theory and democratic politics in arguing for a pluralist and democratic ethos of engagement, 'responsive to both the indispensability of justice and the radical insufficiency of justice to itself'.[19] One of the distinctive features of democratic politics is that even the fundamental convictions expressed in its laws and institutions are open to change: for example, the extension of basic political rights to include those formerly excluded or the priority accorded to certain moral values. It follows that efforts to bring about such changes are a legitimate part of the political process. If we accept that subterranean shifts in the attitudes, sensibilities and beliefs of individuals and populations are among the conditions of such change, then it follows that the micropolitical sphere of such movements is a no less important dimension of democratic politics. Deleuze and Guattari's micropolitical theory provides a language in which to describe movements of this kind. It thereby supplements liberal democratic conceptions of decision-making and challenges these to take into account such micropolitical processes.

Deleuze critical of democracy?

Mengue argues that Deleuze's preference for a minoritarian politics of becoming implies hostility towards and a retreat from the majoritarian politics of the public sphere. He characterises Deleuze's own political involvements as those of an elite, intellectual minority and interprets his criticism of the way in which mass media dominate the public sphere as the pretext for a Platonic gesture of retreat from the agora, and a form of aristocratic disdain for the multitude.[20] Such a characterisation is difficult to reconcile with the history of Deleuze's interventions on matters of public debate in the form of opinion articles, letters and petitions. In one of these interventions, an 'Open Letter to Antonio Negri's Judges', he takes issue with certain questions of legal principle in relation to the charges against Negri: the lack of consistency in the charges themselves, the acceptance of ordinary logical principles of reasoning in the examination of evidence, and the role of the media in relation to this judicial procedure. Deleuze begins this letter with the claim that there are three principles at stake here, and suggests that 'these three principles implicate [are of importance to] all democrats'.[21] The letter implies that he counts himself among those democrats.

Thoburn draws upon Deleuze's *Abécédaire* interview with Claire Parnet, recorded during 1988–9, for evidence to support his contention that Deleuzian politics pose an explicit challenge to social democratic politics: 'For Deleuze, to be "on the left" is not a matter of democracy.'[22] In the section entitled '*G comme*

Gauche', Deleuze responds to Parnet's question, 'What does it mean to be on the left?', by offering a twofold definition of what it means for him. First, he states that it is a matter of perception. Those who are not on the left and who live in the comparative wealth of a relatively privileged first world country perceive problems of inequality and injustice from their own perspective. Sensing that their position is untenable and under threat, they ask 'What can we do to make this situation last?' By contrast, those on the left perceive the situation from the perspective of the horizon, the point farthest from their centre of privilege. These people 'know that it cannot last, that it's not possible, [the fact that] these millions of people are starving to death, it just can't last, it might go on a hundred years, one never knows, but there's no point kidding oneself about this absolute injustice'. Those on the left know that such problems must be dealt with, that the problem is not to find ways to maintain the privileges of Europe but that of 'finding arrangements, finding world-wide assemblages', which address these problems.[23]

To the extent that Deleuze here assumes an egalitarian and indeed cosmopolitan perspective on matters of distributive justice, his position is clearly democratic in the broad sense outlined above. His opposition to existing assemblages is based on the injustice that results from the unequal distribution of wealth and poverty. Similarly, in his interview with Negri, he juxtaposes the sense in which the market as a sphere of exchange of commodities and capital is universal in the sense in which it generates both wealth and misery and distributes these in a manner that is neither universalising nor homogenising. In other words, it is the principle of equality and the idea that such undeserved inequalities of condition are unjust that underpins Deleuze's criticism of both capitalism and the liberal democratic states through which its control of populations is exercised.

The second part of Deleuze's definition of what it means to be on the left is his claim that this is matter of becoming minoritarian as opposed to being majoritarian. It is a matter of knowing that the majority is an abstract and empty representation of an ideal identity that is linked to particular systems of power and control and of knowing that there are minoritarian becomings in which everyone can be engaged and which have the power to disrupt and transform these systems. It is for this reason that Deleuze says that being on the left is not a matter of government, indeed that there are no leftist governments. However, while he clearly aligns leftist politics with minoritarian politics, he nowhere says that this has nothing to do with democracy. There is no telling in advance which processes of deterritorialisation or becoming-minor might lead to fundamental social or political change. There is no privileged minority, such as the proletariat, on which rests the hope for a better future. A legal decision or a sudden imperceptible shift in personal loyalties might set in train processes that lead to the positive deterritorialisation of a given system of power and control. Deleuze neither privileges nor excludes democratic political processes from functioning as agents of revolutionary social change. However, the basis of his opposition to the present socio-political order is that it is fundamentally inegalitarian and therefore undemocratic in the broader sense of the term.

Mengue advances three primary arguments for Deleuze's supposed hostility towards democracy, each related to one of the key principles of his philosophy: preference for immanence over transcendence, preference for minority over majority and preference for becoming over history, where 'history' implies acceptance of the current forms of liberal democratic government based upon consensus. Let us deal with each of these arguments in turn.

Mengue's primary source for the first argument is a series of remarks culled from interviews in which Deleuze is critical of the renewed interest in the rule of law and human rights during the 1980s. For example, in a conversation with Antoine Dulaure and Claire Parnet published in 1985, he describes the way things are going badly in contemporary thought:

> Yet in philosophy we're coming back to eternal values, to the idea of the intellectual as custodian of eternal values ... These days it's the rights of man that provide our eternal values. It's the constitutional state (*État de droit*) and other notions that everyone recognises as very abstract. And it's in the name of all this that thinking is fettered and that any analysis in terms of movements is blocked.[24]

Similarly, in a conversation with Raymond Bellour and François Ewald published in 1988, Deleuze was asked why, unlike Foucault, he took no part in the human rights movement. He replied:

> if you are talking about establishing new forms of transcendence, new universals, restoring a reflective subject as the bearer of rights, or setting up a communicative intersubjectivity, then it's not much of a philosophical advance.[25]

Mengue draws from these remarks an argument against human rights on the grounds of principle. Rights of man are eternal and abstract. As such, they are transcendent values. They suppose a universal and abstract subject of rights, identified with no one in particular and irreducible to singular, existent figures. Deleuze's philosophy is resolutely opposed to transcendence in all its forms. He therefore rejects abstractions such as human rights on the grounds that these serve to stop movement and experimentation on the plane of immanence, in thought as much as in political practice.

While the argument conforms to Deleuzian principles up to this point, it is incomplete in that it does not spell out the reasoning behind the claim that the abstract or the universal stops movement, both at the level of thought and at the level of action. It appears to conclude that Deleuze is opposed to any form of abstraction or to the very idea of rights, when his opposition is only to certain ways of understanding abstraction or rights. Mengue fails to note that, in each case in the remarks quoted above, Deleuze refers to particular historical phenomena. Nothing in what he says implies rejection of human rights, the rule of law or democratic government as such. His criticisms have to do with the manner in which these are represented: as 'eternal values', 'new forms of transcendence, new universals'.

The reasoning behind Deleuze's reticence to embrace the rhetoric of human rights is evident in his remarks about rights and jurisprudence, which Mengue ignores with good reason, since they make it clear that Deleuze is not opposed to rights as such, but only to the a-historical idea that there exists a definitive set of human rights. In the interview with Bellour and Ewald, he points out that rights are created by jurisprudence and that this 'advances by working from singularities'.[26] In the interview with Negri, he comments that it is 'jurisprudence, ultimately, that creates law, and we mustn't go on leaving this to judges'. With reference to a proposal to establish a system of law for modern biology, he says that what is required is not 'an ethical committee of supposedly well-qualified wise men but user groups'.[27] This appeal to jurisprudence and the need to create new rights that reflect the interests of those affected by biotechnology does not sit well with the picture of Deleuze as anti-democratic.

Deleuze takes up this question of rights and jurisprudence again in his *Abécédaire* interviews with Claire Parnet. Here, he elaborates on the emptiness of human rights with reference to the situation of an Armenian population subjected to a massacre by Turks and then to a subsequent earthquake. He raises two objections to the suggestion that human rights are at issue in such situations: first, that when people make declarations about human rights, 'these declarations are never made as a function of the people who are directly concerned'. In this case, the Armenian people concerned have specific needs in the context of a specific, territorial situation: 'their problem is not "the rights of man"'.[28] Second, Deleuze argues that all such abominations to which people are subjected must be considered as *cases* to be decided rather than situations to be subsumed under existing laws. The response to such cases must be creative and not simply the rote application of existing categories. Just as he argues elsewhere that philosophy responds to problems by the creation of concepts, so when we respond to particular situations by legal means we are involved in jurisprudence, meaning the creative modification of existing legal principles or the invention of new ones to fit particular cases:

> To act for freedom, becoming revolutionary, is to operate in jurisprudence when one turns to the justice system ... that's what the invention of law is ... its not a question of applying 'the rights of man' but rather of inventing new

> forms of jurisprudence ... I have always been fascinated by jurisprudence, by law ... If I hadn't studied philosophy, I would have studied law, but precisely not 'the rights of man', rather I'd have studied jurisprudence. That's what life is. There are no 'rights of man', only rights of life, and so, life unfolds case by case.[29]

Deleuze's interest in jurisprudence thus clarifies the sense of his opposition to empty abstractions: it is because these are fixed and a-historical, unable to evolve in accordance with the requirements of a particular case. His preference for jurisprudence over declarations of human rights or their enshrinement in legal codes is a preference for the ongoing and open-ended creative process that leads to the modification of existing laws and the invention of new rights. As such, it parallels the kind of conceptual abstraction that he endorses in philosophy. In law as in thought, this case-by-case approach is a means to introduce movement into abstractions and thereby to approach more closely the conditions of life. It is difficult to reconcile this preference for the ongoing and process of creating new rights in response to particular situations with a hostility towards the rule of law. It is equally difficult to reconcile this interest in jurisprudence with an anti-democratic disdain for the fate of ordinary people, especially when, as Deleuze suggest, the ultimate court of appeal in such situations should be the people most directly affected.

Mengue's central argument for the anti-democratic bias of Deleuzian political philosophy draws together several themes associated with the distinction between majority and minority drawn in *A Thousand Plateaus* and with the remarks about opinion in *What is Philosophy?* He summarises this argument as follows: 'democracy, according to Deleuze, is defined in its essence as the reign of public opinion, of *consensus*, which is essentially majoritarian. It is therefore opposed, and an obstacle, to the powers of minorities which are by nature inventive. Thus, not only is democracy not new but it crushes novelty.'[30] I will take up the issue of Deleuze's hostility towards opinion below, but for the moment let me examine the opposition between majority and minority and its relation to democratic politics.

In *A Thousand Plateaus*, Deleuze and Guattari emphasise the difference in kind between the position of majority and minoritarian becoming, and along with this difference their preference for minoritarian politics. They point to the existence in contemporary societies of a majoritarian 'fact', namely the existence of a standard against which the rights and duties of all citizens are measured:

> Let us suppose that the constant or standard is the average adult-white-heterosexual-European-male-speaking a standard language ... It is obvious that 'man' holds the majority, even if he is less numerous than mosquitoes, children, women, blacks, peasants, homosexuals, etc. That is because he appears twice, once in the constant and again in the variable from which the

Deleuze and democratic politics

constant is extracted. Majority assumes a state of power and domination, not the other way around.[31]

At the same time, Deleuze and Guattari point out that this is 'the analytic fact of Nobody' and contrast it with the 'becoming-minoritarian of everybody'.[32] This becoming-minoritarian is the creative potential of individuals or groups to deviate from the standard. It expresses the sense in which individuals and societies never entirely conform to the majoritarian standard, but exist in a process of continuous variation. It is from the perspective of their political preference for this creative process of minoritarian becoming that they suggest that 'the problem is never to acquire the majority'.[33] Mengue relies upon this comment to support his strongest claim that Deleuze's political orientation is fundamentally hostile towards democracy. Since democracy is the realm of opinion and consensus and since 'the essence of opinion is will to majority',[34] it follows that democracy is in essence majoritarian. If the task of minoritarian politics is never to acquire the majority then it follows that, for Deleuze, 'democracy is definitively and for reasons of principle excluded and radically condemned'.[35]

It is true that Deleuze and Guattari emphasise the difference in kind between majority and minority. However, difference is not the same as opposition and it is important not to overstate the consequences of this difference. In political terms, it amounts to the difference between the constitution or reconfiguration of the majoritarian standard, which is often achieved through democratic and legal means, and the fact and ongoing process of non-coincidence with the standard, however reconfigured. Paola Marrati points out that the emptiness of the majoritarian model is not the emptiness necessary to democracy of which Lefort speaks but the fact that it represents no one. She rightly insists that the emptiness of the majoritarian fact implies a critique of representation, which applies to the identity of minorities as much as it does to that of the majority. Deleuzian micropolitics differs from representative politics, not in the sense that it proposes an alternative, but in the sense that it refers to a different order of political activity: 'Its aim is a *becoming of the world* as a possibility of inventing new forms of life, different modes of existence.'[36]

Mengue turns difference into opposition by suggesting that the position of majority is by nature opposed to the creativity of the minoritarian and that majoritarian and democratic politics inevitably 'crushes' creative becomings. According to this view, to adopt the standpoint of the majority is always to abandon the standpoint of the untimely and the creative in favour of the state and established values. This is an implausible view of democratic politics. What are we then to make of the legislative measures in recent years to broaden the standard to included non-whites, non-males and even to allow equal rights to homosexual partners? These measures suggest that, far from 'crushing novelty' as Mengue suggests, democratic politics can have its own forms of creativity.

[*61*]

Connolly reminds us that, in order to be responsive to new claims for the reconfiguration of the standard, democratic political life needs to be infused with a public ethos of critical engagement.[37] For Deleuze and Guattari, the different forms of minority becoming provide the impulse for change, but this only occurs to the extent that there is adaptation and incorporation on the side of the majority. When they say that the power of minorities 'is not measured by their capacity to enter into and make themselves felt within the majority system, nor even to reverse the necessarily tautological criterion of the majority',[38] they mean that the majorities do not determine the limits of the potential for transformation. They do not mean to suggest that minorities do not enter into and produce effects upon the majority. On the contrary, they insist upon the importance of piecemeal changes to the form and content of a given majority: 'molecular escapes and movements would be nothing if they did not return to the molar organizations to reshuffle their segments, their binary distributions of sexes, classes and parties'.[39]

Deleuze and Guattari's insistence on the transformative potential of minoritarian becomings does not imply a refusal of democratic politics, much less a rejection of democratic principles. The irreducible character of the difference in kind between majority and minority aligns them firmly with the proponents of democratic pluralism. For Connolly, the key to democratic pluralism lies in the 'productive tension' between majoritarian governance, rights and recognition, on the one hand, and minoritarian becoming, on the other.[40] For Deleuze and Guattari, it is precisely those excluded from the majority as defined by a given set of axioms who are the potential bearers of the power to transform that set. These are the source of minoritarian becomings that carry the potential for new earths and peoples, unlike like those found in existing democracies.

The third stratum of Mengue's argument for the anti-democratic character of Deleuze's political philosophy relies upon his highly critical remarks about opinion. It is because democracy is based upon public opinion and consensus, while Deleuze's philosophy is resolutely opposed to opinion in all its manifestations, that 'democracy is definitively and for reasons of principle excluded and radically condemned'.[41] Mengue not only confuses different issues at stake in Deleuze's criticism of opinion, he also confuses criticism of the present state of democratic politics with criticism of democracy as such.

Much of the criticism of opinion in *What is Philosophy?* relates to its difference from philosophy rather than its role in politics. Deleuze and Guattari present philosophical thought as engaged in a struggle on two fronts against chaos and against opinions. Since the latter is the more important front, it follows that philosophy is primarily engaged in a guerrilla campaign against opinion. Mengue relies upon this opposition between opinion and philosophy in order to argue that Deleuzian politics cannot possibly be democratic. Given that democracy implies discussion and public debate, whereas the creation of concepts does not proceed through discussion, it follows that Deleuzian philosophy cannot support democracy: 'If thought or philosophy abhors discussion, it is difficult to see how it would not abhor democracy.'[42] The missing premise in the argument thus far is the equation of Deleuzian politics with a politics of thought. Since Deleuze's criticism of opinion occurs in the context of elaborating a concept of philosophy, this further step in the argument is required in order to connect his criticism of opinion with any position with regard to politics. In an earlier chapter, Mengue does argue that, for Deleuze, politics is reduced to a politics of thought, indeed to thought as politics. He draws upon the brief exergue to *Negotiations* to support his claim that Deleuze collapses the distinction between intellectual and political activity, such that 'the thought of the thinker is directly and in essence political'. This collapsing of politics into a politics of thought provides one basis for the charge that Deleuze is guilty of a 'devalorisation of democracy'.[43]

However, the text cited supports no such conclusion. In this very short Exergue designed to explain the pertinence of the title, 'Negotiations', Deleuze suggests that philosophy is not a power and cannot communicate, or at least not directly, with the powers that be, including the power of opinion. He goes on to suggest that, since these powers 'are not just external things but permeate each of us, philosophy throws us all into constant negotiations with and a guerrilla campaign against, ourselves'.[44] His argument is therefore that philosophy provides at best an indirect form of resistance to the powers that be. It is an aid or a supplement, perhaps a necessary supplement, to political activity in the public sphere, but nothing said here suggests that it is a substitute for political as distinct from philosophical activity. The text provides no support for the claim that Deleuze collapses politics into a politics of thought and therefore no support for the suggestion that he devalues democracy.

What is Philosophy? devotes several pages to distinguishing opinion from concepts and criticising the philosophy of communication that 'is exhausted in the search for a universal liberal opinion as consensus'.[45] Deleuze outlines a rigorous concept of opinion as a function linking perceptual properties of things to particular perceptions or affections, and both of these to subjects of a certain kind (for example, <faithfulness of dogs, detest: dog-haters>, <foul smell of cheese, love it: bon vivants> etc.). Philosophical concepts are not functions and it is in this context that Deleuze ironises about 'the Western democratic popular conception of philosophy as providing pleasant or aggressive dinner conversations at Mr Rorty's'.[46] He is clearly opposed to the idea that the exchange of opinions is a means to create concepts, but not necessarily opposed to the pleasures of conversation as such. Moreover, nothing follows from this sharp distinction between philosophical concepts and opinions about the exchange of opinions or the need for consensus in the political sphere.

As we saw above, Mengue is right to claim that a doxological plane of immanence is necessary for democratic politics. However, it does not follow from this that what passes for public discussion in contemporary liberal democracies is an adequate realisation of this plane. As a consequence, when Deleuze criticises current political forms of public debate as the 'fabrication' of consensus or submission of the masses to the powers in place, he need not be taken to be rejecting the idea of public reason as such, only the forms in which it currently takes place. Mengue claims that, for Deleuze, democracy is the realm of opinion and consensus and, therefore, essentially majoritarian. On this basis, he concludes that Deleuze is opposed to democracy. Nothing could be further from the truth.

Concluding remarks

In *What is Philosophy?* Deleuze says that democracies are majorities and that they do not provide optimum conditions for philosophical criticism: '*We lack resistance to the present.*'[47] However, resistance to the present does not imply the rejection of democracy, but rather resistance to the present state of public opinion, public policy and the existing institutional forms of democratic politics. His critical remarks about opinion do include comments about the conditions under which it is currently produced and circulated. For example, he suggests that we find in the consensus opinions of liberal societies 'the cynical perceptions and affections of the capitalist'.[48] The implication here is that opinion is fabricated by the powers that be and as such is an instrument of domination rather than genuine democracy. However, this is a criticism of the present-day reality of public opinion rather than of the idea of public reason, and Deleuze is not the first or the only philosopher to advance such views. In the aftermath of the invasion of Iraq undertaken by a coalition of governments, largely in the face of public opinion in their own countries and around the world, many would be inclined to think he has a point. Such criticism implies opposition to the current state of what passes for democratic deliberation in the public sphere of liberal capitalist societies. It implies the manipulation and perversion of what passes for the consensus of a majority. But it does not imply rejection of the principle that government should reflect the opinions of all of the governed.

Indeed, Deleuze's call for resistance to the present is advanced not, as Mengue suggests, in the name of some anti-democratic principle of minority rule, but in the name of a 'becoming-democratic that is not to be confused with present constitutional states'.[49] This becoming-democratic bears the same relationship to actually existing democracy that becoming-revolutionary bears to actual revolutions: it refers us to a pure event that is both expressed in and betrayed by its actual historical manifestations. The task of philosophy, according to Deleuze and Guattari, is the counter-actualisation of present historical states of affairs through the creation of new concepts or the modification of old ones. There is no reason to deny them recourse to a philosophical concept of democracy that would express a pure event that is both actualised and betrayed by its present incarnation in liberal democratic states. We could describe this as the concept of a democracy to come, but only on the condition that we take this to mean a future form of democracy that never in fact arrives.[50] In Deleuzian terms, this would be a concept of the pure event of democracy, a virtual democracy, which is irreducible to its past or present actualisations. For Deleuze, it is not lack but the inexhaustible excess of this inner, virtual realm of being that ensures the permanent possibility of change. There is an internal connection between the ontological principle of absolute deterritorialisation at the heart of being and the orientation towards new earths and new peoples at the heart of philosophy. Deleuze's criticisms of contemporary democracies should not be confused with a refusal or a condemnation of democracy as such. They amount to resistance to the present in the name of a virtual democracy or a democracy to come.

Notes

1 I am grateful to Moira Gatens and to the editors, Lars Tønder and Lasse Thomassen, for helpful comments on earlier drafts of this chapter.
2 G. Deleuze and F. Guattari, *A Thousand Plateaus*, trans. B. Massumi (Minneapolis, MN: University of Minnesota Press, 1987), footnote p. 531.
3 *Ibid.*, p. 143.
4 J. Rawls, *Justice as Fairness: A Restatement* (Cambridge, MA.: Harvard University Press, 2001), pp. 3–5.
5 G. Deleuze and F. Guattari, *What is Philosophy?*, trans. H. Tomlinson and G. Burchell (New York: Columbia University Press, 1994), p. 99 (emphases in original).
6 *Ibid.*, pp. 112f, translation modified.
7 N. Thoburn, *Deleuze, Marx and Politics* (London: Routledge, 2003), p. 11.
8 *Ibid.*, p. 142.
9 Philippe Mengue, *Deleuze et la question de la démocratie* (Paris: L'Harmattan, 2003), p. 43.
10 *Ibid.*, pp. 67, 89.
11 *Ibid.*, pp. 107–10.
12 See, for example, those mentioned by A. M. Smith, *Laclau and Mouffe: The Radical Democratic Imaginary* (London: Routledge, 1998), pp. 19–22.
13 For example, E. Laclau and C. Mouffe, *Hegemony and Socialist Strategy: Towards a Radical Democratic Politics* (London: Verso, 1985); J. Derrida, *Specters of Marx*, trans. P. Kamuf (London: Routledge, 1994); R. Peffer, 'Rawlsian theory, contemporary Marxism and the difference principle', in M. Evans (ed.), *The Edinburgh Companion to Contemporary Liberalism* (Edinburgh: Edinburgh University Press, 2001), pp. 113–32; F. Cunningham, 'Whose socialism? Which democracy?', in M. Howard (ed.), *Socialism* (Amherst, NY: Humanity Books, 2001).
14 Mengue, *Deleuze et la démocratie*, p. 47. Mengue refers to Lefort's idea that democracy is the sole political regime to function without foundations. See C. Lefort,

Democracy and Political Theory, trans. D. Macey (Cambridge: Polity Press, 1988), chapter 1.
15 See, for example, the discussion of micropolitical movements which constitute 'masses' of various kinds, *A Thousand Plateaus*, p. 221.
16 Mengue, *Deleuze et la démocratie*, p. 52.
17 *Ibid.*, p. 53.
18 *Ibid.*, p. 56.
19 W. E. Connolly, *Why I Am Not A Secularist* (Minneapolis, MN: University of Minnesota Press, 1999), p. 68. See also his discussions of the 'politics of becoming' and the 'ethos of critical responsiveness', in *The Ethos of Pluralization* (Minneapolis, MN: University of Minnesota Press, 1995); and in *Neuropolitics: Thinking, Culture, Speed* (Minneapolis, MN: University of Minnesota Press, 2002).
20 Mengue, *Deleuze et la démocratie*, pp. 41f, 99–101.
21 G. Deleuze, *Deux Régimes De Fous* (Paris: Minuit, 2003), p. 156. This letter was published in *La Repubblica* 10 May 1979.
22 Thoburn, *Deleuze, Marx and Politics*, p. 142; see also p. 9.
23 'L'Abecedaire de Gilles Deleuze avec Claire Parnet' is unpublished in literary form but available on video cassette (1996) and CD Rom (2003) from Vidéo Editions Montaparnasse. These remarks are from the section entitled 'G as in Gauche'. I am grateful to Charles J. Stivale for his help in translating them.
24 G. Deleuze, *Negotiations 1972–1990*, trans. M. Joughin (New York: Columbia University Press, 1995), pp. 121f.
25 *Ibid.*, p. 152
26 *Ibid.*, p. 153.
27 *Ibid.*, pp. 169f.
28 *L'Abecedaire*, 'G as in Gauche'.
29 *Ibid.* I discuss Deleuze's interest in jurisprudence with reference to the role of law in colonisation in *Deleuze and the Political* (London: Routledge, 2000), pp. 120–31. See also the comments on this discussion and these passages from *L'Abecedaire* in Daniel W. Smith, 'Deleuze and the liberal tradition: normativity, freedom and judgement', *Economy and Society*, 32:2 (2003), 312–17.
30 Mengue, *Deleuze et la démocratie*, p. 102
31 Deleuze and Guattari, *A Thousand Plateaus*, p. 105.
32 *Ibid.*, p. 106.
33 *Ibid.*
34 Deleuze and Guattari, *What is Philosophy?*, p. 146
35 Mengue, *Deleuze et la démocratie*, p. 103.
36 Paola Marrati, 'Against the doxa: politics of immanence and becoming-minoritarian', in P. Pisters (ed.), *Micropolitics of Media Culture: Reading the Rhizomes of Deleuze and Guattari* (Amsterdam: Amsterdam University Press, 2001), p. 214 (emphases in original).
37 Connolly, *Why I am Not a Secularist*, p. 51.
38 Deleuze and Guattari, *A Thousand Plateaus*, p. 471.
39 *Ibid.*, pp. 216f.
40 Connolly, *Neuropolitics: Thinking, Culture, Speed*, p. 172.
41 Mengue, *Deleuze et la démocratie*, p. 103.
42 *Ibid.*, p. 43.
43 *Ibid.*, p. 41.
44 Deleuze, *Negotiations*, Exergue.
45 Deleuze and Guattari, *What is Philosophy?*, p. 146.

46 *Ibid.*, p. 144.
47 *Ibid.*, p. 108.
48 *Ibid.*, p. 146.
49 *Ibid.*, p. 113 (translation modified).
50 Although this expression is widely used by Derrida, Deleuze and Guattari also describe the kind of concept that philosophy creates as 'the contour, the configuration, the constellation of an event to come', in *What is Philosophy?*, pp. 32f. I argue for a partial convergence between the philosophical vocabularies of Deleuze and Derrida with respect to their orientation towards an open future in 'Future politics', in P. Patton and J. Protevi (eds), *Between Deleuze and Derrida* (London: Continuum, 2003), pp. 24–7.

4 • Romand Coles

The wild patience of radical democracy: beyond Žižek's lack

Introduction

As the governmental–corporate–media incantational complex intensifies, it often looks like democracy is sailing into the leading edge of a 'perfect storm'. To be sure, insurgent democratic mobilisations are in the process of developing a vast array of new modes, networks and visions – new tricks – that promise serious resistance and prefigure brighter days. Yet you have to really squint your eyes to generate a visual field in which these are not swamped.

Much radical democratic theory today is, precisely, the art of squinting. Yet squinting is not only a blessing; it is also a curse when our vision becomes myopically fixed and unreflective. Decent squinters must also be good *blinkers* and learn to relax periodically their gaze, if they are to prevent other important, violated and often related aspects of life from passing entirely from view.[1] Theories of abundance and lack are two examples of such fixation. Each illuminates something vital about the human condition and modes of power that damage this vitality.[2] Yet in isolation, they greatly misconstrue our condition and the ethical and political contours of radical democracy. Hence, when lack is fundamentalised in ways that ultimately diminish or deny the corporeal abundance of others and world, it tends to misconstrue negativity and the protean character of otherness, and replicate the least-desirable aspects of modern subjectivity, ethics and politics. Similar dangers appear among those who would theorise abundance 'beyond negativity' in ways that tend to diminish the ongoing need to attend to the tragic elements of political life, the importance of contestation in thought, ethics and politics, and so on.[3]

Both lack and abundance provide rich insight into contemporary problems and alternative possibilities. Yet this richness hinges significantly on articulating their *intertwinement* in ways that better illuminate each concept: checking the dangers of their reification and sharpening their ethical and political suggestiveness. In the first part of this chapter, I illuminate some dangers of fixating on one side of this binary through a critique of Žižek, one of the most profound and increasingly influential theorists of lack. In the second part, I sketch an alternative philosophy of abundance *and* negativity, as well as some of the political implications I think are associated with it.

Žižek's lack attack[4]

Žižek seeks to theorise and provoke an Act that would break beyond horizons of global capitalism and redefine political possibility. Increasingly, pluralising modes of democratic engagement appear to him merely as the 'ideological supplement' of corporate capitalism: each post-modern identity merely clamours agonistically for its own recognition, rights, distributions and interests within the system. Such post-modern democracy is not *political* at all, for Žižek's politics happens only when excluded elements step forth as true representatives of the universal, fundamentally subvert the order, and open up radically new horizons of possibility. Far from a radical democracy of receptive engagements amidst alterity that contribute to alliances around multidimensional struggles, Žižek advocates a new 'left Eurocentricism' in which 'the only authentic communication' is that of 'solidarity in common struggle', when I discover that 'the deadlock [global capitalism] that hampers me is also the deadlock which hampers the Other'.[5] Nauseated by post-modern 'undecidablity', he now pleas for decisive action that involves 'Leninist intolerance' and 'good forms of terror'.[6]

My sense is that the radically anti-democratic horizons Žižek evokes are deeply entwined with the philosophical theory of lack that he develops in his idiosyncratic readings of Descartes through Lacan. His theory of subjectivity is linked to his politics of the Truth-Event and his construal of Love. Below I argue that, quite often where Žižek sees an entwinement of philosophical truth and desirable ethics and politics, there are in fact significant philosophical errors and disastrous politics.

Central to Žižek is the 'endeavor to reassert the Cartesian subject' so as to 'bring to light its forgotten obverse, the excessive, unacknowledged kernel of the *cogito*'.[7] Descartes comes close to understanding the *cogito* as a pure substance-less void that can never be included in its system of representations, yet is nevertheless the uncanny condition of its (im)possibility. However, he ultimately reduces the *cogito* to *res cogitans*, and the bare 'I think' becomes a self-possessing positive substance.

Hegel, Žižek argues, pushes Descartes' deepest insight and becomes the consummate philosopher of subjectivity as dissolution. Hegel shows that inherent in subjectivity *as such* is a profound madness, a 'night of the world' – or radical negativity of imagination – in which being is dissolved by the 'pure self' into 'phantasmagorical representations'.[8] Žižek claims Hegel was able to articulate this insight because he moved beyond Kant's theory of the imagination.

Kant describes the most fundamental world-constituting power as the transcendental faculty of the imagination, which synthetically runs through and holds together the manifold given by receptive sensibility.[9] Yet Žižek claims that Kant's account of synthetic imagination conceals the radically *transgressive* character of subjectivity by depicting a cooperative relation between the pre-worldly manifold of intuition given by sensibility and the synthetical activity of the imagination. '[I]t is not possible to pass directly from the purely "animal soul" immersed in its natural life-world [the "pre-synthetic", "pre-symbolic" manifold of intuition] to "normal" subjectivity dwelling in its symbolic universe'.[10] The problem is not simply that there is 'a kind of elementary violence ... already at work ... in the most elementary synthesis of imagination ... in so far as it consists in an order imposed by the subject's synthetic activity on the heterogeneous disarray of impressions'.[11] For this view itself harbours the fantasy of 'a "secret connection between things", a utopian Secret Harmony beyond phenomenal causal links ... the temporal-spatial non-violent unity of pure diversity', which covers 'the pre-ontological abyss of freedom' at *the core* of subjectivity and *all* connectivity.[12]

Prior to this violence of synthesis is 'the more fundamental violence of dismemberment, of tearing the natural continuity of experience apart', in which subjectivity is born and to which the violence of synthesis is already an answer.[13] This violent primordial negativity of the 'presynthetic imagination' is '"the mightiest of powers", the power of disrupting the unity of the Real', of '*tearing apart* sensible elements out of their context, of *dismembering* the immediate experience of an organic Whole'.[14] Without this radically disruptive imagination we would be '*embedded*' and '*caught*' in a context of the tacit lifeworld and explicit representations.[15] At the heart of every symbolically connected world, as its condition of (im)possibility, is the abyssal lack of subjectivity, which smashes the spell of sensibility and renders the production of the symbolic world necessary, yet radically undecidable and incomplete. There simply 'is' nothing inherently substantive imbued with aspects of patterning alterity prior to the subject's lack-provoked/lack-ridden fantastic synthesis.

Žižek elaborates his claim in contrast to what he views as 'the' other, 'substantialist', understanding (attributed to Adorno and deconstruction) of the 'unfathomable excess of a Thing eluding symbolic grasp'. 'The substantialist [claim] is ... that ... there is something in the object that forever resists being translated into our conceptual network'.[16] Thus, when Judith Butler describes the incompleteness of the subject most fundamentally as 'the inability of the social category to capture the mobility and complexity of persons' – the generative abundance of corporeality,[17] Žižek counters that she thus reduces incompleteness 'to the *empiricist* problematic ... opposition between the infinite wealth of reality and the abstract poverty of the categories by means of which we try to grasp reality',[18] which is 'ontologically unexplained'.[19] Žižek charges that such arguments incoherently make assertions about the very reality (for instance, its 'complexity', 'mobility', etc.) that is said to be beyond conceptual limits.

In Žižek's alternative 'lack' reading of the 'unfathomable excess of a Thing eluding symbolic grasp' every particular has always already been translated – and the excess emerges as a lack in relation to the *subject's desire*:

> What if what eludes our grasp ... are the traces of what in past history, this 'object' ... *might have* become, but failed to do so? To grasp a historical situation 'in its becoming' is *not* to perceive it as a positive set of features ... but to discern in it the traces of failed 'emancipatory' attempts at liberation ... In this case however ... that which eludes our grasp in the Thing, is *no longer* the excess of its positive content over our cognitive capacities but, on the contrary, its *lack*, that is, the traces of *failures*, the *absences* inscribed in its positive existence ... Consequently, this excess/lack is *not* the part of the 'objective' that is in excess of the subject's cognitive capacities; rather it consists of the traces of the subject himself (his crushed hopes and desires) in the object, so that what is properly 'unfathomable' in the object is the objective counterpart/correlative of the innermost kernel of the subject's own desire.[20]

I emphasise the 'not's' and 'no longer' here, because the negative thesis is every bit as interesting to me as the affirmed thesis concerning lack (which neither Adorno, Derrida nor Butler would deny). I am interested in how Žižek's abyssal lack operates less as a supplement or transformative juxtaposition to alternative renderings of excess, than as their radical *nullification*. Hence excess is *not at all* a characteristic of things but *solely* of the 'subject himself' – the subject's lack at the core of the object. Every object has always already been translated (synthesised) by the subject in response to the subject's own destructive Big Bang, so the excess can in no way be a characteristic of things as such, but *only our own* unfulfilled yearnings etched in the scars of things.[21] How the above 'what if' is to support and legitimate these *total negations* of alternative theories that are not necessarily or obviously mutually exclusive is unclear. Nevertheless, this move is central to Žižek's account. Žižek develops this theme through readings of what he calls 'the Christian legacy', because he thinks that 'love' articulates the supreme ethical relation in the midst of lack thus understood. Yet his effort to radically reconfigure democracy in light of a Žižekian-Christian love amplifies many of the worst dangers of some Christian nullifications of all non-Christian otherness.

Žižek's St Paul's 'dying to the Law' emphasises 'love beyond the Decologue'; love beyond the Law and the desire for transgression ('obscene supplement') that many think it generates.[22] Love '*beyond* the confines of the Law' is not the insidious love for the neighbour as our mirror image upon whom we impose our Good, but rather love for other's abyssal power of negativity, 'the Other in the very abyss of its Real, the Other as a properly *inhuman* partner, "irrational", radically evil, capricious, revolting, disgusting ... in short beyond the Good. This enemy neighbor should not be punished (as the Decalogue demands), but accepted as a "neighbor"'.[23] But, what or how does this love love?

Žižek's freedom and love involve 'the passage from extreme egoistic *contraction* to boundless *expansion*' – 'a loving acceptance' that 'finds full realization' in relation to others.[24] Yet love has two sides. For the loving *acceptance* of others 'in the very abyss of the Real' involves a certain hatred akin to radical *withdrawal*. Drawing on St. Luke's Gospel (14:26) where Christ links discipleship to hatred, Žižek follows Kierkegaard's line that we must, '*hate the beloved* out of love and in love'.[25] 'I hate the dimension of his inscription into the socio-symbolic structure *on behalf of my very love for him as a unique person*'.[26] The unique person here is not to be understood in humanist terms (still symbolic): rather the humanist 'individual' must be unplugged and 'reduced to the *singular point of subjectivity*'.[27] With this loving reduction/expansion, self and other undergo a 'symbolic death' in which not just social hierarchy, but every bit of every tradition, social location, historical substance pass away and 'everything has become new' (Corinthians 5:16–17).[28] The neighbour who is accepted is not the neighbour entangled in symbolically substantively mediated thoughts, visions, desires, habits, practices and so on, but rather the neighbour whose abyssal negativity can withdraw entirely and start something radically new and terrifying, and who in turn can lovingly accept the others in *their* terrifying singularity. Loving the other, I hate her substantive attachments in favour of her power for unplugging and becoming 'a singular member of the community of believers'.[29]

Yet in what and how do these believers believe? They worship at the altar of *Lack*. 'In love *I am ... nothing* but, as it were, a Nothing humbly aware of itself, a Nothing paradoxically made rich through the very awareness of its lack. Only a lacking vulnerable being is capable of love: the ultimate mystery of love is therefore that incompleteness is in a way *higher than completion*'.[30] Awareness of lack is the condition of love: love of the lack in oneself and the lack in the other, which, as lack, is indistinguishable from and the foreign body in the lack that I am (not). Henceforth, this community of lovers – higher and richer than the others insofar as the others falsely identify through symbolic and substantive attachments – engages in the *work* of love: repeatedly disengaging themselves, 'from the inertia that constrains us to identify with the particular order we were born into', discerning and engaging subjects with 'crushed dreams and desires'[31] – *not* the (partly) *un*crushed dreams and desires that find *some* symbolic and substantive points of support and animation in the heterogeneous world of being, but the crushed ones, which evince the abyssal lack truly worthy of love.

Yet, paradoxically, this fragile community must repeatedly work to perceive and bring forth the miraculous and thus must not, ultimately, remain unnamed and entirely beyond the symbolic. Indeed, in a world that threatens to obliterate all traces of lack, the task is precisely to 'stage the void' – to represent it, without freezing it into a new positivity. For Žižek, the performance of this task goes back to Christ, the Gospels and Paul, who most fully named Christ's Event. Christianity *truly transcends* pagan idolatry in which the divine is reduced to its positive representation, 'through the reduction of the representative content to the lowest imaginable level: at the level of representation, Christ was the "son of a man", a ragged, miserable creature crucified ... and it is against this background of this utterly wretched character of his earthly appearance that his divine essence shines through all the more powerfully'.[32] In the Christian sublime, purely formless lack-love finds symbolic expression, endurance and efficaciousness through its appearance as the crucified of all symbolic order. The depth of 'God *is this gap itself*, this 'monstrous distortion of the surface', the absolute height that is only achievable by turning downward through the remainder *beneath* symbolic categories.[33]

Paul's narrative transforms Christ's Act (loving rejection of positivised being) into a 'universal symbolic framework that guarantees and accomplishes ... fidelity' by orienting us toward the cross.[34] Yet crucifixion is only part of Christ's story. Resurrection is the other. It is the 'highest religious expression of the power of symbolic fiction as the medium of universality'.[35] Christ's rebirth in a community of believers – the forgiving incarnation of grace that comes from far beyond our individual efforts at self-realisation and ushers in a New Beginning – utterly disrupts the claim of balanced economy that is inherent in the symbolic *as such*. Christ's miracle – the divine – is that he teaches us how to 'give body' to the void of negativity and new beginning, to deploy the symbolic to subvert rather than reinforce hierarchical frozenness.[36]

Vital to democracy based on this Christian inheritance is a '"democratic unplugging": we are all directly members of the democratic collective, irrespective of our place in the intricate set of relations that form our respective communities'.[37] Central to this is Rancière's *singulier universel*, in which a particular group excluded from the order seeks not to be recognised as an equal partner in governance, but 'present[s] [itself] as the representative ... for the Whole of Society, for the true Universality ("we – the nothing" ... are the people, we are the All against others who stand only for their particular privileged interest)'.[38] Politics happens when those with no place disrupt the order in the name of Balibar's *egaliberté*, the empty universal that solicits all those excluded to seek to undermine and transform power's horizon of false universality. Precisely the emptiness of democratic universality prevents any order from monopolising justice. Rather than seeking a universalism in our 'common humanity' (which merely reinforces systems of power), Žižek implores the left to '*identify universality with the point of exclusion*', the Void in the order, those displaced from the social whole.[39]

Žižek asserts that every political-economic field has a single 'fundamental structuring principle' that provides the unacknowledged horizon for all the contenders within it. Today, capitalism is this unquestioned horizon constitutive of both the particular struggling political identities and their most basic modes and terms of engagement (interest group liberalism, abstract universals corresponding to commodity fetishism, acceptance of capitalist markets, progressive agenda reduced to solving particular problems and so on). Postmodern politics seeks only to 'shift the limit that divides our identity into the acknowledged and the disavowed part more in the direction of the disavowed part',[40] while leaving the basic structure untouched by marginalising revolutionary *politicised* economic critique and transformation. In contrast, the truly *political* Act, Žižek imagines, would radically transform the foundational principle. The aim is to disrupt fundamentally present horizons by taking what are typically viewed as particular and marginal malfunctions within the existing regime and casting them as structurally necessitated violence that fundamentally de-legitimates the order and suspends its 'Law'.

Žižek, following Badiou, locates the exemplary Truth-Event in Paul's Christ, though modernity's democratic revolutions and the Leninist October Revolution provide other good examples. Every contingent order has a single fundamental horizon and thus '*one and only one* Truth', which is the Event that names and dissolves it.[41] This truth is unperceivable in the positive terms of an order, and hence the Event in which it is revealed and suspended is miraculous – utterly unanticipatable in the current order of things. Indeed, there is no remotely neutral place of decidability from which to judge the Truth-Event: 'An Event is thus circular in the sense that its identification is possible only from the standpoint of … "an *interpreting intervention*"'.[42] 'Truth is discernible only for the potential members of the new Community of "believers", for their engaged gaze',[43] based on a 'previous decision for Truth'[44] and fidelity to it: 'what if…the Truth-Event *is* at its most radical, a purely formal act of decision, not only not based on an actual truth, but ultimately *indifferent* to the precise status (actual or fictitious) of the Truth-Event it refers to?'.[45] True Universalists are 'not those who preach global tolerance of differences … but those who engage in a passionate fight for the assertion of the Truth that enthuses them', 'proto-Leninist militant[s] fighting different deviations'.[46] The struggle is a radically subjective one between those who advocate the extant order and those who recognise and live in fidelity to the Truth-Event, which is 'irreducible to (and unaccountable in terms of)' it.[47]

Žižek's stance is in marked opposition to a politics of difficult agonistic dialogue aimed at fashioning more generous and receptive judgments and modes of co-existence among different constituencies with different political visions. For Žižek, communication has little to do with post-colonial efforts to open new possibilities through double-translation and responsiveness to otherness. Rather, 'the only authentic communication is that of "solidarity in a common struggle", when I discover that the deadlock which hampers me is also the deadlock which hampers the Other'.[48]

Many affirm the negative, episodic and marginal character of subversive politics. Marginalist politics, Žižek argues, fears taking responsibility for a new order because it thinks it will forfeit the negativity of subversion for a new positivity of Being. In contrast, Žižek emphasises how every extant order is, in fact and contrary to its claims, not the coherent whole that it claims to be, but rather an inconsistency constituted by the void of a prior Act that must repeatedly be re-enacted as a 'disavowed and obscene supplement' that sustains the order through exercise of arbitrary violence against those excluded. Hence, rather than succumbing to the illusion that the order is apolitical, the revolutionary should provoke the system in ways that increasingly bring its hidden political support to the fore. Yet beyond this provocation, 'the test of the true revolutionary ... is the heroic readiness to endure the conversion of the subversive undermining of the existing System into the principle of a new [not really] positive Order which gives body to this negativity'.[49] However, in contrast to those who seek to convert the Act-sustained character of their order into a new positivity that disavows the contingency of the Act, Žižek urges us to assume responsibility for the undecidable Void of our contingency, thus radicalising the 'democratic invention' in which the contingency and gaps of power are transformed from being merely obstacles, into becoming the condition of power's legitimate exercise.

Yet a true recognition of contingency should not hystericise the revolutionary into a state of indeterminacy. Rather, truly embracing the ineliminable contingency and violence of our Act – 'ex nihilo, without phantasmic support' – means that we should, like 'a true Leninist [be] not afraid of all the consequences, unpleasant as they may be, of realizing his political project' (secret police to fight counter-revolutionaries, and 'cruelty' are offered as analogues here).[50] Because every Act will be indecipherable in the terms of the extant system, the Act will inevitably appear as a 'choice for the worst' and seem wholly unaccountable to those ensconced in existing discourses. Radically reconfiguring the rules of the game is inherently 'terroristic', and though we should not re-enact the bad forms of Stalinist terror, we should search for 'good terror' that will radically transgress the limits most associate with progressive politics: We must 'ground a new political universality by opting for the *impossible* ... with no taboos, no a priori norms ("human rights", "democracy"), respect for which would prevent us also from "resignifying" terror, the ruthless exercise of power, the spirit of sacrifice ... if this radical choice is decried by some bleeding-heart liberals as *Linksfaschismus*, so be it!'.[51] These a priori norms are merely the 'freedom of choice *within* the coordinates of the existing power relations, while actual freedom designates the site of an intervention that undermines these very coordinates'.[52] The only criterion of the political act is whether, as viewed from within, it is an 'enacted utopia' where 'we *already are free while fighting for freedom, we already are happy while fighting for happiness*'.[53] Insofar as 'love' is the movement of revolutionary abyssal subjectivity that embraces others shorn of their substantive finitude, there can be no criteria with any determinacy beyond the experienceless experience of love itself – and the sublime hatred it inspires.

Pluralising negativity and abundance

I begin my critique at the 'beginning', by interrogating Žižek's 'big bang' account of subjectivity, drawing from an alternative philosophy of negativity and abundance that must remain sketchy and suggestive here.[54] Žižek claims there is an abyss between the 'animal soul', embedded in a totalising Whole, and human subjectivity, which is born/e through a 'night of the world' dissolution of all tacit and explicit orders. Yet this account is not compelling and seems to fall for the bluff of positivism in a manner analogous to Žižek's claims about some post-modernists.

Contra regimes of power-knowledge – and those they bluff – we do not find ourselves trapped in an experiential world of inseparably connected flat parts of a closed totality. Rather, as Merleau-Ponty depicts more plausibly, the flesh of the world and our flesh amidst it, has more the character of a 'perpetual pregnancy' of open depths that repeatedly generate newness through movements of folding-back, crossing and overlapping. Merleau-Ponty articulates a philosophy of abundance, but simultaneously a philosophy of negativity, as the thickness, density and resistance of each bit of flesh to every other is integral to both the non-identity and the generativity of our world. Negativity and generativity are co-generative. Each corporeal–perceptual crossing of this being that we agonistically share with the world is articulated through a foreground–background structure, in which the world appears always with a thickness, depth, negativity, such that it is at once radically proximate yet inexorably beyond our complete grasp. Every thing appears not only against a structuring background of other things, but also with its own-most background: its other sides, undersides, insides. This depth is entwined with – and paradoxically both makes possible and is made possible by – the depth of intercorporeality.

Each sentient thing appears as an 'other' opening on to the world, sensing from flesh I cannot peer out of – a sentience that is never mine. Each sentient being's embodiment also prevents it from sensing itself as others sense it, and so each human is significantly a background to itself – a depth sensed by others in ways we cannot sense. As each of us gains intercorporeal depth through our encounters, simultaneously the world of things blossoms into its depth, as it entwines with the gazing and touching of myriad unique others to announce an inexhaustible excess, irreducible to our sensual openings. As we humans move through the world, crossing our flesh with that of the world around us – crossing our openings with the openings of others – its appearance alters as unwonted perceptions spring from the background depths and reorders the perceptual field. Even where this happening is suppressed by modes of power that invest the body, affect, perception, language and sociality in ways that persistently freeze and misrecognise the foreground–background structure of the experienced world, they cannot eradicate this dynamical intercorporeal structuring of the perceptual field of being *as such*. The background depths remain, indeterminately haunting, pregnant, resisting, threatening to break into the foreground and restructure our perceptual field.

Let me emphasise a few interrelated points that pertain most directly to Žižek's argument. First, Žižek's (philosophical, ethical, political) *dichotomy* between changing *parts* and changing *basic frameworks or horizons* is false. As elements in perceptual and political fields change, they modulate their relationships to other elements around them *and* alter (sometimes subtly, sometimes radically) the horizon of their sense. An element (either sentient or nonsentient) can become a horizon (or 'world', or lens) for other elements, as the world appears through it and under its sway. Sometimes these changes are minor and nearly imperceptible, and often they are deeply constrained by power-saturated habituations. Nevertheless, power acts upon, but cannot fundamentally eradicate, this basic structure of wild being; and not infrequently elements distend the structure and limits of a horizon quite significantly – occasionally radically. Often several elements interact to form a *manifold* horizon with *inconsistencies and instabilities*. There is a vast range of degrees of reciprocal transformation between a framing horizon(s) and that which appears within this frame. Indeed, 'particular' and 'fundamental horizons' are not dichotomous, but can morph into one another, as, say, capitalism, race and sexuality, each frame the others, but are also framed by the others. Transformation centrally involves difficult *judgments* concerning these interactions, connections, disruptions, the extent of their salience, fluidity, rigidity and so on. What is rarely if ever involved is an either/or choice between changing a part that leaves the horizon static, or *absolutely* changing the fundamental horizon (we have only Walter Benjamin's '*weak* messianic power').[55] Our affective, perceptual, cognitive, ethical-political *work*, takes place *in* this contestable transformative play between elements and structure.

Second, this dynamism – and the miraculous – emerges through a co-(de)generativity between self, world and others, rather than through a subject's absolute withdrawal into an abyss of pure negativity and lack. Negativity, the dissolution and cancellation of a perception or a horizon of sense, emerges through the *intertwining* between self and world – it is a power uncannily dispersed between my depth and the depth of things. Think, for example, of when what I thought was a standard immovable wall begins to open slowly as I lean on it, thereby negating and changing my sense of the 'wall' and my entire sense of this house in relation to the underground railroad, or provoking my imagination concerning the need for trickster architectures for democratic agency. How far and deeply this particular intertwining transforms my perceptual-political field depends, of course, on a slew of other experiences, practices of power and how we manage to craft modes of living and story-telling in the zones of determinacy and indeterminacy disclosed therein. To be sure, I have singular powers of critical resistance, rearticulation and decision, which I am able to mobilise with varying degrees of efficacy, intensity and duration, but they are inspirited and nurtured in this dispersed intertwining in which things and others negate, transgress, tempt, vivify, inform and radically reform my experiences. It is not that power does not saturate our perceptual field to produce, contain, conceal and forget experience. Yet we should not bow to and replicate it by accepting its false flattening of the ontological character of experience and its rendering of subjectivity in ways that conceal precisely the dynamic intertwining that is the source of our capacity for ethical-political judgment and action.

Third, the negativity of subjectivity is neither absolute nor pure, but rather a power animated, informed *and marked, and thus limited,* by the chiasm of our singular historicity with the world. It is a dynamic working power of indeterminate finitude that both transgresses and is etched by the specific relations in which it is born/e as well as the specificity which it resists. The singular historicity of these relations acquires a power that gains a certain autonomy of its own. But in everything, from its degree of intensity, ferocity and frequency of deployment, to its focus, range, the persistent blindness that tend to decommission it at certain points and so on, 'my' negativity bears limiting traces of the historical specificities of its emergence that infuse and resist it even as they are conditions of its possibility.[56]

Thus, contra the 'Big Bang' theory of negativity, our critical and generative powers are nurtured in and indebted to the tension-laden indeterminate interstices within and between beings. There is, contra Žižek, a generative mobility and complexity in beings that resists full translation and exceeds our comprehensive grasp. This claim can*not*, as Žižek rightly notes, be completely 'ontologically explained' – yet this does not damn it. It is a projection nurtured by endless retrospective readings of how things always appear later to be more and other than we thought they were. It is a 'faith' thus nurtured that the corporeality of the world will continue significantly to exceed our perceptual and conceptual renderings; a faith that it is wise (or at least less stupid) to anticipate this and cultivate modes of receptivity toward it; a faith that the myriad reductions of the world's alterity – including Žižek's – will continue to be, as they always have been, hubristic dangerous illusions repeatedly disclosed as false, yet relentlessly and insistently reinvented.

Hence, as Butler argues, 'there is no recourse ... to a single lack ... Our exile in heterogeneity is, in this sense, irreversible'.[57] Relatedly, this goes for ethics and politics too, where Žižek's work similarly obliterates heterogeneity amidst the 'singular members of the community of believers': one either has/is had by the faith in this singular exemplary Lack, or not. For all his talk of vulnerability and dispossession, it seems that Lack itself becomes the ultimate *possession*. It becomes property in a most radical sense: something possessed so intensely that it is absolutely invisible to those beyond the charmed circle. Those outside the 'engaged' gaze do not see it, and those within the Truth are utterly unaccountable to them.

Hence, in response to William Hart's perceptive criticism of Žižek's reiteration of the centuries-old unsubstantiated colonial denunciation of heterogeneous voices world over, Žižek's only response is: yes, so what? Žižek is so possessive of/possessed by his Lack, that he fancies the burden of proof is on Hart to show that there is plausibly anything worthwhile on the globe beyond Žižekian–Christian–Marxian–Eurocentricism. 'Where is the judgment?' – Žižek replies to Hart. The judgment is that there is no negativity when it is monopolised by a single community and language that takes itself to be beyond the risks of accountability to exteriors and reciprocal translation. Nothing extinguishes negativity more than this construal of negativity. Yet let us ring Žižek's question in a different way: Where is the judgment? Indeed, where is *judgment*? The judgment is precisely that, if we accept Žižek's position, *there is and can be no judgment*, simply decisionistic warfare and, ultimately, absolute terror. And it is precisely *this* lack, this absence of the vulnerable and receptive interplay between discrepant negativi*ties*, concerning complex and mobile situations that exceed their grasp and even their dreams, that is of greatest concern.

Radical democracy, ecology, and political judgment

Too many theorists use 'decisionism' polemically to dismiss other positions as irrational[58] and that is not my aim here. Hence, by judgment, I refer to an activity that takes place across numerous entwined registers – from the excited gut and pounding heart, to both peripheral and precise perceptions, to the most abstract conceptualisations – in which we, with others, try to assess how the world is and ought to be changed. Central to this activity is a polymorphous process in which we seek to translate different registers of our sensual being into other registers, and attempt to translate our faiths, thoughts, feelings perceptions into the faiths, thoughts, feelings and perceptions of the others. This is a wild, risky, painful and exciting, and uncertain activity. But it is the best we can do ethically and politically, in a world where negativity and generative possibility are messily dispersed beyond belief.

Among the aims of this judging activity are two: First, through a long-winded process of critical adjustments and cancellations, to better inform our decisions –which *remain decisions* because of the inexpugnable ambiguities and contestabilities – but *resist decisionism,* because experience overwhelmingly shows that judging is least violent and most conducive to justice and flourishing when it suffers and develops thus. This process has some kinship to Rawls's reflective equilibrium. We must forge democratic judgments leading to political action and we do this best by striving toward a certain transfiguring comprehensiveness regarding discrepant considerations.

Yet the very character of existence that demands *this activity* – our radical finitude, our murky mobile depths and the way power invests in our misrecognition of things – also chastens our sense of its capacities and conclusions, and thus solicits *another activity*, which disrupts and informs the first. I have in mind the pursuit of reflective *disequilibrium*: crafting stories and bodily practices of unresolved and perhaps irresolvable remainders and paradoxes between different registers and people(s). These call us to re-open our deep conclusions, to cultivate receptive generosity to those who contest them, to re-work them and so on. Without the first dimension, there is little hope for less dogmatic and more responsive democratic judgment and action. Without the second, the latter tends, in spite itself, inexorably toward the dogmatism it would resist (for instance, Rawls).

Politically, given the relentless effort of hierarchical power to impede democratic sensibilities, judgment and action by freezing horizons, I think we should pursue radical democratic politics through an *ecology* of different modes that work on extant limits in markedly different ways. Each mode is necessary yet insufficient for performing and cultivating a democratic counter-culture. Alone, each cultivates essential insight and energy, yet shifting ethical and political horizons requires work from a variety of different angles across a variety of different registers. Woven together these practices offer hope for more sustained engagements of the democratic promise.

This politics is significantly informed by a grassroots social movement in which I am involved in Durham, North Carolina.[59] Our long-term aims are about intergenerational and fundamental radical democratic change, including political economy. Yet we are working on this by building a democratic counter-culture around pressing concrete issues facing many people. These issues have allowed us to build a large and growing coalition that cuts across lines of race, nationality and religion; includes poor, working and middle-class people; and is increasingly capable of tackling deeper and broader issues. Among the practices in the radical democratic ecology that we are fashioning, I focus here upon three: *receptive practices* that bend our ears and bodies toward other people's voices, places, historical narratives and modes of being; *exuberant Dionysian enactments* of utopic being-together in an (im)possible beloved community of differences; and *pragmatic research, deliberation and negotiation* (some cooperative, some agonistic) concerning particular issues in power-saturated highly constrained contexts.

Crucial among practices of receptivity, are those I call 'moving democracy'.[60] Negativity and abundance – critical energy, pregnant anger and creative spark – are widely dispersed, and democracy requires that they be provoked and gathered in capillary fashion through responsive engagements across the manifold terrain of our heterogeneous city. Yet our densely gated spaces, narrowly scripted paths, clogged ears and bound-foot imaginations greatly impede receptivity across differences. Hence, it is imperative that we cultivate *arts of radical receptivity*. Among these arts, are thousands of one-on-one meetings and small house gatherings, where the aim is largely to hear other people's stories, angers and dreams. Each meeting is a differently nuanced sound chamber in which we develop our capacities for receiving voices across lines that typically render others inaudible. Yet listening is often insufficient in a gated and oblivious world, for it is often nearly impossible to hear others well if you have not spent discerning time in their very different spaces, been proximate to their discrepant conditions and modes of being – especially when our spaces and modes of being have been constituted in opposition to these possibilities. Difficult receptivity requires bodily practices that transfigure our striated condition through new and more responsive modes of encountering different spaces. Hence we constantly move meeting spaces, so that we find ourselves listening to people speak, pray, sing, tell stories and work hard, and (im)patiently move toward democratic power from those places etched everywhere with discrepant suffering and tattered rising dreams. We engage in 'neighbourhood audits', practices of walking more receptively in strange neighbourhoods with diverse strangers, taking inventory of the condition, gaining an initial sense of the shape of lives we have never experienced. This actual world travelling bends, broadens and nurtures our receptivity, imagination and capacities for power-action in ways that deliberation within more fixed horizons does not.

We entwine receptive practices with gatherings that enact a *Dionysian conjuring of utopic possibility*. At these events of radical critique and reconstruction, we experience transformed modes of being-together and vivify a sense that far-reaching change is miraculously proximate to our approaching capacities for action. Let me excerpt from my notes depicting such a frenzied event in the Spring of 2003:[61]

> Rev. Battle is delivering the 'closing talk'. For a few minutes he's carefully deliberative, but soon he's shouting about how 'God works with our hands. God walks with our feet.' Then he throws the room into a guttural 'love jam'

incantation with Corinthians: 'LOVE ... LOVE ... LOVE ... ' The call and response pulsations start from a part of the room where several members of his church are seated. These are entwined with exuberant echoes of every phrase by a Hispanic organizer translating into a small microphone as electronic pulses carry the evocations through headphones to the ears of newly arrived Mexicans. Even white folks and atheists are starting to join in ecstatically in response to this counterpointal motif of preacher, church members, translator, Mexicans. I'm wanting to leap up but instead confine myself to twitching various muscle groups, shuddering, squirming, and clapping my hands. Battle growls into the ecstatic room: 'With *LOVE* we will find the possible in this impossible!' The contours of the world are beginning to blur, shift, melt away. Many of us have moved through listening *to* this cicada we are, to being *in its insides*. With each pulse we are growing a cicada confidence. Emerging in inimitable prime number cycles – 13, 17, and 23 years, these are among nature's ultimate tricksters. Too irregular for any predator to map its life-rhythm successfully onto theirs and make them 'prey', they detach from roots they've sucked for years, dig up out of the moist earth when their time comes, big red eyes emerging under a bowl of stars, they climb trees and sing their wings. We are of prime numbers; cicada torso, leg, and wing. Cicada confidence.

This sensibility flows into the hard work of coming months, much of which is centred on practices of patient constrained deliberation and negotiation that is receptive and transcendent in far more modest ways than the practices described above. However, this deliberation is informed and inspired by them, gives them substance and is no less important. As we sit negotiating with elected officials and bureaucrats, we focus carefully on more pragmatic explorations of micro-possibilities, patiently seeking to translate bigger visions into littler packages in ways that will in turn heighten future possibilities for broader transformations. We practice a political jujitsu in which status quo terms and interests are seized and directed toward an accumulation of changes that might gradually disrupt the current political economic horizon. Uninformed and uninspired by practices of radical receptivity and utopic conjuring, this deliberative work risks degenerating into myopic reformism stuck within an unchallenged world-disclosive horizon. Yet without this 'patient labor giving form to our impatience for liberty',[62] our utopic conjuring will quickly ring hollow and lose its soliciting power; our receptivity will fail to transfigure the political structures that stifle it.

Dionysian utopic being-together risks obliterating many significant differences when it is severed from practices of attentive receptivity. Difficult receptivity risks a politics that is insufficiently capable of mustering up prophetic energy, sensibility, voice, refusal and transformative passion and action, when divorced from utopic Dionysian conjuring. Both must inspirit deliberative reform if the latter is to avoid degenerating into a flaccid pragmatism. In turn, the wild patience of these deliberative practices enacts in the capillaries of our work a way of engaging agonistic others and concrete circumstances in our daily work that gives enduring body to democratic possibilities. Moreover, the modest victories achieved in these negotiations bear witness to the reality and power of the more ineffable moments of other practices. Each practice in this ecology nurtures and agonistically checks the others. Judgement is cultivated *in-between*.

Democracy's difficult hope is like this. It endures only in the tensions of a mobile ecology of ethical-political practices, because negativity and abundance are too heterogeneous to be served by formalist theories, which, squinting, unblinking and disengaged, fetishise one dimension of damaged life and solicit the worst. Shifting power-fortified political horizons requires hard and manifold work; it requires the surging pressures and transcending ecstasy of experience and vision of those already democratically engaged: the ebbing pulls in which others within and beyond a movement receive each other in radically new modes; and patient capillary work on our limits – informed by this ocean of experiences and aspirations flowing from myriad springs beyond all bounds.

Notes

1 See J. Derrida, 'The principle of reason: the university in the eyes of its pupil', *Diacritics*, 13:3 (Fall 1983), 3–20.
2 I discuss some important contributions of lack theorists in my sympathetic yet critical treatment of Laclau and Mouffe, in 'Liberty, equality, and receptive generosity: neo-Nietzschean ethics and the possibility of caritas', *American Political Science Review*, 90:2 (1996), 375–88.
3 See, for instance, my critique of Milbank's Deleuzian Christianity, in 'Storied others and the possibilities of *Caritas*: Milbank and neo-Nietzschean ethics', *Modern Theology*, 8:4 (1992), 331–51. Not all who theorise from a stance of abundance make this mistake.
4 I focus on some of his most relevant and important philosophical and political writings: Žižek's contributions in J. Butler, E. Laclau and S. Žižek, *Contingency, Hegemony, Universality: Contemporary Dialogues on the Left* (London: Verso, 2000); S. Žižek, *The Fragile Absolute – Or, Why is the Christian Legacy Worth Fighting For?* (London: Verso, 2000); S. Žižek, *Tarrying with the Negative: Kant, Hegel, and the Critique of Ideology* (Durham: Duke University Press, 1993); S. Žižek, *The Ticklish Subject: The Absent Centre of Political Ontology* (London: Verso, 1999); S. Žižek, 'A leftist plea for "Eurocentrism"', *Critical Inquiry*, 24:3 (1998), 988–1009; S. Žižek, 'Melancholy and the act', *Critical Inquiry*, 26:4 (2000), 657–81; S. Žižek, 'A plea for Leninist intolerance', *Critical Inquiry*, 28:2 (2002), 542–66; S. Žižek, 'Critical response: a symptom – of what?', *Critical Inquiry*, 29:3 (2003), 486–503; (see related essay by G. G. Harpham, 'Doing the impossible: Slavoj Žižek and the end of knowledge', in same volume, 453–85; S. Žižek, 'I plead guilty – but where is the judgment?', *Nepantla: Views from South*, 3:3 (2002), 579–83. See the excellent related essays by W. D. Hart: 'Slavoj Žižek and the imperial/colonial model of religion', in the same volume, 553–78, and 'Can a judgment be read?: a response to Slavoj Žižek', in

Nepantla: Views from South, 4:1 (2003), 191–4.
5 Žižek, *The Ticklish Subject,* p. 220.
6 See Žižek, 'A plea for Leninist intolerance'.
7 Žižek, *The Ticklish Subject,* p. 2.
8 Ibid., pp. 29f.
9 See my discussion of this issue in *Rethinking Generosity: Critical Theory and the Politics of Caritas* (Ithaca, NY: Cornell University Press, 1997), chapter 1.
10 Žižek, *The Ticklish Subject,* p. 35.
11 Ibid., p. 37.
12 Ibid., p. 61.
13 Ibid., p. 37.
14 Ibid., p. 31.
15 Ibid.. p. 62.
16 Ibid., p. 89.
17 Butler, Laclau and Žižek, *Contingency, Hegemony, Universility,* p. 29.
18 Ibid., p. 216.
19 Ibid., p. 311.
20 Žižek, *The Ticklish Subject,* pp. 89f, my emphases.
21 Of course Žižek also writes of the subject as, 'nothing but the very gap which separates phenomena from Thing' (*Tarrying with the Negative,* p. 21). Yet this gap is not grasped as somehow ontological in relation to an excess of multiplicity or generativity inhering in things, but rather as '*sustained only by the space of desire as structured by the intervention of the signifier*'. 'Reality' is retrospectively posited against the background of the 'lost Thing' which would bring about the 'full satisfaction of the drive' – which can never be filled due to the lack at the heart of the subject–object (*Ibid.,* p. 37).
22 Žižek, *The Fragile Absolute,* p. 111.
23 Ibid., p. 112.
24 Ibid., p. 103.
25 Ibid., p. 126.
26 Ibid., my emphasis.
27 Ibid., p. 127.
28 Ibid.
29 Ibid.
30 Ibid., pp. 146f.
31 Ibid., pp. 128f.
32 Žižek, *Tarrying with the Negative,* p. 50.
33 Ibid.
34 Žižek, *The Ticklish Subject,* p. 164.
35 Ibid., p. 331
36 Žižek, *The Fragile Absolute,* pp. 104f.
37 Ibid., p. 126.
38 Žižek, *The Ticklish Subject,* p. 188.
39 Ibid., p. 224.
40 Butler, Laclau and Žižek, *Contingency, Hegemoney, Universality,* p. 124.
41 Žižek, *The Ticklish Subject,* p. 131.
42 Ibid., p. 135.
43 Ibid., p. 140.
44 Ibid., p. 136.
45 Ibid., p. 144.
46 Ibid., p. 226.

47 *Ibid.*, p. 227.
48 *Ibid.*, p. 220.
49 *Ibid.*, p. 238.
50 *Ibid.*, p. 236.
51 Butler. Laclau and Žižek, *Contignecy, Hegemony, Universality*, p. 326.
52 Žižek, 'A plea for Leninist intolerance', p. 544.
53 *Ibid.*, p. 559.
54 For my efforts to support this position, see for instance: *Self/Power/Other: Political Theory and Dialogical Ethics* (Ithaca, NY: Cornell University Press, 1992), especially chapter 4 (on Merleau-Ponty); *Rethinking Generosity*, especially the chapters on Kant and Adorno; and *Moving Democracy* (Minneapolis, MN: University of Minnesota Press, 2005), especially Chapters 6 and 7 (on Derrida and Chicana feminists respectively).
55 W. Benjamin, *Illuminations*, trans. H. Zohn (New York: Schocken Books, 1969), p. 254.
56 Related to this, Judith Butler argues contra the formalism of Žižek's negativity, that 'abstraction [or negation] cannot remain rigorously abstract without exhibiting something of what it must exclude in order to constitute itself as abstraction … Abstraction is thus contaminated precisely by the concretion from which it seeks to differentiate itself' (Butler, Laclau and Žižek, *Contingency, Hegemony, Universality*, p. 19; see also p. 272).
57 Butler, Laclau and Žižek, *Contignecy, Hegemony, Universality*, p. 171.
58 Habermas takes this to the extreme when he floats this charge toward Thomas McCarthy, as I discuss in 'Of democracy, discourse, and dirt virtue: developments in recent Critical Theory', *Political Theory*, 28:4 (2000), 540–64.
59 Durham CAN (Congregations, Associations, and Neighborhoods), an Industrial Areas Foundation affiliate.
60 See my 'Moving democracy: IAF social movements and the political arts of listening, traveling, and tabling', *Political Theory*, 32:5 (2004), 678–705.
61 I am indebted to Laura Grattan's notes and insights.
62 M. Foucault, 'What is Enlightenment?', in P. Rabinow (ed.), *The Foucault Reader* (New York: Pantheon Books, 1984), p. 50.

5 • *Aletta J. Norval*

Theorising hegemony: between deconstruction and psychoanalysis[1]

OUR current intellectual milieu more often than not demands fidelity to a single author or style of thinking. More a theoretical bricoleur than a purist, Laclau has consistently developed his work in defiance of this demand. Ever since the publication of *Hegemony and Socialist Strategy* (with Chantal Mouffe), the influence of both deconstruction and psychoanalysis, as specific modes of thinking, have remained constant in Laclau's work. Indeed, three relatively distinct phases can be discerned in Laclau's work: the early Marxist writings up to and including *Politics and Ideology in Marxist Theory*; a middle phase in which post-Marxist arguments were developed, including *Hegemony and Socialist Strategy*, and in which the impact of deconstruction is already clearly felt; and a later phase in which both deconstruction and Lacanian psychoanalysis began to take on a more explicit role, starting with *New Reflections on the Revolution of Our Time*.[2] Laclau has developed insights drawn from the deconstructive and psychoanalytic traditions without giving way to the demand for purity and adherence to particular mode of thinking. It is precisely in this difficult conjunction that the distinctiveness of Laclau's work in general, and his account of hegemony in particular, are to be found. In this chapter, I explore the trajectories of these influences on his theorisation of hegemony and critically assess the productivity of the articulation between them.

It could safely be suggested that the main contribution of Laclau to political thought today consists in his emphasis on the centrality of hegemony to any understanding and analysis of politics. As he puts it, hegemony defines the terrain in which a political relation is actually constituted.[3] This claim can only be understood once one regards the terrain of the political as that of a contingent articulation of relations, identities and interests. It is only if nothing is seen to be determined in advance, that hegemony can emerge as a central category of analysis. Laclau's work gives considerable attention to the conditions – ontological, theoretical and historical – in which hegemony as a political logic becomes thinkable and visible. His outline of these conditions resonate strongly with the outstanding features of our contemporary political landscape: the emphasis on contingency and the need to think hegemony through a process of articulation captures something of the difficulty and complexity of constructing common political projects in a world fragmented and individualised by the forces of globalisation.

This conceptualisation is informed by a wide array of developments in contemporary continental philosophy and post-structuralist theory, including the works of Derrida, Lacan, Foucault, Heidegger, Husserl, Žižek, in addition to the Marxist precursors, which remain a consistent and important presence. The bringing together of insights from sometimes diverging traditions produce both a distinctive vision of politics and a fecund analytical toolbox. This is done through and coheres around a precise set of ontological presuppositions, which defines the distinctiveness of the hegemonic account of politics. However, these bodies of thought inevitably also produce certain tensions, some of which will be explored in the course of this chapter. In the terms framing this volume, the articulation between deconstruction, as thought of abundance,[4] and psychoanalysis, as thought of lack, is one that is both productive and challenging. Several issues may be raised in respect of this articulation. In this chapter, I seek to make clear the terms of the articulation, the analytical consequences and the remaining unresolved tensions between them. I start by placing the theorisation of hegemony in the Marxist theoretico-political context from which it emerges. I then proceed to outline the key developments in this theorisation, as influenced by the deconstructive and psychoanalytic traditions. I conclude with some critical reflections on the grammar of politics that emerges as a result.

Hegemony: the emergence and radicalisation of a category

A hegemonic account of politics and ideology focuses attention on the logic of articulation: it seeks to make visible the contingency of political structures (institutions, discourses, identities and ideologies are all treated as sedimented structures of different sorts on this account) and provides us with theoretical and methodological tools that allows us to break with both topographical and essentialist assumptions concerning the character of such institutions and ideologies. Hence, Laclau's claim that political logics are articulatory in character: they put together elements with no prior and necessary connection. Thus, what we need to understand and account for is the constitution and dissolution of identities and ideologies resulting from the contingent articulation of elements.[5] This emphasis on contingent articulation shapes every dimension of Laclau's political theory, and is progressively deepened as Laclau's work becomes more influenced by deconstruction and psychoanalysis.

It is precisely this emphasis on articulation, as opposed to mediation,[6] which allows Laclau to separate his insights from those inspired by more traditional Marxist orientations.[7] Accounting for the emergence of 'hegemony' as a category marking the failure of the logic of necessity in Marxist theory, Laclau and Mouffe show how a progressive separation between structural positions (class) and historical 'tasks' occur. Their deconstruction of this logic opens up the role and formation of the subject and questions the presumption of historical necessity, be that in the form of a logic of history generally or of the development of productive forces in particular. Problematising any remainders of historical necessity and structural determination, yet also eschewing voluntaristic accounts of subjectivity, Laclau and Mouffe put forward an argument for understanding politics in terms of hegemonic logics. Thus, their critique of the Marxism of the Second International leads them to draw out the underlying *logic* of the argument concerning hegemony, such that hegemony no longer refers to the dominance of one class over another, but to a generalised political logic: 'hegemony is a *type of political relation* and not a topographical concept ... its effects always emerge from a surplus of meaning which results from an operation of displacement'.[8] Laclau reiterates this point some years later: the point is to move from 'a purely sociologistic and descriptive account of the *concrete* agents involved in hegemonic operations to a *formal* analysis of the logics involved in the latter ... The really important task is to understand the logics of their constitution and dissolution.'[9]

The logic of hegemony has been worked out in Laclau's writings over some three decades. Here I wish only to draw out some of the key features of his treatment of hegemony as political logic,[10] and to focus on a number of the central concepts that together help define this logic. Of particular interest in this respect is the extent to which the conceptual development of the category of hegemony displays, as Laclau points out in *New Reflections*, a progressive incorporation of articulatory logics into different areas of the social. The radicalisation of 'hegemony' consists in conceiving, first, of key signifiers, then of political projects and, finally, of the structure itself as incomplete and thus open to political articulation.[11] These different moments, whose development one can locate in different key texts in Laclau's *oeuvre*, each takes the thought of 'openness' a stage further, and each of these stages are clearly influenced by Derrida and Lacan respectively.

Though both these influences are present from an early period in Laclau's writings, their respective imprints are visible in particular dimensions of the account of hegemony and different aspects of deconstruction and psychoanalysis are drawn upon at different points, only some of which I can touch upon here. The argument concerning the constitutive incompletion of the social and its centrality to understand the working of hegemonic logics, for instance, takes its key from Derrida's deconstruction of structuralism.[12] This insight is later deepened by drawing on Gasché's reading of deconstruction as infrastructural accounting.[13] Specifically, Laclau focuses on the infrastructure of undecidability to conceptualise, more fully, the incompletion of the structure.[14] This also

Theorising hegemony

facilitates the emergence of a new concern with, on the one hand, the character of hegemonic decisions and their relation to destructured terrains and, on the other, the subject taking decisions. The influence of Lacan is similarly present throughout Laclau's work. Following Žižek's important intervention in 'Beyond discourse analysis',[15] Laclau draws more explicitly on Lacan in recasting the subject as 'distance between the undecidable structure and the decision'.[16] Similarly, his early reading of the key nodal points around which political projects are articulated draws on Lacan's insight into the functioning of *points de caption* in holding discursive elements together. Finally, the nature of the objects of identification around which hegemonic projects are constructed also later receive further elaboration via a reading based upon the *objet petit a*, a reading this time inspired by Copjec's Lacan.[17] These arguments are all drawn together and inform his treatment of hegemony as a mutual articulation between the universal and the particular.

The status of the theoretical articulation: an exercise in ontology

These specific insights, on which I will elaborate below, are accompanied by reflection on the nature and condition of the combination of these distinctive bodies of thought.[18] Three points are of particular importance in this respect. First, there is no eclecticism involved here. Laclau submits the logics he draws from both deconstruction and psychoanalysis to the theoretical questions inspiring his work: these are articulated with one another and this, inevitably, means that the categories are subjected to a certain amount of re/deformation. As I have argued at the outset, this is not an operation aiming to retain some original 'purity' of argumentation. Rather, the emphasis is on thinking through the rationale for a certain mode of argumentation.

The second point concerns the substance of the arguments. Laclau emphasises the role of lack and its introduction of unfixity and contingency as preconditions for the combination of a hegemonic and psychoanalytic approach to politics:

> The ultimate point which makes an exchange between Lacanian theory and the hegemonic approach to politics possible and fruitful is that in both cases, any kind of unfixity, tropic displacement, and so on, is organized around an original lack which ... opens the way to a series of indefinite substitutions which are the very ground of a radical historicism.[19]

A very similar point regarding unfixity is made with regard to deconstruction and its relation to hegemony:

> To conceive of politics in terms of hegemonic articulations involves showing 1) that sedimented social forms are inherently contingent; and 2) that the

language games that it is possible to play starting from these contingent articulations presuppose relations between entities that far exceed what was thinkable within the implicit political ontology of classical political theory. From this point of view, the notion of undecidability as developed by deconstruction is crucial. The infrastructures – supplementarity, iteration, re-mark, and so on – as systematized by Rodolphe Gasché are invaluable for rethinking the strategic operations presupposed by a hegemonic logic.[20]

The third point concerns the status of the resulting interventions. In both cases Laclau is at pains to emphasise that it is not ontic or regional, but work of an *ontological* character:

> I think that the psychoanalytical discovery of the unconscious is one of these epoch-making events whose ontological dimensions we are only starting to glimpse. So I do not think that the *objet petit a* or the subject of lack are ontic categories limited to a particular region of human reality. When one realises their full ontological implications they transform *any* field, the political field included.[21]

Similarly, deconstruction is viewed as a body of thought that deepens ontological insights in that it facilitates a making visible of the non-essential character of any social ordering.[22] This argument is already clearly present in Laclau and Mouffe's *Hegemony and Socialist Strategy*, where they draw on Derrida to develop their argument concerning the 'non-closure' of the social. I now turn to a discussion of these themes in greater detail.

The initial impact of deconstruction

The deconstructive intervention, from the outset, eschews all voluntarism and subjectivism.[23] It takes place, tracing out and so making visible, relations of force in the particular text or discourse under discussion. This work of deconstruction plays a formative role in the development of Laclau and Mouffe's writings. I will argue that a key characteristic of their writings in this respect consists of bringing the impurity of thought to bear on the theorisation and analysis of politics. Before turning to this specific argument, I will briefly outline the manner in which a deconstructive mode of thinking has shaped Laclau's – in conjunction with Mouffe's – work since the early 1980s.

In their treatment of the Marxist tradition, in particular the Marxism of the Second International, Laclau and Mouffe consistently deploy what could only be characterised as a deconstructive argumentative strategy. The key features of this strategy consist of a reading that, firstly, seeks to make visible the unthought, constitutive tensions at the heart of Marxist theory. Secondly, the effects of their recasting of these conceptual tensions are disseminated to other

Theorising hegemony

conceptual fields, leading to a rethinking of categories central to political theory more generally.[24] Take, for example, the reworking of the relation between necessity and contingency in Marxist theory already mentioned. Laclau and Mouffe make visible the dependence of relations of necessity on those of contingency, and the privileging of the former as dependent upon the exclusion and subordination of the latter. Importantly, this does not proceed through a rejection of the categories of Marxist analysis. It works through these categories, showing how their mutual imbrication sustains precise political logics, logics put into question by their reading.[25] Generalising the insights they gained from this deconstructive account of the relation between necessity and contingency, Laclau and Mouffe trace out the consequences of a generalised contingency and facticity for an understanding of politics. In so doing, they do not replace an emphasis on necessity with one on contingency in a simple movement of reversal. Laclau argues in this respect: 'We are dealing not with a head-on negation of necessity ... but with its subversion ... In this sense, it is the contingent which subverts the necessary: contingency is not the negative other side of necessity, but the element of impurity which deforms and hinders its full constitution.'[26]

Laclau and Mouffe then proceed to provide a structured genealogy of key concepts, in which the impossibility of a pure logic of necessity, uncontaminated by contingency is shown, and the logic of impurity is put to work. From this a more general argumentative strategy emerges that takes full account of the aporias constitutive of political theorising, but which does not attempt to supersede them in any simple fashion. Akin to what Gasché characterises as Derrida's infrastructural accounting,[27] Laclau and Mouffe delineate a series of concepts within the Marxist tradition marked by similar tensions as those outlined above. This strategy is not, however, limited to the Marxist tradition. In their later works both Laclau and Mouffe respectively emphasise the import of the deconstructive insights developed in their early writings. For instance, Laclau engages with such key concepts as power and representation,[28] illuminating key aporias in these concepts and logics. Taken together, their works provide a panorama of concepts that have been subjected to deconstructive interventions so as to show their impurity and the extent to which their transcendental aspirations must always already be frustrated.

Apart from this general deconstructive argumentative strategy, Laclau and Mouffe also develop more substantive insights from Derrida's analysis. One of the key insights of *Hegemony and Socialist Strategy* relates to what has become known as the 'impossibility of society' argument. Drawing on Derrida's argument concerning the decentering of the structure,[29] Laclau and Mouffe argue that an ineradicable *excess*, which escapes it, marks the representation of societal unity, as positive and fully present. This opens up the space for a hegemonic form of politics. As Laclau puts it already in his seminal article, 'The impossibility of society',[30] any structural system is limited and is always surrounded by an *excess* of meaning that it is unable to master. For Laclau, this excess must be understood primarily in terms of signification. *Hegemony and Socialist Strategy* abounds with references to the 'surplus of meaning'. The discussion of floating signifiers, as well as of the 'field of discursivity', to mention but two concepts, is marked by references of 'polysemy', a 'proliferation of signifieds', an 'overflowing' of discourses by the field of discursivity and so on.[31] As a consequence of this excess, there is an ultimate impossibility of fixing any meaning. Hence, any attempt to stabilise meaning has to take the form of an act of hegemonisation; that is, a partial and incomplete act of articulation of this excess of the social. This argument holds, not only for the identity of society, but also for identity *tout court*; that is, every identity is constitutively marked by non-closure.[32] This thought of openness is taken further in Laclau's subsequent writings, where he sets out to develop the implications of 'undecidability' – as worked through in Derrida's writings – for the theorisation of hegemony.

Undecidability and hegemony

For Laclau, the issue of the relation between deconstruction and hegemony arises in the context of undecidability and the need for the stabilisation of what is essentially unstable. He holds that a deconstructive approach is highly relevant to two dimensions of the political. The first is the notion of the political as the instituting moment of society, and the second is the incompletion of all acts of political institution. That is, what makes politics possible – the contingency of acts of institution – is also what makes it impossible. Ultimately, no instituting act is fully achievable. In short, deconstruction widens the field of structural undecidability, so clearing the field for a theory of the decision taken in an undecidable terrain.[33] On this reading, hegemony requires deconstruction because without the radical undecidability that the deconstructive intervention brings about, many strata of social relations would appear as essentially linked by necessary logics and there would be nothing to hegemonise. Conversely, deconstruction requires hegemony, since it needs a theory of the decision taken in an undecidable terrain.[34] Given this formulation, three key areas need to be addressed: the nature of the undecidable terrain, the decision taken in this terrain and the nature of the subject of the decision.[35] I will deal with them in turn.

As is clear from the brief introduction above, for Laclau, the undecidable terrain amounts to nothing more and nothing less than a destructured social field, one in which previous social logics have been put into question by a dislocatory event.[36] In taking up the logic of undecidability, Laclau's main concerns are to question two prevalent tendencies in political theorising today, coming from quite distinct directions. The first rejects anything that we might learn from deconstruction and holds that there are certain social logics that predetermine and structure all possible political decisions in a situation of crisis. The second, proceeding from within the horizon of deconstruction, suggests, in a not dissimilar fashion, that the destructured terrain is already shaped by a certain ethical demand.[37] Both these positions have the consequence of putting into question the primacy of the political, a central tenet of Laclau's work and a key influence on his theorising of the decision.

For our purposes here, it is crucial to note that for Laclau, the 'undecidable terrain' is the corollary of a 'lack' in the structure. They are, so to speak, two sides of the same coin: 'the structure is not fully reconciled with itself ... it is inhabited by an original lack, by a radical undecidability that needs to be constantly superseded by acts of decision. These acts are precisely what constitute the *subject*.'[38] The 'excess' and 'abundance', identified in Laclau's writings with the Lacanian understanding of 'lack' and Derrida's work on the decentring of the structure respectively, are thus not to be understood in diametrically opposed ways.[39] For Laclau, in contrast to some other contemporary political theorists, they simply constitute two different ways of approaching the same issue. In both cases, Laclau identifies two areas standing in need of further theorisation: that of the 'decision' and the subject of the decision.

The passage from undecidability to the decision is thought of as an act of politics through and through. Refusing to ground the decision in an ethical moment, Laclau posits a conception of it based on power. For him, a decision taken in a terrain of structural undecidables means: (a) that the decision is self-grounding; (b) that it consists in 'repressing possible alternatives that are not carried out'; and (c) that it is internally split (this/a decision), emphasising the interplay between the universal and the particular in the production of any hegemonic discourse.[40] The terrain of the decision, on this account, is the terrain of the political proper: there is nothing in the dislocated terrain that determines the decision. If it did, it would not be a decision proper:

> A true decision escapes always what any rule can hope to subsume under itself ... in that case, the decision has to be grounded in its singularity. Now, that singularity cannot bring through the back door what it has excluded from the main entrance – i.e. the universality of the rule. It is simply left to its own singularity. It is because of that, as Kierkegaard put it, the moment of the decision is the moment of madness.[41]

Thus, for Laclau, to take a decision 'is like impersonating God',[42] since this act cannot be explained in terms of any underlying rational mediation. This moment of the decision is then, simultaneously, that of the subject.[43] As Laclau puts it, the 'lack is precisely the *locus* of the subject, whose relation with the structure takes place through various processes of *identification*'.[44] For the deepening of the theorisation of the subject, Laclau turns to Lacan rather than to Derrida.[45]

Bringing the subject back in – introducing Lacan

Contra his earlier account of the subject in terms of subject positions, where Foucault's influence was quite clear,[46] Laclau now offers a more fully developed psychoanalytic-inspired account of the subject as the distance between the undecidable structure and the decision.[47] Since the structure is dislocated, the subject cannot be presumed to have a positive identity. Instead, it can only construct an identity through acts of identification: 'we do not simply have subject positions within the structure, but also the subject as an attempt to fill these structural gaps. That is why we do not have just *identities* but, rather, *identification*.'[48]

Three consequences relevant to our discussion follow from this. First, if the emergence of the subject is the result of a 'collapse of objectivity', it means that 'any subject is, by definition, political'.[49] Second, since the structure with which it may identify is dislocated, any act of identification will be partial and incomplete. Third, this means that the act of identification is simultaneously a hegemonic act through which the fullness of the community is constructed in its absence: 'We, "mortal gods" ... have to fill the gaps resulting from the absence of God on earth, simulating being Him and replacing with the madness of our decision on omniscience that will always elude us.'[50] Despite the decisionistic and voluntaristic tones of these passages, Laclau tempers his account of the decision by finally emphasising that it is always taken in a context. Thus, it is not entirely free: '[W]hat counts as a valid decision will have the limits of a structure which, in its actuality, is only partially destructured. The madness of the decision is, if you want, as all madness, a regulated one.'[51] Together these elements – hegemony, decision and subject – furnish the initial contours of the morphology of Laclau's conceptualisation of hegemony as a political logic. The final piece of the puzzle is provided by his introduction of the logic of the partial object to re-theorise the project.

The role of the partial object

In his latest work, *The Populist Reason*, Laclau deepens his reading of the nature of hegemonic projects further by drawing on the reading of Lacan developed by Joan Copjec. In *New Reflections*, where Laclau discusses the theoretical radicalisation of the category of hegemony, he points out that the signifiers – such as 'democracy' – around which hegemonic projects are articulated, are, in principle, 'floating'. That is, they can be articulated to different projects, and the projects themselves equally lack essential characteristics. These insights are now considerably complicated by introducing, first, an account of the processes of identification of the subject, via a discussion of the affective dimensions of such identification; second, further reworking what is involved in the hegemonic project itself;[52] and, third, the role of naming in these processes.

Laclau argues that the character of investment in a hegemonic project rests on rhetorical form, on the one hand, and affective force, on the other. The operation of rhetorical relations of substitution and combination play a central role in Laclau's analysis of the constitution of political identities from the 1980s. This is evident in the key role given to the logics of equivalence and difference in his account of identity formation. The introduction of these logics also broadens out the categories that can legitimately be used to think about social relations: 'Synonymy, metonymy, metaphor are not forms of thought that add a second sense to a primary, constitutive literality of social relations; instead, they are the part of the primary terrain itself in which the social is constituted.'[53] These insights are generalised in his 'Glimpsing the future: a reply', where he argues that 'rhetoric is constitutive of discourse' and, further, the affective components of discourse are now treated as an integral part of the signifying process.[54] As Laclau argues in *The Populist Reason*: 'Affect is not something which exists of its own, independently of language, but it only constitutes itself through the differential cathexes of a signifying chain. This is exactly what "investment" means.'[55] Moreover, if 'an entity becomes the object of an investment – as in being in love, or in hatred – the investment belongs necessarily to the order of *affect*'.[56] Hence, the importance of focusing on the nature of naming – understood as a 'highly cathected rallying point'[57] – and the role of subjective identification in the account of hegemony. The different elements of the argument are brought together in the following extract, which I quote at length:

> My theory of hegemony asserts: 1) that there is a constitutive dislocation in any structural arrangement which ultimately makes impossible any kind of full symbolic identification; 2) that the object able to fill that structural lack, being both necessary and impossible, can only be a *particular object* which assumes the role of bringing about a fullness incommensurable with itself (this is the hegemonic link); 3) that, this link being essentially contingent, there is no logical connection between representative and what it represents – there is no 'natural' passage from one to the other (this is why a 'radical investment' is required, the latter involving an *affective* link between two objects); 4) that, as a result, there is no permanent attachment between the signifier of fullness and the various objects incarnating it.[58]

This extract draws out two further dimensions of the argument, on which it is necessary to focus. The first concerns the fact that in politics, identification takes place more successfully with some objects rather than others. That is to say, though there is no possibility of a necessary link between the 'signifier of fullness' and the objects incarnating it – this link is essentially contingent – there are some objects that lend themselves more clearly or easily to the task than others.[59] Which objects may fulfil this role will be determined by the precise political context in which it operates. Following Gramsci, Laclau argues:

> which social force will become the hegemonic representation of society as a whole is the result of a contingent struggle; but once a particular social force becomes hegemonic, it remains so for a whole historical period. *The object of the investment can be contingent, but most certainly is not indifferent – it cannot be changed at will.*[60]

This argument is crucial since it directly contests Žižek's position, which holds that the object of identification is more or less irrelevant. What is crucial for Žižek is the lack in the subject itself, which is covered over as a result.[61]

The second point of importance is the emphasis Laclau puts on the particularity of the object, which nevertheless has to fulfil a universal task. It is here that his earlier arguments on the imbrication of particularity/universality receive a new Lacanian dimension. Following Copjec, Laclau argues that the *object a* – the partial object – is not a part of a whole, but 'a part which is the whole'.[62] The partial object does not evoke a totality, but rather becomes the *name* of that totality. Thus, hegemony is 'nothing more than the investment, in a partial object, of a fullness which will always evade us'.[63] To put it differently, the object with which one identifies (the hegemonic project) can only ever be a particular object 'which assumes the role of bringing about a fullness incommensurable with itself' and there can be no permanent attachment between this signifier of fullness and the various objects incarnating it.[64] Consequently for Laclau, as opposed to Žižek, the object of identification must play a crucial role in any analysis; it cannot simply be reduced to its function of covering over the lack in the subject.

Critical conclusions

Above I have outlined the broad substance of the arguments seeking to articulate together a certain reading of psychoanalysis, deconstruction and a hegemonic approach to politics. There remains, of course, a series of issues relating to the more detailed uptake of the traditions in Laclau's work. Here the key questions revolve around the overall integration of theoretical terms into a coherent conceptual morphology, on the one hand, and more precise questions concerning his interpretation of specific philosophemes, on the other.[65] Important as these questions are, I wish to conclude, not with a detailed consideration of the minutiae of conceptual development and the morphology of hegemony, but with the broader issues arising out of this combinatorial theorisation.

As has been argued above, Laclau articulates the thought of abundance or excess, on the one hand, and lack, on the other, by drawing on insights derived from Derrida and readings of Lacan. This combination is made possible, in large measure, as a result of the fact that his readings of both these traditions focus on their opposition to the thought of structural completion and fullness. In the case of deconstruction, this arises out of its critique of the metaphysics of presence, whilst in the case of psychoanalysis its source is the destructuring effects of the unconscious. Thus, both deconstruction and an appropriation of Lacanian psychoanalysis – here the readings of Žižek and Copjec respectively[66] – theorise, and so make visible, the constitutive character of incompletion. At this deep ontological level, there is nothing that prevents a productive articulation between them.

However, once one moves away from this general insight, to the particular theoretical tools each of these traditions brings to bear analytically, this situation potentially changes. An analysis of a political discourse that takes as its starting-point an undecidable terrain as opposed to a terrain that is 'lacking' will produce readings that are quite different in character. In the first instance, the analytical task, for instance, will have to focus retroactively on revealing the multiple possibilities constitutive of a terrain, which has been covered over by the institution of a particular hegemonic discourse. In other words, analysis will concentrate on recovering the richness of dimensions of political life that have been submerged and/or excluded by dominant political forces so as to make visible alternative ways of thinking about a political order or a political project. In the second instance, the focus on lack shifts attention away from an alternative, genealogical mapping of the structure, to the intervention of the subject and an analysis of modes of identification and their failure or success. The focus and object of analysis thus changes significantly. While these analytical tasks are clearly complementary, they are not the same, and any worthwhile analysis of a hegemonic project would have to take all of these dimensions into account. Moreover, one would do well to take heed of the possible different analyses that may follow from the respective treatments of subjectivity in deconstruction and psychoanalysis. Deconstructive analyses tend to maintain a critical, if not sceptical, engagement with 'the subject', questioning the very possibility of talk of 'the subject', while giving serious attention to the minutiae of relations constituting different subjectivities. In contrast, some Lacanian inspired works have tended to propose heroic models of identification, where 'the subject' very much forms the foreground of discussion.[67] This, it seems to me, is not accidental, and is a source of potential tension in the articulation between psychoanalysis and deconstruction. This particular difference may also be suggestive of a more general differentiation in approach. Deconstruction by definition pushes the analyst to give attention to finer points, which are treated as indicative, and sometimes constitutive, of important distinctions. The broad brush with which some Lacanian analyses operate, tend to favour larger gestures and more abstract explanations. These differences may become particularly problematic in the hands of a political analyst not sufficiently attuned to the specificity of arguments and contexts, and they will be exacerbated where there is a clear preference for one of these intellectual (re)sources.

Where one is emphasised at the expense of the other, this is often done via a pre-theoretical authorial allegiance.[68] There is ample evidence of this in contemporary readings and debates on the relation between psychoanalysis, deconstruction and a hegemonic account of politics.[69] Both Butler and Žižek, for instance, have objected to dimensions of Laclau's theoretical articulation of deconstruction, psychoanalysis and politics, Žižek being particularly vehement in his denunciations of so-called post-modern approaches (to which he often wrongly assimilates Derrida) and Butler questioning the sensitivity of Lacanian approaches to historical context. These debates are both wide-ranging and address quite specific issues. This is not the place to recount and respond to these criticisms. However, given that they are marked by some recurring themes, they are worth addressing in some more detail.

The first concerns the 'strength' of the logics deployed by Laclau. The formulation of this problem takes on many different guises, ranging from questioning the apparently a-historical character of some of the insights on which Laclau draws (the Lacanian account of the subject is one such candidate)[70] to berating him for what appears to be excessive 'formalism' (a term disguising many different concerns). The key concern here is the ontological status of the theorisation of his hegemonic account of politics and the fact that it seemingly militates against historical and contextual nuances and sensitivity. Laclau has responded to these criticisms by emphasising the need in any theorisation for formalism: 'Formal analysis and abstraction are essential for the study of concrete historical processes – not only because the theoretical construction of the object is the requirement of any intellectual practice worthy of the name, but also because social reality itself generates abstractions which organize its own principles of functioning.'[71]

A further response may also be possible here, one that does not seek to question either the articulation between the traditions under discussion by falsely opposing one against the other or the very relevance and fecundity of these traditions for thinking about politics. This response seeks to draw out the similarities in some of the logics of both the deconstructive and psychoanalytic traditions, but in a manner favouring *theoretical articulation* rather than philosophical wholeness. This should not, however, be regarded as a license for imprecision, vagueness and eclecticism, as pointed out earlier. There is much scope for very precise and detailed consideration of argumentative forms that, whilst retaining their singular insights, could potentially enrich our understanding of hegemony. In this respect, the treatment of 'infrastructures' in deconstruction and the theorisation of relations between objects in psychoanalysis immediately spring to mind. The complexification of the relation between the inside/outside in deconstruction through the infrastructures of remark, iterability, supplementarity and so on, which are also visible in the Lacanian treatment of *extimité*, is extremely suggestive in two respects. Firstly, each of these depicts in a different way the relations between political identities or projects: breaking with all thought of wholeness they open up a complex array of possible forms that relations may take. Secondly, this refiguring is dependent upon a willingness to embrace impurity of thought in a precise sense: the interpenetration and imbrication of relations – conceptual and otherwise – are foregrounded. In this universe, the demand for wholeness and purity has been superseded by a recognition of the opacity and complexity penetrating all relations, a complexity that resists simplification in principle.

Finally, close consideration of these infrastructures puts into question the association between deconstruction and the thought of abundance, on the one hand, and psychoanalysis and that of 'lack', on the other. The infrastructure of supplementarity, for instance, combines both presence and its self-deficiency.[72] As Gasché puts it, supplementarity puts great emphasis on 'the structural necessity of the addition to a difference to a "full" entity such as an origin by showing it to be a consequence of the fact that "full" terms compensate for their *lack* of another origin'.[73] Similarly, *extimité* captures the sense in which the unconscious never only refers to an interior psychic system but to an intersubjective structure 'overflowing', having effects beyond 'itself'.[74] Here abundance captures the heart of what is at stake in the psychoanalytic intervention. Hence, it would be mistaken to treat the terms 'abundance' and 'lack' as simple opposites. As any good deconstructionist knows, each of these terms may shade into their opposite, insofar as they are treated as one another's 'constitutive outsides'. This deconstructive logic, as I have argued, deeply permeates Laclau's conceptual work and, in particular, it shapes his reading of Lacanian psychoanalysis, subverting any simplistic appropriation of arguments concerning 'lack'. Once one is in the terrain of theoretical articulation, multiple possibilities open up, such that simplistic mappings become redundant and even stifling of innovative thought. Though there are many respects in which Laclau's new conceptual grammar needs development and refinement in its details, it has opened up a new terrain of theorising, which is unsurpassed in its potential fecundity.

Notes

1 I would like to thank Jason Glynos, David Howarth, Lasse Thomassen, Lars Tønder and Jacob Torfing for comments on earlier drafts of this chapter.

2 E. Laclau, *Politics and Ideology in Marxist Theory* (London: Verso, 1978); E. Laclau and C. Mouffe, *Hegemony and Socialist Strategy* (London: Verso, 1985); E. Laclau, *New Reflections on the Revolution of Our Time* (London: Verso, 1990).

3 Laclau in J. Butler, E. Laclau and Slavoj Žižek, *Contingency, Hegemony, Universality: Contemporary Dialogues on the Left* (London: Verso, 2000), p. 44.

4 It should be noted that Laclau here differs from for instance, Connolly, in his reading of Derrida. Connolly thinks abundance through the work of Deleuze and treats Derrida as a theorist of lack. See W. E. Connolly, *The Ethos of Pluralization* (Minneapolis, MN: University of Minnesota Press, 1995), pp. 94–7.
5 Laclau in *Contingency, Hegemony, Universality*, p. 53.
6 For a fuller discussion of the distinction between articulation and a Hegelian conception of mediation, see Laclau and Mouffe, *Hegemony and Socialist Strategy*, p. 94.
7 For an overview of Laclau and Mouffe's earlier arguments, see, D. Howarth, 'Theorising hegemony', in I. Hampsher-Monk and J. Stanyer (eds), *Contemporary Political Studies 1996* (Glasgow: PSA, 1996), pp. 944–56; and D. Howarth, 'Hegemony, subjectivity and radical democracy', in S. Critchley and O. Marchart (eds), *Laclau: A Critical Reader* (London: Routledge, 2004).
8 Laclau and Mouffe, *Hegemony and Socialist Strategy*, p. 141.
9 Laclau, *Contingency, Hegemony, Universality*, p. 52
10 For a further discussion of this matter, see D. Howarth, 'Theorising hegemony'.
11 Laclau, *New Reflections*, pp. 28f.
12 Laclau argues that Derrida starts from 'a radical break in the concept of structure, occurring at the moment in which the centre ... is abandoned, and with it the possibility of fixing a meaning which underlies the flow of differences'. Laclau and Mouffe, *Hegemony and Socialist Strategy*, pp. 111f. See also J. Derrida, *Writing and Difference* (London: Routledge & Kegan Paul, 1978), pp. 278–94.
13 R. Gasché, *The Tain of the Mirror: Derrida and the Philosophy of Reflection* (Cambridge, MA: Harvard University Press, 1986), esp. Part 2.
14 E. Laclau, *Emancipation(s)* (London: Verso, 1996), chapter 5.
15 S. Žižek, 'Beyond discourse analysis', in Laclau, *New Reflections*.
16 E. Laclau, 'Deconstruction, pragmatism, hegemony', in C. Mouffe (ed.), *Deconstruction and Pragmatism* (London: Routledge, 1996), p. 54.
17 J. Copjec, *Imagine There's No Woman* (Cambridge, MA: MIT Press, 2002).
18 See, Laclau in L. Worsham and G. A. Olson, 'Hegemony and the future of democracy: Ernesto Laclau's political philosophy', in L. Worsham and G. Olson (eds), *Race, Rhetoric and the Postcolonial* (Albany, NY: State University of New York, 1999), p. 159.
19 Laclau, *Contingency, Hegemony, Universality*, p. 71
20 Laclau in C. Pessoa, M. Hernández, S. Lee and L. Thomassen, 'Theory, democracy, and the Left: an interview with Ernesto Laclau', *Umbr@* (2001).
21 E. Laclau, 'Glimpsing the future: a reply', in Critchley and Marchart (eds), *Laclau: A Critical Reader*, p. 36.
22 Laclau, 'Deconstruction, pragmatism, hegemony'.
23 See J. Derrida,'"Eating well", or the calculation of the subject: an interview with Jacques Derrida', E. Cadava, P. Connor and J.-L. Nancy (eds), *Who Comes After the Subject?* (New York: Routledge, 1991), pp. 96–119.
24 These moves echo almost precisely the two-tiered Derridean strategy of setting aside and re-inscribing terms. See J. Derrida, *Positions* (Chicago: University of Chicago Press, 1981), p. 36.
25 For a summary of this argument, see Laclau, *New Reflections*, pp. 27f.
26 Laclau, *New Reflections*, pp. 26f.
27 Gasché, *Tain of the Mirror*, pp. 142–54.
28 Laclau, *Emancipation(s)*, chapter 6.
29 Derrida, *Writing and Difference*, pp. 278–94.
30 E. Laclau, 'The impossibility of society', *Canadian Journal of Political and Social Theory* 7:1–2 (1983), 21–7.

31 Laclau and Mouffe, *Hegemony and Socialist Strategy*, pp. 111–13.
32 For a fuller discussion of how these arguments relate to antagonism, dislocation and undecidability, see A. J. Norval, 'The impurity of politics: deconstructive interventions', *Essex Papers in Government and Politics, Sub-series in Ideology and Discourse Analysis*, no. 18, Department of Government, University of Essex (2002).
33 Laclau, 'Deconstruction, pragmatism, hegemony', p. 48.
34 *Ibid.*, pp. 59f.
35 The first two subsections here roughly follow the argument presented in A. J. Norval, 'Hegemony after deconstruction: the consequences of undecidability', *Journal of Political Ideologies*, 9:2 (2004), 139–57.
36 Laclau, *Emancipation(s)*, p. 78. It should be noted that Laclau's conceptualisation of dislocation draws both on Henry Staten's reading of the 'constitutive outside' in Derrida, and on the Lacanian conception of the real. See Laclau, *New Reflections*, pp. 41–61 and 212. See also H. Staten, *Wittgenstein and Derrida* (Lincoln, NE: University of Nebraska Press, 1984), p. 24.
37 For a discussion of the ethicization of Derrida's work via a reading of Levinas, see, *inter alia*, S. Critchley, *The Ethics of Deconstruction. Derrida and Levinas* (Oxford: Blackwell, 1992); S. Critchley, 'Deconstruction and pragmatism – is Derrida a private ironist or a public liberal?', in Mouffe (ed.), *Deconstruction and Pragmatism*, pp. 19–40. For Laclau's response to this, see, *inter alia*, 'Ethics, politics and radical democracy – a response to Simon Critchley', *Culture Machine*, 2002, http://culturemachine.tees.ac.uk/Articles/laclau.htm.
38 Laclau, *Emancipation(s)*, p. 92
39 In this Laclau and Žižek are in agreement. See Žižek's discussion of readings of Lacan focussing on 'lack' in *The Indivisible Remainder* (London: Verso, 1996), pp. 95–7.
40 See Laclau, 'Deconstruction, pragmatism, hegemony', p. 48.
41 *Ibid.*, p. 53.
42 *Ibid.*, p. 55.
43 These views were first expressed in the first essay of *New Reflections*, which bears the clear imprint of Lacanian inspired account of the subject.
44 Laclau, *New Reflections*, p. 210.
45 It is important to note that there is a whole literature on Derrida's account of and relation to 'the question of the subject'. See, for instance, Derrida's responses in "Eating well", pp. 96–119; and the detailed discussion of Derrida in S. Critchley, *Ethics, Politics, Subjectivity* (London: Verso, 1999).
46 Laclau and Mouffe, *Hegemony and Socialist Strategy*, p. 115.
47 Laclau, *New Reflections*, p. 60.
48 Laclau, *Contingency, Hegemony, Universality*, p. 58.
49 Laclau, *New Reflections*, p. 61.
50 Laclau, 'Deconstruction, pragmatism, hegemony', p. 56.
51 *Ibid.*, p. 57.
52 This follows on his earlier work, which characterises a hegemonic project as 'not ... external to the structures, but ... the result of a movement generated within them ... to achieve an articulation ... that can only be partial'. Laclau, *New Reflections*, p. 28.
53 Laclau and Mouffe, *Hegemony and Socialist Strategy*, p. 110.
54 Laclau, 'Glimpsing the future', p. 27; and E. Laclau, 'Paul de Man and the politics of rhetoric', *Pretexts*, 7:2 (1998), 153–70.
55 E. Laclau, *The Populist Reason* (London: Verso, 2005), p. 112 (all references are to draft manuscript).
56 *Ibid.*, p. 111.

57 *Ibid.*, p. 7 ('Concluding remarks').
58 Laclau, 'Glimpsing the future', pp. 19f.
59 For a detailed conceptual treatment of the relation between empty signifiers and *objects petit a*, see J. Glynos and Y. Stavrakakis, 'Encounters of the real kind: sussing out the limits of Laclau's embrace of Lacan', *Journal for Lacanian Studies*, 1:1 (2003), 110–28.
60 Laclau, *The Populist Reason*, p. 116 (emphasis added).
61 For a fuller discussion of this problem in Žižek's work, see A. J. Norval, 'Review article: the things we do with words – contemporary approaches to the analysis of ideology', *British Journal of Political Science*, 30:2 (2000), 313–46.
62 Laclau, *The Populist Reason*, Appendix 1 'Affect, object a and hegemony'. It should be clear that this object fulfils a dual role: it is both particular and acts as universal. See Laclau, *Contingency, Hegemony, Universality*, pp. 302f.
63 Laclau, *The Populist Reason*, Appendix 1 'Affect, object a and hegemony'.
64 Laclau, 'Glimpsing the future', p. 20. Laclau points out that this argument is entirely commensurate with the Lacanian argument on enjoyment: 'there is always going to be a gap between the jouissance expected and the jouissance obtained'.
65 Detailed discussion of Laclau's reading of Derrida and Lacan can be found in the following texts: A. J. Norval, 'Frontiers in question', *Acta Philosophica*, 18:2 (1997), 51–76; Norval, 'Hegemony after deconstruction'; and Y. Stavrakakis, 'Antinomies of formalism: Laclau's theory of populism and the lessons from religious populism in Greece', F. Panizza (ed.), *Populism and the Mirror of Democracy* (London: Verso, 2005). See also the various contributions to *Laclau: A Critical Reader*.
66 Whilst Žižek and Copjec do not disagree fundamentally in their readings of Lacanian psychoanalytic theory, Laclau draws on Copjec to reach a set of conclusions for political analysis – as well as politics – that differ from those reached by Žižek .
67 I would argue that this 'heroism' remains trapped in a revolutionary conception of subjectivity, fundamentally at odds with a deconstructive ethos. See, for instance, S. Žižek, 'Melancholy and the act', *Critical Inquiry*, 26:4 (summer 2000), 657–81.
68 In an insightful comment on Žižek, Bennington notes that for Žižek 'Hegel and Lacan really already are what Derrida would like to be'. He calls this a need to maintain a 'pre-theoretical concept of authorial identity (without which this distribution of praise and blame would make no sense)'. G. Bennington, *Legislations* (London: Verso, 1994), p. 6.
69 See, in particular, the exchanges between Butler, Žižek and Laclau in *Contingency, Hegemony, Universality*.
70 Butler, *Contingency, Hegemony, Universality*, p. 12.
71 Laclau, *Contingency, Hegemony, University*, p. 86.
72 J. Derrida, *Speech and Phenomena* (Evanston: Northwestern University Press, 1973), p. 88.
73 Gasché, *Tain of the Mirror*, p. 206 (emphasis added).
74 See, for instance, Evans's discussion of both 'extimité' and the unconscious in D. Evans, *An Introductory Dictionary of Lacanian Psychoanalysis* (London: Routledge, 1996), pp. 58f and 217–19.

6 • *Lasse Thomassen*

In/exclusions: towards a radical democratic approach to exclusion[1]

WE LIVE in times of exclusion. In a time when, after the end of the Cold War, one would have thought that we were breaking down walls and becoming one world, it nonetheless seems that our Western liberal democracies rely on the exclusion of a number of Others: the (Muslim) fundamentalist, the subversive immigrant, the (Muslim, again) terrorist and so on and so forth. Even at the end of history, it seems, we are not at the end of exclusion or at the end of thinking in terms of 'us' and 'them'. My aim in this chapter is to ask what a radical democratic alternative to discourses that divide the political space into 'us' and 'them', friend and enemy, would look like. More specifically, I propose to do so through a discussion of Ernesto Laclau's theory of hegemony.

Developed in collaboration with Chantal Mouffe, the theory of hegemony seeks, among other things, to provide an answer as to how one can build a radical democratic project. Yet, hegemony necessarily involves closure, and the question is therefore whether the theory of hegemony and the Laclauian version of radical democracy provide an adequate radical democratic alternative. This is all the more so as some of Laclau's critics have argued that Laclau tends to emphasise the creation of clear limits between an inside and an outside, which, they argue, is precisely what should be put into question from a radical democratic standpoint.[2] Thus, in the following, I shall critically reconstruct Laclau's notions of hegemony and antagonism. My answer to the question whether Laclau's theory of hegemony provides an adequate radical democratic alternative to questions of exclusions is affirmative. Yet, I shall also argue that it is the notion of heterogeneity from his most recent work – as something escaping any attempt to create a clear line of separation between an inside and an outside – rather than that of antagonism that is central to a radical democratic approach to exclusion.[3]

Hegemony, community and empty signifiers

Laclau's theory of hegemony seeks to show, among other things, how it is possible to think the identity and limits of a community in a non-essentialist fashion.[4] Laclau starts from a post-Saussurean notion of meaning – and, hence, of identity – as constituted through relations of difference. Accordingly, the identity of a community is not the reflection of an underlying essence of History, race, fate and so on. Since the differential elements that make up the community do not belong together by virtue of any essence they share prior to and beneath their differences, the identity and limits of the community – the community as a *whole* – depends on a hegemonic relation: the articulation of different elements into what Laclau calls a chain of equivalence. In order for hegemonic articulation to be possible, both the identity of each element and the relations among elements must be relatively unfixed and floating.

The identity of the community as a whole, or the equivalence of the chain of equivalence, is established through the emptying of the differential content of one of the elements. This is what Laclau has referred to as an empty signifier in his work subsequent to *Hegemony and Socialist Strategy*.[5] The empty signifier solves a number of problems. First of all, while no particular element can represent the community as a whole in a direct or immediate fashion (that would assume an essential relationship between the particular element and the community as a whole), the community as a whole cannot be represented by signifying what is beyond it as yet another positive difference either. If the community stood in a relation of difference with what is beyond it, its identity would depend on the latter, and two consequences would follow.[6] First, it would not be possible to say where the community ends and the beyond starts, as the latter is constitutive of the former (and *vice versa*). Indeed, one could say that this would be an inclusive exclusion as the exclusion of what is beyond the community would simultaneously be included, because the identities of both would refer to a larger field of which they would be but two parts. Second, if the community stood in a relation of difference with what is beyond it, one would have to ask for the beyond of the beyond in order to determine the beyond. That is, if the totality of the field of differences has not been determined, the identity of the community would be dissolved into the infinite play of differences.

The empty signifier solves these problems, because it interrupts difference, thereby establishing an equivalence among different elements of a chain. The empty signifier representing the community as a whole does not stand in a relation of difference with what is beyond it, and in this way it is able to establish a clear distinction between inside and outside, between the fullness of the community and an antagonistic Other: 'True limits are always antagonistic.'[7] The outside will appear as an antagonistic threat to the community as a community: 'the actualisation of what is beyond the limit of exclusion would involve the impossibility of what is this side of the limit'.[8] Moreover, as the empty signifier does not stand in relations of difference *vis-à-vis* the other elements within the community, the community is One and devoid of internal divisions. Thus, the emptiness of the representative of the community and the fullness and clear limits of the community go hand in hand. Here one can think of the example of George W. Bush, the so-called War on Terror and the situation after 11 September 2001. Only months after being elected by a minority of the US voters in an election, whose legitimacy was strongly contested, Bush was able to unite not only the United States, but also the whole 'Free World'. The creation of the coalition against terror in the aftermath of 9–11 was an example of the creation of a chain of equivalence, whose uniting signifier – 'Freedom', and sometimes 'democracy' – nobody could be against. Of course, later the chain of equivalence was broken, and this is not only an empirical possibility, but also an essential theoretical possibility.

Differential remainders and tendentially empty signifiers

The condition of possibility of hegemony is that the elements being articulated into a chain of equivalence are relatively unfixed and floating; if all elements were completely fixed either in a differential system or in a chain of equivalence, then no hegemonic articulation would be possible. Of course, this is simultaneously the limit of hegemony, as the ultimate unfixity of elements means that no hegemony is entirely stable. Indeed, the hegemonic articulation of different elements does not establish the identity, but only the equivalence of the different elements of the chain, thus suggesting that the elements retain part of their differential relations *vis-à-vis* one another.[9] Although the two logics of equivalence and difference subvert and interrupt one another, they also require one another: without difference, we would have identity, not equivalence; and without equivalence, the play of difference would not be able to stabilise itself. As a result of this unstable tension between equivalence and difference, the elements are, at least in part, floating. In the terms of *Hegemony and Socialist Strategy*, 'a discursive totality never exists in the form of a simply *given and delimited* positivity, the relational logic will be incomplete and pierced by contingency ... A no-man's-land thus emerges, making the articulatory practice possible'.[10] A discursive totality – for instance, a community – is constituted in the field of discursivity, that is, it is made possible and simultaneously undermined by the floating character – the 'surplus of meaning' – of any element.[11] As a result, 'the logic of difference never manages to constitute a fully sutured space, [and nor] does the logic of equivalence ever achieve this'.[12] We are always somewhere in between the two ends of a continuum ranging from full equivalence to pure difference, both of which would have the same result, namely the complete fixation of meaning and the end of hegemony.[13]

In his later work, Laclau has reformulated the notion of the field of discursivity and the inherent tension between equivalence and difference as the *tendentially empty signifier* and as an inherent split in the representative of the community; that is, in the so-called empty signifier.[14] In order to understand this, it is important to remember that the hegemonic relation is essentially a relation of representation, where the representation is not the representation of an original presence but what brings about the represented – in short, it is a relation of articulation. The fullness of the community is absent and lacking, which is why the hegemonic representation of it is both necessary and possible. If the identity and limits of the community can only become present through a constitutive representation, this introduces a constitutive difference (the 're-' of re-presentation), which it is not possible to recuperate later; that is, what we in the Introduction to this volume called a radical difference. The community is constituted through the relation of representation; hence, the representation, which proceeds through the emptying of a signifier, has a performative character to it. It is not a pure act of naming, however, since it relies on the citation of an existing element with a particular differential content (say, a particular party's presidential candidate).

Although the creation of equivalence is only possible through the relative emptying of the particular element or signifier, the limit of this is the contingency of the particular element that is being emptied and comes to stand in for the whole. Since the representative does not stand in an immediate relation with the community that it represents, it is a matter of contingency, not necessity, which particular element represents the community as a whole. However, the fact that there is no *necessary* relation between the representative and what it represents does not mean that this is a purely *accidental* matter or that any element is equally able to take up this representative role (making it a pure act of naming). Since the act of representation takes place in a terrain already partly sedimented and partly penetrated by relations of power, the particular representative must not only be available, but also compete for the chance to represent the whole.[15] Consequently, the relation of representation (hegemony, articulation) involves power and exclusion: although the tendentially empty signifier stands in for the other elements in the chain of equivalence, it does so at their expense to the extent that it retains a 'differential remainder'.[16] For instance, there is a point when it becomes evident that the 'freedom' representing the community is not the freedom of everyone, and where one person's terrorist is not another person's terrorist. Thus, when Laclau writes that 'a chain of equivalence can in principle expand indefinitely, but once a set of core links has been established, this expansion is limited',[17] this is not quite the case. The infinite expansion of the chain of equivalence, which would correspond to the total emptying of the empty signifier, is impossible both in principle and in practice, because the chain of equivalence depends for its condition of possibility on what is simultaneously its limit, namely the citation of one particular signifier rather than another. This is 'the materiality of the signifier' and of representation: the non-transparency of representation (which should not be confused with an essential remainder of the tendentially empty signifier isolated from hegemonic articulation).[18]

In/exclusions

The differential remainder in the tendentially empty signifier means that the latter is inherently split between its role of representing the community as a whole and its differential content. This split or tension is constitutive and cannot be overcome; indeed, hegemony would be impossible without it. The constitutive split – which can also be expressed in terms of a tension between equivalence and difference, a differential remainder, the field of discursivity and a constitutive or radical difference – means that the community is internally divided, and the limits of the community are unstable: the line between inclusion and exclusion is blurred. If antagonism refers to a clear-cut line of division between the community and an external threat, then it would seem that antagonism is impossible. I want now to turn to the ambiguities in Laclau's formulation of the notion of antagonism.

Antagonism

The initial formulation of antagonism in *Hegemony and Socialist Strategy* is marked by a fundamental ambiguity: on the one hand, it refers to a discursive construction; on the other hand, it refers to the limit of discursive objectivity. In the first sense, as a discursive form, antagonism is presented as the result of the creation of a chain of equivalence or what Laclau will later refer to as the emptying of a signifier representing the fullness of a community.[19] Yet, the overwhelming thrust of Laclau and Mouffe's argument in *Hegemony and Socialist Strategy* is that antagonism should be understood as the limit of discursive objectivity. As Laclau later formulated it, 'antagonism is the *limit of all objectivity* ... antagonism does not have an objective meaning, but is that which prevents the constitution of objectivity itself'.[20] As opposed to real opposition and logical contradiction, in the case of antagonism we are dealing with a more radical exclusion. Real opposition and contradiction presuppose that the poles as well as the relationship between the two poles can be objectified and the exclusion of one by the other is therefore one which is inclusive in the sense that it assumes as an objectifiable totality the field of the included and the excluded.[21] As opposed to this, antagonism arises from the failure of the constitution of identity; for instance, from the failure of the identity of a community. However, the problem with *Hegemony and Socialist Strategy* is that it is not clear in what sense 'antagonism, as a witness of the impossibility of a final suture, is the "experience" of the limit of the social'.[22] We are presented with two possibilities. First, antagonism *qua* the subversion of difference by equivalence is presented as the expression of the impossibility of the community to establish itself as One with clearly demarcated limits in the sense explained in the previous section.[23] At the same time, however, it is clear that antagonism, as the complete suspension of difference and, hence, the elimination of the tension between difference and equivalence, would fix the limits and identity of the community.

The same ambiguity is also expressed in the following terms: 'in the case of antagonism ... the presence of the "Other" prevents me from being totally myself. The relation arises not from full totalities, but from the impossibility of their constitution.'[24] Antagonism is supposed to both *prevent* the fullness of identity and *arise from* the failure of fullness. Yet, in so far as antagonism is only possible through the representation of the fullness of the community, it in fact helps constitute and sustain, rather than threaten, the identity of the community, even if the antagonistic Other is represented as a threat: if only we could get rid of Saddam Hussein, we would be able to realise the community of freedom. Instead of conceiving antagonism as the limit of objectivity or as a threat to identity, one can then think of antagonism as one possible discursive representation among others. In fact, antagonism is an extreme, which is never achieved as it would require the elimination of difference. Following Slavoj Žižek one may argue that antagonism is a way to externalise the ineliminable divisions within the community and, in this way, discursively master the dislocation of identities.[25] As an example, one need only think about what would happen to George W. Bush's claim to represent 'America' and 'the Free World' if the antagonistic threat of terrorism disappeared. Bush needs this threat to be absolute and to reappear – as a videotape, a security alert or a bomb – on a regular basis in order to suppress the differential remainders in his chain of equivalence. Indeed, since *New Reflections on the Revolution of Our Time* (1990), Laclau has thought of identity as inherently dislocated because constituted around a lack in the Lacanian sense. In this sense, antagonism is one way to master discursively the limit of representation – namely the lack – even if this always ultimately fails. Of course, in order to be able to distinguish between dislocation and antagonism, the latter cannot follow automatically from the former; hence, antagonism cannot be the necessary expression of the always already dislocated character of identity.[26]

In *Hegemony and Socialist Strategy*, Laclau and Mouffe argue that 'Antagonism as the negation of a given order is, quite simply, the limit of that order, and not the moment of a broader totality in relation to which the two poles of the antagonism would constitute differential – that is, objective – partial instances.'[27] Yet, we can now see that, although this type of antagonistic exclusion is not a positive, differential relation, this does not preclude its objectivity (to the extent that it would in fact be possible to represent it, of course). 'Antagonism' precisely refers to and presupposes 'a broader totality in relation to which the two poles of the antagonism would constitute', if not differential, then at least objective 'partial' instances. Since antagonism presupposes the fullness of the identity of the community, with a clear division between inside and outside, antagonism presupposes the space of representation within which both the community and its antagonistic Other are constituted. In this sense, the antagonistic exclusion too is an inclusive exclusion. Therefore, Laclau and Mouffe are both right and wrong when they write that the '"experience" of the limit of all objectivity [has] a form of precise discursive presence, and this is *antagonism*.[28] Antagonism can only exist as a 'precise discursive presence', but, as such, it is not the limit of objectivity or representation. The reason why Laclau and Mouffe think of antagonism as a threat to identity and as the limit of objectivity is that, in *Hegemony and Socialist Strategy*, they think of objectivity and meaning as relations of difference. Hence, what disrupts difference – namely equivalence and antagonism – comes to be seen as the limit of objectivity and meaning. When Laclau and Mouffe theorise limits and exclusion, the dominant strategy is to do so in terms of equivalence and antagonism, which is as the disruption of difference. The same pattern arises from the initial formulation of the notion of an empty signifier as the limit of signification and representation in *Emancipation(s)*. As argued above, and as Laclau now recognises, the limit of objectivity does not arise from either equivalence or difference, but from their tension.

The critique of the original formulation of antagonism, which is partially a self-critique on Laclau's part, also functions as a response to those of Laclau's critics who have argued that Laclau (and Mouffe) risks reducing hegemony, politics and radical democracy to the creation of antagonistic exclusions.[29] It would certainly be a mistake to reduce exclusion, let alone politics, to antagonism. Antagonism is only one among other possible discursive representations of the identity and limits of a community (even if, as I have argued, the construction of antagonism always ultimately fails). To be sure, a radical democratic approach to exclusion would have to put into question any attempt, successful or not, at the construction of antagonistic frontiers, as this would rely on a notion of identity as stable and clearly delimited. Likewise, it is necessary to distinguish between, on the one hand, antagonism as a discursive representation and, on the other hand, the limit and the expression of the limit of discursive representation. The introduction of the notion of dislocation (or lack) as the limit of representation in *New Reflections* made Laclau able to make this distinction as one between antagonism and dislocation. However, even in this work, as well as in some of his later works, antagonism continues to have an ambiguous character: it is referred to both as a concrete discursive construction and as the limit of representation. And even with the introduction of the notion of heterogeneity as the limit of representation in Laclau's most recent work, antagonism continues to have an ambiguous status.[30] Before turning to a more precise characterisation of heterogeneity, it is first necessary to look at the notion of 'constitutive outside', which has been important to Laclau's (and Mouffe's) work, and which is of interest to the question of exclusion.

Of constitutive outsides

'Constitutive outside' is a notion introduced by Henry Staten[31] and taken on board by Laclau, Mouffe and some of their interpreters. In *New Reflections*,

Laclau uses the term 'constitutive outside' – 'a *radical* outside, without a common measure with the "inside"'[32] – to refer to the antagonistic Other. 'It is an "outside" which blocks the identity of the "inside" (and is, nonetheless, the prerequisite for its constitution at the same time).'[33] However, the way that Laclau (and Mouffe) use the term opens itself to the same confusions as the formulation of antagonism. On the one hand, the constitutive outside is presented as an enemy or some other discursively constructed antagonistic other. On the other hand, however, the constitutive outside is said to have no common measure with the identity it threatens. That is, the constitutive outside is irrepresentable within the discourse of the identity, yet constitutive of it, and *as such* it threatens the latter's identity. If conceived in the latter sense, it is the discursive exclusion of the constitutive outside as an outside of an inside that makes possible the purity of the identity (of the inside).

There is an interesting ambiguity in Henry Staten's original use of the term 'constitutive outside', an ambiguity analogous to the one found in Laclau's and others' use of it. Staten introduces the notion of constitutive outside in the context of a discussion of the relationship between essence and accident. He uses the notion of constitutive outside as a non-synonymous substitute for 'a regulated overflowing of established boundaries'; that is, for the different aporias found in deconstructed texts.[34] Yet, he uses the term in two distinct ways.

First, there is a '"general" law'[35] of the constitutive outside, referring to a general condition of contingency or to the fact that, since there is no transcendental signified, the play of signification is ultimately infinite. This is similar to the idea expressed with Laclau and Mouffe's notion of the field of discursivity or, indeed, as I shall argue below, with the notion of heterogeneity. Conceived in this sense, Staten's notion of constitutive outside is a constant threat to any identity: it is an undecidable excess that must be dealt with – for instance, by excluding it as a threatening Other.

Staten uses constitutive outside in a second way to refer to the particular outside that a particular discourse or identity may have: 'each particular thing will also have a "special" accident that will be the limit appropriate to its own as-such and that will constitute it as that particular kind of as-such. In this sense of a "constitutive outside", the outside is not "accidental" as indefinite, since it is necessary for a given kind of as-such.'[36] This constitutive outside refers to the determination of an outside – for instance, the discursive construction of an external Other, who serves to account for the threat that the constitutive outside in the first sense poses to the identity – something that is only possible through the simultaneous determination of an inside in its 'as-such'. Staten concludes: 'X is constituted by non-X. X here means essence or self-identity as conceived by philosophy, and non-X is that which functions as the "outside", or limit, to the positive assertion of this self-identity, that which keeps ideality from complete closure, yet in *limiting* it remains the *positive* condition of possibility of the positive assertion of essence.'[37] The constitutive outside in this sense – as a determined outside – does not threaten my identity, but is rather comforting: 'The "dialectics" of the same and the other, of outside and inside, of the homogeneous and the heterogeneous, are, as you know, among the most *contorted* ones. The outside can always become again an "object" in the polarity subject/object, or the reassuring reality of what is outside the text; and there is sometimes an "inside" that is as troubling as the outside may be reassuring.'[38] Again the post-9–11 discourses on security, terrorism and Muslims provide good, if discouraging, examples of this.

In conclusion, the constitutive outside only threatens the purity of the inside (my identity), because 'the [constitutive] outside [is] *necessary* to the constitution of a phenomenon in its as-such, a condition of the possibility of the "inside"'.[39] But notice that it is only insofar as it is determined as excluded (as antagonistic, for instance) that the constitutive outside helps constitute the inside as an inside. As a matter of fact, 'constitutive outside' is in a certain sense a misnomer, because we do not start with a pure inside with a constitutive *outside*. The constitutive outside dislocating the inside is not an outside of the inside, it is not a determined outside beyond a fully constituted inside, but rather an internal limit, thus subverting the inside/outside distinction. It is only the 'negation' of this dislocation – its externalisation – that creates the purity of the inside.

Heterogeneity

In the previous sections, I have referred to a number of expressions – a tension between equivalence and difference, a differential remainder, a constitutive split in the so-called empty signifier, the field of discursivity and the constitutive outside in Staten's first sense of the term – which all, in one way or another, refer to the ultimate impossibility of the representation of clear lines of inclusion and exclusion. I would now like to link these expressions and the question of inclusion/exclusion to the notion of heterogeneity from Laclau's most recent work.

The condition of possibility of the hegemonic production of clear lines of division between an inside and an outside – for instance, in the form of the production of an empty signifier or an antagonistic frontier – is the suppression of the tension between equivalence and difference, of the differential remainder, and so on. Yet, the disappearance of the latter would simultaneously make hegemony impossible. Hence, we have an undecidability or aporia, where the conditions of possibility of the constitution of the identity and limits of a community are simultaneously their conditions of impossibility. This aporia appears as discursive heterogeneity. The existence of this aporia does not mean that inclusion and exclusion, identity and limits do not exist. On the contrary, exclusions of people, practices, opinions, worldviews and so on and so forth *are* made, and these exclusions and limits have real consequences. For instance, sometimes even wars are fought on the basis of these exclusions: 'you are either with us, or you are with the terrorists'. Yet, from any attempt to establish lines of division between inclusion and exclusion there will be a discursive excess or heterogeneity, which 'is in an undecidable tension between internality and externality'[40] and escapes the lines of division governing the political space. In Laclau's terms, what cannot be included into any chain of equivalence is the reverse side of the differential remainder; if the latter is constitutive of the chain of equivalence, there will be a number of elements in the discursive field, which cannot enter into any chain of equivalence.

The heterogeneous elements are not simply excluded, for instance as opposed or antagonistic to the community. Heterogeneity is not a relation of exclusion if we by that mean the exclusion of the dichotomy of exclusion and inclusion, because heterogeneity puts into question the categories of inclusion and exclusion, inside and outside. As such, heterogeneity is a radical exclusion. Moreover, heterogeneity is a radical exclusion in the sense that it is fundamental or constitutive. The heterogeneous is excluded from a community, yet at the same time it is internal to the community because constitutive of it. Again it is important to stress that the 'exclusion' of heterogeneity does not constitute the community by being determined as an outside to an inside; rather, the 'exclusion' of heterogeneity is what makes it possible to speak of an inside and an outside in the first place. In this sense, heterogeneity is undecidable according to the distinction between inside and outside. The heterogeneous is not something lying on the other side of the limit of the community; in fact, the two do not share the same space of representation, even if they do 'touch' at the point of the constitution of the identity and limits of the community. It may be objected that both antagonism and heterogeneity help constitute the division between inclusion and exclusion. However, the difference between the two becomes clear when we ask for the condition of possibility of antagonism – this is precisely the 'exclusion' of heterogeneity.

Heterogeneity does not only refer to the failure of the constitution of the identity and limits of a community. Although heterogeneity is the limit of discursive objectivity and, hence, of the representation of the identity and limits of the community, it cannot be thought of as the simple negation, lack or failure of an already constituted identity. Nathan Widder has argued that Laclau reduces difference and, by implication, questions of exclusion to negation, and that he reproduces a dichotomy between identity and difference, where the former is implied as either the ground or the *telos* of the latter.[41] While this is certainly a potential danger with the notion of antagonism, there are in Laclau's work the theoretical resources to go beyond it with the notion of heterogeneity. Like the Lacanian lack, heterogeneity should not be understood simply as the failure of identity. Instead, like the lack at the heart of the constitution of any identity, heterogeneity simultaneously subverts and constitutes that identity.

A good example is the figure of the *Lumpenproletariat* in Karl Marx's work. The *Lumpenproletariat* is a discursive excess, escaping the conceptual categories of the analysis of capitalism. It is heterogeneous to these categories, a discursive remainder from the determination of the antagonistic relation between the proletariat and the capitalist class. However, as Peter Stallybrass has argued, the *Lumpenproletariat* not only shows the limit of the attempt to objectify the relation between proletariat and capitalists; it is the exclusion of the *Lumpenproletariat* from the other conceptual categories that makes Marx able to theorise the latter as determined by their antagonistic opposition.[42]

So, heterogeneity is close to this understanding of lack, although heterogeneity refers simultaneously to a lack (the split in the tendentially empty signifier, for instance) and to a discursive excess. This is not to say that the distinction between abundance and lack is dissolved in the notion of heterogeneity. First of all, theorists of abundance do not link abundance to lack; and, in addition, as opposed to Deleuzean notions of abundance, representation is central to the notion of heterogeneity.[43]

Thinking about hegemony in light of heterogeneity, one should not only focus on the paradigmatic relations of substitution that result from the identification with a particular object taking the place of, and temporally filling, the lack. This would lead to a one-sided emphasis on the creation of equivalential chains and antagonistic exclusion. These relations of substitution are always interrupted by syntagmatic relations of difference.[44] Here one may find a crucial difference between theories of abundance and theories of lack. Generally speaking, theories of abundance tend to emphasise syntagmatic relations and, hence, horizontal combination and networks, and they tend to think of radical democratic politics as building bridges between constituencies. Theorists of lack, on the other hand, tend to emphasise paradigmatic relations and, hence, hierarchical substitution, and they tend to think of radical democratic politics in terms of the occupation of the symbolic place of the community as a whole. Heterogeneity refers to the undecidable tension between equivalence and difference, and between paradigmatic substitutions and syntagmatic combinations, and, so, we have here something breaking with the identity/difference dichotomy.

Before moving on to the implications of theorising exclusion and politics, it is necessary to raise a note of caution. The notion of heterogeneity should not be confused with or reduced to the examples given of it; for instance, heterogeneity should not be reduced to the *Lumpenproletariat*, in Marx's texts or elsewhere. Related to this and to the point made above about the relationship of heterogeneity to representation, heterogeneity is a category for the analysis of discourse. It is a structural feature of the constitution of the identity and limits of a community, but it does not simply precede the concrete analysis of discourse but is, rather, constituted through its use. Thus, it is not a transcendental structure underlying and determining the constitution of identity and limits, and it is not an underlying structure, which examples of heterogeneity merely reflect. 'Heterogeneity' is simply a term – a non-synonymous substitute, in Derrida's terms – that I use in order to speak about different discursive aporias, especially those pertaining to exclusion. As such, although the use of the term heterogeneity is already a partial representation of what is supposed to resist representation, heterogeneity does not claim to grasp anything in its 'as-such'. Heterogeneity precisely refers to an *internal* limit of representation and not to a beyond or an outside of representation.[45]

Heterogeneity, exclusion and radical democracy

In addressing the question of the relationship between heterogeneity, exclusion and radical democracy, I am not concerned with writing a cookbook for a future radical democratic politics of exclusion. Rather than providing answers, the aim is to show how the notion of heterogeneity gives us a way to think differently about the question of exclusion and the boundaries of our communities.

Here one must caution against any fetishisation of heterogeneity. There is nothing inherently progressive about heterogeneity. For instance, although Marx saw some revolutionary potential in the spontaneity of the *Lumpenproletariat*, it nonetheless became the foundation of the power of conservative Bonapartism. Hence, the heterogeneous may be articulated and managed in a variety of ways, and there are no guarantees to a politics that takes heterogeneity as its starting point. Heterogeneity does provide a point of entry for normative intervention, however, because highlighting it shows the contingency of things and that they could be otherwise. By highlighting the contingent nature of the present organisation of the political space, heterogeneity simultaneously points to the way that exclusion and power have shaped the present.

Heterogeneity, then, is related to radical democracy in two ways. First, heterogeneity points to the possibility that things may be otherwise, and that changing things is a matter of political struggle. Second, heterogeneity concerns the very fundamentals of political space, community and identity, because it concerns their constitution. Although any radical politics will have to start from the present order of things and take it seriously, the notion of heterogeneity gives us a way to think a form of radical democracy and politics that does not take the limits of the present as its ultimate – and fundamental – horizon of possibility. Radical politics is not the art of the possible, but the art of making possible what is impossible in the present.

What, then, does heterogeneity mean for how we, as radical democrats, relate to exclusion? First of all it means that exclusion is ineliminable, and that, therefore, it is not a question of exclusion or no exclusion, because there is always some exclusion. Yet, we should not proceed too quickly from acknowledging the ineliminability of exclusion to actual exclusions; between these two moments, there are several intermediary considerations, such as: *What* exclusions? *How* to exclude? *How* can we institute mechanisms for the contestation of exclusion? – and so on and so forth.[46] Just as we should not oppose concrete instances of exclusion to a general situation of non-exclusion, similarly we should not take concrete exclusions as either given or necessary. Hence, nothing in this view leads automatically to conservative resignation.[47] Furthermore, the argument about heterogeneity means that exclusion is constitutive of inclusion, which has two implications. First of all, it means that the relation between inclusion and exclusion is not simply a plus-sum game, where the less exclusion we have the more inclusion we automatically have. If exclusion is constitutive of inclusion, then inclusion cannot simply proceed as the extension of symmetrical relations to a point where we reach universal inclusion. However, and secondly, we should not accept this as an apology for any concrete exclusions – for instance, the argument that only by establishing a clear line of division between 'us' and 'them', between who belong to the nation and who do not, is it possible to create an inclusive political community.[48] Although there is no inclusion without exclusion, this does not mean that it is a simple zero-sum game, where it is either us or them.

In relation to Laclau's theory of hegemony, the argument about heterogeneity means that a radical politics of exclusion must take into consideration the hegemonic relation itself. This relation involves heterogeneity: a constitutive difference, the differential remainder, the ineliminable tension between equivalence and difference, and so on. Hegemony must, then, be paired with sensibility towards its own contingency and the resulting exclusions. Here the work of William Connolly may serve as a supplement to Laclau, because Connolly provides a vocabulary for the required sensibility towards the excluded: the politics of becoming, the ethic of cultivation and critical responsiveness.[49]

Related to this, and to the point above about the relationship between inclusion and exclusion, there is a paradox in how we deal with exclusion. On the one hand, exclusion is unavoidable; on the other hand, we are looking for sensitive ways to relate to the excluded. The trouble is that the constitutivity of exclusion is not something that can be overcome at a later stage, or by relating to the excluded in a different way. Related to radical democracy, we may say, with Laclau, that it is 'a type of regime which makes fully visible the contingent character of the hegemonic link',[50] and hence of exclusion. Here I would only add that the contingent character of exclusion is only made visible from a particular point of view, namely radical democracy, and hence making visible contingency also requires some closure. Radical democracy cannot provide us with a point of view that itself avoids exclusion.

With regard to this, Robert Goodin has put forward an interesting critique of contemporary models of inclusion. According to Goodin, one of the problems with current uses of the terms inclusion and exclusion is that they work with a flawed notion of unity. 'The true source of our anxieties', Goodin writes, 'lies not in the practice of exclusion but in that of inclusion', because 'the problem of exclusion is that there *is* an inclusive community'. Hence, 'the solution is not to make our communities more inclusive but rather to change their nature'.[51] Since we tend to think of inclusion as emanating from a (nation-state) centre, the inclusion of the otherwise excluded merely confers a marginalised status upon the latter.[52] Consequently, Goodin proposes a new concept of the state, but at this point he pulls back from a more radical conclusion. He envisages 'a system of multiple, overlapping "sovereignties", with lots of different levels and places one might lodge an application or an appeal'.[53] For the people who nonetheless fall outside the sovereignty and protection of any state, 'we will need some agency ... to take residual responsibility for those who find no one else to take care of them'. 'This would not be an overarching authority. It stands beneath, not above, the other elements of this larger network', in order 'to pick up the pieces that inevitably get left behind'.[54] For Goodin, inclusion becomes a matter of simply adding new institutions – 'with lots of different levels and places' – as well as institutions to pick up the pieces, the residue and leftover. Although Goodin acknowledges the constitutivity of exclusion for inclusion, the problem with his proposal is that it will leave those who are thus residually included still marginalised relative to a centre of inclusion, which was what Goodin wanted to avoid in the first place.

The task cannot be simply to add yet another inclusive institution. If we must respond to heterogeneity, but heterogeneity is what escapes attempts to divide the political space into an inside and an outside, then the task must be to rethink the inclusion/exclusion constellation, and to rethink the way we build our institutions. Rather than relegating the residuals to residual and marginal positions within the system of inclusion or denoting them as foreign and thereby excluding them, thinking *differently* about inclusion/exclusion involves rethinking our notions of community, limits and inclusion in light of the heterogeneous remainders from our traditional ways of thinking about these things.[55] A radical democratic approach to exclusion should not be a politics of heterogeneity, if by that we understand a politics that aims only at the heterogeneous; such a politics would remain at best marginal, at worst impotent. But neither is this a politics of heterogeneity, if by that we understand a politics that can do justice to the heterogeneous. That would precisely assume that the heterogeneous is something that could be represented within a given space, before justice, and that it is something that could eventually be eliminated.

Needless to say, there are no guarantees that the perspective of heterogeneity will take us in a progressive direction, but that is perhaps what radical democracy is about: politics without ultimate guarantee.

Notes

1 I would like to thank Lars Tønder, Aletta Norval and Ernesto Laclau for their conversations about earlier versions of this chapter. I would also like to thank the participants at the conferences where I initially presented this argument for their comments and questions.
2 See R. Coles, 'Liberty, equality, receptive generosity: neo-Nietzschean reflections on the ethics and politics of coalition', *American Political Science Review*, 90 (1996), 375–88; A. J. Norval, 'Frontiers in question', *Filozofski vestnik*, 18:2 (1997), 51–75; N. Widder, 'What's lacking in the lack: a comment on the virtual', *Angelaki*, 5:3 (2000), 117–38; C. Barnett, 'Deconstructing radical democracy: articulation, representation, and being-with-others', *Political Geography*, 23 (2004), 503–28. See also William E. Connolly's critique of Mouffe in 'Review essay: twilight of the idols', *Philosophy and Social Criticism*, 21:3 (1995), 127–37.
3 For Laclau on heterogeneity, see E. Laclau, 'Paul de Man and the politics of rhetoric', *Pretexts*, 7:2 (1998), 154–6; Laclau, 'Democracy between autonomy and heteronomy', in O. Enwezor *et al.* (eds), *Democracy Unrealized: Documenta11_Platform1* (Ostfieldern-Ruit: Hatje Cantz, 2002), p. 381; C. Pessoa *et al.*, 'Theory, democracy, and the Left: an interview with Ernesto Laclau', *Umbr@*, (2001), 9f; and E. Laclau, 'Identity and hegemony: the role of universality in the constitution of political logics', in J. Butler, E. Laclau and S. Žižek, *Contingency, Hegemony, Universality: Contemporary Dialogues on the Left* (London: Verso, 2000), p. 68.
4 The most relevant works in this regard are: E. Laclau and C. Mouffe, *Hegemony and Socialist Strategy: Towards a Radical Democratic Politics*, 2nd edition (London: Verso, 2001), chapter 3; E. Laclau, *Emancipation(s)* (London: Verso, 1996), chapter 2; E. Laclau, 'The death and resurrection of the theory of ideology', *Journal of Political Ideologies*, 1:3 (1996), 201–20; and E. Laclau, 'Constructing universality', in J. Butler, E. Laclau and S. Žižek, *Contingency, Hegemony, Universality: Contemporary Dialogues on the Left* (London: Verso, 2000), pp. 301–5. Although relevant to the questions I raise in the following, I shall leave Mouffe's work out of consideration, as it deserves a separate treatment.
5 See especially Laclau, *Emancipation(s)*, chapter 2.
6 Laclau and Mouffe, *Hegemony and Socialist Strategy*, p. 126; and Laclau, *Emancipation(s)*, pp. 37f.
7 Laclau, *Emancipation(s)*, p. 37.
8 Ibid.
9 Laclau, 'The death and resurrection of the theory of ideology', p. 206.
10 Laclau and Mouffe, *Hegemony and Socialist Strategy*, pp. 110f.
11 Ibid., p. 111.
12 Ibid., p. 129.
13 Laclau, 'Constructing universality', p. 305.
14 Laclau, 'The death and resurrection of the theory of ideology'; and Laclau, 'Constructing universality', pp. 301–5.
15 Compare Laclau, *Emancipation(s)*, pp. 41–3; and E. Laclau, *New Reflections on the Revolution of Our Time* (London: Verso, 1990), p. 66.
16 The term is Laclau's, cf. E. Laclau, 'On the names of God', in Sue Golding (ed.), *The Eight Technologies of Otherness* (London: Routledge, 1997), p. 262. Laclau also refers to it as 'a remainder of particularity', cf. Laclau, 'The death and resurrection of the theory of ideology', p. 219; and Laclau, 'Constructing Universality', p. 305.
17 Laclau, 'The death and resurrection of the theory of ideology', p. 219.

18 Laclau, 'Identity and hegemony', pp. 70f.
19 Laclau, 'Constructing universality', pp. 301–5.
20 Laclau, *New Reflections on the Revolution of Our Time*, p. 17.
21 Laclau and Mouffe, *Hegemony and Socialist Strategy*, pp. 122–5.
22 *Ibid.*, p. 125.
23 *Ibid.*, p. 128.
24 *Ibid.*, p. 125.
25 S. Žižek, 'Beyond discourse-analysis', in E. Laclau, *New Reflections on the Revolution of Our Time* (London: Verso, 1990), pp. 251–4.
26 Widder, 'What's lacking in the lack', p. 133.
27 Laclau and Mouffe, *Hegemony and Socialist Strategy*, p. 126.
28 *Ibid.*, p. 122. See also *ibid.*, p. 146.
29 Connolly, 'Review essay: twilight of the idols', pp. 130–6; Norval, 'Frontiers in question', pp. 56–61; and Widder, 'What's lacking in the lack', pp. 118, 133.
30 See, for instance, Laclau, *New Reflections on the Revolution of Our Time*, p. 69; E. Laclau, 'Politics, polemics and academics: an interview by Paul Bowman', *Parallax*, 5:2 (1999), 103; Laclau, 'Identity and hegemony', pp. 72, 77; and E. Laclau, 'Can immanence explain social struggles?', *Diacritics*, 31:4 (2001), 5. For an ambiguous characterisation of heterogeneity, see also E. Laclau, 'Democracy between autonomy and heteronomy', p. 382.
31 Henry Staten, *Wittgenstein and Derrida* (Lincoln, NE: University of Nebraska Press, 1984), pp. 16–18, 24.
32 E. Laclau, *New Reflections on the Revolution of Our Time* (London: Verso, 1990), p. 18.
33 *Ibid.*, p. 17. See also *ibid.*, pp. 172f.
34 Staten, *Wittgenstein and Derrida*, p. 24.
35 *Ibid.*, p. 16.
36 *Ibid.*
37 *Ibid.*, p. 17.
38 J. Derrida, *Positions*, trans. A. Bass, 2nd edition (London: Continuum, 2002), p. 67. On the dangers of 'spatialising' politics, see also L. Thomassen, 'Reading radical democracy: a reply to Clive Barnett', *Political Geography* 24:3/4 (forthcoming 2005).
39 Staten, *Wittgenstein and Derrida*, p. 16.
40 Laclau, 'Paul de Man and the politics of rhetoric', p. 156.
41 Widder, 'What's lacking in the lack', pp. 117f, 123. See also his contribution to this volume.
42 P. Stallybrass, 'Marx and heterogeneity: thinking the Lumpenproletariat', *Representations*, 31 (1991), 69–95. For Laclau's use of this example of heterogeneity, see Pessoa *et al.*, 'Theory, democracy, and the Left', pp. 9f; and Laclau, 'Democracy between autonomy and heteronomy', pp. 381f.
43 Faced with the choice between Lacan and Deleuze, my choice would be Derrida. For the latter on abundance and lack in relation to the supplement, see J. Derrida, *Writing and Difference*, trans. A. Bass (London: Routledge, 1978), pp. 289f; and J. Derrida, *Of Grammatology*, trans. G. C. Spivak, Corrected edition (Baltimore: Johns Hopkins University Press, 1997), pp. 144f. For Laclau on negativity and excess, see Laclau, 'Can immanence explain social struggles?', p. 5.
44 Cf. Norval, 'Frontiers in question', p. 60.
45 Laclau and Mouffe, *Hegemony and Socialist Strategy*, p. 126; and Laclau, 'Identity and hegemony', pp. 66–8.
46 Widder, 'What's lacking in the lack', p. 131.
47 See L. Thomassen, 'Lacanian political theory: a reply to Robinson', *British Journal of*

Politics and International Relations, 6:4 (2004), 583–6.
48 For an example of this position, see M. Walzer, 'The distribution of membership', in P. G. Brown and H. Shue (eds), *Boundaries: National Autonomy and Its Limits* (Totowa, NJ: Rowman & Littlefield, 1981), pp. 1–33.
49 See, for instance, Connolly, 'Review essay: twilight of the idols'.
50 E. Laclau, 'Democracy and the question of power', *Constellations*, 8:1 (2001), 5. Laclau is referring to democracy here. It is not always clear when he is referring to radical democracy, and when he is referring to democracy, hegemony or just politics; see also *ibid.*, pp. 8 and 10.
51 R. Goodin, 'Inclusion and exclusion', *Archives Européennes de Sociologie*, 37 (1996), 344.
52 *Ibid.*, p. 348.
53 *Ibid.*, p. 364.
54 *Ibid.*, p. 366.
55 See also Laclau in Pessoa *et al.*, 'Theory, democracy, and the Left', 20; and in L. Worsham and G. A. Olson, 'Hegemony and the future of democracy: Ernesto Laclau's political Philosophy', in L. Worsham and G. A. Olson (eds), *Race, Rhetoric, and the Postcolonial* (Albany, NY: State University of New York Press, 1998), p. 153.

II

THE POLITICS OF RADICAL DEMOCRACY

7 • *Chantal Mouffe*

For an agonistic public sphere

Introduction

MY AIM in this chapter is to offer some reflections concerning the kind of public sphere that a vibrant democratic society requires, an issue particularly relevant to the type of questions raised by this volume. In particular, I want to scrutinise the dominant discourse, which announces the 'end of the adversarial model of politics' and insists on the need to go beyond left and right toward a consensual politics of the centre. The thesis that I want to put forward is that, contrary to what its defenders argue, this type of discourse has very negative consequences for democratic politics. Indeed, it has contributed to the weakening of the 'democratic political sphere' and has led to the increasing dominance of a juridical and moral discourse, a dominance that I take to be inimical to democracy. I submit that the increasing moralisation and juridification of politics, far from being a progressive step in the development of democracy, should be seen as a threat to its future existence.

The demise of the political

There are many reasons for the weakening of the democratic public sphere, some having to do with the predominance of a neo-liberal regime of globalisation, others with the type of individualistic consumer culture now pervading most advanced industrial societies. From a strictly political perspective, it is clear that the collapse of Communism and the disappearance of the political frontiers that structured the political imaginary during most of the twentieth century have led to a crumbling of the political markers of society. The blurring of frontiers between right and left that we have witnessed in Western countries constitutes, in my view, one of the main reasons for the growing irrelevance of the democratic political public sphere.

Elsewhere, I have shown how the current celebration of centrism and the lack of effective democratic alternatives to the present order have strengthened the appeal of right-wing populist parties.[1] When passions cannot be mobilised by democratic parties, because these parties privilege a 'consensus of the centre', those passions tend to find other outlets around particularistic demands or non-negotiable moral issues in diverse fundamentalist movements. When a society lacks a dynamic democratic life with genuine confrontation among a diversity of democratic political identities, the groundwork is laid for other forms of identification to take their place, identifications of an ethnic, religious or nationalist nature that generate antagonisms which cannot be managed by the democratic process.

Here I will focus on the reasons and consequences of the decline of a properly political discourse and its replacement by a moral and, in many cases, even a moralistic one. I see this phenomenon as signalling the triumph of a moralising liberalism, which pretends that antagonisms have been eradicated, and that society can now be ruled through rational moral procedures and remaining conflicts resolved through impartial tribunals. Hence, the privileged role of the judiciary and the fact that it is the legal system which is seen as being responsible for organising human coexistence and for regulating social relations. Since the problems of society can no longer be envisioned in political terms, there is a marked tendency to privilege the judicial and to expect the law to provide solutions to all types of conflict.

As a political theorist, I am particularly troubled by the pernicious influence of political theory in this displacement of politics by morality and law. Indeed, in the theoretical approach that is rapidly colonising the discursive terrain under the name of 'deliberative democracy', one of the main tenets is that political questions are of a moral nature and therefore susceptible to rational treatment. The objective of a democratic society is, according to such a view, the creation of a rational consensus reached through appropriate deliberative procedures, the aim of which is to produce decisions that represent an impartial standpoint equally in the interests of all. All those who put into question the very possibility of such a rational consensus and who affirm that the political is a domain in which one should always rationally expect to find discord are accused of undermining the very possibility of democracy. Habermas, for instance, asserts: 'If questions of justice cannot transcend the ethical self-understanding of competing forms of life, and existentially relevant value conflicts and oppositions must penetrate all controversial questions, then in the final analysis we will end up with something resembling Carl Schmitt's understanding of politics.'[2]

This theoretical tendency to conflate politics with morality, understood in rationalistic and universalistic terms, has very negative consequences for democratic politics because it erases the dimension of antagonism, which I take to be ineradicable in politics. It has contributed to the current retreat of the political and to its replacement by the juridical and the moral, which are perceived as ideal terrains for reaching impartial decisions. There is, therefore, a strong link between this kind of political theory and the demise of the political. In fact, the current situation can be viewed as the fulfilment of a tendency, inscribed at the very core of liberalism, which, because of its constitutive incapacity to think in truly political terms, must always resort to another type of discourse: economic, moral or juridical.

This perspective is exemplified in the work of John Rawls, who extols the US Supreme Court as a model of what he calls the 'free exercise of public reason', which, in his view, is the essence of democratic deliberation. Another example can be found in the work of Ronald Dworkin, who gives primacy to the independent judiciary, seen as the interpreter of the political morality of the community. According to Dworkin, all the fundamental questions facing a political community in the arenas of employment, education, censorship, freedom of association and so on, are best resolved by judges, providing that they interpret the Constitution by reference to the principle of political equality. There is very little left for the political arena.

Even pragmatists like Richard Rorty, despite carrying out a far-reaching and important critique of the rationalist approach, fail to provide a forceful alternative. Indeed, the problem with Rorty is that, albeit in a different way, he also ends up privileging consensus and missing the political dimension. To be sure, the consensus that he advocates is to be reached through persuasion and 'sentimental education', not rational argumentation, but he nevertheless believes in the possibility of an all-encompassing consensus and therefore in the elimination of antagonism.

But this is to miss a crucial point, not only about the primary reality of strife in social life and the impossibility of finding rational, impartial solutions to political issues, but also about the integrative role conflict plays in modern democracy. A well-functioning democracy calls for a confrontation of democratic political positions. Absent this, there is always the danger, as I pointed out earlier, that this democratic confrontation will be replaced by a battle between non-negotiable moral values or essentialist forms of identification. Too much emphasis on consensus, together with an aversion to confrontation, engenders apathy and disaffection with political participation. This is why a democratic society requires debate about possible alternatives. In other words, while consensus is necessary, it must be accompanied by dissent. Consensus is needed on the institutions that are constitutive of democracy and on the ethico-political values that should inform political association, but there will always be disagreement concerning the meaning and methods of implementing those values. In a pluralist democracy, such disagreement should be considered legitimate and indeed welcome. They provide different forms of citizenship identification and are the stuff of democratic politics.

Antagonism and agonism

In order to defend and deepen the democratic project, what is urgently needed is an alternative to the dominant approach in democratic political theory, one that would help revitalise the democratic public sphere by stimulating awareness of the need for political forms of identification around clearly differentiated democratic positions and the possibility of choosing between real alternatives. This is why, against the two existing models of democratic politics, the aggregative and the deliberative, I have argued for a model of 'agonistic pluralism', which acknowledges the role of power relations in society and the ever-present possibility of antagonism. According to such a view, the aim of democratic institutions is not to establish a rational consensus in the public sphere, but to defuse the potential of hostility that exists in human societies by providing the possibility for antagonism to be transformed into 'agonism'. By this I mean that, in democratic societies, while conflict neither can or should be eradicated, nor should it take the form of a struggle between enemies (antagonism), but rather between adversaries (agonism).

This is why, in my view, the central category of democratic politics is the category of the 'adversary', the opponent with whom we share a common allegiance to the democratic principles of 'liberty and equality for all', while disagreeing about their interpretation. Adversaries fight against each other because they want their interpretation to become hegemonic, but they do not question the legitimacy of their opponents' right to fight for their position. This confrontation between adversaries constitutes the 'agonistic struggle', which I take to be the very condition of a vibrant democracy.[3]

The specificity of this approach is that it is a way of envisioning democracy, which – contrary to the other conceptions – recognises the dimension of what I have proposed to call 'the political'; that is, the potential antagonism inherent in social relations, antagonism which can take many forms and which can never be absolutely eradicated. I have distinguished this notion of 'the political' from that of 'politics', which refers to the ensemble of discourses, institutions and practices, the objective of which is to establish an order, to organise human coexistence in a context that is always conflictual because of the presence of 'the political'. The aim of democratic politics, as I have already indicated, is to create the institutions through which this potential antagonism can be transformed into 'agonism'; that is, a situation defined by a confrontation between adversaries, not the relation 'friend/enemy'.

Let me stress that this notion of the adversary needs to be sharply distinguished from the understanding of that term found in liberal discourse. According to my conception of 'adversary', and contrary to the liberal view, the presence of antagonism is not eliminated but 'tamed', so to speak. What liberals call an 'adversary' is actually a 'competitor'. They envision the field of politics as a neutral terrain in which different groups compete for power; that is, their objective is to dislodge others in order to occupy their place, without challenging the dominant hegemony and attempting to transform the existing relations of power. This is merely a competition among elites. In my case, however, the antagonistic dimension is always present, since what is at stake is the struggle between opposing hegemonic projects, which can never be reconciled rationally – one of them must be defeated. It is a genuine confrontation but one that is played out under conditions regulated by a set of democratic procedures accepted by the adversaries.

Of course, such a view would be anathema to the advocates of deliberative democracy and promoters of the Third Way, who will no doubt condemn it as 'Schmittian'. But I submit that this is the condition for revitalising democratic institutions that we are witnessing today. This would indeed provide a way in which passions could be mobilised toward democratic designs.

Post-politics

So far, I have concentrated on the shortcomings of current theories of democratic politics in order to show how they contribute to shaping the end-of-politics *Zeitgeist*, which prevails today and which prevents us from envisioning a properly democratic public sphere. Now I would like to examine a different but related trend, the fashionable thesis put forward by Ulrich Beck and Anthony Giddens that we have entered a new phase of 'reflexive modernity' in which the adversarial model of politics has become obsolete. I intend to highlight the consequences of such a perspective and its strong connections with the current dominance of a moralistic discourse. Those who announce the death of the adversarial model claim that the friend/enemy relation in politics is characteristic of classical industrial modernity, the 'first modernity', but that we now live in a different, 'second' modernity, a 'reflexive' one, in which the emphasis should be placed on 'sub-politics', the issues of 'life and death'. For Beck, these are '[a]ll the things that are considered loss, danger, waste and decay in the left–right framework of bourgeois politics, things like concern with the self, the question: who am I? what do I want? where am I headed?, in short all the original sins of individualism, lead to a different type of identity of the political: life and death politics'.[4]

In the same vein, Giddens distinguishes between old-fashioned 'emancipative politics' and 'life-politics', which he defines in the following way: 'Life politics concerns political issues which flow from processes of self-actualisation in post-traditional contexts, where globalising tendencies intrude deeply into the reflexive project of the self, and conversely where processes of self-realisation influence global strategies.'[5]

As in the case of deliberative democracy, at the basis of this conception of reflexive modernity is the possibility of elimination of the political in its antagonistic dimension and the belief that relations of friend/enemy have been eradicated. The claim is that in post-traditional societies, we no longer find collective identities constructed in terms of us/them, which means that political frontiers have evaporated and that politics must therefore be 'reinvented', to use Beck's expression. Indeed, Beck assumes that the generalised scepticism and doubt prevalent today preclude the emergence of antagonistic relations, since the latter depend on strong commitments to notions of truth, impossible in an era of ambivalence. Any attempt to speak in terms of right and left or to organise collective identities on the basis of common objectives and to define an adversary is thereby discredited as being 'archaic' or 'Old Labour' (to speak like Tony Blair).

Discourses like deliberative democracy or reflexive modernity are usually presented as the truly progressive ones, or, at least, better suited to the present stage of democracy. In fact, the chief consequence of envisioning our societies in such a 'post-political' manner is an inability to articulate any alternative to the current hegemonic order. These approaches render us incapable of thinking in a political way, of asking political questions and proposing political answers.

We should also be aware of the fact that this incapacity is reinforced by the centrality of human rights discourse, which has displaced all other discourses. Indeed, the discourse of human rights currently serves as a substitute for the socio-political discourses, which have been discredited. As Marcel Gauchet has argued,[6] it has become the organising norm of collective consciousness and the standard of public action. As he indicates, the problem is that such a discourse is not interested in – nor does it allow us to grasp – why things are as they are and how they could be changed. In fact, the insistence on human rights in many cases tend to disqualify the very idea of searching for explanations, because to try to understand is seen as excusing what is deemed 'unacceptable'. This is why, very often, the ideology of human rights thrives on denunciation. It commands a politics of intentions that is indifferent to the consequence of its actions, a politics of virtuous sentiment that is therefore not vulnerable to criticism.

Towards an agonistic public sphere

Putting together all these different elements, the ideological framework in which the dominant consensus is inscribed becomes visible. Such a consensus has two faces: neo-liberalism on one side, human rights on the other. Do not misunderstand my point. I am not saying that the discourse of human rights is simply an ideological cover for neo-liberalism. I do believe that human rights represent a constitutive component of modern democracy, and that they should be valued and fought for. The problem arises when they become a substitute for a truly political discourse and when democracy is reduced to the defence of human rights at the expense of its other dimension, that of popular sovereignty. Such a move impedes a grasp of the nature of modern democracy, which consists in the articulation of two different traditions: the liberal tradition of rule of law and individual liberty with the democratic tradition of equality and popular sovereignty. The tendency to privilege exclusively the liberal component and to treat the democratic element as obsolete has serious political consequences. It is the source of the growing success of right-wing populist parties, which pretend to re-establish popular sovereignty against elites.

It is also in the context of the current hegemony of liberalism that we can make sense of the now-dominant moralistic discourse, which has displaced any real political argumentation. Such a displacement is seen as proof that democracy has entered into a new, more mature phase in which morality has replaced outmoded confrontational politics. However, if we examine the question closely, it is immediately evident that this is far from being the case. Politics, with its supposedly old-fashioned antagonisms, has not been superseded by a higher stage of moral concerns. Politics, with its antagonisms, is still very much alive, except that it is now played out in the moral register. Indeed, frontiers between us and them, far from having disappeared, are continually re-inscribed, but since the 'them' can no longer be defined in political terms – given that the adversarial model has supposedly been overcome – these frontiers are drawn in moral categories, between 'us the good' and 'them the evil ones'.

Put another way, the consensus at the centre, which ostensibly includes everyone in our so-called post-traditional societies, cannot exist without the establishment of a frontier because no consensus – or common identity, for that matter – can exist without drawing a frontier. There cannot be an 'us' without a 'them' and the very identity of any group depends on the existence of a 'constitutive outside'. So the 'us of all good democrats' must be secured by the definition of a 'them'. However, since the 'them' cannot be defined as a political adversary, it can only be defined as a moral enemy, as the 'evil them'. In most cases, it is, of course, the 'extreme right' that provides the 'evil them' required by the very existence of the good democrats. This reference to the 'extreme right' is not very helpful, however, because it has become a nebulous category in which many different movements – from skinheads to right-wing populist parties – are lumped together indiscriminately. This blurs their differences and specific characteristics, and hinders the development of effective strategies for fighting them politically. But, of course, from the point of view of the 'good democrats', such differences are irrelevant. What is at stake for them is not political analysis but the delimitation of a 'them', which will provide the conditions of possibility for the 'us'.

This type of politics played out in the moral register is not conducive to the creation of the 'antagonistic public sphere', which I have argued is necessary for a robust democratic life. When the opponent is defined in moral rather than political terms, he cannot be envisioned as an adversary but only as an enemy. With the 'evil them', no agonistic debate is possible – they must simply be eradicated. They are usually conceived as the expression of a moral plague, therefore it is not necessary to try to understand the reasons for their existence. This is why moral condemnation often replaces a proper political analysis, and solutions are limited to the building of a 'cordon sanitaire' to quarantine the affected sectors.

It is ironic that, in the end, the political theory that claims that the friend/enemy model of politics has been superseded contributes to the revitalisation of the antagonistic model of politics, but this time in a way not amenable to a transformation of antagonism into agonism. Rather than helping to construct a vibrant agonistic public sphere, thanks to which democracy can be kept alive and deepened, those who proclaim the end of antagonism and the arrival of a consensual society might in fact be jeopardising democracy by creating the conditions for the emergence of antagonisms that cannot be contained by democratic institutions.

Beyond the nation-state

I will end by addressing another issue that also concerns the way we should envision the conditions of a democratic public sphere. It is clear that we are today confronted with a set of problems that cannot be tackled at the level of the nation-state but only in a wider context. If we accept the theoretical perspective that I have been delineating here, however, it is evident that this wider context cannot be coextensive with the whole planet. Democratic governance requires the existence of units, *demoi*, where popular sovereignty can be exercised, and this entails boundaries. It is in my view a dangerous illusion to imagine the possibility of a cosmopolitan citizenship that would be based exclusively on an abstract idea of humanity. To establish the conditions for effective democratic self-governance, citizens need to belong to a *demos* where they can exercise their rights of citizenship and this would not be available to a cosmopolitan citizen. Of course, this does not mean that political units must be identical with the nation-state. There are good reasons to argue in favour of the coexistence of smaller and larger units, according to diverse forms of belonging and the kinds of issues that need to be decided. So, globalisation could be structured in terms of a 'double regionalisation': on one level, the formation of a number of regional unions of diverse nation-states like the European Union, which would themselves be composed of sub-regions made up of parts of various nation-states. This would create the conditions for a new form of pluralism that would greatly enhance the capacities for popular participation at different levels.

In this respect, I find the diverse attempts to elaborate a new form of federalism particularly interesting. Here I have in mind several proposals made by

For an agnostic public sphere

Massimo Cacciari, the former mayor of Venice, who calls for a Copernican revolution that would radically deconstruct the centralist–authoritarian–bureaucratic apparatus of the traditional nation-state.[7] According to Cacciari, the modern state is being torn apart as a consequence of two movements, one micro-national, the other supranational: on the one hand, from the inside, under the pressure of regionalist or tribalist movements; on the other hand, from the outside, as a consequence of the growth of supranational powers and institutions and of the increasing power of world finance and trans-national corporations. Cacciari proposes federalism as the answer to such a situation. But his is a very special type of federalism, which he calls federalism 'from the bottom', as opposed to federalism 'from the top', the type proposed as a model for the European Union. This federalism from the bottom would recognise the specific identity of different regions, of different cities, not to isolate them, to separate them from each other, but, on the contrary, in order to establish the conditions of an autonomy conceived and organised on the basis of multiple relations of exchange between those regions and those cities. Such federalism would combine solidarity and adversarial competition, constituting a form of autonomy exercised in systems that are integrated in a conflictual mode.

Such ideas, of course, require further development, but I find them very suggestive. If our project is to contest the imposition of a single, homogenising model of society and the parallel decline of democratic institutions – both consequences of neo-liberal globalisation – it is urgent that we imagine new forms of association in which pluralism would flourish and where the capacities for democratic decision making would be enhanced. Against the anti-political illusions of a cosmopolitan world-governance, and against the sterile and doomed fixation of the nation-state, I believe that the type of federalism advocated by Cacciari provides promising insights. By allowing us to envision new forms of solidarity based on recognised interdependence, it might constitute one of the central ideas around which democratic forces could organise in a plurality of democratic public spheres. This would breathe new life into the agonistic struggle, which, as I have argued, is the defining characteristic of democratic politics. Moreover, this federalism should not be seen as being specific to Europe – it could stimulate the development of other regional units with their specific identities, units in which the global and the local could be articulated in many different ways and in which diverse types of links could be established within a context that respects differences. This would allow us, not to finish the democratic process – which by nature must remain open and therefore 'unfinished' – but to keep it alive and to envision how it could be deepened in a radical democratic direction.

Notes

1 C. Mouffe, 'The "end of politics" and the challenge of right wing populism', in F. Panizza (ed.), *Populism and the Mirror of Democracy* (London: Verso, 2005).
2 J. Habermas, 'Reply to symposium participants', *Cardozo Law Review*, 17:4–5 (1996), 1493.
3 For a development of this argument, see Chantal Mouffe, *The Democratic Paradox* (London: Verso, 2000).
4 Ulrich Beck, Anthony Giddens and Scott Lash, *Reflexive Modernization: Politics, Tradition and Aesthetics in the Modern Social Order* (Cambridge: Polity Press, 1994), p. 45.
5 Anthony Giddens, *Modernity and Self-Identity: Self and Society in the Late Modern Age* (Cambridge: Polity Press, 1991), p. 214.
6 M. Gauchet, 'Quand les droits de l'homme deviennent une politique', *Le Débat*, 110: 2 (2000), 258–88.
7 Some of the ideas can be found in an interview with M. Cacciari, 'The philosopher politician of Venice', *Soundings*, 17 (2001).

8 • *Jane Bennett*

In parliament with things[1]

They want to keep science and technology as distinct as possible from the search for values, meaning and ultimate goals. Is this not a tragedy if ... the present trend leads precisely in the opposite direction and that the most urgent concern for us today is to see how to fuse together humans and non-humans in the same hybrid forums and open, as fast as possible, this Parliament of things?[2]

[S]ome have suggested a parliament that includes non-human voices ... At first it is difficult to see beyond the medieval comedy of endangered Amazonian forests tapping microphones to be heard above the bellowing megafauna. Yet, such a mind change is necessary if the planet is not to be speedily consumed by the interests of short-term capital.[3]

Nonhuman actants

LET ME begin with a story about trees, soil, and worms, which Bruno Latour tells in *Pandora's Hope*. The line between the savannah and the rainforest in Amazonia is usually quite clear. But one day a botanist notes the presence, about ten meters *into* the forest, of several trees typical of the savannah. How can this be? An interdisciplinary, international team of scientists is called in, and inspection of the soil along the savannah-forest border reveals that it is 'more clayey than the savanna but less so than the forest. It would appear that the forest casts its own soil before it in order to create conditions favorable to its expansion. Unless, on the contrary, the savanna is degrading the woodland humus as it prepares to invade the forest.'[4] What the scientists understand themselves to be encountering is decidedly *not* nature as a mechanism automatically proceeding according to fixed laws. What they see, rather, is a set of actors – savannah, forest, soil and a host of unnamed others – all responding, in real time and without predetermined outcome, to each other and to the collective force of the whole configuration. The scientific task, as they conceive it, is to discern the agents involved and to get a better sense of the styles of action they practice. After consulting the testimony of a variety of plants, animals, books, spread sheets and soil sampling devices, the men and women on the scene conclude that it is the forest that is advancing, and they identify the earthworms as particularly efficacious agents in this forward march. The worms, who had gathered there for reasons still unknown to the humans, were producing the aluminium necessary to transform the silica of the sandy soil into clay.[5]

It is not controversial to say that the worms are participants in the *ecology* of the rainforest. But can it be said that they are also participants in its *politics?* Can there be a parliament of things? It is hard to deny that their activities make a difference to *homo sapiens'* debates about the rainforest: they speak, for example, to questions about the resilience of a forest known to support indigenous human populations, exotic nonhuman species and, more indirectly, all life. But does the ability to make a difference qualify something as a political actor? This question turns, I think, on both how one conceives of politics and how one conceives of agency. Is politics an exclusively human domain? Can nonhumans possess agency? The two questions are related.

Perhaps some light can be shed on the matter by looking at what we mean when we say that *humans* have political agency. Implicit here is the requirement that something more than an automatic causality is operative: if a human is to qualify as a political agent, her act must participate in a less deterministic kind of causality. But this need not rise to the level of full-blown intentionality: all we ask is that the act makes a difference to collective life and that it be *irreducible* to a knee-jerk reaction or instinctual response. For example, when people distribute themselves into racially and economically segregated neighbourhoods, it is said that they are engaging in politics, even when the actors do not intend or endorse the impact it has, say, on municipal finances, crime rates or transportation policy.

In this chapter, I experimentally endorse the view that nonhumans possess agential capacities, capacities irreducible to automatic functioning. It seems to me that there are enough affinities (though not an equivalence) between, say, the acts of worms migrating to the savannah-forest border and the acts of people moving to the suburbs to warrant greater attention to the role of nonhumans in collective life. I ask, more specifically, what would a democratic theory look like that acknowledged nonhumans as political participant-actors? It is difficult to find the right vocabulary here. 'Actor' may connote more autonomy than I mean to imply; 'participant' better captures the sense in which action is a collective endeavour in which nonhumans act alongside or with humans. But 'participant' may connote more *intentionality* than is warranted when characterising the activities of nonhumans. Perhaps the best term is Bruno Latour's 'actant', or that which has sufficient coherence to perform actions, produce effects and alter situations. Actants can be either human or nonhuman.[6]

I include in the category nonhumans both natural entities and technological objects. Examples of the former, in addition to those worms, include anthrax spores, the flowers sticking out of the rifles of National Guardsmen during the Vietnam War, the wind currents that bring drought, the whale songs that galvanised an international protest against Japanese fishing practices. Examples of high-tech nonhumans include the mobile phones in public places lamented by social theorists of the face-to-face encounter, the tanks on the streets during the US invasion of Iraq, the genetically modified seed corn rejected by some European farmers, the roar of commercial refrigeration units located in poor, urban neighbourhoods.

Contemporary Euro-American societies are very good at making refined and complex artefacts. Our artistic productions display a sophisticated appreciation for the beauty, eccentricities and wonders of nature. But political theorists lag behind in acknowledging the political potency of technological gadgets and natural objects. It seems to me that the agential power of nonhumans, because it is too often reduced to automatic instinct or deterministic mechanism, is less carefully woven into human agendas and democratic ideals than it should be.

Ontology and democratic theory

Democratic theory today rests largely upon an implicit onto-story, wherein humans are radically distinguished from other entities, upon a scenography of subjects and objects, of active Mind and inert Matter.[7] In this world picture, human forms of communication, human modes of intelligence and creativity and human structures of order are given such pride of place that the centrality of humanity appears, not as a powerful tradition, but as an inevitability, as, say, an irrevocable fact of consciousness or perception. Such anthropocentrism shapes the range of ethical and policy concerns taken up by theories of democracy. It focuses attention, for example, upon the problem of the unequal participation of different human groups, especially economic and racialised classes. But to me it also lacks thick descriptive power, for its image of political life as one where active (or potentially active but currently disempowered) human subjects confront passive (or, in the case of technology, dangerously autonomous) nonhuman objects does not ring true to the high-tech, commodity-laden, germ-infused world with which we are exquisitely enmeshed.

Perhaps I can intimate the connection between democratic theory and a human-centred ontology by looking briefly at the concept of 'association' advanced by Mark Warren in *Democracy and Association*. Warren affirms Tocqueville's judgment that voluntary associations (neighbourhood groups, religious congregations, bowling leagues) are crucial to a vibrant democratic culture. 'The concept of association', he writes, 'evokes the possibilities of collective action, but in a way that retains social (as opposed to legal/bureaucratic or market) modes of mediation among people.'[8] *Democracy and*

Association is an excellent book, which draws attention to non-state and non-electoral practices of governance, and which shows how 'even today democracy might be re-thought and even radicalized within the vast array of participatory spaces that large-scale, complex and differentiated societies now offer'.[9] But I am also struck by the way Warren's account tends to discount the political role played by nonhumans (in dissonant conjunction with humans), including, for example, natural entities like deer or anthrax populations or technologies like video files of prisoners at Abu Ghraib. This exclusion is linked to the way Warren figures what counts as communication, or the ability to be present in an association. Association 'thrives on talk, normative agreement, cultural similarity, and shared ambitions – that is, forms of communication that are rooted in speech, gesture, self-presentation'.[10] Warren imagines 'speech, gesture, self-presentation' as acts of humans alone. But, even when communication issues from human bodies, it is not an exclusively human affair – think of the activity of electrical charges in the brain, of recollection-provoking scents in the air or of the microchips of hearing aids. And a case could also be made for the communicative capacities of nonhumans – think here of the voice of birds or chimps, and also of microbes acting as disease and beer cans speaking as trash.[11] But the vitality of such materialities is obscured for theorists like Warren, for whom communication is framed as a communicative rationality unique to humans.

The exclusion of a whole set of operatives is normal within an ontology that assigns agentic capacity to only one side of a human–nonhuman divide. Later in this chapter, I draw upon the work of Jacques Rancière and Bruno Latour to explore how a notion like democratic association might meaningfully be extended to acknowledge the activities of nonhumans. Let me first say something about the onto-story from which this alternative approach to democracy emerges.

This onto-story, which I have described elsewhere as an enchanted materialism, pictures the world as a web of lively and mobile matter-forms of varying degrees of complexity. It posits multiple sites of agency, including the intentions of human and nonhuman animals, the temperament of a brain's chemistry, the momentum of a social movement, the mood of an architectural form, the propensity of a family, the style of a corporation, the drive of a sound-field and the decisions of molecules at far-from-equilibrium states.[12] This materialist tale draws upon an eclectic set of figures and claims: Henry Thoreau's notion of the Wild, Lucretius's contention of a swerve or unpredictable motility intrinsic to matter, Spinoza's claim that bodies have a natural propensity to form groups and complexity theory's accounts of the autopoetic or self-organizing capacity of some physical systems.

I seek a conception of materiality that acknowledges the moments of recalcitrance, vitality and efficacy within nonhumans – their 'thing-power' or the curious ability of 'inanimate' things to animate humans, to surprise us, impinge upon us and propel us to engage in movements, moods or utterances that we otherwise would not.[13] Within this imaginary, humans are figured as themselves materialities inextricably enmeshed with nonhuman entities and forces, for humans can operate only if accompanied by a bevy of nonhumans (from foodstuffs to intestinal bacteria to the metal/plastic/silicon of tools). It might even be said that humans need nonhumans to function more than nonhumans need humans, for many nonhumans – from a can rusting at the bottom of a landfill to a colony of spores in the Arctic – fester or live beyond the proximity of humans.

If human life is inextricably enmeshed with that of nonhumans, and if the powers of the co-participants to some degree overlap, then perhaps the most appropriate unit of analysis for democratic theory is neither the individual human nor the human group but what Gilles Deleuze calls an 'assemblage' or what Bruno Latour terms a 'collective'. The focus shifts to what Karen Barad calls the intra-action of humans and nonhumans, whose ensembles are edged by porous membranes. These functioning wholes are open systems that are continually disrupted by, but also always reforming in response to, the entrance and exit of new participants or actants.[14]

Actants are creatures of what Lasse Thomassen and Lars Tønder term an 'ontology of abundance', that is, a world-picture where everything participates in becoming and thus every thing tends to overreach its current form.[15] This focus on process makes it less salient to distinguish sharply between types of parties to the action, between, that is, human and nonhuman participants. Moreover, from this perspective, it is *action* that acts as much as any individual. Latour puts the point this way: 'whenever we make something *we* are not in command, we are slightly overtaken by the action: every builder knows that'. Likewise, the momentum of nonhumans is also slightly overtaken by *us*, by 'the *clinamen* of our action'.[16]

In addition to the image of matter as a vital and dynamic force, there is a second ontological assumption embedded in my approach to radical democracy, and that is the idea that there exists what might be called a *structural parallel* between formations in nature and cultural formations. A particularly vivid sense of this is expressed in the *Great Treatise on Supreme Sound*, a fourteenth-century Chinese music textbook in which each hand position of the lute-player is understood to be a repetition of a natural movement of an animal. Music is the result of making this ontological parallel explicit: the lutist renders the silent parallel between nature and culture audible – he performs it. Unlike the European system of assigning each musical note a figure on a musical score, 'Chinese musical notation does not indicate the sounds themselves … but simply the precise gesture required to produce them.' For example, to make the staccato sound of two notes played on the same string in rapid succession, the lutist is instructed to reproduce the motion of 'an emaciated crow perched on a bare tree or pecking at the snow in hope of finding something to eat'. Or, to make the sound that comes when the index, middle and third finger grip two strings at once, the lutist is to render his hand in the image of 'the nonchalant flick of a carp's tail'. Likewise, a 'floating sound' will be produced by arranging the fingers in the successive movements of a 'white butterfly fluttering at flower level' that 'lingers but does not stay'.[17]

Complexity theory offers a contemporary version of such a view. According to it, natural and technological systems, at least for a wide range of spatial and temporal frames, parallel each other. Both are governed by analogous processes of structuration and correlative modes of evolution – for both are subject to the intrinsic limits, tendencies and fortuitous opportunities of a common, though variably expressed, materiality. For example, clusters of neurons in a human brain, groupings of buildings in a city and colonies of slime molds all follow similar organisational rules. They are all instances of what Steven Johnson calls 'organized complexity'. In contrast both to simple systems where 'billiard ball causality' reigns and also to vast systems whose structure is best described in terms of statistical probability, systems of organised complexity are marked by self-organised patterns created from the bottom up, where no single element plays the role of a centralised or higher authority. There is no 'pacemaker' but only a 'swarm'. But it is a swarm that exhibits a collective intelligence; that is, the capacity to create an effective and adaptable order for its elements.[18] Organised complexity exists whenever a system – be it biological, social, technological, human or nonhuman – produces outcomes that cannot be explained as issuing from *either* a consummate central agent *or* an automatic process. The outcomes are better described through terms like 'assemblage decision' and 'emergent choice'.

Let me now return to the self-organising system called democracy and to the question of the role of nonhumans within it. What existential endowment, what kind of embodiment, is required for events to count as acts of participation? I proceed, first, by way of Rancière, for whom the essence of democracy (and politics *per se*) is the eruption of those who protest their exclusion, an exclusion constitutive of the polity. The defining characteristic of a *demos* is, for Rancière, its capacity to barge in and reject the order's claim to have accounted for all parties. This democratic act *par excellence* exposes the contingency of the dominant 'partition of the sensible', or ontological frame that renders some groups and acts visible and locates others below the threshold of note. This is, I claim, a capacity that nonhumans too possess. The second theory of democracy I consider is that of Bruno Latour, who imagines the *demos* as an instance of organised complexity: it is a productive, creative force with an inherent capacity to negotiate and re-negotiate settlements, to build socio-natural collectives in which nonhumans and humans engage and enter into each other. I appreciate the role of disruption and interruption that Rancière emphasises as the key to democracy. But I side with Latour in extending the capacity for disruption to nonhumans, and in adding a dimension of positive action to the democratic agenda.

The eruptive *demos*

Democracy, says Rancière, is not to be understood as a way of arranging and managing 'places, powers, and functions'. (That is the function of 'the police'.) Democracy is instead 'the name of a singular disruption of this order of distribution of bodies ... It is the name of what comes and interrupts the smooth working of this order.'[19] This destructive force is unruly in that the chain of effects it unleashes cannot be predicted, but it is not a blind eruption wholly unhinged from human intentionality or political strategising. Rancière tries to position 'disruption' between these two extremes of fate and freedom by casting it as a *theatrical* act. The *demos*, when it exercises its disruptive essence, constructs 'a *polemical scene*' so that the 'noises that come out of ... [the excluded individual's] mouths could count as argumentative utterances'.[20] What such a scene stages is a very specific kind of confrontation: one between the order, with its hierarchical distribution of rights and privileges, and the sheer fact of 'the equality of speaking beings'.[21] These performances declare 'the ultimate secret of any social order': 'there is no natural principle of domination by one person over another'.[22]

The *demos* engages in a distinctly *political* act, then, when it rudely interjects itself as qualified to join the group of parties to the debate. 'One does not practice democracy except under the form of these mise-en-scenes that reconfigure the relations of the visible and the sayable'.[23] Rancière's point is this: what distinguishes *political* exchange from other forms of inter-action is not the aim of consensus but the existence of a fundamental *lack* of agreement about the number and form of those parties who are to count *as* parties to the discussion. In other words, politics is the introduction *by* the *demos* of a new political subject now proclaimed *as* the *demos*; it is the making-visible of this actor within 'the field of experience, which then modifies the regime of the visible'.[24] Politics happens when the invisible leftovers, the remainders ignored in the official count of disputants, make themselves apparent.

Are there nonhuman actants among the *demos*? Is it possible for an animal, a technology, or a sound to redraw the 'partition of the sensible'? When I posed this question to Rancière at a conference celebrating his work, his answer was a clear 'no'. He did not want to extend the concept of the political that far; it ought not, he said, to be stretched beyond the realm of the human. Any political efficacy (apparently) associated with nonhuman entities is ultimately a function of human agents.[25] Despite Rancière's reply, his theory opens a conceptual space for nonhumans to appear as political actants.

Take, for example, the terms he uses to describe the activity proper to the *demos*. One set of verbs mark acts of nay-saying: the *demos* refuses, resists, dissents, objects, repudiates and rejects. It negates the existing partition of the sensible, or way the world is carved up and accounted for. But do things as well as people not possess this negating power? Indeed, a passive and non-negotiable recalcitrance or defiance is often cited as the very essence of thinghood, as, for example, the rock of Sisyphus's labour. The refusing-power of things is, as well, a basic assumption of the scientific method: Latour notes how his Amazonian scientists fear that the soil and plant samples will reject their hypotheses.[26]

Rancière also uses a second set of verbs to describe the behaviour of the *demos*. These are the more active and violent acts of rupture, eruption, interruption, disruption: 'Politics is a specific *rupture* in the logic of *arche*. It does not simply presuppose the *rupture* of the "normal" distribution of positions ... It also requires a *rupture* in the idea that there are dispositions "proper" to such classifications.'[27] Davide Panagia, in an interview with Rancière, describes this rupturing as a 'speaking out of turn in a cacophonous manner'.[28] Here again, nonhumanity seems quite capable of wielding this power. Indeed, the rupture verbs of *Disagreement* evoke the traditional imagery of a natural sublime (volcanos, whirlwinds, sexual drives) that overwhelms human reason, speech and comprehension.

Though Rancière sometimes describes the rupturing act as a theatrical performance (thus entailing more self-consciousness than things like volcanos can muster), the plot of this performance is not particularly subtle. Rather, the *demos* bursts on to the stage and bluntly proclaims the equality of all linguistic beings. The gruff inelegance of its utterance is a function of the fact that the *demos* must labour to be heard at all, for it is still the victim of the Platonic prejudice, which views it as a repellent group of noise-making animals, in contrast to men with *logos*. For Rancière, the *demos*, as a group of 'floating subjects' forced to live below the threshold of political agency as currently defined, is in fact the *only* entity capable of political action, for politics consists precisely in the rearing up of this nether-worldly group, a rearing up which reveals sounds to be human voices.[29]

In thinking about whether nonhumans might be included within the *demos*, we also might examine the *process* through which that political association comes into being. The *demos*, says Rancière, does not pre-exist its act of disruption, but is constituted by its very refutation of the order's claim to have already accounted for all parties to the polity. The *demos* emerges from forces and voices so disenfranchised that they are not even on the official list of disenfranchised subjects. Rancière does elaborate upon this difficult notion of a proto-entity with enough coherence to stage a disruptive encounter but not enough to be

In parliament with things

discernible to the order's sensibility. William Connolly's account of 'pluralization' in *The Ethos of Pluralization* offers theoretical amplification: in contrast to a pluralism conceived solely in terms of the aggregation of relatively stable interest groups, Connolly advocates a politics also alert to the emergence of groups that currently exist just below the register of identity. These are clusters of forces and persons that are not yet objects of political recognition. He argues for an ethos of anticipatory responsiveness to them, which

> responds to a movement to pluralize even before the constituency in question has become fully consolidated into a recognized, positive identity. For the positive identity is an effect at the end of a political struggle, not quite a fact or implicit concept at its beginning ... Each pluralizing movement, if and as it succeeds, migrates from an abject, abnormal, subordinate, or obscure Other *subsisting* in a nether world *under* the register of justice to a positive identity now *existing* on the register of justice/injustice.[30]

Connolly's description of the *demos* as a pluralising movement is echoed in Rancière's claim that the *demos* is 'neither the sum of the population nor the disfavored element within', but 'an excessive part – the whole of those who are nothing, who do not have specific properties allowing them to exercise power'.[31] But could not this description of an 'excessive part' – which exerts a force but is not yet recognised as actant – apply to nonhumans as well as humans? Many of the discursive interruptions Rancière valorises – the outbursts of enslaved, female or gay people – were once themselves treated as the noises of creatures below the threshold of viable political agency.

But even if one were to allow that a tree, a viral epidemic or a subtle change in climate could disrupt the existing partition of the sensible, it is a separate question whether such a rupture qualifies as an objection to a wrong, which is a second *sine qua non* of political agency for Rancière. The paradigmatic wrong, he says, is the unequal treatment of equals – which he understands as the unequal treatment of beings *equally in possession of the power of human speech*. Injustice thus defined, there can be no 'wrong' done to nonhumans. They are barred from the *demos* (and from the status of political actants) by virtue of the fact that only *linguistic* forms of objection qualify. Nonhumans can make noise but only humans can produce '*argumentative utterances*'.[32] Rancière's *demos* consists only in 'beings engaged in a collective destiny through words'.[33]

In defining the *demos* as a linguistically competent, though currently unrecognised practitioner of human language, Rancière both demeans the non-linguistic elements of human expression and excludes nonhumans from political participation. When he says that 'politics exists because those who have no right to be counted as speaking beings make themselves of some account',[34] his formulation seems to leave open the possibility that nonhumans could enter the polity, that nonhumans too have the power to stage a scene. But Rancière

[141]

then forbids this particular re-partitioning of the sensible when he restricts what it takes to stage a scene to demonstrations of one's possession of *logos* or rational speech. Though he challenges the Habermasian model of communicative action because it 'presupposes the partners in communicative exchange to be pre-constituted' whereas 'the particular feature of political dissensus is that the partners are no more constituted than is the object or the very scene of discussion',[35] Rancière shares with Habermas an anthropocentric prejudice. They share a model of participation that restricts itself to the range of powers made possible by a distinctly human kind of embodiment – indeed, their understanding of what participation entails is formed on the basis of a model of linguistic competence. And this when language-use is but one of the many modes of *human* communication. Here again we see how the judgment of whether or not to count nonhumans as political actants is shaped by an ontological imaginary. Like Warren's associations, Rancière's *demos* presumes a radical divide between, on the one hand, humans, who are always worthy (but not always bestowed with) the status of subjects and, on the other hand, nonhumans, which are mute objects. A more radical theory of democracy could soften this distinction while reducing its perceived salience to politics, admitting nonhumans into the ranks of 'contentious objects whose mode of presentation is not homogeneous with the ordinary mode of existence of the objects thereby identified'.[36]

The self-brewing *demos*

In contrast to Rancière, Bruno Latour defines democratic action not only as the (negative) power of disruption or the accusation of a miscount, but also as the (productive) activity of forming a working whole or 'cosmos' – a cosmos that is an assemblage of human *and* nonhuman actants. This cosmos is a construction, but not merely a *social* construction; not, that is, something made by and of humans only. Rather, 'humans, for millions of years, have extended their social relations to other actants with which, with whom, they have swapped many properties, and with which, with whom, they form collectives'.[37] The *demos* is one such collective.

Like Rancière, Latour defends the disorder of democratic politics, where politics is understood not as the application of fixed and abstract principles but as the trials and errors of 'clothed and living bodies assembled in the agora'. Unlike Rancière, however, the *demos* must not only interrupt the police-order but also 'decide, on the spot, in real time, what to do next'. Humans in the *demos*, in collaboration with the nonhumans in which they are bound up, must have the courage to see 'policies through to the finish'.[38]

But how is it possible for such an ontologically diverse *demos*, which includes actants with little or no self-consciousness, and in which even human actants must act 'without the benefit of proof, of hindsight, of foresight, of repetitive experiment',[39] to pursue a positive agenda? Latour responds by claiming that the *demos* is guided by a self-organising power intrinsic to all assemblages of sufficient size and diversity. A democratic assemblage comes to a decision through a process akin to that of brewing or fermentation. The *demos* engages in:

> a completely ad hoc sort of activity that is neither transcendent nor immanent but more closely resembles a fermentation through which the people brews itself toward a decision – never exactly in accordance with itself, and never ... commended or directed from above.[40]

Latour here begins to articulate a model of action that does not rely on an anthropocentric onto-tale, with its fundamental distinction between human subjects capable of making decisions in accordance with criteria set out in advance, and nonhuman objects manipulated in the service of implementing these decisions. Rather, democratic action entails a long and convoluted series of 'negotiations', 'mediations' and 'translations' involving the actions and effects of a rich mix of actants. There is no other way for these negotiations to proceed except through impure means: 'rumors, condensations, displacements, accumulations, simplifications, detours, transformations – a highly complex chemistry that makes *one* stand for the *whole*'.[41] What it means to participate in a democracy, then, is to engage in a process akin to the 'kneading of a dough – except that the *demos* is at once the flour, the water, the bakers, the leavening ferment, and the very act of kneading'. Democratic decision-making is a kind of *autophuos*, 'the power to "grow by themselves" into what all the others are doing and willing.'[42]

For Latour, the relationship between human and nonhuman members of the *demos* is close, for each human is continuously enmeshed with a set of other humans and other (sub-assemblages of) microbes, plants, climatic forces, handicrafts and technologies. Each individual is a participant in a collective, though not all collectives are equally democratic or worthy of endorsement: some are more richly 'vascularized' than others, less hierarchically structured.[43] Latour figures politics as a series of call-and-response engagements between humans and nonhumans: 'Action is not what people do, but is instead the "*fait-faire*", the making-do, accomplished along with others in an event, with the specific opportunities provided by the circumstances. These others are not ideas, or things, but nonhuman entities, or ... *propositions*.'[44]

But Latour also insists that democracy not a process that we could ever fully master, for there will always be a 'slight surprise of action', an unpredictable element contributed by the action itself, irreducible to the propensity, will, or stubborn inertia of any of the actants:

> there is no object, no subject ... But there are events. I never *act*; I am always slightly surprised by what I do. That which acts through me is also surprised by what I do, by the chance to mutate, to change, and to bifurcate, the chance that I and the circumstances surrounding me offer to that which has been invited, recovered, welcomed.[45]

In insisting upon the 'slight surprise of action' does Latour reveal an 'ontology of abundance' or an 'ontology of lack'? Is the slight surprise a sign of a fecund world of becoming, where all entities are always in the process of exceeding and overreaching themselves? Or does this surprising element signal a profoundly aporetic and ineluctable reality, a lack at the heart of being? I am not sure, though the exuberance of his prose, and the valence of metaphors like brewing, fit an ontology of abundance. And what about Rancière – from what ontological imaginary arises the description of the *demos* as the 'excessive part' that always haunts the order's partition of the sensible? Again, I am not sure, though his preference for the negative, for disruption and rupture, may suggest an ontology of lack. One thing is clear, however. For Latour the slight surprise pertains to actions generated by *collectives* of humans and nonhumans, whereas for Rancière the relevant excess issues from human bodies alone.

For Latour, the nonhumans with which we are enmeshed *propose* to us a direction toward which to proceed; they suggest an open-ended course of action, should they, should we, endeavour to join up and form a new collective (or enrich a collective already in progress). By describing humans and nonhumans alike as propositions and propositioners, Latour, it seems to me, is attempting to name the *momentum* that action itself seems to possess, a directionality irreducible either to human intentionality or to the propensity of the materialities with which it engages. Action carries with it its own kind of trajectory, pull or vector-ality.

In parliament with things

> Are you ready, and at the price of what sacrifice, to live the good life together? That this highest of moral and political questions could have been raised, for so many centuries, by so many bright minds, *for human only* without the nonhumans that make them up, will soon appear, I have no doubt, as extravagant as when the Founding Fathers denied slaves and women the vote.[46]

The exclusion of nonhumans from democratic theory may seem a rather exotic concern, especially given the dismal state of ordinary democratic practice today. (I write as an American living under the regime of George W. Bush.) And I would gladly defer the attempt to speak a word on behalf of the political salience of nonhumans if doing so would produce a stronger, old-fashioned kind of democracy, with, for example, national elections where all human votes are counted, or Presidents who considered themselves accountable to the human electorate, or a news media that was independent, intelligent and critical or a system of taxation that did not produce a vast and obscene gap between rich and poor humans. But it does not seem that the two kinds of democratisation, one human-centred and one not, are related in this way. I have nothing new to say about how to strengthen old-fashioned democracy: I think Internet initiatives such as MoveOn.org make great sense; there is promise in attempts to use the courts to render the executive branch more open to public scrutiny, and in the direct action of groups like the cyclists of Critical Mass or the Industrial Areas Foundation.[47] My hope, however, is that such tactics might benefit from the radical shift in ontological imaginary that I seek. It is a shift in our images of agency and efficacy, of who or what is capable of possessing those vital powers and what kinds of inter-species collaborations they today entail.

Let me close by returning to the worms of Amazonia, my example of how one set of nonhumans participated in a political debate about the rain forest. The human population of Amazonia, and by extension all humans enmeshed with the climate regulated by rain forests, are unwitting and often unwilling partners with earthworms, as well as with the technical means through which we come to hear them *as* speakers and see them *as* communicative partners. Indeed, we participate in collectives made up of an 'increasingly large number of humans ... mixed with an increasingly large number of nonhumans'.[48] If we are ever to cope successfully with the complexities of this collective, and with the ecological threats posed by it and by ourselves to our survival, we had better start respecting the nonhumans with which we are always already in league.

'We'? The prose governing the paragraph above discloses something about the limits built into such a radical democracy. The first task is to recognise ourselves as in league with a wide and changing variety of natural and technological things. The second is to acknowledge these other things as actants in the world, even if the degrees and forms of agency vary among the participants. The third is to generate new ways of consulting nonhumans, new ways to listen to them and respond more carefully to their outbreaks, objections, testimonies and propositions. For these offerings are profoundly important to the health of the world assemblage upon which we utterly rely. Because their modes of embodiment differ, humans and nonhumans cannot participate equally or in the same way in political affairs. But surely the scope of democratisation can be broadened to acknowledge nonhumans, in something like the way we have come to hear the political voices of teenagers, or Founding Fathers or divine Persons.

Notes

1 The author gratefully acknowledges the comments and criticisms of William Connolly, Lisa Disch, Mark Ingram, Norma Kriger, George Shulman, Lasse Thomassen and Lars Tønder.

2 B. Latour, 'What rules of method for the new socio-scientific experiments?', lecture prepared for the Darmsdadt Colloquium plenary lecture, 30 March 2001, www.ensmp.fr/~latour/poparticles/poparticle/p095.html.
3 K. Murray, 'The Cabinet of Helmut Lueckenhausen', in *Craft Victoria* (1999), 17–19.
4 The story is told in B. Latour, *Pandora's Hope* (Cambridge, MA: Harvard University Press, 1999), chapter 2. The quotation is from p. 53.
5 *Ibid.*, p. 76.
6 Sometimes, says Latour, as in laboratory experiments, a proto-actant emerges that does not yet have a stabilised identity and is describable only as a list of effects or performances. Here the term 'name of action' is more appropriate than actant, for 'only later does one deduce from these performances a competence', that is, an entity congealed enough to engage to make a difference in the situation (*ibid.*, pp. 303, 308).
7 Though a wariness of self-confident 'grand narratives' persists, there has been what might be called an ontological turn within social and political theory. By this I mean a willingness to make *explicit* the ontological imaginary – the picture of the basic character of nature/life/existence – that informs a theory's more specifically political set of claims, criticisms and analyses. Such onto-stories are, in contrast to traditional metaphysics, presented as speculative and contestable, though also as a valuable and perhaps indispensable part of thinking. Just as Hobbes's onto-story of a world of matter-in-motion and a distant, Jobian God enables his distinctive notions of sovereignty, contract and civil peace, contemporary works such as Deleuze and Guattari's *A Thousand Plateaus* and Lyotard's *A Postmodern Fable* link their political conceptualisations to a metaphysical imaginary. My approach follows this trend. See G. Deleuze and F. Guattari, *A Thousand Plateaus: Capitalism and Schizophrenia*, trans. B. Massumi (Minneapolis, MN: University of Minnesota Press, 1987); and J. F. Lyotard, *Postmodern Fables*, trans. G. Van Den Abbeele (Minneapolis, MN: University of Minnesota Press, 1999).
8 M. E. Warren, *Democracy and Association* (Princeton, NJ: Princeton University Press, 2001), p. 8.
9 *Ibid.*, p. 13.
10 *Ibid.*, p. 39.
11 For accounts of nonhuman animal speech and self-presentation, see, for example, F. De Waal's *Good Natured: The Origins of Right and Wrong in Humans and Other Animals* (Cambridge, MA: Harvard University Press, 1996), and his *The Ape and the Sushi Master: Cultural Reflections of a Primatologist* (New York: Basic Books, 2001); F. De Waal and P. L. Tyack (eds), *Animal Social Complexity: Intelligence, Culture, and Individualized Societies* (Cambridge, MA: Harvard University Press, 2003); T. Barber, *The Human Nature of Birds* (New York: Penguin, 1993).
12 See J. Bennett, *The Enchantment of Modern Life* (Princeton, NJ: Princeton University Press, 2001); I. Prigogine, *The End of Certainty: Time, Chaos, and the New Laws of Nature* (New York: Free Press, 1997); I. Prigogine and I. Stengers, *Order Out of Chaos: Man's New Dialogue with Nature* (Toronto: Bantam Books, 1984); M. De Landa, *A Thousand Years of Non-Linear History* (New York: Swerve Editions, 2000); Deleuze and Guattari, *A Thousand Plateaus*.
13 I develop this claim in J. Bennett, 'The force of things: steps toward an ecology of matter', *Political Theory*, 32:3 (2004), 347–87.
14 Unlike the term society, collective 'refers to the associations of humans and nonhumans. While a division between nature and society renders invisible the political process by which the cosmos is collected in one livable whole, the word "collective" makes this process central' (Latour, *Pandora's Hope*, p. 304). Karen Barad coins the

notion of intra-action in order 'to signify *the inseparability of "objects" and "agencies of observation"* (in contrast to "interaction", which reinscribes the contested [subject–object] dichotomy).' K. Barad, 'Scientific literacy → agential literacy', in M. Mayberry, B. Subramaniam and L. H. Weasel (eds), *Feminist Science Studies* (London: Routledge, 2001), p. 232.

15 See L. Thomassen and L. Tønder, 'Introduction: rethinking radical democracy between abundance and lack', pp. 6f (in this volume).

16 Latour, *Pandora's Hope*, p. 281 (emphasis in original).

17 F. Jullien, *The Propensity of Things: Towards a History of Efficacy in China*, trans. J. Lloyd (New York: Zone Books, 1995), pp. 113, 115, 116.

18 S. Johnson, *Emergence: The Connected Lives of Ants, Brains, Cities, and Software* (New York: Touchstone Books, 2001), p. 18. Organised complexity is like a 'dance – not ... a simple-minded precision dance with everyone kicking up at the same time ..., but ... an intricate ballet in which the individual dancers and ensembles all have distinctive parts which miraculously reinforce each other and compose an orderly whole' (*ibid.*, p. 51). In systems of organised complexity, the individual elements 'follow specific rules and through their various interactions create a distinct macrobehavior, arranging themselves in a specific shape, or forming a specific pattern over time' (*ibid.*, p. 48).

19 J. Rancière, *Dis-agreement: Politics and Philosophy*, trans. J. Rose (Minneapolis, MN: University of Minnesota Press, 1999), p. 99.

20 J. Rancière, with D. Panagia, 'Dissenting words', *Diacritics*, 30:2 (2000), 125, my emphasis.

21 Rancière, *Dis-agreement*, p. 33. Democracy is the 'staging of the very contradiction between police logic and political logic', as when the feminist Jeanne Deroin presented herself, in 1849, 'as a candidate for a legislative election in which she cannot run' (*ibid.*, p. 41).

22 *Ibid.*, p. 79. Democracy happens when the incommensurability between 'the order of the inegalitarian distribution of social bodies' and 'the order of the equal capacity of speaking beings in general' becomes visible (*ibid.*, p. 42).

23 Rancière, 'Dissenting words', p. 125.

24 Rancière, *Dis-agreement*, p. 99.

25 The conference was called 'Fidelity to the Disagreement', sponsored by the Post-Structuralism and Radical Politics group of the British Political Studies Association, held at Goldsmiths College, London, 16–17 September 2003.

26 When humans exercise the power to thwart, it is typically viewed as an active decision and not an instance of passive, automatic functioning. Latour objects to this asymmetrical treatment, and describes the geographer Heloisa Filizolas, who kept the field notebook, as one 'guarantor of the standardization of experimental protocols' amidst other nonhuman actants. See Latour, *Pandora's Hope*, pp. 34, 46.

27 J. Rancière, 'Ten theses', *theory & event*, 5:3 (2001), Thesis 3, my emphasis.

28 D. Panagia, '*Ceci n'est pas un argument*: an introduction to the Ten Theses', *theory & event*, 5:3 (2001), 5.

29 The example Rancière likes to give of this irruption on to the scene is the activity of the plebeians of Aventine Hill, who forced the patricians to relate to them as if they had intelligence, as if they were worthy of discoursing with. The plebs erected 'a sphere for the name of the people to appear', carving out 'in the heart of the city [a] ... place where liberty is to be exercised ... where the power of the demos that brings off the part of those who have no part is to be exercised' (Rancière, *Dis-agreement*, p. 66).

30 W. E. Connolly, *The Ethos of Pluralization* (Minneapolis, MN: University of

Minnesota Press, 1995), p. 184 (emphasis in original). Connolly, unlike Rancière, treats a pluralist democracy as a politics in which interdependence and tension is maintained between existing pluralist settlements and new drives to 'pluralization'.
31 Rancière, 'Dissenting words', p. 124.
32 Ibid., p. 125, my emphases.
33 Rancière, Dis-agreement, p. 25.
34 Ibid., p. 27.
35 Rancière, 'Ten theses', Thesis 8, paragraph 24.
36 Rancière, Dis-agreement, p. 104.
37 Latour, Pandora's Hope, p. 198.
38 Ibid., pp. 227, 239.
39 Ibid., pp. 241f.
40 Ibid., p. 247, my emphasis.
41 Ibid., p. 250.
42 Ibid., pp. 251f.
43 A democratic collective is one 'which brings together starts, prions, cows, heavens, and people ... into a "cosmos" instead of an "unruly shambles"' (ibid., p. 261). For Latour, all politics is cosmopolitics, that is, 'the management, diplomacy, combination, and negotiation of human and nonhuman agencies' (ibid., p. 290).
44 Ibid., p. 288, my emphasis.
45 Ibid., p. 281.
46 Ibid., p. 297, emphasis in original.
47 See www.buildiaf.org. See also R. Coles, 'Moving democracy: IAF social movements and the political arts of listening, traveling, and tabling in a heterogeneous World', paper presented at the 2002 American Political Science Association Annual Meeting.
48 Latour, Pandora's Hope, p. 214.

9 • *Jon Simons*

The radical democratic possibilities of popular culture[1]

Introduction: radical democracy, liberalism and Marxism

RADICAL democracy, in the sense referred to in this volume, is distinct from both alternative notions of democracy and radical democratic theory in general, which is best understood in terms of its emergence in the New Left. Of the two theoretical versions of radical democracy identified in this volume, theories of abundance are a better resource for the political project of radical democracy. They focus on the potentialities and forces that make popular democracy possible, whereas theorists of lack provide a sobering if not pessimistic critique of how the 'people' are led astray. I find it instructive to see some parallels and differences between the political moods and attitudes that characterise ontologies of lack and abundance, on the one hand, and pessimism and populism in cultural studies, on the other. This focus helps to draw out the political stakes of the debate conducted in this volume, but also points the way to two significant theoretical moves. First, the articulation of the theory of hegemony, which is central to the debate in cultural studies, together with the ontology of lack is only contingent. Subsequently, I identify Lacanian theorists of lack as lacking the resources for the radical, popular democracy. By re-articulating hegemony with the ontology of abundance, radical democratic theories of abundance gain a political direction currently missing. Second, a radical democratic theory of the media identifies popular culture as a hospitable terrain for democratic politics. On this account, appeals for consent are couched in popular cultural forms, and the public of mass democracies is constituted by means of communication technologies that depend on and disseminate popular culture.

Radical democracy as a theoretical and practical project contrasts with both liberal democracy and Leninist revolutionary democratic centralism. It is an alternative to both the form of 'actually existing' democracy that has developed in the West, and to the Soviet-style rule by a single party claiming to represent the 'people'. The significance of radical democracy lies in the political context of the second half of the twentieth century, particularly the growing disillusionment on the Western Left with Soviet socialism, and the increasing global hegemony of capitalist, liberal democracy, especially after 1989. Radical democracy has emerged in distinction from the socialist and especially Marxist tradition, because, although it is of the Left, it is not traditionally left, in the sense of being concerned primarily with class struggle, economic equality or alienation from production. The New Left arose from circumstances that challenged the 'hegemony' of Marxism as the critical discourse in the West. Ernesto Laclau's and Chantal Mouffe's theory of hegemony was a theory of the new social formations that included the American civil rights movement and other anti-racist protests, anti-Vietnam war protests, anti-colonial protests, student revolts, the women's movement and ecological politics that constituted the New Left. Radical democracy, however, does not abandon the socialist tradition, nor does it become uncritical of liberal democracy. Radical democrats regard the issues around identity politics that were taken up by the New Left as challenges to liberalism as well as socialism. They advocate a pluralism in which respect for others does not depend on the extent to which those others belong to the same community as us, or deserve rights because they share universal human features.

Radical democracy is also a product of the breakdown of the post-Second World War social democratic consensus and is thus opposed to the New Right, its doctrine of the free market, its nationalist cultural conservatism and populist hostility to 'minority' ethnic and sexual groups and its global ambitions. 'Actually existing' liberal democratic government is not a neutral tool of the will of the people, but one attuned to the logic of capitalism and the demands of cultural conservatism. But unlike the revolutionary Left, radical democracy holds that no meaningful form of socialism can be achieved without liberal democratic institutions and freedoms, though the philosophical orientations or ethos which guide them must be radicalised. While the institutions and practices of liberal democracy as it is currently constituted and constrained are inhospitable to radical democracy, the ideals of liberal democracy are not alien to it.

Radical democratic theorists return to the point before Marx gave up hope with liberal democracy, as a result of which the Marxist tradition has tended to overlook its advantages and strengths. Radical democracy entails furthering the democratic revolutions of the past, thus continuing the struggles for democratisation that tended to run out of steam when civil and political rights seemed to have been achieved. Civil and political rights were not granted by the liberal state but won in hard struggles by the labour, women's and civil rights movements. As Slavoj Žižek points out, most of the demands at the end of *The Communist Manifesto* are today part of the liberal democratic consensus.[2] Yet, radical democratic theory does not wish to go as far as Marx and many of his followers did in considering liberal democracy *per se* to be a fraud in the sense

Radical democratic possibilities

that its ideals are unrealisable under capitalism and hence ideological. According to the story I am telling, Žižek's Leninist turn, in which liberal parliamentary democracy is reduced to being capitalism's political form, and Jacobin terror is endorsed, takes him beyond the scope of radical democracy and into revolutionary socialism.[3] Sarah Kay poses the question on Žižek's behalf of whether liberalism is better than totalitarianism.[4] The answer for me and for radical democratic theory is a resounding 'yes!'

Radical democracy is democratic socialist, in that it holds that democratic control of the economy is both desirable and possible (though very difficult on a global or transnational level). Socialism in this sense means social or popular (not state) government of the economy, which could bring about the conditions in which the ideals of liberal democracy could be achieved. Radical democracy thus inhabits a tricky terrain between faith in the realisation of democratic ideals under capitalist conditions and revolutionary disdain for democracy that turns into disdain for the people whose emancipation is at stake. Radical democratic theorists of abundance and of lack, however, (who have no monopoly to the term 'radical democracy'), tend to be drawn towards these two poles. Theorists of abundance such as Bill Connolly and Jane Bennett often seem to imply that democracy's ideals can be achieved by cultivating an 'ethics of generosity', without suggesting anything by way of a collective anti-capitalist political strategy to change the minds of citizens and elites. Theorists of lack such as Žižek, by contrast, dismiss the new social movements as a 'marginal disturbance' in the absence of party organisation, insisting that today's 'working class', as in Lenin's time, needs the 'traumatic experience' or 'foreign kernel' of the Party, acting as its analyst, to become revolutionary, because it is never 'fully itself'.[5] The abundant version of radical democratic theory offers the better hope of fulfilling democratic ideals on condition that it is articulated with a theory of hegemony to give it a political strategy.

Radical democracy in a general sense has often distinguished itself from conventional democracy by defining itself in terms of direct or participatory democracy. Behind those ideas lies a notion of popular democracy, in the sense of people making their own laws and governing themselves. Popular democracy has always competed with other modes of liberal democracy that became democratic only because of popular pressure. Whereas direct, participatory democracy locates sovereignty with the people, as a sum of all wills, as consensual democratic will-formation or as the general will, conventional democracy detaches sovereignty from the people. Sovereignty might be said to rest with the body of representatives of the people, such as the British Parliament, or to be dispersed in mixed government or the separate powers. Conventional liberal democracy finds ways to mediate popular sovereignty through institutions that prevent the people from ruling itself. According to radical democracy in this general sense, democracy should be genuinely popular, living up to Abraham

Lincoln's wonderful sound bite: 'of the people, by the people, and for the people'.

Radical democracy and the non-identity of the people and its government

The versions of radical democratic theory in this volume, whether theories of lack or abundance, have some qualms about the version of direct, participatory, radical democracy outlined above. As the editors of the volume explain in their introduction, radical democratic theory is distinguished from liberal theory because of its alertness to the ubiquity of the political and insistence on 'a difference that goes beyond the dualism of identity and difference'. There are two ways in which the theories of radical democracy uphold their 'slogan' that 'difference constitutes identity' in respect of popular democracy.[6] First, 'the subject' of popular democracy, 'the people', is never identical to itself, but is a subject constituted by difference. All attempts to define it singularly as the bearer of sovereignty (such as 'the nation', or 'the general will') obscure (that is, de-politicise) not only the ways in which the identity of 'the people' is constituted through exclusion of its others, but also the differences among and between 'the people' (class antagonisms, ethnic domination, sexual oppression).

Second, the government and the governed are never identical. 'The people' that is not identical to itself is therefore never sovereign. Radical democratic theorists of abundance and lack deny the possibility of 'the people' ruling itself in accordance with liberal, communitarian or nationalist principles of popular sovereignty, because 'the people' does not exist as an entity. It is neither the sum of all individuals who have come together in a social contract, nor a collective historical or racial being that is more than the sum of individual citizens. This gap between ruler and ruled in democracy is certainly recognised by liberal, representative democratic theory, which regards it as a blessing that the 'will of the people' (if such a thing exists) is mediated through a body of elected representatives.

Unlike liberal democratic theories, radical democratic theorists of abundance and lack do not regard individual citizens, the state, political elites or institutions as self-identical agents. The democratic gap is not between 'the people' and 'the government', but is constitutive of the democratic relation itself. These forms of radical democratic theory take the lack of finality of the democratic relation as the concrete condition for the lack of finality institutionalised by democracy. Democracy has radical potential, cherished by theorists of abundance and lack, in that it institutionalises changes of law, policy, leadership, collective identities and shared values. Just as the legitimacy of democracy cannot be grounded in the sovereignty of the people if 'the people' does not exist as a unitary subject, so can the legitimacy of democracy not rest on the solidity and unity of the autonomous individual self, individual rights or on any other principles that precede the democratic relation itself. Political entities, institutions and practices do not exist until they are made, their shape being determined not by values that transcend our world but by what we humans make of that which is in the world.

The democratic openness mentioned above does not guarantee that democracy will tend toward popular rule of the people by the people or the realisation of the liberal democratic ideals of liberty and equality. Democratic openness is merely a condition of possibility for the ongoing contestation of who the people are, who should govern and legislate, how the economy should be governed and so on. Democratic openness also does not guarantee that popular rule will be exercised in the ways that revolutionary socialists would prefer, or even that popular governance of the economy would be preferred at all times of popular rule to a neo-liberal market economy. All that democratic openness guarantees is that when 'the people's' identity, the nature of democracy and its ideals or the proper way to govern society and the economy are said to be finalised, to transcend or precede the democratic relation, or to be natural, then that which should be determined democratically has been depoliticised and democracy has been curtailed. Popular democracy as understood by theorists of lack and abundance is never finally achieved, because it must always be ongoing, always deciding again that which has been decided before.

Theories of abundance and lack, cultural populists and pessimists

This volume is premised on a fundamental theoretical distinction, not only between radical and liberal democratic theory (to which I have added a distinction between radical theory in general and in the sense used in this volume), but also within radical theory, between ontological imaginaries of abundance and lack. The differences between theorists of abundance and lack make the ontology of lack an unlikely intellectual resource for radical democracy. I am more concerned with the political than theoretical differences between radical democrats, which can best be understood as a difference of political mood, or a different estimation of the political possibilities of achieving democracy, which Jane Bennett defines as 'affective constellations'.[7] These differences are analogous to a well-worn but fundamental division in cultural studies, between cultural pessimists and cultural optimists or populists. Drawing on this analogy (which does not work perfectly) helps to grasp the political stakes of the debate conducted in this volume between ontologies of abundance and lack. It is also useful for making the theoretical move of disarticulating hegemony from theories of lack and connecting it to theories of abundance, thereby giving a political direction to what otherwise remain as open-ended possibilities for democracy.

Jon Simons

Cultural pessimism and theories of lack

A key (but not defining) overlapping point of difference between theorists of abundance and theorists of lack, and between critical cultural populists and pessimists, is that, in each case, the former often consider popular culture to be a resource of abundant creative forces for radical democracy, while the latter consider it to be an obstacle. Cultural pessimists and theorists of lack regard popular, mediated culture as ideology, or as late capitalist industry, that prevents the possibility of democratic control of human destiny. Critical cultural populists and theorists of abundance and hegemony regard popular culture as at least a site of contestation, in which, in spite of the uneven character of the struggle, that possibility is fought for.

Frankfurt School theorists Adorno and Horkheimer presented the pessimists' credentials for cultural studies. Their focus is on the commodified, fetishist character of popular culture and the capitalist conditions of cultural production and consumption. Democracy that operates under the conditions of such 'mass culture' cannot be genuine, since it offers the same ideological forms of false consensus and fantasy or manufactured needs fulfilment as commodified culture. By organising conformism and promoting a substitute gratification, the culture industry 'impedes the development of autonomous, independent individuals who ... would be the precondition for a democratic society'.[8]

Lacanian theorists of lack share in this cultural pessimism and in the conception that popular mediated culture is ideological, though there are theoretical differences between them, notably in respect of ideology. The media are regarded as an obstacle to the development of radical democracy in that they enthral the populace with idols, with unfulfillable fantasies of collective and personal satisfaction. The media lure the populace into unrealisable attempts to fill the lack and attain the Real (of fullness of identity, of satisfaction of needs, of popular sovereignty, of freedom) by re-presenting the absent Real.

The fantasies disseminated by the media structure an economy of desire and 'administration of enjoyment' on which 'the hegemony of the market depends'. Advertising, for example, on which most contemporary media depend, works with experiences of social lack, whose 'condition of possibility' is 'the prohibition ... of a "mythical" pre-symbolic enjoyment (*jouissance*) which stands at the Oedipal roots of (social) subjectivity'. Advertising produces fantasies projected on to a particular product that 'is offered to us as an object that can satisfy our desires'. Though the product cannot fulfil our desires or realise the fantasy, that is not a failure of advertising as ideology, as 'through fantasy, we learn how to desire', that is, by postponing it indefinitely. Some significant points to note here are, first, that the theory of lack treats desire or *jouissance* as an inevitable feature of subjectivity, which is administered and structured by capital, by

Radical democratic possibilities

racism and nationalism, often through the media, to reproduce themselves. Second, the logic of the deferment of desire, that is entailed by lack, by the non-identity of the subject with its desire, is also an ideological operation that promises 'an encounter with the lacking *jouissance* in the future' (equivalent in effect to blaming a hated Other for the lack). Deferment of desire sustains the fantasy that desire can be fulfilled. Third, because desire cannot ever be denied or fulfilled, ideology critique is unlikely in itself 'to effect a displacement in the social subject's psychic economy'. Subjects are so enthralled by their own unfulfillable desire that they 'cannot help themselves; they cannot stop repeating'. While an 'alternative administration of enjoyment' is conceivable, it depends on a post-analysis, disillusioned way of relating to lack.[9]

The radical democratic theory of lack is a useful analytical tool for analysing the ways in which 'the people' is mistakenly taken to be identical with itself and with its government (as in nationalist and totalitarian regimes). But the theory of lack is so good at explaining why people enjoy their own oppression that change seems impossible. Alternatively, theorists of lack may be tempted, as is Žižek, by a revolutionary vanguard party helping those who cannot help themselves. After all, a revolution of desire is needed, aimed at the whole field of *jouissance*, so that new desiring subjects can exist. Incremental and partial transformations seem unlikely and untenable so long as the old structure and economy of desire remain intact.

Pessimism is built in to the ontology of lack because the ideal of radical popular democracy, according to which 'the people' is identical to itself as both that which governs and that which is governed, is impossible, yet the deferment of that enjoyment sustains the fantasy of liberal democracy. Theorists of lack consider that their form of ideology critique makes visible the impossibility of full democracy. Ideology critique of the cultural products disseminated through the mass media and the very forms of mass media (especially television and cinema) shows that lack and impossibility are constitutive of popular democracy. Rather than regarding that as a pessimistic approach to democracy, theorists of lack consider radical democracy to be an institutionalisation of lack, of the non-identity of governed and government, that both precludes the totalitarian identification of ruler and ruled (as in the fascist perversion of democracy) and the illusion that liberal democratic government can re-present the people. But that leaves the theory of lack as a negative radical attitude, unable to propose forms of popular democracy in place of the illusionary forms it criticises. As the editors argue in the introduction to this volume, theories of lack remain theories limited to criticising those ideologies seeking to cover up the constitutivity of lack and of distortion when a particular signifier stands in for the universal.[10] Theorists of lack would regard any sense of popular power as an ideological misrecognition. Similarly, cultural pessimists argue that individuals are alienated from their own desires and needs, which have 'already been suppressed by the control of individual consciousness'.[11] Theorists of lack are political pessimists, for whom democracy can never be achieved, even contingently and temporarily.[12]

The theory of lack shares with cultural pessimists a low regard for the possibilities of radical agency. Cultural pessimists would maintain that corporate, commodified culture systematically overwhelms the agency of cultural consumers. The degree of powerlessness experienced within the culture industry is expressed in the last sentence of Adorno and Horkheimer's famous essay on the culture industry: 'The triumph of advertising in the culture industry is that consumers feel compelled to buy and use its products even though they see through them.'[13] Even though consumers are not deceived ideologically, they cannot resist the power of the culture industry. This view is echoed in Žižek's notion of the fantasy structuring social reality according to which 'they know that, in their activity, they are following an illusion, but still, they are doing it'.[14]

Lacanian theorists of ontological lack (when that theory is disarticulated from a theory of hegemony) share with cultural pessimists the view that the people do not have the capacity or agency to overcome the conditions of their own oppression and exploitation and thus to bring about their own emancipation. Perhaps unwittingly, the underlying Borg message is that 'resistance is futile', because even if the capitalist political-economic system was the historical result of human activity, it has become beyond humans to remake their own history. Or rather, the only humans who could remake history are the revolutionary vanguards.

There is, however, a hugely significant difference between cultural pessimists and theorists of lack. Cultural pessimists are also pessimists about democracy, but not for ontological reasons, but because of the social, political and cultural conditions identified with capitalism. Just as Marx argued that political emancipation would not itself bring human emancipation, so pessimistic cultural theorists argue that what is described as popular or mass culture is nothing like 'a culture that arises spontaneously from the masses themselves, the contemporary form of popular art'.[15] In both the case of mass culture and the case of democratic politics under capitalist conditions, the enlightened, emancipatory potential of popular action is frustrated. Should those conditions change (through historical necessity or political struggle), then genuinely popular culture and democracy would be achievable. Because lack is perceived ontologically in the Lacanian schema, however, the absence of identity of people and popular sovereignty is grounds for permanent pessimism. As lack is a feature of desire as such, then alienation is not, as Adorno would claim, a result of current conditions of capitalist domination.[16] This pessimism explains the curious mix in Žižek's politics between pragmatic acceptance of neo-liberalism and his Leninism.[17]

Yet the radical democratic theory of lack insists that it does have a constructive feature, which, as the editors of this volume argue, is provided by the Gramscian notion of hegemony. I argue, though, that the link between lack and hegemony is contingent. Hegemony is a tool for understanding both how popular sovereignty is blocked by the ideological power of capital and how 'the people' might be constituted out of different elements that are articulated into a contingent, contestable and temporary whole. Readers familiar with debates and trends in cultural studies (or with Gramsci) will probably already be asking themselves why or how hegemony should be associated with cultural pessimism. The use of the term 'hegemony' in cultural studies signifies that however strong the ideological power of commodified culture may be, that does not amount to domination. Hegemony is always contingent, its articulations always contestable by counter-hegemony. The abundance of popular energies always exceeds the limits of domination. The adoption of 'hegemony' in British cultural studies, especially by Stuart Hall, was designed to counter the cultural pessimism of the Frankfurt School thesis about the culture industry as an implacable tool of mass deception. While Hall stands somewhere between the extremes of cultural pessimism and populism, his work consistently makes the case that the culture industry cannot completely dominate popular culture, and that popular culture is both 'where hegemony arises and ... one of the places where socialism might be constituted'.[18] For Gramsci too, while the analysis of hegemony might provoke 'pessimism of the intelligence', it is also cause for 'optimism of the will'.[19] Radical democratic theory needs some of each, but perhaps more of the latter.

Theorists of radical democracy should take the hint from cultural theory that there is no necessary articulation between the Lacanian ontology of lack and the Gramscian notion of hegemony, as there is a case for unstitching these two theoretical principles. Laclau and Mouffe do state that: 'This original lack is precisely what the hegemonic practices try to fill in.'[20] But the context of their introduction of Lacanian terminology is to argue against the structural determination that was the orthodoxy of the Second International and for the principle of historical contingency. The principle that they take from Lacan is a broader post-structuralist one of the contingent connection between signifier and signified, which they translate into political terms. The 'hegemonic' version of radical democratic theory does not rest on an ontology of lack, but an historical 'empiricism' (in a materialist sense) of contingency. Indeed, at the time, Laclau and Mouffe seemed to owe as much to Derrida as to Lacan. It would appear not to be the ontology of lack that shapes the contingency at the heart of the radical democratic theory of hegemony, but 'the absence of the transcendental signified [that] extends the domain and play of signification infinitely'.[21]

Laclau and Mouffe introduce Derrida's notion of the 'surplus of meaning' as an *example* of several currents of post-structuralist thought that 'have insisted on the impossibility of fixing ultimate meanings'. For them, Lacan's notion of nodal points explains the 'partial fixations' that 'arrest the flow of differences' and enables 'society' to take contingent form. So, although 'society never manages to be identical to itself' the partial fixation, or articulation, of social relations '*proceeds from the openness of the social, a result, in turn, of the constant overflowing of every discourse by the infinitude of the field of discursivity*'.[22] The overriding logic in their account of hegemony is thus not one of lack but excess. The poststructuralist sense, that meaning exceeds intended and official interpretations, was adopted in cultural studies to argue that the messages of cultural products are not always interpreted as intended by different categories of cultural consumers. The excess of meanings in popular culture translates politically into the abundance of popular energies that can exceed the forces of domination. The radical democratic theory of hegemony can and should be articulated with 'abundance'. That theoretical move significantly changes the balance between theories of lack and abundance, leaving lack to Lacan. What matters most to counter-hegemonic formations is not the way they coalesce around nodal points (empty signifiers) and are constituted antagonistically in relation to an outside (though this does occur), but the abundance of social resources whose articulation is contingent and underdetermined. Coalitions are not totalities, which is why they are so difficult to manage, just like democratic polities.

Cultural populism and theories of abundance

Theorists of abundance share with cultural populists an optimistic view of the capacities of the people for resistance to domination, if not ultimately to form a counter-hegemonic force that overcomes hegemony. According to the 'populist' perspective, the apparent one-way technological flow of the mediation of culture is resisted by the active interpretation of messages by the people who retain their ideological or cultural agency. The way the populists figure popular culture indicates that they consider their agency to be diverse and multiple rather than unified or self-identical. Fiske describes the necessary features for popularity in television, which apply to other mass media and to democratic politics too. From the side of the audiences, he notes their activity in producing a range of meanings and pleasures in relation to a variety of social positions. He also notes that television can only be popular, appealing to many different audiences, if it is polysemic and prone to semiotic excess. Although corporate media producers may seek to control polysemy and ensure that their message is decoded the way they encoded it, their products are only popular if they allow for meanings that show the contradictions of capitalism or the antagonisms that fissure any hegemonic articulation. Hence, television 'promotes and provokes a network of resistances to its own power whose attempt to homogenize and hegemonize breaks down on the instability and multiplicity of its meanings and pleasures'.[23]

Radical democratic possibilities

The cultural populists thus, to some extent, parallel the ontology that conceives of difference in relation to abundance understood as 'networks of materiality, flows of energy, processes of becoming, and experimenting modes of affirmation'.[24] They do so partly by considering the differences that exist between cultural elites and 'the people', but also by conceiving of popular culture in terms of pleasure, polysemy and excess. The 'popular' is not a single taste or style attributable to an undifferentiated mass, but a multitude of tastes, which resist elite prescriptions of 'good taste' and find pleasure in the abundance of popular culture by appropriating it for 'the people's' purposes. There is some correspondence between the figuration of the 'popular' in cultural studies and Michael Hardt and Antonio Negri's figuration of 'the multitude' (a representative ontology of abundance). Popular resistance to corporate media culture might be said to 'reside ... in the creative and productive capacities of the multitude' from which arises 'a horizon of activities, resistances, wills, and desires that refuse the hegemonic order, propose lines of flight, and forge alternative constitutive itineraries'. For Hardt and Negri the multitude does not stand outside Empire but, from the point of view of the ontology of abundance, is immanent to it as the 'real productive force of our social world' in relation to which Empire is parasitical. Although Empire dominates the multitude, regulating, disciplining and exploiting its 'productivity and creativity', the 'power of the multitude is the productive force that sustains Empire'. They go as far as to say that: 'The multitude called Empire into being.'[25] In doing so, they go further than to claim, as cultural populists do, that the people always resist domination by capitalism. But the key feature of the common ground that both cultural populists and theorists of abundance share is that they attribute a significant share of the abundant productive and creative forces in the world to 'the people' or multitude. 'Resistance is fertile' is the message of both cultural populists and theorists of class and other anti-hegemonic agency.[26]

In cultural studies, the populists reacted against the Marxist political economists, whom they regarded as pessimists, because they seemed to hold out no hope (or only a distant utopian hope) of social and cultural change, while analysing the effectiveness of domination. Populists went in search of consumer agency, finding it everywhere, in sub-cultures, in decoding of cultural texts contrary to their encoding, in re-appropriation of fashion. Cultural populists are confident that consumers of popular culture make their own meanings and find their own pleasures, and that there is ubiquitous evidence of popular resistance to dominant meanings disseminated by the culture industry. Similarly, theorists of abundance accentuate the possibility that an articulated popular hegemony or a productive and creative multitude could resist oppression or govern its own destiny.

Jane Bennett, one of the theorists of abundance, argues against Adorno and Horkheimer's 'mass deception' thesis saying that they have over-coded with a disembodied intellectualism the active, affective and bodily relationship of consumers to cultural commodities. For them, the pleasures consumers experience with cultural commodities mean only affirmation of domination and a denial of the effort of critical thought required for demystification. They overlook what Hardt and Negri would call the productivity and creativity of the multitude that Bennett understands, in terms of a Deleuzian 'enchanted materialism', to include animated commodities. Adorno and Horkheimer overlook the possibility that 'commodity fascination' does not (only) dull human critical reflection and the capacity to resist. They do not see that 'part of the energy needed to challenge injustice comes from the reservoir of enchantment'.[27] Bennett's ontology of abundance lends support to the radical project opposed to the economic system of commodity fetishism by disarticulating the commodity from fetishism and articulating it with enchantment.[28] She argues that the energies required for radical democratic practice inhere in popular culture, even in its commodified form. I take that also to be the thrust of Hall's conviction that socialism might arise from within popular culture.

Bennett's optimism about the potential to be found in commodity culture parallels the optimism of the cultural populists. This parallel can also be observed in the similarity of criticisms that are made of cultural populists and of the optimism of political theories of abundance. These criticisms are by no means groundless, so the optimism needs to be tempered and an appropriate balance found between cultural pessimists and populists, as well as between theorists of lack and abundance. Populists were criticised for underestimating the constraints imposed by the capitalist system on the agency and creativity of consumers in their enjoyment of the satisfaction of needs that cannot actually be fulfilled. In part, then, the critique of the populists draws on the psychoanalytic theory of lack, of desires that can never be fulfilled.[29] Most criticisms of cultural populism, however, focus on its inattention to political economy and the constraints that the means and modes of production of culture impose on its consumption. The populism that was intended to locate power and agency among audiences and consumers had become uncritical, arguing that popular culture is fashioned by the consumers in their use of it.[30] The radical intent behind populism in cultural studies had become indistinguishable from conservative populism, which is a 'celebration of popular culture' as expressed and 'legitimated by the evidence of the market'.[31] For instance, Jim McGuigan argues in respect of tabloid journalism that 'popular pleasure is routinely articulated through oppressive ideologies that operate in fertile chauvinistic ground'.[32] Populists also overlook their responsibility as cultural critics to discriminate between instances of popular culture, and not simply to assume that all 'popular cultural goods and services are somehow the same in the empowering value'.[33]

Cultural populists, then, have rightly been criticised for being uncritically populist. Although populists such as Fiske are 'aware of countervailing commercial forces which constrain the interpretations that any cultural item may acquire',[34] the overall impression given by reading much cultural populist research is that Donald Duck has been so deconstructed that global capitalism must have no hold whatsoever on popular consciousness. Similarly, theorists of abundance, for example Hardt and Negri, are criticised for romanticising the power of the multitude compared with empire. On the one hand, they leave the definition of the multitude rather vague, because it is a multiple, rhizomatic entity, but, on the other hand, they endow it with a singular purpose and agency. The question of how the energies of the multitude are organised counter-hegemonically in relation to empire is left unanswered. In Bennett's treatment of a *GAP* advert, she suggests that consumers' pleasure may not be their assent to cultural-economic hegemony, but also a pleasure in the abundant creativity and energy of film-makers and dancers. Perhaps, but why not write also about the organised energy of the anti-sweat campaign that targeted the way that *GAP*, among others, exploited the energy of the workers producing the advertised clothes? For the reservoir of energy to realise any of its radical potential, the energy must be channelled appropriately by those who feel it, not only toward enhancing their own pleasure, but also in combating capitalism.

Democratic possibilities of popular media

There is a middle ground between cultural pessimists and populists for which the notions of hegemony and counter-hegemony are crucial. The British or Birmingham School of cultural studies views culture 'both as being actively created out of the available resources and as constitutive of political relations'.[35] Stuart Hall deploys both some elements of Frankfurt School theory and a Gramscian understanding of hegemony. His work is able to show that there is 'popular' agency and that popular culture can be a resource for radical democracy (or socialism, to use his preferred phrase), without slipping into a romanticised and uncritical populism. His perspective is one between 'the two alternative poles of that dialectic – containment/resistance' or 'pure "autonomy" or total encapsulation'.[36] Ordinary people are not cultural dupes, yet the effects of cultural domination should neither be denied nor simply read off from the capitalist modes of cultural organisation.

Hall's preferred yet uneasy definition of 'popular' 'refers to that alliance of classes and forces which constitute the "popular classes". The culture of the oppressed, the excluded classes ... The people versus the power bloc: this is the central line of contradiction around which the terrain of culture is polarised.'[37] It is this antagonistic relation which makes sense of a descriptive definition of 'popular' as what the people do, because the power relations matter, not the shifting boundaries between and contents of 'popular' and 'elite'. Moreover, whereas the pessimist perspective regards popular culture as a site of class domination, Hall figures it as a site of a struggle, 'necessarily uneven and unequal, by the dominant culture, constantly to disorganise and reorganise popular culture'. As a result, popular cultural forms are contradictory rather than coherent: 'alongside the false appeals, the foreshortenings, the trivialisation and short circuits, there are also elements of recognition and identification'.[38]

Indeed, it is the question of the constitution (and conditions of possibilities of), the agency of the popular that prompts my turn to a theoretical approach that is sensitive to the political significance of both the constraints on and capacities of popular agency. A Foucauldian approach to media as technologies of government leads to a position somewhere between the populists and pessimist positions in the cultural studies debate, though perhaps somewhat closer to the former. Similarly, a Foucauldian position lies, politically, somewhere between the pessimism of lack and the optimism of abundance. A reconceptualisation of media technologies as political technologies highlights the government of the public, meaning the constitution and regulation of political publics, in liberal democratic regimes. Government in the Foucauldian sense cannot be reduced to control or domination, in this case of political publics by the media or the elites that manage them. Government implies regulation, by the institutional and technological forces of the media, of the conduct of political publics which have been constituted as political agents by those same forces. The political public of representative democratic regimes are mediated publics, in that they exist and are constituted as publics through the mediation of technologies of mass media. The public sphere of democratic politics is thus part of, and central to, the mediated sphere of popular culture. Putting the same point in other terms, the political publics of democratic regimes are governed through popular culture, by means of technologies of mediation. The public is only amenable to representation in the form of an electorate, which is an effect of technical organisation that can mediate between people at a distance from each other. The key point of this analysis is that the public does not exist prior to or outside of its constitution. The 'public' is an effect of the construction, maintenance and articulation of audiences by media technologies, which mediate between individuals and groups.

Media technologies work in two directions: they allow the public to govern the government to some extent, at the very least by exchanging one set of representatives for another; and they require the government to constitute the adult population as a political public amenable to representation. If the varieties of liberalism are different governmentalities of different forms of 'population', then they are also various governmentalities of popular consent. Just as media networks compete for larger chunks of market share, those agencies seeking popular political consent try to occupy a position from which they can speak in the name of 'the people' or 'the public interest'. In other words, the ultimate political aim of media technologies is to constitute popular audiences as a 'nation', a 'oneness of imagination that binds citizens to states', even though some audiences are transnational. Although there are many niche audiences as well as audiences made up of broader sectors of the population, and hence although 'the public' is governed differentially, '[c]ultural citizenship becomes the integrative forum, through processes of governmentality inextricably intertwined with tracking the popular'.[39] The integrated national audience is the terrain in which people become citizens by means of cultural practices and media technologies that connect them.

It is difficult for any political agent in advanced liberalism to organise either media production or its audiences in a way that constitutes the public as 'the people', especially in these transnational times. It often takes dramatic contingent events to bring such convergence about, such as the death of Princess Diana in Britain or 9/11 in the United States. Nonetheless, when that does occur, when a relation of democratic equivalence is articulated across a wide assemblage of audiences, the media organise the articulation. As the pessimists claim, such articulation may take the form of a hegemony organised by capitalist media to reproduce class domination. But as the populists believe, it is also an articulation through popular culture.

In Foucauldian terms, the popular public readerships of the tabloid news are constituted with their agency as subjects of the power relations that traverse state, market and culture. It is not only culture that is necessarily contradictory (a point that is argued by cultural populists), but also agency, because the very power relations that constitute subjects with agency also locate them in positions of domination and subordination. A Foucauldian, governmentalist approach differs from both cultural populists and Hall in its focus on the constitution of 'the popular' as cultural styles and the 'public' as both forms of agency and objects of government. The popular public has no agency or autonomy that is not constituted by governmental technologies, including the media. But, at the same time, that there is no guarantee, as some populists might like to believe, that the popular public will be constituted as an agent of resistance to dominant culture, it is also by no means inevitable that it will be governed as a passive consumer of commodified culture. One is reminded of Foucault's dictum that 'where there is power, there is resistance'.[40] Resistance to hegemonic or elite representations exists in the inconsistencies between different media producers, different genres within media, different types of media, between media producers and media consumers, as well as between different audiences. Publics and audiences, both elite and popular, act on each other in efforts to conduct the actions of others. In democratic governance the actions of elites are governed and thus constrained by each other and the resistance of popular publics.

Even in their current states, both liberal representative democracy and commercialised popular culture contain the potential forces that can render democracy and culture truly popular. There are abundant forces circulating in both liberal democracy and popular culture, forces that are governed quite successfully by both the political elites and the culture industry. But because both liberal democracy and the acknowledgement of popular tastes are the results of popular struggles, then political and cultural hegemony is not secure. Among the forces that both political and cultural elites attempt to organise and govern is affect, which directs the energies and investments of people in the world in which they live, in their investments in identities, in their judgements and in politics.[41] Cultural pessimists and theorists of lack focus on the ways that affect is manipulated by elites to channel popular energies in conservative and repressive directions. But as Bennett points out, they turn their back on the creative, energising power of affect, which is needed to challenge injustice.[42] On the other hand, if the radical potential of abundant popular energies is to be realised, it must be organised through popular culture into counter-hegemonic forms. Theorists of abundance, as well as cultural populists, need a notion of hegemony to understand how popular energies are currently misdirected and how those energies can be organised for radical effect.

Organising affect both occurs in popular culture and is needed for radical politics, for resistance and transformation. At the same time, affective energy is currently obviously misdirected. I argue for a notion of radical, popular democracy that is already immanent in existing forms of liberal democracy and popular culture, forms of which cultural pessimists and theorists of lack are rightly critical. But too much critique is not good for the radical spirit, because in its attack on the misdirection of affective energies, it tends to attack affective energy all together. Cultural pessimists and theorists of lack admittedly play only a small cultural role in undervaluing the radical potential of popular energies compared with other media. Though their work has value as critique, this is only part of the radical process. While acknowledging the significance of radical critique of existing forms of democracy and popular culture, cultural populists and theorists of abundance offer the better cultural resource for radical, popular democracy. The latter have the intellectual tools to acknowledge the political resource of popular energies, which have brought democratic revolutions as far as they have, and will one day, perhaps tomorrow, carry them further.

Notes

1 I would like to thank the British Academy for funding my travel to present a version of this chapter at the American Political Science Association Annual Meeting, Chicago 2004, and the editors of this volume for their insightful and constructive comments on earlier versions of the chapter.
2 S. Žižek, 'Repeating Lenin', www.lacan.com/replenin.htm, accessed 11 May 2004.

Radical democratic possibilities

3 Žižek, 'Repeating Lenin'. Žižek does not identify himself as a radical democrat, because he holds that 'it's simply a more radical version of the standard liberal-democratic game'. See S. Žižek and R. Salecl, 'Lacan in Slovenia', in P. Osborne (ed.), *A Critical Sense: Interviews with Intellectuals* (London: Routledge, 1996), pp. 37–8.
4 S. Kay, *Žižek: A Critical Introduction* (Cambridge: Polity, 2003), p. 149.
5 Žižek, 'Repeating Lenin'.
6 L. Thomassen and L. Tønder, 'Introduction', in this volume, pp. 3.
7 J. Bennett, *The Enchantment of Modern Life: Attachments, Crossings, and Ethics* (Princeton, NJ: Princeton University Press, 2001), p. 128.
8 T. Adorno 'Culture industry reconsidered', in J. M. Bernstein (ed.), *The Culture Industry: Selected Essays on Mass Culture* (London: Routledge, 1991), p. 92
9 Y. Stavrakakis, 'Jacques Lacan', in J. Simons (ed.), *Contemporary Critical Theorists: From Lacan to Said* (Edinburgh: Edinburgh University Press, 2004), pp. 28–31.
10 Thomassen and Tønder, 'Introduction' in this volume, p. 5–13.
11 M. Horkheimer and T. Adorno, *Dialectic of Enlightenment* (New York: Continuum, 1993), p. 121.
12 See also A. Robinson 'The politics of lack', *The British Journal of Politics and International Relations*, 6:2 (2004), 259–69.
13 Horkheimer and Adorno, *Dialectic of Enlightenment*, p. 167.
14 S. Žižek, *The Sublime Object of Ideology* (London: Verso, 1989), p. 33.
15 Adorno, 'Culture industry reconsidered', p. 85.
16 See S. Žižek, 'Eastern Europe's republics of Gilead', *New Left Review*, 183 (September/October 1990), 56.
17 See Žižek and Salecl, 'Lacan in Slovenia', p. 32.
18 S. Hall, 'Notes on deconstructing "the popular"', in J. Storey (ed.), *Cultural Theory and Popular Culture*, 2nd edition (London: Prentice Hall, 1998), p. 453.
19 This maxim by Romain Rolland was used by Gramsci as a slogan in the newspaper, *Ordine Nuovo*.
20 E. Laclau and C. Mouffe, *Hegemony and Socialist Strategy: Towards a Radical Democratic Politics* (London: Verso, 1985), p. 88, note 1.
21 J. Derrida cited in *ibid.*, p. 112.
22 *Ibid.*, pp. 111–13 (emphasis in original).
23 J. Fiske, *Television Culture* (London: Methuen, 1987), p. 324.
24 Thomassen and Tønder, 'Introduction', in this volume, p. 5f.
25 M. Hardt and A. Negri, *Empire* (Cambridge, MA: Harvard University Press, 2000), pp. 47f, 62, 61, 43.
26 The slogan 'Resistance is Fertile' appears in *New Internationalist* 365 (March 2004), 28.
27 Bennett, *The Enchantment of Modern Life*, pp. 118, 119, 128.
28 No doubt there are those for whom Bennett's call to 'reform commodity culture to render it more just' (*ibid.*, p. 113) is precisely reformist rather radical.
29 See for example J. Williamson, *Consuming Passions* (London: Marion Boyars, 1986).
30 See J. McGuigan, *Cultural Populism* (London: Routledge, 1992).
31 J. Street, *Politics and Popular Culture* (Cambridge: Polity Press, 1997), p. 152.
32 McGuigan, *Cultural Populism*, p. 174.
33 S. Frith, 'The good, the bad and the indifferent', *Diacritics*, 21:4 (1991), 105.
34 Street, *Politics and Popular Culture*, p. 160.
35 *Ibid.*, pp. 146, 130f.
36 Hall, 'Notes on deconstructing "the popular"', pp. 443, 447.
37 *Ibid.*, p. 452

38 Ibid., pp. 447–8.
39 T. Miller, *Technologies of Truth: Cultural Citizenship and the Popular Media* (Minneapolis, MN: University of Minnesota Press, 1998), pp. 28, 250f.
40 M. Foucault, *The History of Sexuality, Vol. I* (Harmondsworth: Penguin, 1978).
41 L. Grossberg, *We Gotta Get Out of this Place: Popular Conservatism and Postmodern Culture* (London: Routledge, 1992).
42 Bennett, *The Enchantment of Modern Life*, p. 128.

10 • *Torben Bech Dyrberg*

Radical and plural democracy: in defence of right/left and public reason

The political and democracy

IN HER preface to *Dimensions of Radical Democracy*, Mouffe continued the argument she and Laclau launched in *Hegemony and Socialist Strategy*, stating that 'the objective of the Left should be the extension and deepening of the democratic revolution initiated two hundred years ago'.[1] The traditional objective of the Left – socialism – was based on struggles against economic inequality and political domination, where the former was seen as the cause of the latter. But if there were forms of inequality and domination that could not be led back to the economy, it would be unwarranted to claim that a socialist revolution would automatically abolish them. The problem of the Left lay in its inability to account for the autonomy of the political, identified by the democratic revolution, thus making it blind not only to some of the most heinous political crimes in the twentieth century committed in its name, but also to the 'ordinary' repression of rights and attempts to foster democratic movements in communist dictatorships.

Today, the interest in the political seems to go together with a wish to reinvigorate a leftist engagement in extending and deepening democracy, which would seem to indicate that the political and democracy are two sides of the same coin. Democracy is based on the autonomy of the political, which is, in turn, underpinned by democracy. This is not a call to abandon socialist objectives, but to situate them within an overriding concern for democracy. The aim of this alternative strategy for the Left, which is indebted to the pluralist tradition,[2] is to give political voice to any struggle against inequality and domination by creating a political perspective that is 'radically libertarian and infinitely more ambitious in its objectives than that of the classic left'.[3]

The political imaginary of radical and plural democracy, as envisaged by Laclau and Mouffe, is inseparable from their argument concerning the constitutive nature of the political. In the argument presented below, I will not consider radical and plural democracy as one among several other conceptions on offer within democratic theory or radical politics. Rather, the claim is that the democratic insistence on liberty and equality is radical and plural as 'it is not possible to find more radical principles for organizing society'.[4] I will look at the radicalism and pluralism of democracy by focusing on what the autonomy of the political symbolic order means *vis-à-vis* the cultural/religious symbolic order.

In so doing I will focus on the political reversal of a symbolic order structured by cultural/religious codes in which the political has no autonomy.[5] This reversal is implied by the creation of a modern political symbolic order, which attains autonomy by reversing and re-appropriating cultural/religious codes. In the modern era – from the French revolution onwards – the autonomy of the political as an organising matrix of political order is a condition for democracy. A pluralist setting, based on the values of liberty and equality, has been underpinned by the right/left polarity as the only form of political orientation that is able to sustain the autonomy of a democratic political symbolic order.

I will then go on to discuss the radical right, which has gained political influence in recent years and confronts democratic politics with major challenges.[6] By articulating nationalist, racist and populist themes, the radical right moves beyond the right/left polarity. This means that right/left is not assigned the hegemonic task of being the common language for political orientation. The radical right threatens political and democratic values by appealing to nation, culture and the unity of the people as something given prior to politics and which has priority over democracy.

Finally, in contrast to the radical right and, more generally, to discourses 'beyond right/left', I will argue that the right/left polarity has a vital role to play in democratic politics as it sustains the autonomy of the political symbolic order. It is the only type of political orientation that is able to accommodate modern democratic principles of (1) equal political status and equal liberty;[7] (2) pluralism as opposed to monism; and (3) the contingency of identity and signification as opposed to objectivism and fundamentalism. In pursuing this line of thought I will discuss how right/left is able to account for both unity and division, and hence how it is related to public reason based on the political reversal of cultural/religious codes. In my view, radical and plural democracy has to base itself on the autonomy of the political symbolic order and hence on the three principles: political equality, pluralism and contingency.

The political significance of orientational metaphors

In the following, my aim is to discuss the value of the right/left polarity for democracy in relation to three other pairs of orientational metaphors – in/out, up/down and front/back – and to discuss how the articulations among these polarities structure the political terrain.[8] In contrast to a few decades ago, right/left today seems largely unable to capture the imagination of people. If

Radical and plural democracy

right/left cannot articulate the other polarities in a way that hegemonises the political terrain, it will be displaced and political intensity will shift towards the other orientations. Thus its declining significance has gone hand in hand with a political radicalisation along the up/down, front/back and in/out axes. Hierarchical up/down and exclusive in/out orientations represent a democratic problem insofar as they either attack or displace the basic premise of right/left: the mutual recognition and acceptance of differences among agents of equal political status. But the other side of the coin is that the present state of affairs should be seen as a challenge to re-orientate right/left *vis-à-vis* other politically relevant orientations. If this is not done it is hard to see how the Left could become a vibrant pole of identification in today's changing political environment.

Orientational metaphors are politically relevant by structuring identification and discourse. By organising 'a whole system of concepts with respect to one another',[9] they outline the structure of the political terrain and allow individuals to position themselves on this terrain. When power operates at basic levels of understanding and practice and in minute detail (for instance, Foucault's micro-physics of power), it works simultaneously on the individual body and on the body politics in general, feeding bodily experiences into political discourses.[10] Different articulations of metaphors identify political positions and the frontiers between them. The symbolisation of orientation situates the individual in a political terrain, which means that it structures our ability to make a difference.

The idea of discussing four clusters of orientational metaphors is to see power as the structuring of complex strategic situations, which consist of the forces making an impact on a situation, while also being shaped by this situation.[11] In this perspective, focus is on the articulation of limits or frontiers between modalities of power – such as in/out, up/down, front/back and right/left – which structure political identification and map the political terrain. While identification processes articulate various discursive fragments, the ordering of these revolves around these basic forms of orientation, and the structuring of political frontiers is related to how the four pairs of metaphors are articulated with each other. The four pairs of orientational metaphors are structured around:[12]

1 *In/out.* Turns around issues such as member/non-member, us/them, here/there, inclusion/exclusion and important/marginal. Moreover, it involves status, class and sense of belonging (locality, nation, civilisation, and so on).
2 *Up/down.* Deals with, for example, inequality/equality, high/low status, elite/mass, patron/client, active/passive, more/less, in control/being controlled and good/bad.
3 *Front/back.* Concerns time and direction as in modern/tradition, progres-

[169]

sive/reactionary, and state of mind as in open-minded/closed, transparent/obscure and light/dark.
4 *Right/left.* Is the modern democratic polarity in which opposed views are stated and balanced, which is based on the mutual recognition and acceptance of agents having equal political status. Right/left frames and gives voice to the other polarities (for instance, inequality/equality).

I will treat the four sets of polarities as anthropological facts of human existence, which develop gradually in the individual within its first five to six years of existence in the above order of appearance. These terms are employed by each individual as a way to orientate him- or herself to be able to act in an environment of other individuals, society and nature. In each culture they are – according to comparative anthropological studies[13] – invested with dense symbolic significance, which structures social interaction. This means that they play an active role structuring political orientation both at the level of how people orientate themselves politically, and at the societal level where orientations shape trends, developments, social and religious facts and imperatives, habits, traditions and so on. The four pairs of orientational metaphors perform different functions, of course, and they operate differently. For example, in/out orientation might be more basic and more frequently encountered than right/left orientation. This suggests that political identification is structured 'orientationally' and that strategies focusing on in/out have a better chance of making an impact on strong emotional ties than right/left. These orientations have different effects: in/out is more easily associated with something 'existential' and uncompromising than right/left, which not only thrives on opposition, but also on balancing judgements and decisions.

Nevertheless, in the political symbolic order, right/left attains a special status *vis-à-vis* the three other orientational metaphors. The main democratic function of the right/left polarity lies in short-circuiting the domination of the religious/cultural symbolic order in the political realm, and it does so by framing and expressing the other types of orientation. Up/down, for instance, is expressed in the language of right/left because, historically, right has been linked to the defence of high status, privileges and inequality, and left pushes in the direction of equality. Likewise, in/out is voiced in terms of right/left, since right is associated with a restrictive view on civil rights, while left opts for a more inclusive view. Put differently, the stratification of classes, groups and so on, implies an overarching reference point (us). Social class and nation have been particularly strong poles of not only party identification but also of ordinary 'life–political' orientation, both of which operate on the in/out dimension, such as membership and belonging. These poles are supplemented by front/back orientations in both establishment and Left discourses on progress, necessity, rationality, transparency, emancipation and so forth.

Radical and plural democracy

The positive/negative categorisation of opposites provides a basic level of consistency with regard to self- and other-description and suggests that translations among the terms occur within the same cluster of polar opposites. There is a tendency towards congruence among the positive ends of spatial polarities along which self-description and identification are formed, indicating that political struggles are about hegemonising the positive terms. The positive pole is more elaborated and more tightly structured in equivalential links than the negative one.[14] Although the positive 'us' cannot be thought without the negative 'them', they are asymmetrical because the latter is defined solely in terms of its function to boost the former.

Vertical associations between the two poles of each of the four orientational pairs form a reservoir of signification, which is shaped in political articulations. This implies that association forms a continuum from loosely structured signification and identification, which is ordinary, tacit, volatile, *ad hoc*, evasive and so on, to more established and institutionalised patterns of signification and identification, in which associations operating at the level of orientation are formed as equivalential links structuring discourses.[15]

The radical right as political orientation beyond right/left

Since the 1980s, radical right-wing parties have gained considerable electoral success in Western European politics. As opposed to the occasional popping up of radical right parties and movements in the preceding decades, what we see today are not merely country specific protest parties. These parties show marked similarities across countries and they have become part of the established party system.[16] One of their most important common traits is that they have managed to integrate nationalist, racist and populist themes into an antagonistic style of identity politics directed against alien forces and the cultural and political establishment. While radical politics as a form of identity politics was 'the new Left' brand from the mid 1960s and around 20 years onwards, it is today linked to a broad spectrum of culturalist discourses ranging from leftist multiculturalism to 'the new Right' organised around nationalist, racist and populist lines. The latter can be envisaged as a triangle where the articulations between nationalist, racist and populist themes make up friend/enemy antagonisms around front/back, in/out and up/down orientations.[17]

1. The link between *nationalism and racism* focuses on the heritage and the unity of people–nation–culture and depicts multiculturalism, rights and foreign influence as anti-people and anti-nation.
2. The link between *racism and populism* revolves around racial and cultural unity and purity, depicting Muslims and the system as enemies.
3. In the link between *populism and nationalism*, the nation frames the unified

and authentic will of the people and depicts the European Union, globalisation and the system as enemies that destroy this unity.

To construe political antagonisms along these orientations can be seen as answers to the diminished significance of party differences, which goes hand in hand with the blurring of the right/left matrix.[18] Nation, culture and people are branded as existential reference points fuelled by nationalist, racist, and populist resentment against the EU, Muslims and the establishment. The three aspects are explicit in:

1. The argument against political integration in the EU, which symbolises the disintegration of nation state sovereignty and national culture and hence the pillars of the welfare state. Here, in particular, there is a significant similarity between right and left.
2. The argument against Muslims and, more generally, to what is foreign to the national culture and its religious traditions, which among other things imply criticism of globalisation and multiculturalism.
3. The argument against the establishment's unwillingness to resist further integration in the EU and to reduce the influx of refugees, which is depicted as the main causes undermining the unity of political/cultural elites and ordinary people.

The radical nature of the mixture of nationalist, racist and populist discourses lies in their reshuffling of what has otherwise been a fairly stable political configuration of orientational metaphors in the second part of the twentieth century. This happens in the following ways:

Right/left. They displace right/left because they see it as an outdated medium for political identification and attach less emphasis on legality and public reason and more emphasis on populist legitimation and a friend/enemy type of identity politics. The move here is from moderatism to radicalism and from balancing opposites to the either/or choices typical of the three other polarities.

Up/down. They criticise political and cultural elites as exercising repressive ideological power and for having separated from their roots, from those they represent. The frequent use of organic metaphors underlines the '*Blut und Boden*' appeal to national culture and tradition as the site of indigenous and popular authenticity. This is the political frontier between elites and people, discursively structured in terms of up–front–left versus down–back–in.

Front/back. They bring back up–front, as it were, by exposing hypocrisy and manipulation on the part of the establishment and by bringing forth what has been put aside, hidden or excluded. What has been excluded is essentially what we are (in), which goes together with a joyful exposure of the 'beast within' as well as with an emotionalisation of political discourse.

Radical and plural democracy

In/out. Finally, they accentuate the exclusionary mechanisms of nationalism, racism and populism to forge images of a native and homogenous identity with a strong sense of belonging, in which the unity of up/down is a condition for the unity of the state and the political establishment, on the one side, and the nation and the people, on the other. This unity, in turn, is also a condition for distinguishing us from them (in/out).

From right/left to establishment/opposition discourses

The changing patterns of political frontiers tend to break up stable relations between right/left and up–front–in. The ability of the right/left to be a vehicle of political orientation and identification in the twentieth century relied on the political terrain being hegemonised by a political settlement around up–front–in that, for all practical purposes, established centre-right/left as the exhaustive political alternative in Western European politics. Right/left orientation has played a more or less pronounced role in structuring political identification, but, if it loses ground in a situation marked by a destabilisation of the configuration of the orientational metaphors, it will not be able to bend these other orientations towards itself. That is, it will be difficult to voice, say, up/down in right/left terms as an opposition between inequality/equality. It goes for both fascist parties in the interwar period and the radical right today that they undermine the right–up versus left–down configuration and replace it with a right–down versus left–up antagonism.[19] The decline of right/left political orientation creates a political uncoupling between political elites and lay people, such as the antagonism between system politics and identity politics in nationalist, racist and populist discourses. When the two drift apart, up/down conflicts are articulated with in/out and front/back orientations, both of which differ from the right/left polarity.

The problems with right/left arise when we view up–front–in negatively. This inversion of positive/negative valuation is another way of stating a change of perspective and context. This is the situation when:

1 *Up* is associated with the establishment, whose cultural and political elites and experts are seen as a cosmopolitan and leftist threat of power, gain, manipulation and so on, and opposed to ordinary people as powerless objects of control.
2 *Front* is associated with the political correctness, arrogance, manipulation and the rationalism of the system and opposed to entrenched sentiments of ordinary people and their sense of belonging. The criticism is levelled against artificial so-called cosmopolitan communities, such as the EU and the United Nations.
3 *In* connotes access to and presence in political decision-making arenas

instead of referring to 'us', that is, to national and popular culture, identities and traditions of ordinary people.

From this inversion of up–front–in as the positive pole of identification follows a positive revaluation of down–back–out. This is the situation when:

1. *Down* is associated with what is ordinary, popular and common, 'habits of the heart', 'down to earth', rooted, grounded and so on. Organic metaphors are frequently used to buttress the sense of belonging as an authentic expression of existence directed against establishment rhetoric.
2. *Back* is brought up–front, connoting repressed authenticity and truth; real as opposed to artificial community; and caring, belonging and solidarity as opposed to uprooted indifference and egoistic individualism.
3. *Out* takes the place of in. Out maintains its negative value, but its content changes by pointing to what is incompatible with down–back. The distinctions between us/them, inclusion/exclusion and central/peripheral are thus drawn differently than in establishment discourses.

It should be clear that the terms employed here are not univocal, as their connotations vary according to the other metaphors with which they are articulated. 'In', for example, is a target in every political discourse, because it is valued positively. It embodies incompatible sets of orientations as in in_1–up–front versus in_2–down–back, where in_1 could refer to political power and in_2 to popular/national culture. Whereas establishment discourses associate 'in' with taking part in political decision making, being present, seeking influence and so on, it is in euro-sceptic discourses associated with national or popular identity, culture and so on. It is, in other words, an existential category.

With the reshuffling of political frontiers, right/left plays a less significant role for political identification. This might at first look odd given the upsurge of the radical *right*, which move along the up/down, front/back and in/out axes and displace right/left as a relic of class politics. The democratic problem does not, of course, consist in addressing up/down, front/back and in/out as political problems. Rather, the problem is that right/left is confronted with difficulties of becoming hegemonic in the sense of establishing itself as the horizon for democratic politics; that is, of framing and articulating these other polarities.[20] The result is that political intensity tends to be channelled into either/or alternatives couched in an antagonistic style of identity politics.

Some of the major features of this kind of politics are those of a growing emotionalisation and toughening of politics; resentment against political correctness and toleration; stress on closure to ensure national culture and solidarity in the welfare state; emphasis on tribal identity and collectivism along ethnic, national and religious lines – all of which fit neatly with policing public debate by stigmatising internal and external enemies.[21] Multicultural society and European political integration are among the preferred targets, but the Left is also under attack in the anti-system rhetoric as left is associated with the establishment.

How should radical and plural democratic politics respond to the reshuffling of political frontiers along these lines? To be able to go at least some of the way in answering this question the following two sections will look at which role right/left is assigned in the modern political symbolic order and how it is related to democratic public reason. Here it will be useful to look at the overarching functions of political right/left orientation to avoid getting caught up in transient fluctuations of the meaning and significance of the distinction. This will make it possible to argue that right/left has a crucial function in democratic politics, while criticising its inability to renew itself in present-day politics, failing to spark off democratic imagination.

Negativity as the political reversal of cultural/religious codes and the autonomy of the political symbolic order

A major democratic concern is whether political discourses follow an up/down and in/out pattern (such as the radical right that brings together nationalist, racist and populist themes), or whether they follow a pattern of right/left and front/back based on political equality and 'progress'. Changes in the patterns of political orientation make it important to sort out where the lines of political contestation run in order to get a better grasp of the forces that set the political agenda as well as the challenges confronting democratic politics today. An important aspect deals with the differences between cultural/religious and political ways of coding orientational metaphors. It is a near universal pattern that while the former views up–front–in–right as positive and down–back–out–left as negative, the modern revolution and hence democracy dislocate this order by granting parity between right and left.

Before the French revolution the up/down spatial dimension played the dominant role in defining political orientation. 'In this vertically ordered cosmos, the political is subordinated to and inspired by the religious; sovereignty is associated with heaven.'[22] The revolution inaugurates the modern political symbolic order as relatively autonomous compared with the cultural/religious order. The former is brought about in a reversal of the latter, which privileges right over left, associating them with in/central/up/strength/good and out/peripheral/down/weakness/bad, respectively.[23] This is done by reconfiguring right/left, making it a symbol of political differences being accepted as parts of a given whole (the political community), and asserting that opposed parties, interests and values are on equal political footing. The political reversal consists in making right and left equal opposites, something that makes room for representing and dealing with disagreement as constitutive traits of politics, while acknowledging the political imperative of equal liberty (dependent on the dislocation of the cultural/religious coding of right/left.[24] The reversal is partial because the cultural/religious classifications of up–front–in as positive and down–back–out as negative also holds in politics in general, and because right/left takes shape *vis-à-vis* these other polarities. The political dislocation of the cultural/religious symbolic order concerns the right/left polarity, which is not able to eliminate the hierarchical structure of the power of authority. The latter finds its way into the right/left distinction when right is associated with up–back and left with down–front – that is, the defence of either inequality and status quo, or equality and change.[25]

It is because no subsystem can exist independently of the overall system that the reversal of polarities cannot be complete.[26] The ways in which orientational metaphors structure political discourses cannot be isolated from the structuring of discourses in general, as there can be no rigid barriers between different types of categorisation. They slide into each other and produce internal tensions, which are especially clear in relation to right/left, where the incompatibility of the two types of categorisation is most clearly expressed (hierarchy and inequality versus parity and equality).

The significance of the modern political code of right/left lies in the institutionalisation of a political symbolic order that is relatively autonomous in relation to its environment, in which right–up is positive and left–down is negative.[27] The political revolutions of 1776 and 1789 – which dislocated the old system by going from hierarchical to equal status, from order to change and from a religious to a secular order – marked a refusal to accept the inevitability of the up/down hierarchical ordering of politics. A new egalitarian polarity was invoked to underpin the horizontal classification of democratic politics that was political insofar as it was constituted in a rupture in the coding of right/left: from being part of a cultural/religious codex of hierarchical social standing to a political codex of equal status. As a symbol of parity, right/left cleared a space in which opposition and disagreement were legitimate and where contending forces could be balanced against each other. The autonomy of the political order *vis-à-vis* the cultural/religious order constituted a political principle of societal unity in the face of division.[28]

The importance of this principle and hence of right/left for democracy lies in its possibility to support the argument that unity cannot be substantial, but is a heterogeneous set of differences, and that it is illegitimate, democratically speaking, to base political values on a primordial or organic unity as this would eliminate the autonomy of a common political space. Right/left is sufficiently vacuous to find its way into very different political cultures *and* to be structured by the other orientations, for example, right–up–in versus left–down–out. The political reversal states two fundamental demands that are basic for modern democracy: political equality, which emphasises that, say, social or economic differences must be irrelevant with regard to political status; and that matters of common concern must be dealt with politically and that political deliberation, accordingly, has to be based on right/left orientation.

The political revolution that grants the autonomy of democracy means that politics 'as a subsystem, as a system of challenge, opposition, and change [is] located on the negative side of an overall system of perception'.[29] The right/left matrix of the political reversal gives form to negativity, as it were, by not accepting pre-political references in politics as valid, thereby stressing the limit of the acceptability of cultural/religious codes in the political symbolic order. The political institution of order is the precondition for democracy, which is subversive by being conceived in terms of challenge, opposition and change. Negativity thus shows the impossibility of subsuming the political under the cultural/religious symbolic order, which gives way for the proliferation of political orientations in the modern era. 'Democracy thus proves to be the historical society *par excellence*, a society which, in its very form, welcomes and preserves indeterminacy', and which 'is instituted and sustained by the *dissolution of the markers of certainty*'.[30] This dissolution is unthinkable without the political reversal, which, by instituting right/left as the overdetermined hegemonic orientation, displaces up/down orientation associated with hierarchy and religion.

As the symbolic matrix of modern democracy, right/left refers – when articulated with in/out – to a politically based form of commonality that is marked by mutual recognition and acceptance of differences as the governing principle of coexistence. It is thus opposed to letting cultural/religious assumptions govern democratic politics. Mutuality, which is implied in speaking of right/left as symmetrical opposites, refers to a delimitation of those who are equal from those who are not. This is why right/left is entwined with in/out from the outset as it focuses on inclusion/exclusion such as member/non-member, us/them and citizen/non-citizen. Since these distinctions are inherited from the cultural/religious symbolic order, the question is now how they, when reoccupying the political symbolic, are able to sustain the autonomy of politics that makes democracy possible.[31] This is also a question of how the increased political intensity around in/out, up/down and front/back changes the political landscape.

Three levels of right/left orientation in politics

Right/left has been a hegemonising device in politics and has proved particularly suitable for parliamentary democracy, stretching from its origin as a seating principle in parliament to becoming a matrix of political identification and democratic politics. It has managed to link political elites and people through political representation, and has, in this respect, provided a workable frame for governing under conditions of pluralism in which opposition is legitimate in the political regime and differences are recognised and accepted in the political culture.

It is because right/left has been closely related to issues such as class and elites (up/down) and citizenship (in/out) that it is able to voice a democratic concern for the creation of a political environment in which difference and opposition are cherished as political facts that enhance democracy as such. Seen in this light, right/left is imperative for democracy as a hegemonic device that structures other forms of orientation. The right/left polarity maps a political scenario that polarises political orientation, while maintaining the poles as symmetrical opposites within the defining framework. The articulation between the horizontal (right/left), the vertical (up/down), the frame (in/out) and direction (front/back) creates a centre that balances opposites and evokes a distance to a periphery.

In discussing the significance of right/left for democratic politics, it is useful to distinguish between three analytical levels or layers, making it possible to honour the importance of the principle of right/left whilst allowing for criticism of how it is structured.

The first level concerns the identification of right and left in specific contexts. Right/left is part of a broader system of classification with which it is articulated politically as well as culturally, making the meaning of right or left historically contingent. This can be seen in inversion and convergence: for instance, that right and left switch content over time and that they move towards each other, thus blurring the differences between them. In the United Kingdom and Scandinavia, for example, euro-scepticism has been associated with a leftist position, which is gradually changing, whereas euro-scepticism in Continental Europe has been more associated with the right.

The second level concerns what might be termed the prototypes of the right/left polarity, that is, the more general and identifiable attitudes related to right and left. These are typically measured in relation to economic issues, class conflicts and the nation-state.[32] Within this perspective, although primarily a Western European one, right has often been identified with individualism and the market, while left has been identified with collectivism and state intervention. This differentiation captures some of the significant attitudes of right and left, and it shows how they are bound up with the other orientational metaphors.

1. Right/left is articulated with up/down, because it takes a principal stance on the question of inequality/equality, a question that involves issues such as high or low social status, more or less power and so on.[33] Traditionally there has been a close link between right–up and left–down, evidenced by the industrial age of class politics, where mass movements and organisations linked political elites with ordinary people.[34]
2. Right/left is also articulated with in/out as in struggles for women's right to vote and universal suffrage in general as well as citizenship rights for, say,

ethnic and sexual minorities. Struggles such as these revolve around restrictive vs. inclusive views of citizenship – associated with right and left respectively – and, more generally, about the scope of the recognition and acceptance of differences in the political community. Whether citizenship is viewed restrictively or inclusively is, again, related to the issue of inequality and equality.
3 Finally, right/left is articulated with front/back as when left is identified with youth, change and being progressive, and when right is identified with seniority, stability and status quo and with being reactionary.

Political frontiers are shaped *vis-à-vis* the articulations among the four pairs of orientational metaphors making up the political terrain. This is an ideological structuring of orientation, which means that it is a vehicle of political identification in which terms can be associated with each other by forming equivalential links, thereby structuring political discourses. Discursive identification is thus structured by metaphorical orientation, and ideology can be seen as the link between them. It provides a perceptual and interpretative perspective operating at the threshold between awareness and unawareness, and between what appears contestable and what is taken for granted. Although ideology does not rely on consistency in any strict sense of the term, it does play a suturing role for identification *vis-à-vis* the logic of equivalence. This means that the terms can be translated into one another and become hegemonic poles of identification and self-description in a way that a polarity cannot. It is not, then, possible to identify with polar opposites such as right/left, although it is, as I have argued, possible to identify democratic politics in this way. In other words, there is a difference between (1) people identifying with either right or left and (2) people identifying democratic politics in terms of right/left. This brings us to the third level, which is concerned with the function of the right/left polarity.

The third level deals with the single most important aspect of right/left, namely, the overarching function of the polarity in the political symbolic order, which is coined not in terms of positive and negative as in the cultural/religious symbolic order, but instead in terms of parity.[35] This is the political reversal, which implies that right/left is related to fairness and hence to the public reasoning of balancing different and conflicting claims. Three interrelated claims can be made concerning right/left at this level:[36]

1 *Frame*: as symmetrical opposites, right/left stands for mutual recognition and acceptance of differences (everyone has equal political status), coupled with the categorical proposition of equal liberty.
2 *Difference*: right/left is a vehicle of division for the purpose of opposition and conflict, which entails the acceptance of political opposition, disagreement, conflict and so on within explicit and negotiable limits.
3 *Centre*: right/left serves the function of setting apart for the purpose of coop-

eration and exchange, requiring a balance between them; that is, a reaching out for even-handed judgements and reasonable decisions.

The articulation between frame, difference and centre defines the function of right/left orientation in politics as a way of governing in a political regime marked by competition for power and as a way of interaction in the wider political community marked by 'the fact of pluralism'.[37] The three aspects of right/left serve as a vehicle for turning this fact into a 'reasonable' one, by which is meant that it orientates political identification to common concerns. Right/left links in this way links the conceptions of the political and democracy closely together. So even though one might feel that the right/left polarity has an anachronistic touch to it in today's political climate, it cannot be replaced by any of the three other pairs of orientational metaphors without destroying the autonomy of the political symbolic order and democratic politics. In this respect there is no viable democratic strategy beyond right/left. Radical and plural visions of democracy have to be based on this polarity whilst at the same time being able to criticise the general patterns of categorising right and left (the second level).

Radical and plural democracy: right/left and public reason

The political reversal of cultural codes, which underpins the autonomy of the political symbolic order, has been coined in terms of negativity; that is, in terms of the clashes between the codes governing the political and the cultural symbolic orders *within* the political terrain. Political and cultural codes are to varying degrees incommensurable, but they are incompatible with regard to defining and dealing with common concerns (pluralism and contingency versus monism and objectivism). This implies that public reason is based on the imperative that political values must trump cultural ones as this is the only way to ensure a form of commonality that is based on political equality and mutual recognition and acceptance of differences. This is not only a value orientation, but also a matter of securing the autonomy or integrity of the political symbolic order and hence democracy.

The political reversal means that there can be no *political* stance on comprehensive views and ways of reasoning. Instead, there is the political imperative to put them within brackets to ensure the autonomy of the political symbolic order and to sustain a democratic politics based on the mutual recognition and acceptance of differences among members. Public reason based on the equal political standing of participants is the democratic means to regulate the configuration of the four pairs of orientational metaphors mapping the political terrain. As such it is a battleground structuring democratic political orientation in the political community at large.

Radical and plural democracy

A radical and plural democratic strategy has as its primary task to safeguard the autonomy and integrity of the political symbolic order. It has, in other words, to assert the primacy of the political in matters of common concerns. This means that it has to base itself on the right/left divide whilst at the same time being able to adjust to changes in the political terrain if it is going to make a political impact. If the Left cannot deal with political intensity moving on to up/down, front/back and in/out, it will not be able to launch a convincing alternative capable of broad appeal. With the restructuring of the political terrain and the greater political intensity of these metaphors, the identity and relevance of right/left have been questioned. One should be careful not to mix up the second and the third level of the right/left distinction, that is, the general attitudes associated with it and its democratic function. It is crucial not to drop the latter because the former is problematic. Instead, a Leftist approach to democratic politics would give right/left the key role of framing and negotiating political differences between up/down, front/back and in/out.

It is all-important for democratic politics that right/left is able to provide a frame for up/down, front/back and in/out, as this would expose these orientations to democratic public reason. A few examples can illustrate some of the democratic potentials of such a move, directed against both elitist establishment politics and the identity politics of the radical right.

1. In relation to *up/down* it would imply that relations between, say, elites/non-elites, experts/laypeople and system/identity politics are put on the public political agenda and thus exposed to and structured by democratic political concerns as opposed to be the prerogative of populist discourses. A Leftist position would be critical of both 'the rational consensus' of elite politics and of identity politics inasmuch as it is based on culturalist premises.

2. In relation to *front/back* it would imply that relations between responsible, necessary and rational politics, on the one hand, and political culture, popular trends and sentiments, on the other, could clarify what the progressive/reactionary opposition means in a democratic political discourse. A Leftist position would direct its criticism against technocratic elite/expert politics and the '*Gemeinschaftsschwärmerei*' of culturalist and communitarian discourses.

3. In relation to *in/out* it would imply that relations between members/non-members, acceptable/unacceptable as well as issues related to multicultural society, nation-state sovereignty and access to decision making could be based on democratic traditions as opposed to nationalist, racist or populist parameters. A Leftist position would run against any attempt to base inclusion/exclusion on premises other than political ones, as this would compromise the autonomy and integrity of democratic public reason.

These are just a few examples of how right/left could make a difference *vis-à-vis* the other dimensions that have attained political prominence. Instead of considering up/down, front/back and in/out as 'post political' or anti-democratic trends, focus should be on how to reorient, recontextualise and revaluate right/left *vis-à-vis* these orientations. This would dissociate right/left from the oppositions that structured politics in the last century such as national/international, state/market, public/private and collectivism/individualism. The fact that these oppositions are out of tune with political reality today does not warrant the conclusion that right/left is anachronistic, as the overarching function of the distinction cannot be exhausted by its contingent instantiation. It is this gap between the function of the distinction and its particular contingent instantiation that makes it possible to revitalise right/left to see what it could have on offer in today's changing political climate.

Notes

1 C. Mouffe, 'Democratic politics today', in C. Mouffe (ed.), *Dimensions of Radical Democracy: Pluralism, Citizenship, Community* (London: Verso, 1992), p. 1.
2 K. McClure, 'On the subject of rights: pluralism, plurality and political identity', in Mouffe (ed.), *Dimensions of Radical Democracy*, p. 114.
3 E. Laclau and C. Mouffe, *Hegemony and Socialist Strategy: Towards a Radical Democratic* Politics (London: Verso, 1985), p. 152.
4 Mouffe, 'Democratic politics today', p. 1.
5 J. A. Laponce, 'In search of the stable elements of the Left–Right landscape', *Comparative Politics*, 4:4 (1972), 472f; and J. A. Laponce, *Left and Right: The Topography of Political Perception* (Toronto: University of Toronto Press, 1981), pp. 41–6.
6 I will tentatively distinguish between the radical right and the extreme right and only refer to the former, which includes parties such as The Freedom Party in Austria, The Flemish Block in Belgium, The Danish People's Party in Denmark, The National Front in France, and The Progress Party in Norway.
7 The term might be vague and ambiguous as Bobbio argues in his *Left and Right: The Significance of a Political Distinction* (Chicago: The University of Chicago Press, 1996), pp. 75–7. The point is not to downplay tensions between liberty and equality, but to emphasise that they cannot be defined apart form each other in modern democratic discourse, and that they cannot be associated with right and left, respectively. For the Left it is decisive to endorse not only equality but also liberty, because otherwise it cannot defend pluralism. See also H. Graham, *The Vestibule of Hell: Why Left and Right Have Never Made Sense in Politics and Life* (Toronto: Stoddart, 2001), pp. 65f.
8 T. B. Dyrberg, 'Right/left in the context of new political frontiers: what's radical politics today?', *Journal of Language and Politics*, 2:2 (2003), 339–42; J. A. Laponce, 'Spatial archetypes and political perceptions', *The American Political Science Review*, 69:1 (1975), 11–13; and Laponce, *Left and Right*, chapter 3.
9 G. Lakoff and M. Johnson, *Metaphors We Live By* (Chicago: The University of Chicago Press, 1980), p. 14.
10 According to M. Eliade (*A History of Religious Ideas, Vol. 1: From the Stone-Age to the Eleusinian Mysteries* [Chicago: The University of Chicago Press, 1978], p. 3), 'space can be organized around the human body as extending forward, backward, to right,

Radical and plural democracy

to left, upward, and downward. It is from this original and originating experience – feeling oneself "thrown" in the middle of an apparently limitless, unknown, and threatening extension – that the different methods of *orientatio* are developed.' See also Lakoff and Johnson, *Metaphors We Live By*, chapter 4.

11 M. Foucault, *The History of Sexuality, Vol. 1: An Introduction* (Harmondsworth: Penguin Books, 1981), p. 93.

12 Dyrberg, 'Right/left in the context of new political frontiers', pp. 340–42.

13 See R. Hertz, 'The pre-eminence of the right hand: a study in religious polarity', in R. Needham (ed.), *Right and Left: Essays in Dual Symbolic Classification* (Chicago and London: The University of Chicago Press, 1973), pp. 3–32; R. Needham (ed.), *Right and Left: Essays in Dual Symbolic Classification*; R. Parkin, *The Dark Side of Humanity* (Amsterdam: Harwood Academic Publishers, 1996); Laponce, 'Spatial archetypes and political perceptions'; Laponce, *Left and Right*; and C. McManus, *Right Hand, Left Hand* (London: Phoenix, 2002).

14 Laponce, 'In search of the stable elements of the Left–Right landscape', pp. 472f; J. A. Laponce, 'The use of visual space to measure ideology', in J. A. Laponce and P. Smoker (eds), *Experimentation and simulation in political science* (Toronto: University of Toronto Press, 1972), p. 53; and Laponce, 'Spatial archetypes and political perceptions', pp. 18f.

15 The logics of difference and equivalence as the structuring matrix of discourses were introduced by Laclau and Mouffe in *Hegemony and Socialist Strategy*, chapter 3. See also Laponce, *Left and Right*, pp. 73f.

16 H.-G. Betz, *Radical Right-Wing Populism in Western Europe* (London: Macmillan, 1994), p. 23; and T. Bjørklund and J. G. Andersen, 'Anti-immigration parties in Denmark and Norway: the Progress Parties and the Danish People's Party', in M. Schain, A. Zolberg and P. Hossay (eds), *Shadows Over Europe: The Development and Impact of the Extreme Right in Western Europe* (New York: St. Martin's Press, 2002), chapter 6.

17 T. B. Dyrberg, 'Racist, nationalist and populist trends in recent Danish politics', Research Paper No. 19/01, The Department of Social Sciences, Roskilde University (2001); and Dyrberg, 'Right/left in the context of new political frontiers', pp. 346ff.

18 T. B. Dyrberg, 'Racisme som en nationalistisk og populistisk reaktion på elitedemokrati', in T. B. Dyrberg, A. D. Hansen and J. Torfing (eds), *Diskursanalysen på arbejde* (Frederiksberg: Roskilde Universitetsforlag, 2000), pp. 224–7; and C. Mouffe, *The Democratic Paradox* (London: Verso, 2000), pp. 114, 116.

19 J. Schwartzmantel, *The Age of Ideology* (Houndmills: Macmillan, 1998), pp. 124f.

20 Whilst right/left is one among the three other sets of orientational metaphors with which it is articulated, it is also that polarity which takes on the hegemonic democratic task of framing all other political orientations by becoming the medium through which they can be expressed politically. The universality of right/left within a democratic discourse is thus an overdetermined articulation of political orientations. 'Politics', says Laponce in *Left and Right* (p. 24), 'needed dualities and needed an overarching duality that would summarize all others'.

21 Z. Puhovski, 'The moral basis of political restructuring', in C. Brown (ed.), *Political Restructuring in Europe* (London: Routledge, 1994), pp. 208, 211, 215.

22 Laponce, *Left and Right*, p. 77.

23 Hertz, 'The pre-eminence of the right hand'; and McManus *Right Hand, Left Hand*, chapter 2.

24 Laponce, 'In search of the stable elements of the Left–Right landscape', pp. 472f; Laponce, 'The use of visual space to measure ideology', p. 53; Laponce, 'Spatial arche-

types and political perceptions', pp. 16–20; and Laponce, *Left and Right*, pp. 41–6.
25 Laponce, 'Spatial archetypes and political perceptions', p. 17.
26 Laponce, 'In search of the stable elements of the Left-Right landscape', pp. 472f.
27 Hertz, 'The pre-eminence of the right hand'; and Laponce *Left and Right*, chapters 4 and 6.
28 C. Lefort, *Democracy and Political Theory*, trans. D. Macey (Oxford: Blackwell, 1988), pp. 18, 34–35, 39, 41.
29 Laponce, 'Spatial archetypes and political perceptions', p. 17. For a critique of Laponce, see H. F. Bienfait and W. E. A. Beek, 'Right and Left as political categories: an exercise in "not-so-primitive" classification', *Anthropos*, 96:1 (2001).
30 C. Lefort, *Democracy and Political Theory*, pp. 16, 19.
31 E. Laclau, *New Reflections on the Revolution of Our Time* (London: Verso, 1990), p. 74.
32 Schwartzmantel, *The Age of Ideology*, pp. 5f.
33 Bobbio, *Left and Right*, pp. 39, 51f, 58f, and chapter 6.
34 Laponce, 'Spatial archetypes and political perceptions', pp. 17–19.
35 S. Lukes, 'What is Left?', *Times Literary Supplement* (27 March 1992).
36 Laponce, *Left and Right*, pp. 27f.
37 Rawls discusses 'the fact of pluralism' and 'the fact of reasonable pluralism' among other places in J. Rawls, *Collected Papers*, ed. by S. Freeman (Cambridge, MA: Harvard University Press, 1999), p. 425.

11 • Yannis Stavrakakis

Negativity and democratic politics: radical democracy beyond reoccupation and conformism[1]

On negativity

THE CHALLENGES transformative politics and political theory are facing today are obviously of considerable complexity and I hope I will not oversimplify things by saying that one of their most important dimensions is the following: how does one respond to the increasing centrality – and awareness – of negativity in human experience? Negativity, of course, is not new; nor is it a challenge only for the Left. It is hard to deny that personal trauma, social crisis and political rupture are constant characteristics of human experience and everybody has to face them, one way or the other, sooner or later. However, in the context of this chapter, I intend to focus on *negativity* in the ontological sense (in the singular) and not on *negativities* in the ontic sense (in the plural). How can we define this negativity, why is this important, and how can 'negativity' function within theoretical discourse?

In Laclau's words, negativity 'is something which simply shows the limits of the constitution of objectivity and cannot be dialecticized'.[2] Negativity is a figure, a generic category used to discuss a multiplicity of phenomena entailing a disruptive effect, an effect of *dislocation*. This implies a particular type of relation between the ontic and the ontological level, between 'negativity' as an (empty) signifier of theoretical discourse and the (open-ended) multiplicity of disruptive effects punctuating human experience. Obviously the two are related in crucial ways. Indeed, we would not be aware of negativity without our social and political positivities – variable in time and space – being repeatedly destabilised and dislocated by 'something:' by an encounter with the impossible, the uncanny, the unrepresentable, the unconscious, *the real*. Negativity, however, is not the Lacanian real *per se*, it designates an attempt of theoretical reflection to encircle the moments of such encounters, moments when the gap between our limited symbolic/imaginary *reality* and the always escaping *real* – a *non-lack* beyond anything we can think or say to describe, represent and master it – makes its disavowed or repressed presence felt again, and again and again. It is an attempt, furthermore, to register the distinct character of this multiplicity of phenomena. In that sense it is important to stress that *negativity* cannot be reduced to particular *dislocations (negativities)*. This is perhaps the oldest strategy of foreclosing the ontological character of negativity. It also explains why we need to discuss *negativity* in its own right in order to say something revealing about *dislocations (negativities)* as comprising a distinct order of phenomena.

But what about the opposite danger, that of reducing the irreducible multiplicity of dislocations to a singular figure, the danger of positivising or naturalising negativity? Surely, the perceptive reader must have noticed that up to now we have refrained from offering any positive description of negativity. Any such attempt would betray the very principle it is supposed to serve. As Diana Coole has recently put it, 'to name it would be to destroy it; to render it positive, ideal, and thus to fail at the very moment of apparent success'.[3] It is the constitutive failure of all human attempts at offering final positive representations of experience – a failure inscribed in the inability of bridging the gap between the real and the symbolic – that renders possible the recognition of this ontological horizon. Besides, it must already have become clear that we can only acknowledge negativity by following its disruptive traces along the fabric of what societies construct as their positive world, by following the play between positivities and dislocations. In that sense, the 'ontology' of negativity is limited by its 'reliance' on – but not reduction to – the positive aspect of human experience. This is another reason that explains why from the beginning of this chapter we have conceived of negativity as directly linked to what Laclau calls dislocations. While, on the one hand, they threaten and disrupt identities, on the other, dislocations 'are the foundation on which new identities are constituted'.[4] The same is true of negativity. If negativity refers to the horizon of impossibility and unrepresentability that punctuates the life of linguistic creatures, this does not mean that it should be understood as a mere destructive force. In Coole's terms, negativity is also affirmative: 'a creative–destructive force that engenders as well as ruins positive forms. In this sense negativity does tend to operate as (a surrogate for) ontology, although it is far too mobile, too negative, to serve as a foundation for what follows.'[5] Negativity then also indicates the dimension of 'becoming, a productivity that engenders and ruins every distinct form as a creative destructive restlessness'.[6] It is neither an object nor its negation: it is the condition of possibility/impossibility of the constitution of objects.[7] By inscribing a *lack* in our dislocated positivities, it fuels the *desire* for new social and political constructions and identifications.

In that sense, the Lacanian dialectic between lack and desire becomes crucial in clarifying the status of an ontology of negativity and lack. It is important to stress at this point that Lacanian theory does not consider lack in isolation, as a primordial archetype of the psyche. Lack is always inscribed in the fabric of our identifications as a lack of something: of the lost/impossible energy, the excessive enjoyment (*jouissance*) we retroactively project on our existence before socialisation. Even if entering into the world of language and social norms demands the castration of an excessive part of our bodily energy – or rather, precisely because of that – the 'nostalgia' and the associated promise of recapturing our sacrificed enjoyment persists and returns to form the kernel of fantasies that stimulate our desire for new identifications. These imaginarisations of abundance and excess remain the backbone of our fantasmatic life, the vehicle of our (personal, social and political) desire. It is true that in Lacanian theory desire is never seen as an unlimited energy flowing *ex nihilo*, as in some of the modern mutations of the philosophy of immanence (the most recent example being Hardt and Negri), but that does not mean that Lacanians neglect the elements of excess and abundance. On the contrary, the constitutive play between lack and abundance is internal to Lacanian theory, only it never serves the idealisation of desire and abundance, precisely because of the ontological status of lack and negativity. As we shall see, it is conceived in terms of a dialectics of fantasy with important political implications.

In pre-modern societies religious imagination was the predominant discursive horizon for the inscription and administration of negativity. There is no doubt, however, that modernity has signalled a shift in our symbolic and imaginary administration of negativity and contingency. On the one hand, it has highlighted its constitutive nature: a world without God is a world visibly lacking the promise and the guarantee of a final resolution of negativity. On the other hand, unable to assume full responsibility for such a radical recognition, such a disruptive awareness, modernity has 'reoccupied' the ground of a pre-modern ethics of harmony, often substituting God with reason.[8] What are the political implications of these developments? Undoubtedly, 'negativity is already political inasmuch as it signals the vulnerability and contingency of every phenomenon that appears to be fully positive and replete'.[9] Furthermore, experiencing negativity – *qua* the moment of the political – brings forth a play of symbolisation, which invariably takes the form of political (hegemonic) struggles. In fact, the play between the *political* (dislocation and hegemonic re-articulation) and the *social* (the field of sedimented reality) can be characterised as a play of continuous interpenetration and contamination between negativity and positivity,[10] between lack and the promise – the fantasy, of abundance. In particular, it seems that political modernity has oscillated between (at least) three responses *vis-à-vis* negativity. I will refer to them as the utopian, the democratic and the post-democratic response.[11] In what follows I will briefly present what I consider as the defining characteristics of these three strategies with reference to negativity and the play between lack and abundance. I will then try to show that in order to move beyond dangerous and ineffective utopian reoccupations and the conformism of post-democracy, transformative politics in the new century can benefit from a radical democratic argument re-activating the promise of the democratic revolution. I understand such a radical democratic argument along the lines set by Laclau and Mouffe, with an added Lacanian twist. However, this opens the whole question of the hostility of some theorists inspired by Lacan towards such arguments. Thus, in the last section of the chapter, I will discuss the interventions of Žižek and Badiou in order to clarify further the ethical and political status of radical democracy.

The utopian reoccupation

The first response, one reoccupying the ground of pre-modern metaphysics, is best exemplified by some mutations of modern political utopianism. I use utopia here in the strong sense of the word, as a discourse that offers final political solutions from the point of view of a 'subject supposed to know', whose opaqueness and authority is never questioned *per se*. Fascism and Stalinism are two obvious examples. What is dominant here is a fear to encounter negativity without recourse to the certainty of attaining another order, a utopian society, a harmonious future eliminating negativity once and for all.

In fact, whenever a conscious attempt was made to realise utopia, to institute human reality according to a plan promising to resolve social contradiction and dissimulate political antagonism, the results were catastrophic. To use a well-known Lacanian phrase, what was foreclosed in the symbolic appeared in the real; the real of excessive terror and extermination. Here, realising the promise of full positivity, the fantasy of abundance, seems to open the road to a proliferation of negativity. The result is 'the triple knotted effect, of ecstasy, the sacred and terror' that Alain Badiou has called *disaster*.[12]

There are at least two ways to ground such a view on modern utopianism.[13] One can articulate a *historical argument* according to which political attempts to realise modern utopian fantasies (notably the ideal of an Arian Nazi order and that of a proletarian revolution leading to a future Communist society) have only reproduced a pattern typical of pre-modern eschatological discourses, such as revolutionary millenarianism. The way all these discourses deal with negativity is more or less the following. Utopian fantasies promise to eliminate forever negativity in whatever socio-political form it takes (from black death to economic exploitation, poverty and even whatever is perceived as national humiliation). In order to achieve this impossible goal, utopian discourses *localise* the cause of negativity in one particular social group or political actor. Thus, the essential by-product of the utopian operation is invariably the stigmatisation and even the elimination of the social group presented as incarnating negativity (*qua* Evil). This historical argument can be supported by a *psychoanalytic argument* regarding the function of fantasy in politics. From the point of view of a Lacanian ontology – according to which socio-political reality, an imaginary/symbolic construct, is ultimately unable to control, represent or regulate an always escaping real, its own constitutive impossibility – fantasy becomes the explosive union of two contradictory forces. It involves the dream of a state without disturbances and dislocations, a state in which we are supposed to get back the enjoyment (*jouissance*) sacrificed upon entering the symbolic order, while at the same time it relies on the production of a 'scape-goat' to be stigmatised as the one who is to blame for our lack, the *Evil* force that stole our precious *jouissance*. In order to sound credible in its promise to eliminate *negativity* it has to attribute to it a localised, 'controllable' cause. In Slavoj Žižek's words, 'the foreclosed obverse of the Nazi harmonious Volksgemeinschaft returned in their paranoiac obsession with "the Jewish plot". Similarly, the Stalinist's compulsive discovery of ever-new enemies of socialism was the inescapable obverse of their pretending to realise the idea of the "New Socialist Man".'[14]

The democratic revolution

If this is the case, then surely one of the most urgent political tasks of our age is to traverse the fantasy of utopia and reinvent transformative politics in a post-fantasmatic direction. As Žižek has put it, the question of *la traversée du fantasme* – one of the aims of analytic treatment in Lacanian psychoanalysis – becomes 'perhaps the foremost political question'.[15] But what does it mean to move in such a post-fantasmatic direction? Fortunately, it might not entail reinventing the wheel, it might not require a shift of Herculean proportions. One can encounter elements of such a political project in what is usually called the democratic invention or the democratic revolution. This brings us to the second response to negativity present in political modernity, the one closest to assuming – either consciously or unconsciously – the responsibility for its constitutive and irreducible character.

No final resolutions are promised here, no political *Aufhebung*; antagonism is and remains constitutive. 'Democratic revolution' – an expression coming from de Tocqueville but radically refashioned by Lefort and others – marks a discontinuity from the heteronomous legitimacy of the pre-modern *ancien regime* into a new form of the political institution of the social, a society becoming aware of its own historicity. 'The modern democratic revolution is best recognised in this mutation: there is no power linked to a body.' The place of power now appears as 'an empty place', which can be occupied only temporarily: 'There is no law that can be fixed, whose articles cannot be contested, whose foundations are not susceptible of being called into question. Lastly, there is no representation of a centre and of the contours of society: unity cannot now efface social division.' Democracy, according to Lefort, institutionalises 'the experience of an ungraspable, uncontrollable society', in which even the identity of the sovereign people 'will constantly be open to question'.[16] This is clearly the boldest attempt to institute a political order on the lack of ultimate foundations typical of a modernity worthy of its name.

This is not to say that all modern political forms claiming the name 'democracy' obey such a principle of organisation. One can clearly have an essentialist (pre-democratic) or a post-democratic conceptualisation of democracy, which remains blind to negativity. We all know that there is no dictator that has not tried to manipulate, at least once, the vocabulary of democracy. And no citizen of a Western liberal democracy would perhaps instantly identify his own political experience with our picture of the guiding principles of the democratic revolution. This is not surprising. It is because our current experience is marked by a third way of responding to negativity characteristic of political modernity, the response of *consumerist post-democracy* typical of the current articulation between the capitalist order and versions of liberalism.

Consumerist post-democracy

Now, what exactly are the characteristics of a consumerist post-democracy? How does it deal with negativity? If revolutionary and utopian imagination promise the final elimination of negativity and the full encounter with our lost/impossible *jouissance* here and now, consumerist post-democracy follows a more nuanced strategy – the strategy of a *jouissance à venir* to paraphrase Derrida's *democratie à-venir*. Here it is important to examine both components of this hybrid articulation: first post-democracy and then consumerism.

Post-democracy is founded on an attempt to exclude the political awareness of lack and negativity from the political domain, leading to a political order which retains the token institutions of liberal democracy but neutralises the centrality of political antagonism – hence the expression 'post-democracy'. Jacques Rancière has been one of the political theorists who coined this term.[17] A whole chapter is devoted to consensus democracy or 'post-democracy' in his *Disagreement*.[18] According to his schema post-democracy denotes:

> the paradox that, in the name of democracy, emphasises the consensual practice of effacing the forms of democratic action. Postdemocracy is the government practice and conceptual legitimisation of a democracy after the demos, a democracy that has eliminated the appearance, miscount, and dispute of the people and is thereby reducible to the sole interplay of state mechanisms and combinations of social energies and interests.[19]

What, furthermore, underlies post-democracy is an identification of democratic form with the 'necessities' of globalised capital:

> From an allegedly defunct Marxism, the supposedly reigning liberalism borrows the theme of objective necessity, identified with the constraints and

caprices of the world market. Marx's once scandalous thesis that governments are simple business agents for international capital is today an obvious fact on which 'liberals' and 'socialists' agree. The absolute identification of politics with the management of capital is no longer the shameful secret hidden behind the 'forms' of democracy; it is the openly declared truth by which our governments acquire legitimacy.[20]

This brings us directly into the heart of the second component of consumerist post-democracy, capitalist consumerism, insofar as 'the declared success of democracy is then accompanied by a reduction of democracy to a certain state of social relationships'.[21]

The point not to be missed here is that although negativity and antagonism are neutralised within the post-democratic political imaginary, lack and negativity are inscribed within the social circuit of the dominant individualist, consumerist culture regulating social relationships. Inscribed, however, in a particular way. Negativity and the constitutive lack it creates are related to the lack of particular products; to a lack, in other words, that can be alleviated through consumption. Alleviated yes, but not satisfied. However, this non-satisfaction is actually essential in perpetuating desire, and thus sustaining the consumerist circuit of late capitalism. In that sense consumerism – in opposition to traditional utopianism – is not founded on the elimination of lack and negativity at all cost, but, on the contrary, on the cultivation of a particular play between lack and excess/abundance and the domestication of its fantasmatic parameters. A quasi-utopian horizon of fullness and enjoyment remains operative but, crucially, it becomes subordinate to the metonymic passage from product to product, from purchase to purchase, from fantasy to fantasy. The essential by-product of this particular administration of desire is the reproduction of market capitalism. As Lacan has put it, fantasy is not there to fulfil our desire but to constitute it as such. The elimination of lack and negativity is thus to be avoided; it is enough to limit it within an expanding fantasy frame. While in revolutionary utopia, *jouissance* ultimately dominates desire, in the quasi-utopian universe of consumerist post-democracy, desire is given priority over *jouissance*. This is the implicit logic that utopian modernity missed but capitalist consumerism has elevated into its hegemonic rationale.

Re-activating the democratic revolution

The question now is how is one to respond to the increasing hegemony of post-democracy, which after the demise of the utopian political imaginary is now eroding the achievements and the promise of the democratic revolution? A political theory determined to avoid the dangers entailed in the nostalgic politics of reoccupation seems to have only one option: to insist on the radicalisation of democracy on a global scale against de-politicisation and the domestication of negativity and antagonism within the framework of the consumerist play between lack and excess. The fact that capitalist consumerism has colonised democratic institutions should not make us disavow the radical potential of the democratic revolution within political modernity. In fact, it should only serve to reinforce the conviction that the democratic revolution remains the most advanced political invention *vis-à-vis* the recognition of the constitutive character of negativity and its translation into an organising principle for any politics of transformation. If it did not have this potential, then there would be no need for the promotion of the post-democratic agenda on behalf of all those that benefit from the reproduction and globalisation of the present capitalist order. It is also true that most forms of democracy – liberal democracy included – still contain a kernel of that potential – often repressed and marginalised and certainly in need of radical revitalisation and re-activation. I see such a re-activation as one of the most urgent tasks of contemporary political theory.

Where can one locate theoretical projects of this sort?[22] As an example, let me briefly examine radical democracy as formulated by Ernesto Laclau and Chantal Mouffe.[23] What is important here is that radical democracy (as a project re-activating and extending the scope of the democratic revolution), besides involving a set of concrete proposals,[24] involves a particular form of political ethos. This is a point that many have not been able to discern. Seen as a distinct form of politics, this type of radical democracy takes an anti-essentialist ontology of lack and negativity as its condition of possibility.[25] It is not only that one has to acknowledge that 'at the base of any struggle lies ... the experience of dislocation and antagonism'; it is not only that the radical absence of foundation now becomes the basis for a critique of any form of oppression.[26] It is also that accepting the impossibility of any ultimate reconciliation and coming to terms with the irreducibility of antagonism becomes the ethical nodal point of a new political order worthy of the democratic tradition. Worthy because it registers and extends the same democratic principles, the same non-reductive stance *vis-à-vis* negativity. The way radical democracy deals with negativity is by acknowledging its constitutive character and by assuming responsibility for its open, antagonistic administration, resisting at the same time the fantasy of its permanent resolution or its reduction into an advertising spectacle. In Lacanian terms, we can assert that radical democracy's deepening of the democratic revolution involves adopting an ethical position beyond the fantasy of harmony. It is here that the Lacanian ethics of psychoanalysis can lend support to a radical democratic project.[27]

This is not to say, however, that this is an easy task. On the contrary, it is something becoming increasingly difficult. In Jason Glynos' words: 'How does one even begin to bring about this radical democratic ethos? What are the main obstacles to this? Is it sufficient to rely upon intellectualist-cognitivist strategies of persuasion?'[28] These are open questions that require urgent attention. It is

Negativity and radical democracy

clear, in any case, that, at least from a psychoanalytic point of view, persuasion is not enough to shake ethical and political identifications. What underlies such identifications is a particular relation to enjoyment (*jouissance*) structured in fantasy. Thus, a passionate endorsement of radical democracy would require the cultivation and hegemony of a different type of ethical relation to negativity and enjoyment, an ethos beyond the politics of fantasy (in either of its forms: utopian reoccupation and quasi-utopian post-democracy).

It seems, however, that the complexities of such a task have led many on the Left to opt for a nostalgic return to the old – defeated and dangerous – politics of reoccupation. In fact, a substantial part of the Left has never managed to distance itself sufficiently from a particular version of political imagination, utopian revolutionary imagination. Even for someone like Žižek, democracy is 'more and more a false issue, a notion so discredited by its predominant use that, perhaps, one should take the risk of abandoning it to the enemy'.[29] But, if democracy has been discredited by its post-democratic use, is the situation any better with Left utopianism, with the dream of a revolutionary radical re-foundation of the social? Are not the risks involved in the politics of reoccupation substantially higher than those involved in the radicalisation of democracy? Are not the supposed benefits of an illusory and ambiguous nature? It seems that the politics of nostalgia presuppose a very selective memory. In the case of Žižek's Marxism, as Laclau has observed, 'despite his professed Marxism, [Žižek] pays no attention whatsoever to the intellectual history of Marxism, in which several of the categories he uses have been refined, displaced, or – to encapsulate it in one term – deconstructed'.[30] On the other hand, many of those resisting the politics of reoccupation have also opted to disavow the promise of the democratic revolution, this time in a post-democratic direction – I am mainly referring to projects such as the Third Way. In that sense, both the return to the politics of reoccupation and the recasting of some kind of centre-left strategy in a post-democratic direction presuppose the disavowal of the radical potential of the democratic revolution.

What is most troubling in this conjecture is that a big part of the Left still willing to consider the prospect of a transformation of the existing order seems unable to register the distinction between democracy – and the radical promise of the democratic revolution – and post-democracy. Fuelled by the resentment caused by the hegemony of globalised capital, it longs for a supposedly real, positive politics even if such a politics has been proved unable to deal in a consistent way with the intricacies of modernity and negativity. What is most astonishing is that such a course seems to be appealing to theorists that have been instrumental in introducing a Lacanian 'negative ontology' into the social sciences and philosophy, theorists that have also served as our main references in this text. The two cases, which are most instructive in this respect, are surely those of Slavoj Žižek and Alain Badiou.

Žižek, Badiou and radical democracy

Both Žižek and Badiou have been associated with the increasing influence of Lacan in contemporary political theory and philosophy. It is Badiou who has pointed out that Lacan's 'undertaking is an event and a condition for the renaissance of philosophy'.[31] He goes so far as to claim that 'a philosophy is possible today, only if it is compatible with Lacan'.[32] As for Žižek, his whole *oeuvre* – impressive in terms of both volume and dynamism – can be seen as an attempt to demonstrate the importance of Lacanian theory for the analysis of ideology, cultural critique and much more besides. In their recent work, however, they both seem to prioritise a 'positive' politics for the Left, outside the framework of the democratic revolution. It is surely necessary to examine their respective arguments in order to see whether their interventions can indeed be construed as a critique of a radical democratic ethics. Do they really target radical democracy and the democratic revolution? Is their critique based on a consistent understanding of the radical democratic argument; is it in other words justified? Can they enlist Lacan in support of their argument? These are some of the questions we will try to clarify in the remaining part of this chapter. In doing so we will, more or less, limit our attention to two important publications: Badiou's *Ethics*,[33] and Žižek's recent exchange with Butler and Laclau in *Contingency, Hegemony, Universality*. We will start with Žižek, who seems to question the very basis of radical democracy, and then turn to Badiou's treatment of *Ethics* to the extent that it intervenes in the whole discussion around the development of a radical democratic ethos.

Politics ...

Žižek's recent work seems to involve an abandonment of the politics of democracy in favour of a politics in which anti-capitalism is clearly prioritised; his recent projects – for example his critique of the notion of totalitarianism and his resurrection of Lenin – are indicative in this respect. This shift, however, becomes abundantly clear in his exchange with Butler and Laclau. Consider, for example, the concluding remarks of his final intervention included in the exchange: 'either [radical democracy] means palliative damage control measures within the global capitalist framework, or it means *absolutely nothing*'.[34] Here, Žižek attacks radical democracy on the grounds that 'it does not in fact repoliticize capitalism, because the very notion and form of the "political" within which it operates is grounded in the "depoliticisation" of the economy'.[35] His position is that 'the justified rejection of the fullness of post-revolutionary Society does not justify the conclusion that we have to renounce any project of a global social transformation'.[36] Laclau's response is predictable but justified: 'I agree entirely that this short circuit is illegitimate; the only thing I want to add to that is that it is only Žižek who is jumping into it.'[37] Indeed, why should one deny the transformative potential of radical democracy? How can Žižek support his claim that the political potential of radical democracy is limited in such a severe and debilitating way?

Žižek's argument is that, although at the conceptual level the re-politicisation promised by radical democracy's stress on antagonism sounds quite radical, in practice, hegemonic struggle is never played out at an ontological level, at the level of an ontology of negativity. For him *the Political* is split and thus seems to '*be operative only in so far as it "represses" its radically contingent nature, in so far as it undergoes a minimum of "naturalisation"* ... we are never dealing with the Political "at the level of its notion", with political agents who fully endorse their contingency'.[38] In other words, radical democrats cannot assume full responsibility for negativity; they have to rely on a certain positivisation. The price they pay for that is the naturalisation of capitalist relations. Such a view, however, can only be based on a significant omission, something pointed out by Laclau:

> concerning Žižek's assertion of the need for a minimum of naturalisation and the impossibility of representing impossibility as such, my response is qualified ... For in the endless play of substitutions that Žižek is describing one possibility is omitted: that, instead of the impossibility leading to a series of substitutions which attempt to supersede it, it leads to a symbolization of impossibility *as such* as a positive value ... The possibility of this weakened type of naturalization is important for democratic politics, which involves the institutionalization of its own openness and, in that sense, the injunction to identify with its ultimate impossibility.[39]

In other words, Žižek seems to deny the very possibility of institutionalising lack and division, of articulating a *positive* political order encircling – but not neutralising – negativity and impossibility. What is most astonishing here is that such a denial does not seem to be consistent with Žižek's Lacanian framework insofar as Lacan has conceived psychoanalysis as a paradoxical enterprise leading to the identification with the symptom and the traversing of fantasy. Furthermore, Lacan has devoted considerable energy to symbolically inscribing the lack in the Other in a non-totalisable, non-fantasmatic way. The empty place at the centre of (radicalised) democracy constitutes an attempt to discern – and encourage – the political equivalent of such a position within our political experience of modernity.[40] At this point, then, a radical democratic argument can be seen as attempting to draw the political implications of a central Lacanian ethical attitude. Furthermore, this significant omission leads Žižeks politics into a certain ambiguity. Although, as we have seen, he rejects the utopian promise of a post-revolutionary Society, he appears to end up supporting a form of utopian politics: '*demandons l'impossible*' is the title of the closing section of his last intervention in the book. For him, today 'it is more important than ever to hold th[e] utopian place of the global alternative open'.[41]

... and ethics

This brings us to the whole discussion around the ethical turn in contemporary political philosophy. Even if, *contra* Žižek, one concludes that radical democracy can be a viable and fruitful project for a politics of transformation, what about the prioritisation of ethics within recent radical democratic discourse? For example, at a fairly superficial level, it seems as if Žižek questions the importance of ethics in this field, and thus would also seem to question the deployment of the radical democratic attitude at the ethical level. Consider, for example, his outright condemnation of the ethical turn in political philosophy: 'The "return to ethics" in today's political philosophy shamefully exploits the horrors of Gulag or Holocaust as the ultimate bogey for blackmailing us into renouncing all serious radical engagement.'[42] Surely, however, this cannot be a rejection of ethics *in toto*. Even if only because Žižek himself has devoted a considerable part of his work to elaborating the ethics of psychoanalysis in the Lacanian tradition. It follows then that it must be a particular form of ethical discourse that constitutes his target. The same is true of Alain Badiou's argument, to which we will now turn.

Badiou's target is a particular type of ethics, of ethical ideology, which uses a discourse of 'human rights' and 'humanitarianism' in order to silence alternative thought and politics and legitimise the capitalist order. This is an ethics premised on the principle that 'good is what intervenes visibly against an Evil that is identifiable a priori'.[43] What Badiou points to here, is what appears as a strange inversion; here the Good is derived from the Evil and not the other way round.[44] The result of such an inversion is significant for the theory and politics of transformation:

> if the ethical 'consensus' is founded on the recognition of Evil, it follows that every effort to unite people around a positive idea of the Good, let alone identify Man with projects of this kind, becomes in fact the real source of evil itself. Such is the accusation so often repeated over the last fifteen years: every revolutionary project stigmatised as 'utopian' turns, we are told, into totalitarian nightmare. Every will to inscribe an idea of justice or equality turns bad. Every collective will to the Good creates Evil ... In reality, the price paid by ethics is a stodgy conservatism.[45]

This ethic, which is revealed as nothing but a mindless catechism, a miserable moralism,[46] is an ethics that can have no relation to a transformative political agenda.

This ethics are presented in Badiou's argument as a distortion of a real ethic of truths, which attempts to restore the logical priority of Good over Evil. Badiou's ethic of truths is an ethics related to the idea of the event, a category central for his whole philosophical and political apparatus. To put it briefly, the event here refers to a real break, which destabilises a given discursive articula-

Negativity and radical democracy

tion, a pre-existing order. Ethics, in Badiou's sense, implies a particular type of relation to this destabilising event, a relation of *fidelity*: 'An eventful fidelity is a real break (both thought and practiced) in the specific order within which the event took place ... I shall call "truth" (*a* truth) the real process of a fidelity to an event.'[47] Subject, within this schema, is the bearer of such a fidelity, the one who bears a process of truth and, in fact, is constituted and emerges, as a subject, out of this process.[48]

Undoubtedly, Badiou's work introduces a refreshing and challenging tone in contemporary philosophy. However, it is not immune from a certain criticism. From the point of view of a Lacan-inspired radical democratic argument, one could point to the following points of contention:

1. Indeed many of the theoretico-political interventions associated with the so-called 'ethical turn' boil down to the ideological moralism that Badiou so eloquently condemns. So much has been also pointed out by the theorists of radical democracy. Chantal Mouffe, for example, has noted the dangers entailed in the moralisation of political antagonism.[49] As she has recently pointed out, 'democracy can only be endangered when politics is played out in the moral register'.[50] One gets the impression, however, that Badiou draws a very easy distinction between proper ethics and moralism. For example, in order to provide some empirical justification for his condemnation of the discourse of 'human rights' *in toto* he seems to take for granted the ideological manipulation underlying recent attempts to set up an International Criminal Justice system. Consider the following quote: 'The International Tribunal is clearly prepared to arrest and try, in the name of "human rights", anyone, anywhere, who attempts to contest the New World Order of which NATO (i.e. the United States) is the armed guard.'[51] Surely the fact that today both the US and China bitterly resist the creation of an International Criminal Court should lead to a more nuanced position on these issues.

2. Obviously I would be the last to disagree with Badiou's insistence on the importance of Lacan for the development of a proper, non-moralistic, political ethics. I entirely agree with his point that 'ethics must be taken in the sense presumed by Lacan',[52] and I rejoice at his pointing out that 'the ethic of the truth ... [i]s an ethic of the Real' *á la* Lacan.[53] But I have a difficulty in making Badiou's prioritisation of the Good compatible with the Lacanian Ethics of psychoanalysis, which are clearly an Ethics very suspicious of the Good. Badiou's central thesis is that, 'If Evil exists, we must conceive it from the starting point of the Good',[54] but how can this be made compatible with Lacan's assertion that, 'the good as such – something that has been the eternal object of the philosopher's quest in the sphere of ethics', is radically denied by Freud,[55] and that, from an analytic point of view, not only does the analyst not have this Good that is asked of him, but 'he also knows that there

isn't any'?[56] The difference here concerns, in the final analysis, the relation between positivity and negativity. Badiou does not seem to realise that any Good, even the Good of the fidelity to an event, is always irreducibly linked to an ontological negativity. As Žižek has put it: '"Death drive" is thus the constitutive obverse of every emphatic assertion of Truth irreducible to the positive order of Being, that is, the negative gesture which clears the way for creative sublimation ... a sublime object by which we are enthusiastically transfixed is effectively a "mask of death", a veil that covers over the primordial ontological Void.'[57]

3. Badiou, of course, is not completely unaware of the dangers posed by a positive ethics of the Good. The ways in which he attempts to guard against these dangers are multiple, but two feature as the most important. First, as we have just seen, he premises his own ethics on the notion of the event, which brings with it connotations of negativity (break, rupture, etc.). In fact he even goes on to acknowledge, in a very Lacanian way, the *unnameable* kernel of every truth-process. Secondly, he develops a typology of Evil, in which Evil is partly revealed as an excessive positivisation of the Good, of the power of truth(s): 'Every absolutization of the power of a truth organises an Evil', it entails 'a disaster of the truth induced by the absolutization of its power'.[58] One such manifestation of Evil involves wanting, 'at all costs and under condition of a truth, to force the naming of the unnameable. Such exactly is the principle of disaster.'[59] In that sense, behind the strict distinction Good/Evil lies a delicate balancing act of determining the correct degree of positivisation. Too much positivisation (absolutisation) transforms Good to Evil. But, if Evil is an 'unruly effect of the power of truth',[60] don't we have to acknowledge that the possibility of Evil is inscribed in the very process of proclaiming our fidelity to a positive Good? In other words, it is hard to see how 'The genuine militant, whose pursuit of truth is uncertain at every stage ... who manages to avoid converting belief into a religion',[61] can succeed in this effort if the process of fidelity is conceived as driven 'by an intense faith on the part of the subject'.[62] Badiou's ethics can be described as a heroic attempt to reconstitute an enthusiastic positive ethics of the Good purified of the disastrous excesses of the ever-present risk of its absolutisation. This attempt, however, seems to be compromised by his own heroic and excessive, even quasi-religious,[63] rhetoric – Simon Critchley has referred to a certain '*heroism of the decision*' in Badiou's work, a heroism linked to '*the seduction of a great politics*'.[64] Compromised also by the ultimate inability of Badiou's formalist/relativist ethics of the Good to offer any sufficient criteria for distinguishing true from false events.[65] Not that anyone else can offer such *a priori* criteria; however, this constitutive inability – a marker of the continuous interpenetration between Good and Evil – is perhaps the best justification for abandoning a positive ethics of the Good as a matrix for radical politics.

Negativity and radical democracy

This is not to say, however, that Badiou's work is of no use for a radical democratic project situated beyond a political ethics of the positive Good.[66] For example, the following question posed by Badiou strikes me as extremely important: 'There is always one question in the ethic of truths: how will I, as some-one, continue to exceed my own being? How will I link the things I know, in a consistent fashion, via the effects of being seized by the not-known?'[67] From the point of view of a radical democratic ethics it is not enough to encourage fidelity to an event (in practice, any event), but *to cultivate an openness towards event-ness*. Such an openness, premised on a Lacanian negative ontology and alert to the ever-present play of negativity and disaster, will be more adequately equipped to allow and encourage the pursuit of a better future within a political framework founded on the awareness of the dangers of absolutisation. In that sense, fidelity to an event can flourish and avoid absolutisation only within the framework of another fidelity, fidelity to the openness of the political space and to the awareness of the constitutive impossibility of a final suture of the social, within the framework of a commitment to the continuous political re-inscription of the irreducible lack in the Other. This fidelity is not a one-off, a rare occurrence, it is not tied to a great politics of nostalgia, but implies a *permanent democratic revolution* in our political ethos, a sceptical passion that will have to be re-inscribed in every political act: it cannot be reduced to a fidelity to particular acts, not even to those associated with the democratic revolution, but extends its scope to an acknowledgment of the post-fantasmatic political potential opened by them in the direction of a continuous radicalisation of democracy. Badiou is right that today 'democracy' is one of the central organisers of consensus.[68] And this is clearly the consensus of post-democracy. It is obviously necessary to question and interrogate this anti-political normalisation of democracy. The only consistent way of doing that, the only way of making democracy relevant again,[69] without reoccupying the dangerous ground of utopian absolutisations, is by re-activating the radical potential of the democratic revolution, by acknowledging *event-ness and negativity* as the conditions of possibility/impossibility of all transformative political action: 'It is a matter of showing how the space of the possible is larger than the one we are assigned – that something else is possible, but not that everything is possible.'[70]

Notes

1 I would like to thank Jason Glynos, Kurt Hirtler, Lasse Thomassen and Lars Tønder for their valuable comments on earlier drafts of this text. Another version of this chapter has been published in *Parallax*, 92 (2003): 56–71.
2 E. Laclau, *New Reflections on the Revolution of our Time* (London: Verso, 1990), p. 26.
3 D. Coole, *Negativity and Politics: Dionysus and Dialectics from Kant to Poststructuralism* (London: Routledge, 2000), p. 1.
4 Laclau, *New Reflections on the Revolution of our Time*, p. 39.

5 Coole, *Negativity and Politics*, p. 6.
6 *Ibid.*, p. 230.
7 Laclau, *New Reflections on the Revolution of our Time*, p. 36.
8 The concept of reoccupation is used here in the sense introduced by Hans Blumenberg in *The Legitimacy of the Modern Age*, trans. R. M. Wallace (Cambridge, MA: MIT Press, 1983).
9 Coole, *Negativity and Politics*, p. 231.
10 For a more detailed elaboration see Y. Stavrakakis, *Lacan and the Political* (London: Routledge, 1999), chapter 3. I am relying here on the distinction between the social and the political as developed by Laclau in *New Reflections*, p. 35.
11 I do not claim, of course, that this is the only possible way of conceiving the nuances of political modernity. Indeed, it would be possible to complexify this broad typology in a variety of directions. In any case, the ordering of the three directions presented here is logical and not chronological.
12 A. Badiou, *Manifesto for Philosophy*, trans. N. Madarasz (Albany, NY: State University of New York Press, 1999), p. 133.
13 I am relying here on arguments put forward and elaborated in detail in chapter 4 of Stavrakakis, *Lacan and the Political*.
14 S. Žižek, 'I hear you with my eyes', in S. Žižek and R. Salecl (eds), *Gaze and Voice as Love Objects* (Durham: Duke University Press, 1996), p. 116.
15 Žižek, 'I hear you with my eyes', p. 118.
16 C. Lefort, *The Political Forms of Modern Society*, trans. J. B. Thompson (Cambridge: Polity, 1986), pp. 303f. On the importance of the democratic revolution, see also E. Laclau and C. Mouffe, *Hegemony and Socialist Strategy: Towards a Radical Democratic Politics* (London: Verso, 1985), pp. 152–9.
17 J. Rancière, *On the Shores of Politics*, trans. L. Heron (London: Verso, 1995), p. 177.
18 J. Rancière, *Disagreement: Politics and Philosophy*, trans. J. Rose (Minneapolis, MN: University of Minnesota Press, 1999), pp. 95–121.
19 *Ibid.*, pp. 101f.
20 *Ibid.*, p. 113.
21 *Ibid.*, pp. 97f.
22 As for political projects promoting similar goals, the diverse anti-globalisation movement provides many examples.
23 For a general discussion of the politics of radical democracy, see D. Trend (ed.), *Radical Democracy: Identity, Citizenship and the State* (New York: Routledge, 1996).
24 See J. Glynos, 'Radical democracy: democratic theory from an anti-essentialist perspective', *Essex Papers in Politics and Government. Subseries in Ideology and Discourse Analysis*, no. 17 (2001), 4f.
25 *Ibid.*, p. 6.
26 Laclau, *New Reflections*, p. 169; Glynos, 'Radical democracy', pp. 5f.
27 See, in this respect, Stavrakakis, *Lacan and the Political*, chapter 5. See also C. Mouffe, *The Democratic Paradox* (London: Verso, 2000), pp. 129–40.
28 Glynos, 'Radical democracy', p. 14.
29 S. Žižek, *On Belief* (London: Routledge, 2001), p. 123.
30 E. Laclau, 'Structure, history and the political', in J. Butler, E. Laclau and S. Žižek, *Hegemony, Contingency, Universality: Contemporary Dialogues on the Left* (London: Verso, 2000), p. 204.
31 Badiou, *Manifesto for philosophy*, p. 83.
32 *Ibid.*, p. 84.

33 A. Badiou, *Ethics: An Essay on the Understanding of Evil*, trans. P. Hallward (London: Verso, 2001).
34 S. Žižek, 'Holding the place', in J. Butler, E. Laclau and S. Žižek, *Hegemony, Contingency, Universality: Contemporary Dialogues on the Left* (London: Verso, 2000), p. 321 (emphasis in original).
35 S. Žižek, 'Class struggle or postmodernism? Yes please!', J. Butler, E. Laclau and S. Žižekk, *Hegemony, Contingency, Universality: Contemporary Dialogues on the Left* (London: Verso, 2000), p. 98.
36 *Ibid.*, p. 101
37 *Ibid.*, p. 197.
38 *Ibid.*, p. 100.
39 Laclau 'Structure, history and the political', p. 199 (emphasis in original).
40 This connection is elaborated in detail in Stavrakakis, *Lacan and the Political*, chapter 5.
41 Žižek, 'Holding the place', p. 325.
42 Žižek, *On Belief*, p. 127.
43 Badiou, *Ethics*, p. 8.
44 *Ibid.*, p. 9.
45 *Ibid.*, pp. 13f.
46 *Ibid.*, p. iv.
47 *Ibid.*, p. 42.
48 *Ibid.*, p. 43.
49 See, for example, C. Mouffe, 'Democracy, radical and plural', *CSD Bulletin*, 9:1 (2001–02), 13.
50 C. Mouffe, 'The end of politics and the challenge of right-wing populism', unpublished paper, p. 11.
51 Badiou, *Ethics*, p. iv.
52 *Ibid.*, p. 28.
53 *Ibid.*, p. 52.
54 *Ibid.*, p. 60.
55 J. Lacan, *The Ethics of Psychoanalysis* (London: Routledge, 1993), p. 96.
56 *Ibid.*, p. 300.
57 S. Žižek, 'Psychoanalysis in Post-Marxism: the case of Alain Badiou', *The South Atlantic Quarterly*, 97:2 (1998), 258.
58 Badiou, *Ethics*, p. 85.
59 *Ibid.*, p. 86.
60 *Ibid.*, p. 61.
61 J. Barker, *Alain Badiou: A Critical Introduction* (London: Pluto Press, 2002), p. 139.
62 *Ibid.*, p. 84.
63 Notice, for example, his references to immortality in *Ethics* and his general interest in Saint Paul.
64 S. Critchley, 'Demanding approval: on the ethics of Alain Badiou', *Radical Philosophy*, 100 (2000), 23.
65 On this issue, see J.-J. Lecercle, 'Cantor, Lacan, Mao, *meme combat*: the philosophy of Alain Badiou', *Radical Philosophy*, 93 (1999), 12, and Critchley, 'Demanding approval'.
66 We also take for granted the analytical value of Badiou's schema, as it highlights the affective dimension entailed in any identification act.
67 Badiou, *Ethics*, p. 50.
68 A. Badiou, 'Highly speculative reasoning on the concept of democracy', trans. J.

Jauregui, *Lacanian Ink*, 16 (2000), 30.
69 *Ibid.*, 35.
70 A. Badiou and P. Hallward, 'Politics and philosophy: an interview with Alain Badiou', *Angelaki*, 3:3 (1998), 121.

12 • Lars Tønder

Inessential commonality: immanence, transcendence, abundance[1]

Marx helps us to understand that the voice of writing, the voice of the incessant dispute, has continuously to develop and break itself into *multiple* forms. The voice of communism is always *at once* ... total and fragmentary, long away and almost instantaneous. (Maurice Blanchot)

Decisive here is the idea of an *inessential* commonality, a solidarity that in no way concerns an essence. (Giorgio Agamben)

If capitalism/man can be understood as multiple and specific; if it is not a unity but a heterogeneity; not a sameness but a difference; if it is always becoming what it is not ... then noncapital/woman is released from its singular and subordinate status. (J. K. Gibson-Graham)[2]

Introduction

THIS CHAPTER takes issue with the elusive sense of commonality that decides the limit between those who partake in the bond of community and those who must stay outside. What is the character of this commonality? What makes it loveable and possible to affirm? And what kind of politics might it mobilise?

To answer these questions from the perspective of radical democracy is to step outside the traditional paradigms of community. These paradigms, some of which reach their modern acme in the political philosophy of Jean-Jacques Rousseau, demand that we appeal to an essential entity of a sort – an incontestable feature of social life that enables the General Will (or something equivalent) to express the cohesive and unifying nature of human sociability.[3] As this volume demonstrates, theorists of radical democracy make no such appeal, but instead privilege a theoretical framework that highlights the way in which identity-formation depends on difference and otherness (what we in the Introduction to this volume called 'radical difference'). This makes it hard, if not impossible, for theorists of radical democracy to think of community as something that invokes cohesion and unity. Rather, theorists of radical democracy imagine a community that – in the words of Jacques Derrida – puts us 'where the disparate itself *holds together*... without effacing the heterogeneity of the other'.[4] There is little doubt that the image of the disparate represents an important signpost for theorists of radical democracy on both sides of the abundance/lack divide.[5] Even so, the image is still cause for some bewilderment and frustration, for it is not self-evident how we might turn the affirmation of the disparate into a collective endeavour. What is the commonality of the disparate? And what is the link between the conceptualisation of this commonality and the flow of material things and finite human beings?

In what follows, I give one possible answer to these questions by way of what I call 'inessential commonality' – a communal experience of becoming that exposes 'us' (the members of the community) to otherness and difference. Moreover, the notion of inessential commonality says nothing about the way in which members of the community must live their lives in terms of the relationship between the public sphere and the private sphere; nor does it say anything *a priori* about the ethnic or religious bonds that certain members of the community might share. Rather, in opposition to these essentialising versions of community, the notion of inessential commonality suggests an injunction not to close off the disparate itself. This makes it a powerful contribution to the theory of radical democracy, first, because it fosters a care for the disparate across traditional lines of division; and, second, because it situates this care for the disparate within an economic imaginary that turns the heterogeneity of capitalism into a reform of capitalism itself. As we shall see, both of these contributions hinge on a willingness to rework some of the most basic presuppositions of radical democracy. I begin with the question of immanence and transcendence, after which I turn to the issue of capitalism and political economy.

Inessential commonality between immanence and transcendence

The idea of inessential commonality follows from Baruch Spinoza's proposition that what 'is common to all ... and which is equally in a part and in a whole, does not constitute the essence of any particular thing'.[6] In this section, I seek to moderate the ontological presuppositions of this proposition, untying the idea of inessential commonality from its bond to Spinoza's philosophy of immanence. My argument is that the moderation is crucial insofar as the latter – that is, Spinoza's philosophy of immanence – has become the centrepiece of the ontology of abundance.[7] Moreover, without refuting the ontology of abundance, I argue that a strict philosophy of immanence (like the one of Spinoza) harbours its own undoing and, furthermore, that this undoing – itself a mode of transcendence – points to critical dimensions of the very experience of community. Indeed, I suggest that it is from within the space *in between* immanence and transcendence that inessential commonality becomes as a significant contribution to the theory of radical democracy, unearthing what we characterise as a disjunctive junction holding together the disparate. The following discussion of Spinoza sets the stage for this argument.

Spinoza's philosophy of immanence relies on two ideas, both of which point to a 'pure ontology ... of positive forms':[8] first, it relies on the idea that we all emerge from the same source of existence, which, as a God immanent to the world, operates according to the laws of Nature; and second, it relies on the idea that this notion of God makes no categorical distinction between different life-forms, but instead is equally present in human beings and material things alike. The difficulty of these two ideas lies in their multiple interpretations. For example, some contemporary commentators argue that the ideas point to an incontestable feature of social life that all members of the community must affirm in order to be truly communitarian.[9] Certainly, this interpretation adds valuable insights to our understanding of Spinoza. Even so, the interpretation is problematic insofar as it situates the radical weft of Spinozism within a conventional paradigm of community, which fails to take seriously Spinoza's own attempt to destabilise our modern belief in the self-sufficient integrity of individual existence (what we might think of as always already formed individuals).

Instead, it seems that Gilles Deleuze and Félix Guattari provide us with a better interpretation of the two ideas structuring Spinoza's philosophy of immanence. Writing in the vein of Spinoza, reworking his metaphysics in the light of contemporary debates on difference and otherness, Deleuze and Guattari argue that a philosophy of immanence is characterised by the attempt to substitute what they call 'haecceities' for always already formed individuals.[10] More tangible than modern individuality, a haecceity is a composite entity, which receives its consistency from a unique combination of *longitude* (defined as different relations of movement and rest) and *latitude* (defined as different degrees of potentiality).[11] This Spinozist proposition has important consequences for the way in which we are able to conceptualise the production of inessential commonality. The phenomenon of taking a walk illustrates how this might be the case.[12] Along the dimension of longitude, walking is the aggregated result of several relations of movement and rest. Naturally, there is the walker who contributes with one kind of speed defining the tempo of the walk. However, this speed is not independent of its surroundings, but depends, among other things, on the resistance of the road surface (another constellation of movement and rest), wind-direction and its particular speed, and the temperature of the air. Moreover, the phenomenon of taking a walk is also a question of understanding how the interaction of these different constellations of movement and rest produce different degrees of potentiality along the dimension of latitude. For example, one day it may be the dark-blue colour of the road surface that makes us feel melancholic and anxious; another day our happiness of being out in the open air may be what makes a stiff wind feel like a gentle breeze, in the slipstream of which a complicated problem finally reaches its own solution.

But if the combination of longitude and latitude gives the phenomenon of taking a walk its consistency, its unique form and potentiality, then we might also say that this consistency is nothing but the contingent togetherness of otherwise disparate entities (a walker, a stiff wind and a dark-blue road surface). The consistency of taking a walk is thus an example of what I call inessential commonality. Deleuze and Guattari substantiate the community of this commonality with the notion of the rhizome – a notion that breaks with the traditional paradigm of community insofar as it refuses to issue any definite standard according to which we must measure or judge concrete instances of community. Moreover, the rhizome allows us to think of community as a multiplicity of connections that come into being wherever there is a flow of finite yet consistent haecceities. Here is how Deleuze and Guattari summarise their notion of the rhizome:

> Unlike trees or their roots, the rhizome connects any point to any other point, and its traits are not necessarily lined to traits of the same nature; it brings into play very different regimes of signs, and even non-sign states. The rhizome is reducible neither to the One nor the multiple. It is not One that becomes two or even directly three, four, five, etc. It is not a multiple derived from the One, or to which One is added ($n + 1$). It is composed not of units but of dimensions, or rather directions in motion. It has neither beginning nor end, but always a middle (*milieu*) from which it grows and which it overspills. It constitutes linear multiplicities with n dimensions having neither subject nor object, which can be laid out on a plane of consistency, and from which the One is always subtracted ($n-1$).[13]

In sum, this interpretation of Spinoza's philosophy of immanence suggests a place for the holding-together of the disparate (inessential commonality); that is, the disparate is what travels along the infinite dimensions of the rhizome and the dispersive character of its travelling what puts the rhizome into motion. Even so, the interpretation may also carry the contradiction, if not dissolution, of inessential commonality, for, as Jean-Luc Nancy argues, the philosophy of immanence is always in danger of turning into a totalitarian demand. If this is the case, then it is also the case that the philosophy of immanence is what Nancy characterises as a 'stumbling block to the thought of community'.[14]

According to Nancy, the reason for this is that immanence can only become immanent to itself by becoming everything, eliminating any attempt to transcend the ultimate source of existence (for instance, Spinoza's God). No matter how much we refine this source of existence the demand itself leaves the thought of community with the following choice: either the community forces every member to recognise that there is only one source of existence; or the community begins discriminating between those who share its sense of history and those who do not (for instance, the foreigner or the stranger). In both cases the philosophy of immanence ends up closing off the space of the disparate, thereby contradicting its own *raison d'être*. Moreover, in order to become everything, the philosophy of immanence has to become nothing or to become what Nancy – following the work of George Bataille – calls an 'unknowable'.[15] The unknowable comes about insofar as the process of getting to know everything rests on a bird's eye view of the very source of existence. Without this view there is no way that we can assure ourselves that we really know everything. But to get a bird's eye view also requires that we step outside ourselves, even if we are the ones who are trying to see and understand everything. This is because 'we' are just as much part of what 'we' want to know as everything else. Yet to step outside ourselves implies a step into the realm of difference and otherness, a realm that escapes any kind of knowledge. Thus, we end up producing an unruly unknowable that never stops questioning the existence of proclaimed totalities. This questioning includes the philosophy of immanence, which, insofar as it acknowledges that it, too, belongs to a non-totalisable community of relations, has to admit that inessential commonality comes into existence through the *undoing* of immanence (rather than its opposition, the constitution of immanence).

Deleuze and Guattari may not agree with this critique. Their way of formulating a philosophy of immanence is not only one that resists binary thinking, but also one that emphasises the impossibility of reducing the field of ontology (Being) to anything actual. This means that a rhizomatic community is always a community that exceeds its own finite limits as it connects with other haecceities and assemblages. Even so, Nancy's argument against philosophies of immanence in general – what he calls 'immanentism' – points to the contestability of their position and invites us to situate the production of inessential commonality in between immanence and transcendence.[16] The key to this invitation is not only what we mean by immanence, but also what we mean by transcendence.

Traditionally, transcendence signifies the possibility of a world completely different from the world that we currently inhabit, not unlike a super-sensible field free from the contingency of human existence. Nancy himself comes close to this view when he argues that the place of community is so distant from everyday experience that it amounts to imagining what he calls 'the sacred stripped of the sacred'.[17] The problem with this view of transcendence is its insistence on demanding that what lies outside our own world must be truly singular and, as such, without precedence. Among other things, this requires the institution of something exceptional – 'the rule of all rules' – guaranteeing the absence of any attempt to challenge this unprecedented space. Surely, the promise of such an absence is tantalising, if not seducing. Even so, it suggests a view of transcendence that risks becoming host to its own dogmatism, preventing the community of the disparate – that is, inessential commonality – from taking more than just one form. This tendency to totalise the non-totalisable suggests the need to experiment with other views of transcendence.

In particular, I am thinking of a view of transcendence that connotes with transgressing what presently exists without thereby dismissing our connectedness with this presence. Here it is helpful to return to the phenomenon of taking a walk, for what makes walking so interesting is the way in which it situates the production of inessential commonality within a horizon of a sort. To begin with, the horizon makes itself felt by exposing 'us' to what was previously unknown. This exposition appears because the horizon opens up new places, some of which are so surprising that they appear as clues to the existence of an outside, transcendent to lived experience. Even a minor change in the colours of the horizon can change our way of perceiving what we previously took for granted. But the horizon is also what brings us back to the hereness and nowness of our walking. This bringing-us-back to the present occurs because the horizon reminds us of the impossibility of doing away with the horizon as such; it is almost a matter of fact that the horizon is there, immanent to and for itself. So 'we' keep-on walking, looking for new adventures.

The upshot of this argument is a view of transcendence that splits the immanence of the rhizome into contingently constructed points of bifurcation, exposing 'us' to experiences we have never had before. Also, the argument indicates a space *in between* immanence and transcendence – a space that, in the vein of what we in the Introduction of this volume called radical difference, is characterised by a disjunctive junction holding-together the disparate. Two consequences follow from this. First, it is possible to substitute an ethos of creativity and enthusiasm for the kind of nostalgia that circumscribes most traditional paradigms of community. Community is not something we have lost, a notion idea that assumes the possibility of a beginning and an end to very concept of community. Instead, community is an experience of becoming that, constantly deferring its own realisation, allows us to share new modes of otherness and difference. Second, it is possible to imagine a community that refuses to say anything *a priori* about (a) the way in which expressions of being are either private or public; and (b) the need to exclude certain constituencies from participating in the bond of commonality (for instance, the stranger or the mad). Both of these ideas risk stifling the community of radical democracy. Rather, a commitment to the notion of inessential commonality is also a commitment to an ethically motivated injunction not to close off the disparate.[18] The affirmation of this injunction, whose particular expression is subject to contestation, keeps the communal experience of becoming open to new adventures. Furthermore, it enables radical democrats to engage a multiplicity of constituencies, disrupting those hegemonies that pursue an ideology of sameness and totality.

The political economy of inessential commonality

As I have argued in the above, it is the combination of an ethos of creativity and an injunction not to close off the disparate that makes inessential commonality a powerful contribution to the theory of radical democracy. Even so, the contribution does not itself vindicate inessential commonality, for the success of the latter depends to a large extent on the political structures and economic conditions under which it operates. Consequently, we should now move our discussion of community and radical democracy to the field of political economy, a field that puts conceptual innovations, such as inessential commonality, back into the flow of material things and finite human beings. Also, it is a field in which the old Marxist dictum that enthusiasm is a precondition for political change still rings true, confirming what Marx stated in 'Contribution to the Critique of Hegel's *Philosophy of Right*': 'No class in civil society can [change political structures and economic conditions] unless it can arouse, in itself and in the masses, a *moment of enthusiasm* in which it associates and mingles with society at large, identifies itself with it and is felt and recognized as the *general representative* of this society.'[19]

The following section uses this dictum by Marx as its starting-point for an exploration of the kind of political economy that most potently would fortify inessential commonality. My argument follows a dual track. First, I review two prominent discourses on the political economy of radical democracy – one by Michael Hardt and Antonio Negri and another by Ernesto Laclau – and argue that both discourses remain caught in a dilemma between a wish to overthrow capitalism and a tendency to marginalise any alternative that would come after capitalism.[20] The reason for this is, I claim, that both discourses enforce a strict choice between the philosophy of immanence and the philosophy of transcendence, a choice that prevents us from cultivating the potentiality for economic change and political reform that resides within the heterogeneity of capitalism itself. Second, I suggest that we weave what I have said so far about inessential commonality into very the fabric of economic thought. This allows us not only to appreciate the heterogeneity of capitalism, approaching this heterogeneity as a means for change and reform, it also, I argue, opens up an economic imaginary that affirms the communal experience of becoming and its injunction not to close off the disparate. The section concludes with two examples, both of which help us realise how the notion of inessential commonality might change the current flow of material things and finite human beings.

One of the most influential interventions in recent debates on radical democracy is the one by Hardt and Negri. Working from within a strict philosophy of immanence, Hardt and Negri analyse contemporary capitalism as a one-sided mode of economic development that points to what they call a 'smooth world'. The power of this world, which administers the demands of an unlimited world market through an infinite number of de-territorialised societies of control, stems from the ability of capital to operate 'on the plane of immanence, through relays and networks of relationships of domination, without reliance on a transcendent centre of power'.[21] According to Hardt and Negri, it is only because of this ability that capitalism has become a totalitarian force the desire for which is its own accumulation, penetrating and, eventually, taking over all economic relations situated on the plane of immanence. Moreover, from the perspective of radical democracy, the ability of capital to dominate the plane of immanence means that we should not expect capitalism to pursue its own reform. Instead, Hardt and Negri suggest that we commit ourselves to a political revolution that overthrows existing power constellations and replaces capitalism with a desire that is just as powerful as its own (that is, the accumulation of capital). Hardt and Negri call this alternative desire the 'multitude' – a collective political force that, just like the one of capitalism, has 'no reason to look outside its own history and its own present productive power' in its pursuit of a 'new ontological reality'.[22]

We might agree with Hardt and Negri that contemporary capitalism has been successful in spreading a smooth world in which de-territorialised societies of control administer the demands of an unlimited world market. Nevertheless, their alternative – the multitude – appears equally totalising, for the way in which it construes the philosophy of immanence prevents constituencies that do not share its sense of history and purpose from participating in the pursuit of radical democracy. Moreover, from the perspective of the philosophy of transcendence, Laclau criticises Hardt and Negri for turning politics into something 'unthinkable'.[23] The reason is, Laclau argues, that the political itself signifies a split in the social, leaving any identity dependent on its constitutive outside that, insofar as it exceeds definite conceptualisation, defines the limit of discursive signification. This argument, which has much in common with the one of Nancy and other post-structural theorists of transcendence,[24] has two consequences for a possible transformation of capitalism. First, it reduces Hardt and Negri's faith in the immanent power of the multitude to a 'purely fanciful construction';[25] and, second, it opens up an alternative framework of transcendence that emphasises the contingency of political order as well as the multifaceted character of identity and discourse. Indeed, in a recent intervention, Laclau asserts that there is 'nothing in the worker's demand which is *intrinsically* anti-capitalist', an assertion that points in the direction of the neo-Marxist notion of 'combined and uneven development'.[26]

Even so, within this highly developed framework, capitalism remains a relatively stable force that folds rebellious elements into its own mode of organisation. For example, in their seminal work *Hegemony and Socialist Strategy*, Laclau and Chantal Mouffe argue that the introduction of Fordism in the aftermath of World War II transformed society 'into a vast market in which

Inessential commonality

new "needs" [are] ceaselessly created'.[27] Also, in the same work, Laclau and Mouffe argue that the result of this transformation is that there is 'practically no domain of individual or collective life which escapes capitalist relations'.[28] Furthermore, Laclau suggests that insofar as capitalism is 'able to absorb the demands of the subordinated groups in a transformist way – to use a Gramscian expression – that system will enjoy good health'.[29] And, finally, Laclau confirms the idea that, while the struggle for radical democracy is fought on a number of fronts, none of which is privileged *vis-à-vis* the rest, the struggle itself is always 'anti-capitalist' or 'anti-systemic' in nature.[30]

I emphasise these quotations in order to show how Laclau shares at least one idea with Hardt and Negri: the idea that the power of capitalism stems from its ability to move slowly yet steadily toward a complete domestication of the field of economic relations. Furthermore, while Laclau and Hardt and Negri may disagree on who is capable of overthrowing capitalism, they also seem to agree that the overthrow itself demands a political force that is not part of the capitalist system, preventing any intervention into the field of political economy from becoming subject to the 'transformist' logic of capitalism itself. The upshot of this agreement is a set of discursive limitations that undermine the very pursuit of radical democracy. On the one hand, it is not clear how a political collective – whether it is a multitude or a counter-hegemony – would organise itself outside a system of capitalism that appears to be penetrating virtually all social relations. Indeed, both frameworks seem to suggest that the presence of non-capitalist relations is so limited that only a few constituencies would be able to join the collective in the first place. On the other hand, even if it was possible to organise a political collective outside capitalist relations, the collective would soon find itself caught in a dilemma between protecting itself from the transformist logic of what it is fighting and defining itself with reference to this very same logic. Two consequences follow from this. First, radical democrats end up relying on means of change that are non-capitalist in nature, while admitting that these resources are not very powerful in comparison with their capitalist counterparts. Second, radical democrats end up projecting a new economic reality, while admitting that this reality is not only politically peripheral, but also economically unviable.

How do we avoid this dilemma – a dilemma whose logic seems to drown the enthusiasm so critical to the possibility of economic change and political reform? My suggestion is that we modify the choice between the philosophy of immanence and the philosophy of transcendence, approaching capitalism as a process of becoming – what I would call inessential commonality – from which heterogeneous, non-capitalist relations emerge in unexpected ways.[31] A few observations indicate that this approach resonates quite well with current ways of organising the economy. For example, some researchers argue that national accounts overlook more than 50 per cent of all economic activity in both rich and poor countries, suggesting that prevailing depictions of the economy are far from sufficient to the richness of economic relations in general.[32] Moreover, other researchers suggest that almost two-thirds of US citizens belong to some kind of self-employment, unearthing an economic organisation that defies the traditional categories of capitalism, insofar as its participants own the means of production without exploiting wage labourers on any large scale (if any).[33] And, finally, within the economies of both the United States and Western Europe, researchers point to a number of economic agents that, ranging from restaurant-owners to independent truck-drivers, use salary earned on capitalist premises to invest in non-capitalist activities, such as community houses, public schools and alternative health care.[34] Surely, sceptics of these observations would claim that the small size of these subterranean economies make them insignificant compared with large multinational corporations such as Nike or Coca-Cola. Yet, indicating that the economic field is more than a struggle between capitalists and workers, they are nonetheless noteworthy insofar as they operate on labour and capital markets that are distinct from the conventional capitalist enterprise. The latter gives them not only a significant level of financial autonomy; also, it enables them to co-exist alongside the dominant forms of capitalism.

With these examples in mind, my wager is that attention to the heterogeneity of capitalism enables us to see how the latter has the structure of an inessential commonality. Also, my wager is that attention to this heterogeneity enables us to see how the movement between the immanence and the transcendence of capitalism unearths means of change that disrupts capitalism from within. Indeed, we would no longer have to see capitalism as a force that slowly yet steadily penetrates all social relations; rather, we would have to see it as a process of becoming whose self-contradictory nature *might* – and I emphasise *might* – turn into something non-capitalist. J. K. Gibson-Graham is one of those contemporary theorists who have done the most to cultivate this possibility. Mounting a feminist perspective on political economy, which focuses on issues related to the politics of radical democracy, Gibson-Graham suggests an analysis of contemporary identities – what she calls 'class' – that is both critical of capitalism and appreciative of its heterogeneity. The foundation of this analysis is a view of class identity that is similar to what I call inessential commonality, for, as Gibson-Graham says, class is 'a process without an essence; in other words, class processes have no core or condition of existence that governs their development more closely than any other and to which they can be ultimately reduced'.[35] Moreover, Gibson-Graham pursues an analysis that has little to say about the purpose and necessary character of class-identity, replacing this focus with an investigation of the ways in which disparate life-forms connect across disjunctive junctions holding immanence and transcendence together in a productive tension. Interestingly, Gibson-Graham substantiates this suggestion by dividing the process of producing and appropriating surplus labour into two sub-processes, both of which are crucial to the pursuit of economic equality and social justice (and, as such, to the injunction not to close off the disparate). First, Gibson-Graham points to the *process of exploitation* where 'surplus labour is produced and appropriated'; and, second, she points to the *process of distribution* where 'appropriated surplus labour is distributed to a variety of social destination'.[36]

The upshot of this division is an agenda for a progressive political economy that is appreciative of inessential commonality in two important ways.[37] On the one hand, we might say that a progressive political economy is one that not only decentres the appropriation of surplus, refusing the few to exploit the many, but also one that returns the right to appropriate surplus back to those who produced it in the first place. This would most certainly require a major reconstruction of our current way of organising the economy. On the other hand, even if such a reconstruction is impossible here and now, we might also say that a progressive political economy is one that multiplies the sharing of surplus – what Gibson-Graham calls the process of distribution – investing this surplus in a world of economic equality and social justice. Such an investment would not necessarily have to subject itself to the transformist logic that both Laclau and Hardt and Negri find so worrisome. Rather, our previous discussion suggests that to invest in the political economy of inessential commonality is to increase the likelihood of turning the accumulative and commodifying desire of capitalism into something other than capitalism itself. The following two examples fortify this possibility, concluding my discussion of how to embed inessential commonality in the flow of material things and finite human beings.

1 *Financial sector.* The financial sector has an ambiguous position in discussions about radical democracy, embodying the worst traits of capitalist society (for instance, speculation and short-term investment), while being a necessary component in any viable solution to contemporary problems of foreign debt and international economic development. With regard to the politics of inessential commonality, the key to the financial sector lies in broadening its notion of productive investment, so that it becomes legitimate to take into consideration alternative issues, many of which would be related to gender-equality, problems of racial discrimination, environmental sustainability, public health and so on. A potent way of doing this is by democratising money-lending, breaking the link between the production of financial wealth and its allocation. Moreover, to include a variety of constituencies in the process that decides the allocation of loans and other forms of credit is also to re-politicise the production and appropriation of surplus. What are the goals of production? How should we organise the work that goes into it? Do some concerns weigh more than others? If so, which

ones? Eventually, it may be that a politicisation of these questions would foster a sense of community that opposes the demands of world markets and appreciates the injunction not to close off the disparate itself.[38]

2 *Local networks*: But the democratisation of money-lending does not itself guarantee the development of a progressive political economy. Instead, a progressive political economy depends also on the way in which 'we' become economic subjects through the many processes of subjectivation that are at play in any given society. Here the politics of inessential commonality points to the possibility of cultivating a series of local networks where people, who are brought together with no pre-defined purpose other than the pursuit of a new sense of community, begin sharing services and commodities that range from gardening and car maintenance to health care and legal counselling.[39] In the beginning, these projects may seem insignificant compared with 'normal' wage-labour. Nonetheless, they help us to become more familiar with alternative modes of economic organisation and, eventually, might have an effect on how we constitute ourselves as economic subjects. Indeed, they may inspire us to move outside the traditional categories of capitalism. This makes the cultivation of local networks – many of which emerge outside the traditional arenas of politics such as parties and labour unions – crucial to the politics of inessential commonality.

Conclusion: inessential commonality and abundance

It is the efficacy of these initiatives that, although they may seem insignificant in comparison with our prevailing depictions of capitalism, decides the success of inessential commonality, connecting the theoretical insights of the latter with the current flow of material things and finite human beings. Moreover, insofar as the connection is successful, inessential commonality signifies a communal experience of becoming that not only multiplies the limit between those who partake in the bond of community and those who do not, but also invites radical democrats to affirm the injunction not to close off the disparate itself. Importantly, this does not necessarily mean that the community of radical democracy is more inclusive than other paradigms of community (at least not if we by 'inclusion' mean uncritical acceptance of whatever demands and identities might arise in the context of democratic pluralism). Rather, as we have seen, the inclusiveness of radical democracy hinges on the way in which its constituencies combine an ethos of creativity with a moment of enthusiasm, both of which cultivate, first, a critical stance toward capitalism, and, second, a vision of social and economic equality across old and new identities. Ultimately, it is the cultivation of this vision that makes radical democracy a unique contribution to the field of contemporary democratic theory.

Another offshoot of my argument about inessential commonality is a better

Inessential commonality

sense of what defines the ontology of abundance, which, as I mentioned earlier, seems to follow from a philosophy of immanence that emphasises positive forms and rhizomatic assemblages. The discussions of this chapter suggest a more nuanced picture. On the one hand, we have seen how philosophies of immanence harbour their own undoing, insofar as they rely on a bird's eye view forcing them to step outside of the very plane of immanence. On the other hand, we have also seen how the outside of immanence – what I have called the mode of transcendence that exposes 'us' to previously unknown experiences – is much more than a sacred place from which nothing but lack and negativity follow. Indeed, I have argued that the place *in between* immanence and transcendence is one of inessential commonality; that is, the kind of commonality which enables contingently constructed haecceities to connect without having anything essential in common prior to this connection. Also, it is the kind of commonality which augments the positive forms and rhizomatic assemblages that distinguishes the ontology of abundance from the ontology of lack.

In conclusion, we might say that the significance of this connection between inessential commonality and the ontology of abundance lies in its contribution to our understanding of the latter. Three insights are worth emphasising in this regard. First, the connection adds a new dimension of contestability to the ontology of abundance, which not only demonstrates the impossibility of reducing our ontological explorations to a matter of either immanence or transcendence, but also indicates the exuberant richness of these explorations. Second, the connection shows how the ontology of abundance might encourage new practices of democracy, encouraging constituencies of different faiths and beliefs to interact across traditional lines of division (even those that are motivated by either religious traditions or economic interests). And finally, the connection suggests that our approach to the ontology of abundance should be similar to what Maurice Merleau-Ponty calls a style; that is, 'a sort of incarnate principle that brings a style of being wherever there is a fragment of being'.[40] The reason for this is that the ontology of abundance always exceeds its own boundaries on its way to becoming something different from what it is now, something that makes it impossible to define it according to only one form. Instead, we must see it as incarnate principle that informs every aspect of our way of life, colouring even the most mundane connections between immanence and transcendence.

Notes

1 Previous versions of this chapter were presented to the International Society for the Study of European Ideas (ISSEI), 22–27 July 2002, Aberystwyth, Wales, UK; to the graduate student colloquium on justice at the Department of Political Science, Johns Hopkins University, USA; and to American Political Science Association Convention, 28–31 August 2003, Philadelphia, Pennsylvania, USA. I would like to thank Jane

Bennett, William E. Connolly, Paulina Ochoa-Espejo, Sacramento Roselló Martínez, Lasse Thomassen and Hent de Vries for their comments and suggestions.

2 M. Blanchot, 'Les Trois Paroles de Marx', in L'Amitié (Paris: Éditions Gallimard, 1971), p. 117 (my translation); G. Agamben, *The Coming Community*, trans. M. Hardt (Minneapolis, MN: University of Minnesota Press, 1993), p. 18; and J. K. Gibson Graham, *The End of Capitalism (as we knew it): A Feminist Critique of Political Economy* (Oxford: Blackwell, 1996), p. 44.

3 See R. Esposito, *Communitas: Origine et destin de la communauté*, trans. N. Lirzin (Paris: Presses Universitaires de France, 2000) for a critical encounter with the traditional paradigm of community and an attempt to move toward something like the community of radical democracy.

4 J. Derrida, *Specters of Marx: The State of the Debt, the Work of Mourning, and the New International*, trans. P. Kamuf (London: Routledge, 1994), p. 29.

5 See A. Little, 'Community and radical democracy', *Journal of Political Ideologies*, 7:3 (2002), 369–83; and A. Tanesini, 'In search of community: Mouffe, Wittgenstein and Cavell', *Radical Philosophy*, no. 110 (2001), 12–19, for two opposing readings of this alternative imaginary.

6 B. Spinoza, *Ethics*, trans. S. Shirley (Indianapolis: Hackett Publishing Company, 1992), Part 2, Proposition 37.

7 See, for instance, W. E. Connolly, *Neuropolitics: Thinking, Culture, Speed* (Minneapolis, MN: University of Minnesota Press, 2002); G. Deleuze and F. Guattari, *A Thousand Plateaus: Capitalism and Schizophrenia*, trans. B. Massumi (Minneapolis, MN: University of Minnesota Press, 1987); and M. Hardt and A. Negri, *Empire* (Cambridge, MA: Harvard University Press, 2000). Furthermore, see D. W. Smith, 'Deleuze and Derrida, immanence and transcendence: two directions in recent French thought', in P. Patton and J. Protevi (eds), *Between Deleuze and Derrida* (New York: Continuum, 2003), for an outline of the distinction between immanence and transcendence in contemporary French philosophy. As Connolly discusses in his contribution to this volume, the distinction between immanence and transcendence has some affinities with the distinction between the ontology of abundance and the ontology of lack.

8 G. Deleuze, *Expressionism in Philosophy: Spinoza*, trans. M. Joughin (New York: Zone Books, 1992), p. 173.

9 J. I. Israel, *Radical Enlightenment: Philosophy and the Making of Modernity 1650 – 1750* (Oxford: Oxford University Press, 2001), is an important contribution to this interpretation of Spinoza.

10 Hæcceity signifies according to the *Oxford English Dictionary* a 'hereness and nowness' in virtue of which a thing is or becomes a definite individual.

11 Deleuze and Guattari, *A Thousand Plateaus*, p. 260.

12 I use the example of taking a walk in order to illustrate the emergence of inessential commonality (and, hence, community) outside the conventional sphere of politics set by theories of liberalism and communitarianism respectively. Moreover, the example illustrates not only the ubiquity of the political, but also the importance of micropolitics. The latter is of fundamental importance to theorists of radical democracy committed to the ontology of abundance.

13 Deleuze and Guattari, *A Thousand Plateaus*, p. 21.

14 J.–L. Nancy, *The Inoperative Community*, trans. P. Connor (Minneapolis, MN: University of Minnesota Press, 1991), p. 3.

15 *Ibid.*, p. 5.

16 The closest Deleuze gets to an acknowledgment of transcendence is a remark in one

of his last essays, in which he says that transcendence 'is always a product of immanence'. G. Deleuze, 'Immanence: a life', in *Pure Immanence*, trans. A. Boyman (New York: Zone Books, 2001), p. 31.
17 Nancy, *The Inoperative Community*, p. 35.
18 We might argue that the injunction not to close off the disparate represents the limit of radical democracy, although we would also have to say that it is a limit that is constituted through its own process of becoming. As such, the limit of radical democracy is far more malleable than the limit of other models of democracy (for instance, liberalism or communitarianism).
19 K. Marx, 'Contribution to the critique of Hegel's *Philosophy of Right*: Introduction', in R. C. Tucker (ed.), *The Marx-Engel Reader*, 2nd edition (New York: W. W. Norton, 1978), p. 62 (first emphasis added). The context of Marx's comment is a critique of nineteenth-century Germany and an attempt to build a counter-hegemony capable of overturning those in power. I interpret this attempt in light of the ontology of abundance and not in light of the theory of hegemony advocated by Laclau and Mouffe. Instances of the latter are present in Torben Dyrberg's and Simon Critchley's contributions to this volume (chapters 10 and 13).
20 Surely, the two discourses do not exhaust the debate on radical democracy. Even so, they represent two versions of the same issue – that is, the issue of political economy – turning their mutual limitations into a symptom of the debate on radical democracy in general.
21 Hardt and Negri, *Empire*, p. 326.
22 Ibid., pp. 395f.
23 E. Laclau, 'Can immanence explain social struggles?', *Diacritics*, 31:4 (2001), 3.
24 In a lecture Ernesto Laclau gave in Amsterdam, Holland on 'Negativity and Immanence' at a 2004 conference on 'Political Theologies: Globalization and Postsecular Reason', he analysed this kind of transcendence in terms of what he called a 'failed transcendence'.
25 Laclau, 'Can immanence explain social struggles?', p. 6.
26 E. Laclau, 'Structure, history and the political', in J. Butler, E. Laclau and S. Žižek, *Contingency, Hegemony, Universality: Contemporary Dialogues on the Left* (London: Verso, 2000), p. 203 (emphasis in original).
27 E. Laclau and C. Mouffe, *Hegemony and Socialist Strategy: Towards a Radical Democratic Politics* (London: Verso, 1985), p. 161.
28 Ibid.
29 E. Laclau, 'Structure, history and the political', p. 203.
30 Ibid.
31 This alternative conceptualisation of the general field of economics shares many features with Richard McIntyre's concept of uneven development. See R. McIntyre, 'Mode of production, social formation, and uneven development, or Is there capitalism in America?', in A. Callari and D. R. Ruccio (eds), *Postmodern Materialism and the Future of Marxist Theory: Essays in the Althusserian Tradition* (Hanover: Wesleyan University Press, 1996).
32 D. Ironmonger, 'Counting outputs, capital inputs and caring labor: estimating gross household products', *Feminist Economics*, 2:3 (1996), 37–64.
33 G. Steinmetz and E. O. Wright, 'The fall and rise of petty bourgeoisie: changing patterns of self-employment in the postwar United States', *American Journal of Sociology*, 94:5 (1989), 973–1019.
34 See R. Rouse, 'Mexican migration and the social space of postmodernism', *Diaspora*, 1:1 (1991), 8–23, for a discussion of how Mexican immigrants working in the United

States use their US salary to invest in non-capitalist activities in their native hometowns.
35 Gibson-Graham, *The End of Capitalism*, p. 55.
36 *Ibid.*, p. 54. Gibson-Graham defines surplus in general as the result of labour beyond what is strictly necessary for reproduction.
37 The economic imaginary that I outline in the following helps us to distinguish radical democracy from, for example, the political liberalism of John Rawls. While Rawls limits the discussion of political economy to issues of redistribution, theorists of radical democracy challenge the way in which society produces and eventually appropriates surplus. Compare J. Rawls, 'Distributive justice', in *Collected Papers* (Cambridge, MA: Harvard University Press, 1999).
38 In 'The promise of finance: banks and community development', in J. K. Gibson-Graham, S. Resnick and R. Wolff (eds), *Re/Presenting Class: Essays in Postmodern Marxism* (Durham: Duke University Press, 2001), Carole Biewener mentions the Spanish bank *Caja Laboral Popular* (a credit-union serving worker-controlled cooperatives in northern Spain) as a successful way of democratising money-lending.
39 J. K. Gibson-Graham discusses some of the ethical and practical implications of these projects in 'An ethics of the local', in *Rethinking Marxism* (forthcoming).
40 M. Merleau-Ponty, *The Visible and the Invisible*, trans. A. Lingis (Evanston: Northwestern University Press, 1968), p. 139.

13 • *Simon Critchley*

True democracy: Marx, political subjectivity and anarchic meta-politics

POLITICS, then. For reasons that will hopefully become clear, I would like to frame the following discussion of politics by looking at Marx. Let me begin by stating what I see as the first truth of Marx's work, namely the analysis of capitalism, an analysis that is truly prophetic and where the economic form of life, that began in some corners of north-western Europe, in Holland, England and some of its former colonies has, through processes that we all too easily call globalisation, spread its movement of expropriation all across the world. In the opening pages of the *Manifesto of the Communist Party*, Marx and Engels write of the revolutionary role of the bourgeoisie. This shouldn't be forgotten: the bourgeoisie are the outcome of the revolutions of the 1600s in England, the Dutch Republic, and the somewhat retarded 1789 revolution in France, and they play a revolutionary role in history. As Marx and Engels emphasise, in making profane all that is sacred, in establishing connections, colonies and settlements everywhere, through the power of trade, commerce, colonialism and transport (think of Marx's wonderfully eulogistic remarks on the importance of shipping, railways and canals), the bourgeoisie globalises itself, becoming *cosmopolitan*. In sharp contrast to the current vogue that the concept of cosmopolitanism enjoys amongst so many writers and theorists, Marx sees cosmopolitanism as the *pseudo-internationalism* of atomised individualism, which would have to be contrasted with a true international.

In stripping the veneer of naturalness from all social relations, including family relations and the formerly prized professions and hierarchies of feudal society, in making the experience of labour unbearable and indeed crippling through industrial organisation, the bourgeoisie reveal the *contingency* of social life and what we might call its *historicity:* the possibility that the particular set of social arrangements through which we are living are the outcome of a transformative social process and therefore capable of being transformed. Through the extraordinary energy that they expended on the overthrow of feudalism in its various forms, the bourgeoisie unwittingly reveals the *political* character of social life. In reducing those social relations to essentially monetary relations, in creating a world market based on the abstract universality of money and the experience of self-estrangement and alienation, the bourgeoisie is the condition of possibility for anti-bourgeois political struggles. Marx and Engels write in the *Manifesto*:

> Where it has come to power the bourgeoisie has obliterated all relations that were feudal, patriarchal, idyllic. It has pitilessly severed the motley bonds of feudalism that joined men to their natural superiors, and has left intact no other bond between one man and another than naked self-interest, unfeeling 'hard cash'. It has drowned the ecstasies of religious fervour, of zealous chivalry, of philistine sentiment in the icy waters of egoistic calculation. It has resolved personal worth into exchange value, and in place of countless attested and hard-won freedoms it has established a single freedom – conscienceless free trade. In a word, for exploitation cloaked by religious and political illusions, it has substituted unashamed, direct, brutal exploitation.[1]

Ours is a universe where human relations have been reduced to naked self-interest, to unfeeling hard cash, and where all social life is governed by one imperative: conscienceless free-trade, a life of open, unashamed, direct and brutal exploitation. We inhabit what Marx would see as an M-C-M' (money for commodities for more money) matrix of the increasingly centralised expropriation of the vast majority of humanity. In one of the striking scientific metaphors with which Marx begins *Capital*, the commodity is described as the cell-form in the body of the capitalist economy, its basic element or unit.[2] Money is the universal equivalent by virtue of which commodities are exchanged; it is the blood that feeds the circulatory system of capitalism. If the first volume of *Capital* were to be brutally reduced to a formula, we might say that money circulates commodities.

Reading Marx on the genesis and emergence of capital and its political corollary, the modern representative state; reading him on the function of money as the universal, yet alienated, capacity of humankind; on commodity fetishism and the mystified nature of exchange capitalist society; on the massive structural dislocations of capitalist society and the yawning inequalities that it produces, one is simply persuaded of the massive prescience and truth of these analyses. History has proven Marx more successful than he could possibly have imagined in his intention, in another of those metaphors from the beginning of *Capital*, in laying bare the economic law of motion of modern capitalist society.[3]

Dislocation – capitalism capitalises

Sadly, what I have just said is the easy part. For me, Marx's analysis of capitalism remains the *sine qua non* for the understanding of contemporary socio-economic life. However, what follows from this for our thinking about politics? That is the question.

Are we witnessing, as Marx and Engels foresaw with particular clarity in the *Manifesto*, a simplification of the class structure into the opposed poles of bourgeoisie and proletariat? Are we witnessing the emergence of a revolutionary class whose seizure of power, whose dictatorship, will entail the withering away of the state and the implementation of socialism? Are the undoubted and massive dislocations of capitalist globalisation – and just think about what Marx would have said about what has been happening over the past few years in South China or regions of India – producing a classless class, a class who will bring about the overcoming of the division of labour and the achievement of communism? In Marx's famous words at end of the first volume of *Capital*, will the expropriators be expropriated?[4]

Let us just say that I have my doubts. It is here that Ernesto Laclau's work can be extremely instructive. Rather than a simplification of class positions, one might talk, with him, of a multiplication of class actors in society, of society being made up by an increasingly complex fabric of class identifications, rendered even more intricate by other sets of identifications, whether gender, ethnicity, sexual orientation or whatever. In such a situation, we cannot hope, as classical Marxist economism maintained, that once the economic laws of motion of capitalist society have been laid bare, then revolution will follow quasi-automatically from the contradictions and crises of the capitalist system. Crisis-ridden as it doubtless is and has been since at least the 1850s, capitalism is wonderfully persistent and can morph into new shapes at the least sign of resistance, brilliantly recuperating anything that seems to place it in question. Since the time of the Situationist International in the 1960s, we have begrudgingly come to admit that *recuperation* is the fate of all forms of revolutionary avant-gardism, whether aesthetic or political. So, rather than evolving towards a revolution that would take us beyond it, one might say that *capitalism capitalises itself*; it simply produces more capitalism. It makes rather quaint, sad reading to look at accounts of Marx from the 1970s, where figures as sophisticated as Ernest Mandel wrote that 'capitalism's heyday is over'.[5] On the contrary, capitalism under the guise of globalisation is spreading its network to every corner of the earth. If someone found a way of overcoming capitalism, then some corporation would buy the copyright and the distribution rights.

In other words, we cannot sit back and hope that the structural contradictions of capitalism will do the job of political transformation on our behalf. We cannot reduce the sphere of the political to the socio-economic, as is suggested by a crude base-superstructure model with which Marx flirted in the 'Preface' to *The Contribution to the Critique of Political Economy* and which became an article of faith for Engels and the Marxism of the Second International.[6] On the contrary, in my view it is a question of reactivating the *political* dimension of

Marxism, a dimension that will require all our capacities for political invention and political imagination, a political imagination at which the Right have been spectacularly more successful than the Left since the late 1970s. Whether one thinks of Thatcher, Reagan and the New Right of the 1980s; of the various post-Soviet nationalisms in Russia and its former satellite states; of the multiple and flourishing xenophobic parties and regimes in Continental Europe, the most alarming example being Silvio Berlusconi's Italy; of the sheer political tenacity of the Republican campaign against Gore and the *coup d'état* in Florida in 2000; of the ideological mobilisation of 9/11 into a war against terror with its sweeping and swaggering disregard for international law, then there can be little question that it is the Right that has best understood the nature of politics in recent history.

To be clear, when I speak about re-activating the political dimension of Marxism, I do not say this in order to embrace what some have called 'disco-Marxism', that is, an approach that abandons the socio-economic dimension by reducing all experience to modes of discourse, a gesture that politicises Marxism at the price of leaving capitalism unquestioned. On the contrary, I think that the goal of communism as articulated in the *Manifesto* – namely what Marx and Engels call, in a nuanced way, the '*Aufhebung* of private property'; that is, both its maintenance *and* its overcoming, but not an abolition, *Abschaffung* – is an entirely legitimate political aspiration.[7] The issue with regard to capitalism is therefore the establishment of capital as a social product and not a personal one, of removing the class-character of private property. But this is also a political task.

Let me turn to an important line of argument in Laclau's work, namely his rethinking of the category of dislocation. Another way of thinking about what I called a moment ago the first truth of Marx's work is in terms of the accelerating dislocatory power of capitalism. To assert, as I did, that capitalism capitalises itself is to say that it produces more and more extensive and aggravated social and economic dislocations, all over the surface of the earth. This entails increasing demographic movements from the country to the city or from the south to the north, the creation of vast shanty towns of the dislocated poor, but also the dislocation of local industries and practices by cut-price commodities from overseas. In what is for me his most important programmatic theoretical text – his manifesto, if you will – the title essay from the 1990 book *New Reflections on the Revolution of Our Time*, Laclau writes:

> In one sense, our analysis keeps within the field of Marxism and attempts to reinforce what has been one of its virtues: the acceptance of the transformations entailed by capitalism and the construction of an alternative project that is *based on* the ground created by those transformations and not on *opposition* to them. Commodification, bureaucratization, and the increasing dominance of scientific and technological planning over the division of labour should not necessarily be resisted. Rather, one should work within these processes so as

True democracy

to develop the prospects they create for a non-capitalist alternative.⁸

Despite the fact that, for Marx, the dislocations of capitalist society are orientated structurally or systemically by the misguided teleology of a simplification of the class structure and emergence of a revolutionary subject, the proletariat, this should not disguise the great virtue of Marx's work, which is its radically unsentimental, un-romantic and anti-conservative diagnosis of capitalism. The dislocatory power of capitalism must be affirmed and not resisted by a retreat into some sort of romantic and ultimately reactionary anti-capitalism – for which, incidentally, there seems to be a great affection on the American left, which perhaps explains the interest, fascination even, with Heidegger in North America. On the contrary, the more dislocated the ground upon which capitalism operates, the less it can rely on a framework of supposedly natural or stable social and political relations. Capitalist dislocation, in its ruthless destruction of the bonds of tradition, local belonging, family and kinship structures that one might have considered natural, reveals the contingency of social life, that is its constructed character, that is its *political* articulation. This is the moment of what Laclau, after Gramsci, calls hegemony. Once the ideological illusions of the natural have been stripped away and revealed as contingent formations by capitalist dislocation, where freedom, for example, becomes the precarious experience of insecurity when one sells oneself on the labour market, then the cement that holds political identities together is a hegemonic link. Whereas, for Gramsci, hegemony is the activity of the formation of 'collective will' out of the divergent groupings that make up civil society, Laclau expands the concept of hegemony to mean a general logic of the political institution of the social.⁹

The ever-widening dislocations of an increasingly disorganised capitalism do not, however, entail political pessimism, as is the case for an Adorno or a Heidegger from opposite sides of the philosophical looking-glass. On the contrary, such dislocations *can* (I emphasise 'can' as there is no necessity to this operation) be linked to the emergence of a range of alternative political possibilities opposed to capitalism and are thus, as Laclau says, the condition for 'a new militancy and a new optimism'.¹⁰ He writes: 'The fragmentation and growing limitation of social actors is linked to the multiplication of the dislocations produced by 'disorganized capitalism'. It follows from this that more and more areas of social life must become the product of *political* forms of reconstruction and regulation.'¹¹ The radical and perhaps disquieting thought here is for a co-implication of the dislocatory force of capitalist globalisation, a multiplication of social actors and, thus, of political possibility. This co-implication *can* lead to the emergence of an alternative left, but this is a hegemonic operation, it is a construction, it is work that needs to be done. All of which has significant implications for our thinking of the subject of politics, as we will now see.

[223]

Simon Critchley

The names are lacking – the problem of political subjectivity

Politics is always about nomination, about naming a political subjectivity and organising politically around that name. Marx's name for the political subject is the proletarian, more specifically the proletarian as communist. Can this be our name? Are we united around the fact of our proletarian identity? I do not think so. Despite the sociological fact that the industrial working-class no longer plays an obvious hegemonic role in a revolutionary politics, my reasons for doubting Marx's position would take us deep into a critique of Marx's ontology. By ontology I mean Marx's conception of the being of being human, which is expressed in a cluster of related concepts: the idea of species being (*Gattungswesen*), being as production, being as praxis, or being as the practical self-activity of the subject. These are ideas which Marx owes to the 'autonomy orthodoxy' of Kant, Fichte and Hegel, a tradition that Marx both completes and completely overturns. If Hegel can be said to socialise the purported solipsism of Kantian or Fichtean autonomy, locating it in relations of intersubjectivity, then Marx can be said to communise autonomy locating it in the activity and life-praxis of the proletariat. The point here is that, for Marx, communism is an ontological category before it is that around which any political activism can orientate itself, and it is the link between ontological and political activity that allows Marx to claim that the proletariat are the classless class who represent the interests of humanity. To put it bluntly, I do not believe that we are united around the fact of our proletarian identity. I think that the category of the proletarian as revolutionary subject has decisively broken down sociologically and is hostage to a highly dubious ontology. I therefore think that we lack a name around which a radical politics can take shape.

The political task is, then, one of inventing a name around which a political subject can aggregate itself from the various social struggles through which we are living. This act of the aggregation of the political subject is the moment of hegemony. More accurately still, following through on the thought of the multiplication of social actors in the contemporary world, it is a question of inventing *names* for that around which politics can hegemonise itself and then aggregating those names into some sort of association, common front or collective will. The logic of political nomination, I take it, is that a determinate particularity in society is hegemonically constructed into a universality. This is what Laclau calls 'hegemonic universality'. That is, the universal is not read off from the script of some pre-given ontology but is posited in a specific situation. Marx does get close to this thought in an unnervingly contemporary sentence from his 1843 'Introduction' to the *Critique of Hegel's Philosophy of Right*, where the logic of the political subject is expressed in the words: '*I am nothing and I should be everything* [*Ich bin nichts, und ich müßte alles sein*]'.[12] That is, beginning from a position of emptiness, a particular group posits the fullness of the universal, and hegemonically articulates that universality in political action, thereby becoming a political subject. In Europe, at this conjuncture, immigrant, asylum seeker or refugee could be candidates for political names.

While I am on this topic, some people think that 'multitude' in the sense of Michael Hardt and Antonio Negri has become for us a political name. This is clearly the implicit ambition of the powerful analysis of the emergent form of network sovereignty given in the hugely influential *Empire* from 2000, which is made explicit in the 2004 sequel, *Multitude,* which argues that the multitude is the new political subject and political alternative that grows with empire.[13] Yet, I would dispute this view, both because the analysis given in *Empire* at the ontological level risks retreating into the very anti-dialectical materialist ontology of substance that Marx rightly criticised in his early work and also because it makes the work of politics too systemic where both empire and multitude; that is, both capitalism and the resistance to capitalism originate in the same ontological substance. It is rather rare for books to be refuted empirically, but I think this happened to *Empire* on 11 September 2001. More generally, if we are doing politics, we cannot and should not pin our hopes on any ontology, whether a Marxian notion of species-being, a Spinozo-Deleuzianism of abundance, a Heideggero–Lacanianism of lack or any version of what Stephen White has recently called 'weak ontology' in politics.[14] In my view, politics is a disruption of the ontological domain and separate categories are required for its analysis and practice.

Politics as interstitial distance within the state

I would like to move on to the question of the state. We inhabit states. The state – whether national like Britain, transnational like the EU or imperial like the USA – is the framework within which conventional politics takes place. Now, it is arguable that the state is a limitation on human existence and we would be better off without it. It is arguable that without the state systems of government, bureaucracy, the police and the military, human beings would be able to cooperate with each other on the basis of free agreement and not merely through obedience to law. Such is, of course, the eternal temptation of the anarchist tradition, particularly someone like Kropotkin, and I will come back to anarchism below. However, it seems to me that we cannot hope, at this point in history, to attain a complete withering away of the state, either through concerted anarcho-syndicalist action or revolutionary proletarian praxis through the agency of the party. Within classical Marxism, state, revolution and class form a coherent set: there is a revolutionary class, the universal or classless class of the proletariat whose communist politics entails the overthrow of the bourgeois state. But if class positions are not simplifying, but on the contrary becoming more complex through processes of social dislocation, if the revolution is no longer conceivable in Marx's manner, then that means that, for good or ill, let us say for ill, we are stuck with the state, just as we are stuck with capitalism. The question becomes: what should our political strategy be with regard to the state, to the state and states that we are in?

In a period when the revolutionary subject has decidedly broken down, and the political project of a disappearance of the state is not coherent other than as a beautifully seductive fantasy, politics has to be conceived at a *distance* from the state.[15] Or, better, politics is the praxis of taking up distance with regard to the state, working independently of the state, working in a situation. Politics is praxis in a situation and the work of politics is the construction of new political subjectivities, new political aggregations in specific localities, new political sequences. This is arguably a description of the sort of direct democratic action that has provided the cutting edge and momentum to radical politics since the days of action against the meeting of the WTO in Seattle in 1999 and subsequently at Genoa, Cancun and elsewhere. Despite the massive reterritorialisation of state power in the West after 9/11, this movement has continued in the huge mobilisations against US intervention in Iraq and the recent protests against the Republican National Convention in New York in late August and early September 2004.

However, to forestall a possible misunderstanding, this distance from the state is within the state, that is, within and upon the state's territory. It is, we might say, an *interstitial* distance, an internal distance. What I mean, seemingly paradoxically, is that there *is* no distance within the state. In the time of the purported 'war on terror', and contrary to Hardt and Negri's diagnosis of network sovereignty, state sovereignty threatens to saturate the entirety of social life. The constant ideological mobilisation of the threat of attack from outside has permitted the most draconian curtailments of traditional civil liberties in the name of internal political order, so-called 'homeland security'. Such is the politics of fear. Against this, the task of a radical political articulation is a matter of the creation of interstitial distance within the state territory. Political activism around the so-called illegal immigrants in Paris, the *sans papiers*, is a powerful instance of the attempt to create an interstitial distance whose political demand – 'if one works in France, one is French' – invokes the principle of equality at the basis of the French republic. One works within the state against the state in a political articulation that attempts to open a space of opposition.

Perhaps it is at this intensely situational, indeed local level that the atomising, expropriating force of capitalist globalisation is to be met, contested and resisted. That is, resistance begins by occupying and controlling the terrain upon which one stands, where one lives, works, acts and thinks. This need not involve millions of people. It need not even involve thousands; it could involve just a few at first. Resistance can be intimate and can begin in small affinity groups. The art of politics consists in weaving such cells of resistance together into a

True democracy

common front, a shared political subjectivity. What is going to allow for the formation of such a political subjectivity – the hegemonic glue, if you like – is an appeal to universality, whether equality, freedom, legality or whatever. It is my hope that what I call the ethical demand – the infinite responsibility that both constitutes and divides my subjectivity[16] – is the hegemonic glue that will motivate the subject into political action.

True democracy

Politics is praxis in a situation that articulates an interstitial distance from the state, which allows for the emergence of new political subjectivities. Now, and here I would like to return to Marx, I think this distance from the state is democratic. By democracy I therefore do not mean the state-form, in the sense of liberal or constitutional democracy, nor do I mean democracy in the mouth of neo-imperialists, where it is no more than a fetish-object in a legitimating discourse of capitalist expropriation and the *Realpolitik* of war – I refer to the breathtaking metaphysical audacity of the *National Security Strategy of the United States of America*, published in September 2002.[17]

By contrast, I mean democracy as a movement of democratisation, which is – dialectically expressed – the truth of the state, a truth which no state incarnates. As I hear it, this talk of democracy as democratisation picks up on a strand of the young Marx's thinking that can be found in his 1843 critique of Hegel's *Rechtsphilosophie*, written when Marx was only about 25. In these extensive notes, which were first published in 1927, Marx tries to conceptualise what he calls 'true democracy', '*wahre Demokratie*', against the order of the state. By truth, Marx clearly does not mean propositional or empirical truth, but truth as true to democracy, truth in the sense of the German cognate *treu*, fidelity or loyalty to democracy. He writes: 'It is self-evident that all forms of state have democracy as their truth and for that reason are untrue to the extent that they are not democracy.'[18]

Marx claims that democracy is the resolved enigma of all political constitutions, and by democracy what he means is that in true democracy the political state as a formal apparatus operated by the bureaucratic class, who are the universal class, disappears (*untergehe*) and what takes its place is a conception of democracy as democratic self-determination, what he calls the *Selbstbestimmung des Volks*, the self-determination of the people. With a word that remains a constant feature in the vocabulary of Marx's critique of Hegel from 1843 to the 'Preface' to *Capital* in 1873, he argues that Hegel 'mystifies' the state. Whereas, for Hegel, the family and civil society are conceived as mere component of the higher actuality of the state, Marx argues that it is precisely the other way round: 'The fact is that the state issues from the mass of human beings existing as members of families and members of civil society.'[19] Hegel therefore mistakes the ideal for the material: the state is not the condition of possibility for the family and civil society, but is conditioned by them. It is the mass, the material *Menge*, which is the active principle in political life. This entails that the activities and functions of the state are attached to the lives of individuals; that is to say, not their physical being, as in the crude eighteenth century materialism that Marx powerfully and persistently rejects, but their political or social being. Hegel forgets that:

> particular individuality is a human individual and that the activities and functions of the state are human activities. He forgets that the nature of the 'particular personality' is not his beard, his blood, his abstract *physis*, but rather his *social quality* and that the activities etc. of the state are nothing but the modes of existence and operation of the social qualities of men.[20]

For Hegel, political sovereignty is incarnated in the person of the monarch; 'the monarch is', Marx writes, 'personified sovereignty'.[21] Standing this idea on its head, Marx claims that sovereignty is located in the *mass* of individuals that make up society. In a witty allusion to Hamlet's soliloquy, Marx writes, '*Souveränität des Monarchen oder des Volkes, das ist die question.*'[22] Marx wants to defend the idea of popular sovereignty and universal suffrage against Hegel's rejection of both. In a *Zusatz* towards the end of the *Philosophy of Right*, Hegel rejects popular sovereignty as 'one of the confused notions based on a wild idea of the people', and goes on to claim that the idea of the people is a 'formless mass and no longer a state'.[23] Slightly later, Hegel argues that to accept the idea of universal suffrage is tantamount to putting, 'the democratic element without any rational form into the organism of the state'.[24] It is precisely this formless mass of the *demos* that Marx wants to claim is the subject of politics, the subject of what, thinking of Merleau-Ponty, we might want to think of as 'wild democracy'. True democracy, in this sense, would be a *deformation* of the state in the name of material principle, the mass of the people, what Marx refers to in a highly suggestive way as 'the drive [*Trieb*] of civil society'.[25]

For Marx, then, the state is an *abstractum*; the people alone is the *concretum*.[26] From here, in a series of extraordinarily rich and speedily formulated texts from 1843 and 1844, this idea of popular democratic self-determination receives the name 'communism', and I have my reservations about that name. But the thought that I want to retain is the idea of true democracy as not being incarnated in the state, but rather enacted or even simply acted – practically, locally, situationally – at a distance from the state. I am trying to think of democracy as a movement of *disincarnation* or *deformation* that works concretely beneath the state's abstraction. It is that material drive of social being that calls the state into question and calls the established order to account, not in order to do away with the state, desirable though that might well be in some utopian sense, but in order to better it or attenuate its malicious effects. True democracy would be the enactment of cooperative alliances, aggregations of conviviality and affinity at the level of society that materially deform the state power that threatens to saturate them.

Thinking about true democracy in this way would be one way of thinking and reactivating the moment of the political within Marxism; that is, within a Marxist heritage that has tended to reduce the political to the socio-economic and superstructure to base. It would be a way of recovering what Miguel Abensour calls, after J. G. A. Pocock, 'the Machiavellian moment' within Marxism, the moment of decision, articulation, reactivation and event.[27]

I think that it is around such a notion of true democracy, as subjective praxis in a situation, that a gathering, an organisation, an aggregation, an association can emerge. I am very interested in this figure of 'association' or 'coalition' in Marx, which appears in many texts, in *The German Ideology*, the *Manifesto* and *The Poverty of Philosophy*, where in the face of the socially atomising brutality of capitalism, Marx understands political organisation as what he calls 'the power of united individuals'. This is also what Marx calls in the first volume of *Das Kapital*, 'einen Verein freier Menschen', an association of free human beings.[28] (To be honest, it is the *ver* that interests me more than the *ein* in this formulation; that is, the one is that towards which we progress without ever constituting the fantasy of the society as one, as a unity or fullness.) Such a *Verein*, working in common at a certain distance from the state, working towards a control of the place from which one speaks and acts, working together in a situation as a political subject committed to a plan, a place, a space, a process, an event, I think is not just possible, it is actual, and, where it is not actual, it is actualisable. In the interstitial spaces occupied by the dispossessed in the great metropolitan centres, or more generally in the workplace, in housing projects, in schools, in universities, in hospitals, in shelters for asylum seekers, all over. It is a question of the political articulation of these spaces into a common front.

However, against Marx, I would not want to call such forms of association communist. For me, the idea of communism remains ontologically suspect because of the essentialist idealist metaphysics of species-being that determines the concept in Marx's work. Communism is a word that, for me, remains captive to an essentially aestheticised and organicist notion of community that can be traced back to Schiller's *Aesthetic Education of Man* and the 'Oldest System-Programme of German Idealism' and traced forward to any number of utterly pernicious social fantasies of what Jean-Luc Nancy calls 'immanentism'; that is, a conception of social relations based on the fantasy of fusion, unity, fullness and completion. For me, on the contrary, it is a question of trying to conceive of forms of political gathering, coalition, association or organisation, that is to say, contingent political articulations in relation to a more wild and formless conception of social being, what we called above the socio-economic reality is dislocation. If I do not want to call this communist, then I am perfectly happy still to call it socialist, or associationist or whatever.

Ethics as anarchic meta-politics

Let me conclude this chapter by looking at the theme of ethics, and outline how we might think together an ethics with what I have just said about politics.

In my view, what has to be continually criticised in political thinking is the aspiration of a full incarnation of the universal in the particular, or the privileging of a specific particularity because it is believed to *embody* the universal: for example, the classical Hegelian idea of the state, the modish and the vague idea of a European super-state, or the fantasy of the *Weltstaat*, the world-state. By contrast, democratisation is the moment or movement of *disincarnation* that challenges the borders and questions the legitimacy of the state. I conceive of democratisation as a dual sequence of both micro-political articulations, movements and blocs at the level of civil society, and as a sequence of macro-political trans-national articulations, non-state based forms of internationalist intervention. Good examples of this would be the forms of direct action that took place in Seattle and elsewhere. Democratisation is dissensual praxis that works against the consensual horizon of the state. It is action based on an ethical injunction, an ethical demand and not an eschatology, the cunning of reason or some idealist or materialist philosophy of history. It is political action that feeds from what I will now describe as a meta-political moment.

My claim is that at the heart of a radical politics there has to be a *meta-political* ethical moment, the experience of conscience, which provides the force or propulsion into political action. To be clear, meta-political does not mean non-political or pre-political. Although we can analytically distinguish ethics from politics, experientially we always face an ethico-political synthetic manifold. My point is that if ethics without politics is empty, then politics without ethics is blind. We need ethics to see what to do in a political situation. In this chapter, I have sought to describe one conception of ethics. There are others, this is mine. Ethics my way may not be ethics your way. In fact, I imagine that most readers of this chapter will probably be unconvinced about signing up to my exquisite moral vision. My point is that it could not be otherwise. Ethics is not like logic or even like science; it is dependent upon assent or approval, otherwise it is reduced to being the submission to some external command such as the will of God. So, I can try and persuade you, even exhort you, into ethics my way, but I cannot and should not force you. There is a limit to moral argumentation or moral rationality and it is here that we move closer to an experience of acknowledgement. I recommend it to you most warmly, although I am fully aware that I cannot force you to agree with me.

It is here that Levinas's thematic of anarchism takes on great interest, partic-

True democracy

ularly the way in which that theme is handled by Miguel Abensour, when he speaks of an anarchic disturbance of politics.[29] This is the anarchy of the relation of proximity and substitution with the other that introduces what we might call a *metapolitical* moment into politics. In my view, Levinasian ethics is not ethics for its own sake in the manner of what we might call 'angelic' readings of Levinas, but nor is it ethics for the sake of the state, which we might think of as the right-wing Levinasian option, whether that is linked to the logic of Zionism or indeed a quasi-Gaullist, quasi-Chiracian argument for French exceptionalism. In my view, ethics is ethics for the sake of politics. Better stated perhaps, ethics is the metapolitical disturbance of politics for the sake of politics; that is, for the sake of a politics that does not close over in itself, becoming what Levinas would call totality, becoming a whole. Following Levinas's logic, when politics is left to itself without the disturbance of ethics it risks becoming tyrannical.

The problem with much thinking about politics is that it is *archic*, it is obsessed with the moment of foundation, origination, declaration or institution that is linked to the act of government, of sovereignty, most of all of *decision* that presupposes and initiates a sovereign political subject capable of self-government and the government of others. Such is arguably the intent of a tradition of political philosophy that begins in Plato's *Republic*. I would contend that political philosophy in this sense is essentially antipolitical: in Hannah Arendt's terms it consists in the reduction of the political to the social, or in Jacques Rancière's terms it is the reduction of *la politique* to the order or *la police*. That is, the political manifestation of the people is and has to be reduced to their allotted social function in the state as soldier, worker, guardian or university professor – the social division of labour given in Plato's *Republic* that finds a faithful and deeply troubling echo in Heidegger's *Rektoratsrede*. What such a tradition of political thinking fears most is the people, the radical manifestation of the people, the people not as *das Volk* or *le people* shaped by the state, but as *die Leute*, or *les gens*, the people in their irreducible plurality, what we saw Hegel call above the 'formless mass' of the people.

One way of thinking about Levinas and politics, and I think it is the most convincing way, is in terms of ethics as an anarchic, metapolitical disturbance of the antipolitical order of the police. It would here be a question of linking what Levinas sees already in *Totality and Infinity* as the 'anarchy essential to multiplicity'[30] to the multiplicity that is essential to politics. As far as I'm concerned, politics is the manifestation of the multiplicity that is the people, of the *demos*. Who are the people? They are not the alleged unity of a race, the citizens of a nation-state, the members of a specific class like the proletariat, or indeed the members of a specific community defined by religion, ethnicity or whatever. The people cannot be identified and policed by any territorialising term. Rather the people is that which Jacques Rancière describes as that empty space, that supplement that exceeds any social quantification or accounting. The people are those who do not count, who have no right to govern whether through hereditary entitlement like the aristocracy or by wealth and property ownership like the bourgeoisie.

If the activity of government continually risks pacification, order, the state, and what Rancière refers to as the 'idyll of consensus', then politics consists in the manifestation of *dissensus*, a dissensus that disturbs the order by which government wishes to depoliticise society.[31] If politics can be understood as the manifestation of the anarchic demos, then politics and democracy are two names for the same thing. Thus, democracy is not a fixed political form of society, but rather what I called above the *deformation* of society from itself through the act of material political manifestation. Democracy is a political process, the movement of democratisation, which comes very close to the idea of direct democracy. In my view, democratisation consists in the manifestation of dissensus, in demonstration as *demos*-stration, manifesting the presence of those who do not count. Democratisation is politicisation, it is the cultivation of what might be called *politicities*, sites of hegemonic struggle that work against the consensual idyll of the state.

Ethics is anarchic meta-politics. It is the anarchic moment of democratic dissensus articulated around the experience of the ethical demand, the infinite, unfulfillable, universal and overwhelming demand at the heart of my subjectivity that defines that subjectivity by splitting it open. Now, this demand is not some theoretical abstraction. Hopefully, the link to Marx has made clear the way in which this demand takes place in a situation, a political situation, a situation of globalised expropriation and violent injustice, a situation of what I call 'political disappointment'.

This disappointment provokes an experience of injustice or indeed a feeling of anger. I think anger is very important, it is the first political emotion, it is what moves the subject to action, it is the emotion that produces motion, that literally e-motes. But such anger at the treatment of so-called unlawful combatants in Guantanamo, at the tawdry shambles in Iraq, at the mystifying and cynical complacency of a Tony Blair are experiences of a *wrong*, a wrong that provokes an ethical response. The problem with contemporary ethics, particularly the radically devalued currencies of freedom, human rights and liberal democracy – which are at the heart of that *National Security Strategy* document – is, as Chantal Mouffe would rightly say, the risk of a moralisation of politics and hence the risk of depoliticisation.[32] I agree completely, but I do not think that the fact of moralisation should lead to the suspension of ethics. On the contrary, I think it should lead to the development of alternative ethical frameworks, it should lead towards an intensification of ethics and the cultivation of a political ethics that can face and face down depoliticising moralisation. Such is the far from humble ambition of this chapter.

True democracy

Conclusion

Let us now ask: how might a politics of the type I have described happen? How might it become effective? What are the conditions for its emergence?

One might say that politics just happens, but that it is not happening now, ours are not favourable times. One might say, like some post-Heideggerian leftists, that it is necessary to wait and await the advent of the saving power of the revolution, the *Ereignis* will one day come to pass. One might say, like some post-Adornian leftists, that Auschwitz or the death camps are the *nomos* of modernity, and basically *on est foutu*, although we can still enjoy the exquisite aesthetic teasings of high modernism. One might say, like some post-Althusserian leftists, that politics is rare, the last great example being 1968, and we have to acknowledge that we are living in a de-politicised, post-democratic era. One might say, like Slavoj Žižek, pretty much anything you like, as there are so many contradictions in what he has said about politics over the years. But one might also say the following: politics is not rare or seldom and to adopt such a position is finally defeatist. Politics is now and many. The massive structural dislocations of our times can invite pessimism, even forms of active or passive nihilism, but they can also invite militancy and optimism, an invitation for our capacity of political invention and imagination, an invitation, finally, for our commitment, a category that I want to put back at the centre of theoretical and practical debate.

In order not to be defeatist, in order not to participate in the *Kulturpessimismus* or Eeyorism that is the self-defeating speciality of the intellectual left, in order to be affirmative and even a little optimistic, I think we have to acknowledge that such a conception of politics requires an experience of empowerment, an empowerment that is irreducibly ethical. To recall, on my view ethics is the experience of an infinite demand at the heart of my subjectivity, a demand that defines that subjectivity by splitting it open and which requires sublimation in the form of conscience. The motivation that propels a subject into participation in a political sequence comes from the bite or the kiss of conscience.

In these dark times, in these times of war, in this period of the increasingly desperate shoring up of the *imperium* as the provinces burn and our leaders see enemies everywhere, even in their sleep; in these dark times, we can no longer trust our political destiny to quasi-automatic inner contradictions of socio-economic laws of motion, a spontaneously emerging social movement that would lead to the overthrow of the state. Nor can our guide in politics be some set of ontological or metaphysical presuppositions, whether Marx's notion of species-being or Negri's idea of the emancipatory effulgence of the multitude. The revolution is not going to be generated out of systemic or structural laws. We are on our own and what we do, we have to do for ourselves. Politics requires subjective invention, imagination and endurance, not to mention cunning. No ontology or eschatological philosophy of history is going to do it for us. Working at an interstitial distance from the state, a distance that I have tried to describe as democratic, we need to construct political subjectivities in specific situations, subjectivities that are not arbitrary or relativistic, but which are articulations of an ethical demand whose scope is universal and whose evidence is faced in a concrete situation. This is dirty, detailed, local, practical and largely unthrilling work. It is time we made a start.

Notes

1 K. Marx and F. Engels, *Manifesto of the Communist Party*, in T. Carver (ed.), *Marx. Later Political Writings* (Cambridge: Cambridge University Press, 1996), p. 3.
2 K. Marx, *Capital. Volume 1*, trans. B. Fowkes (London: Penguin, 1976), p. 90.
3 *Ibid.*, p. 92.
4 *Ibid.*, p. 929.
5 *Ibid.*, p. 12.
6 In Carver (ed.), *Marx*, pp. 159f.
7 For this distinction, see K. Marx and F. Engels, *Werke, Band 4* (Berlin: Dietz Verlag, 1990), p. 475; and Marx in Carver, *Marx*, p. 13.
8 *New Reflections on the Revolution of Our Time* (London: Verso, 1990), p. 55.
9 For a much fuller account of hegemony, see D. Howarth, 'Hegemony, political subjectivity and radical democracy', in S. Critchley and O. Marchart (eds), *Laclau. A Critical Reader* (London: Routledge, 2004), pp. 256–76.
10 Laclau, *New Reflections on the Revolution of Our Time*, p. 82.
11 *Ibid.*, p. 81.
12 In J. O'Malley (ed.), *Marx. Early Political Writings* (Cambridge: Cambridge University Press, 1994), p. 67; and K. Marx and F. Engels, *Werke, Band 1* (Berlin: Dietz, 1988), p. 389.
13 M. Hardt and A. Negri, *Empire* (Cambridge, MA: Harvard University Press, 2000); and M. Hardt and A. Negri, *Multitude. War and Democracy in the Age of Empire* (New York: Penguin, 2004).
14 See S. White, *Sustaining Affirmation: The Strengths of Weak Ontology in Political Theory* (Princeton, NJ: Princeton University Press, 2000).
15 I borrow this line of thought from Alain Badiou. For an overview of Badiou's political thought, see *Abrégé de métapolitique* (Paris: Seuil, 1998) and an anonymous pamphlet, *Qu'est-ce que l'organisation politique?* (Paris: Le Perroquet, no date). It should be noted, however, that the views I go on to develop on anarchic meta-politics are very much at odds with Badiou, in particular with his critique of the so-called 'anti-globalisation movement' ('Interview with Alain Badiou', Radical Politics Group, University of Essex, unpublished typescript 2003).
16 See S. Critchley, *Ethics, Politics, Subjectivity: Essays on Derrida, Levinas and Contemporary French Thought* (London: Verso, 1999).
17 See www.whitehouse.gov/nsc/nss.html.
18 K. Marx, 'Critique of Hegel's doctrine of the state', in L. Colletti (ed.), *Karl Marx. Early Writings* (London: Penguin, 1975), p. 89. For the phrase 'true democracy', see Marx and Engels, *Werke, Band 1*, p. 232.
19 Marx, 'Critique' p. 3.

20 *Ibid.*, p. 4.
21 *Ibid.*, p. 7.
22 Marx and Engels, *Werke, Band 1*, p. 230.
23 G. W. F. Hegel, *Philosophy of Right*, pp. 182f.
24 *Ibid.*, p. 200.
25 Marx, 'Critique', p. 188.
26 *Ibid.*, p. 85.
27 M. Abensour, *La démocratie contre l'État. Marx et le moment machiavélien* (Paris : Presses Universitaires de France, 1997).
28 K. Marx and F. Engels, *Werke, Band 23* (Berlin: Dietz, 1970), p. 92.
29 Abensour, *La démocratie contre l'État*.
30 E. Levinas, *Totality and Infinity: An Essay on Exteriority*, trans. A. Lingis (Pittsburgh: Duquesne University Press, 1969), p. 294.
31 J. Rancière, *Disagreement: Politics and Philosophy*, trans. J. Rose (Minneapolis, MN: University of Minnesota Press, 1999).
32 See C. Mouffe, *On the Political* (London: Routledge, 2005).

III

AFTERWORDS

14 • William E. Connolly

Immanence, abundance, democracy

Immanence and transcendence

IN A RICH and compelling essay, Daniel Smith reviews a series of differences between a philosophy of transcendence and one of immanence. He selects Jacques Derrida and Gilles Deleuze as exemplars. The terms of comparison between them are fascinating because each has significant affinities to the other and develops a subtle version of the tradition he invokes. Derrida, for instance, does not support a traditional monotheistic image of transcendence, in which the commands of God are revealed through scripture and the human obligation to obedience follows from those commands; nor does he adopt a Platonic view of Ideas realised by exceptional figures through arduous work. Rather, the transcendence Derrida seeks is constantly sought but never attained and urgently demanded but essentially uncertain in content. For the idea of pure transcendence exceeds possible experience.

> Whenever we speak of something 'pure' or 'absolute' or 'infinite', as Derrida often does, we are in the realm of transcendence, since we never encounter the pure or absolute in our experience, it is never something that can be present to experience. The Idea of a pure mother, for instance, would be the idea of a mother who would not be something other than a mother – not a daughter, not a lover, not a wife. We can *think* this idea, but we don't encounter it in experience.[1]

The experience of moral responsibility, for Derrida, conforms to such an aporetic structure. You find yourself participating in a rather closed practice of responsibility, and through deconstruction you become more open to a higher call that cannot be articulated closely but does make a difference to your future possibilities of action toward others whose mode of being and faith has confused or offended you in some way.

Deleuze is also impressed by several of his own predecessors who project the immanence of being. But, paralleling Derrida's movement with respect to transcendence, he does not think that they have come to terms sufficiently with the complexity and evanescence of immanence. In a way that recalls Kant while reversing him, a philosopher of radical immanence can *think* the swarm of differences that subsist below actuality, but cannot *know* or *represent* difference in itself. Deleuze projects a 'genetic principle of difference' that subsists within and below existence or 'actuality'. He thus thinks difference as that which exceeds and helps to propel novel entities into actuality: immanence without transcendence. Moreover, again unlike Derrida, he does not define ethics in the first instance in terms of obligation, responsibility, obedience, debt or lack; he binds ethics in the first instance to a love of the world that flows from the abundance of being over any specific identity.[2] Deleuze is wary of philosophies of transcendence that speak of a constitutive 'debt', a 'lack' between identity and being, or a law 'deferred' into the indefinite future:

> The ethical themes he finds in transcendent philosophies such as those of Levinas and Derrida – absolute responsibility for the other that I can never assume, or an infinite justice that I can never satisfy – are ... imperatives whose effect is to separate me from my capacity to act from the viewpoint of immanence, in other words transcendence represents slavery and impotence reduced to its lowest point: the absolutely impossible is nothing other than the concept of impotence raised to infinity.[3]

As may already have been intimated, I concur with much of what Smith says about both thinkers. But I also need to probe a few points further.

I suggest that there is (at least) a three-way debate here. And the terms of this enlarged debate intimate how profoundly contestable each of the philosophies faiths is in comparison to the others. There is, first, the view of transcendence associated with Derrida and Levinas (even though another line of difference could be drawn between these two); second, a philosophy of immanence associated with Nietzsche and Deleuze (and again further divisions could be elaborated here); and, third, an image of transcendence associated with William James and Henri Bergson.

The third philosophy complicates the contest between the first two. James, for instance, concurs in advance with Derrideans in finding radical immanence to be insufficient to life. But the transcendence he embraces is linked to faith in a 'limited God' who participates in the world without being a creator of it. James believes 'that there is a God, but that he is finite, either in power or in knowledge or in both at once'.[4] The world and this limited God co-exist. Such a God is transcendent in that it is irreducible to humanity. But it is not a God to whom we are deeply indebted, or who is the repository of absolute justice, or whom we can only engage through the ideas of indebtedness or lack. We can be inspired as we enter into fugitive communication with it. Accordingly, James does not define morality in the first instance through concepts of command, obligation

Immanence, abundance, democracy

or debt. Touching a chord in Deleuze, James defines ethics (in the first instance) through inspiration, attraction and attachment to an abundance that courses through us as well as around us. We are connected to the larger world through multiple lines of affinity, including affinities between limits in our capacities of agency and the variable powers of agency the available in other forces in the world, including God.

James' link to Derrida is defined through his commitment to the fugitive experience of transcendence. His distance from Derrida may be defined by his tendency to endow love of the world with more priority than a primordial experience of obligation. The connection of James to Deleuze is discernible through the notion of 'litter' he introduces to break up the image of an explicable in principle through efficient causation in favour of a world always 'in the making'. James complains that 'philosophers have always aimed at cleaning up the litter with which the world apparently is filled'.[5] Litter serves as the signature idea in his philosophy.

According to *Webster's Ninth Collegiate Dictionary* litter is 'decaying matter on the forest floor'; 'trash, wastepaper or garbage lying scattered about'; 'an untidy accumulation of objects'; or 'a shabby writing desk covered with scattered articles'. It functions in James to introduce an element of energetic inexactitude into the world, to appreciate how new things enter the world over time, and to challenge the twin images of traditional finalism and a world subject to a system of efficient causation. The Jamesian idea of litter invites comparison with the Deleuzian theme of 'difference in itself', as those chaotic energies that inhabit things, beings and processes and without being knowable and help to compose a world of torsion between being and becoming. Indeed, Deleuze moves close to the Jamesian idea of 'a pluralistic universe' when he says that 'Diversity is given, but difference is that by which the given is given'. And, when he asserts: 'It is therefore true that God makes the world by calculating, but his calculations never work out exactly, and this inexactitude or injustice in the result, this irreducible inequality, forms the condition of the world.'[6] In a world of 'inexactitude' or 'irreducible inequality' some entities, species and political institutions may endure for millennia, but no mode of being survives forever.[7] Deleuze and James are both indebted to Bergson in this regard, as they attend to the process of 'duration' through which past and present resonate together to foment variations within repetition that enable becoming to puncture established stabilisations from time to time.[8] Both agree that we are neither in debt to difference in itself nor to litter, nor is our relation to the limited God from which James draws inspiration principally one of indebtedness or obligation. For it is not an omnipotent God.

Some differences between these two are notable. While Deleuze seeks attunement to those fugitive junctures at which the immanent reserve surges into actuality, he does not pursue a mystical relation to a limited deity. There is no such deity in the Deleuzian world. James pursues subliminal lines of communication to a limited God in which both human beings and the deity strain to open communication under shifting circumstances. He asserts that when 'the threshold lowers or the valve opens, information ordinarily shut out leaks into the mind of exceptional individuals'.[9]

The most telling differences among James, Deleuze, Derrida and Smith, however, may not lie in the respective commitment of each to transcendence or immanence, they lie rather in the *status* each philosophy is given in the eyes of its defenders. In a lecture Smith gave at Trent University on 'Deleuze and Immanence' at a 2004 conference on 'Experimenting with Intensities', he suggested that Deleuze had devised transcendental arguments to establish the superiority of a philosophy of immanence over that of transcendence.[10] Derrida, too, sometimes appears to think that he has accomplished that mission with respect to transcendence, though during the early period when both Nietzsche and Levinas circulated actively in his thought he may have kept the issue open. My own reading of Deleuze on this score is consonant with Smith's reading. At least, one does not find in Deleuze those focal points in Nietzsche, in which Nietzsche both expresses his commitment to a philosophy of immanence (as will to power and eternal return) and acknowledges it to be a 'conjecture' that is profoundly contestable. At any rate, while this question may be open to debate with respect to Derrida and Deleuze, the issue is clear with respect to James and Nietzsche. The latter two affirm faith in transcendence and immanence respectively; each strives to give the best arguments possible in support of that faith; but each also acknowledges that the faith he affirms is contestable, one open to alternative investments, expressions and articulations by others.

James contends that a contestable faith of some sort is regularly inserted into philosophy, pushing it in this way and nudging it in that. 'A conception of the world arises in you somehow, no matter how', James says.[11] A faith 'arises in you' through the give and take of daily life with parents, teachers, police, bosses, priests, philosophers, unexpected events, urgent calls to loyalty and so on. You can test it by recourse to new arguments and evidence. You might even go through a conversion experience, prodded by objections posed by others, a new source of inspiration, events that shake and transform you, or a combination thereof. But James doubts that the new philosophy will itself be entirely separable from the hopes, fears and anxieties now encoded into the soft tissues of your life. *Given the embodied character of human being, to overcome one faith is to set the stage for emergence of another, even if it, too, is punctuated by ambivalence and hesitation.* So James's philosophy of a 'pluralistic universe' is simultaneously supported by comparative argument, infused with a faith that inclines him toward it, and acknowledged to be contestable. Late in the book we are reviewing, James characterises the standing that his 'pluralistic image' of the universe

Immanence, abundance, democracy

has in his own eyes: 'The only thing I emphatically insist upon is that it [pluralism] is a fully coordinate with monism. This world *may* in the last resort, be a block-universe; but on the other hand it *may* be a universe only strung-along, not rounded in or closed. Reality may exist distributively just as it sensibly seems to, after all. On that possibility I do insist.'[12]

Where do I stand with respect to Smith, Derrida, Deleuze and James? With Deleuze and Smith I am drawn like a magnet to the idea of radical immanence, and I find the interpretations of immanence given by many who do not participate in that faith/philosophy to be deficient. Further, I find myself striving to overcome arguments that purport to show the necessity of transcendence and to bolster those on behalf of immanence. The ideas of litter and difference in itself, therefore, resonate with the way of the world as I experience it; and I am impressed with the extent to which that experience is supported today in complexity theory in fields such as thermodynamics, biological evolution and neuroscience. Moreover, with Deleuze and Smith I connect ethics in the first instance not to a primordial debt or responsibility to alterity but to an abundance of being that exceeds the specific identity I cultivate as, say, male, nontheistic, a former athlete, and professorial. With James, however, I concur that a particular faith becomes infused into you as you participate in the induction routines, rewards, punishments, theo-philosophical debates, public rituals, existential surprises and earthy shocks of everyday life, that the creed/philosophy emerging is sometimes susceptible to further work through a mixture of argument and experimental tactics of the self, and, above all, that no specific philosophy/faith to date, including radical immanence, has been demonstrated so convincingly that it is foolish to have faith in other orientations. Like James, I soften the lines of differentiation between faith, creed, doctrine and philosophy that have stalked the academy since the Enlightenment. And I do not spend too much time worrying about how to define a strict line of demarcation between philosophy/faiths that fall inside the charmed circle of contestable possibility and those that fall outside it. I allow the give and take of lived debates to settle that last issue in a provisional way, even as I expect to be startled periodically by an unexpected competitor that disrupts the established terms of engagement, as I was the first time I read Wittgenstein, and then again Foucault.

The introduction of James into the debate between Deleuze and Derrida itself points to the contestable character of fundamental philosophical stances. Once we see that Derrida and Deleuze do not exhaust the options here, it becomes possible to mix and match themes from this trio in diverse ways. You move from two options to three, and then from three to four, setting the stage for others yet to emerge. You might, for instance, become a Jamesleuzian, supporting Deleuze's philosophy of immanence, while acknowledging its comparative contestability in a Jamesian way, embracing Deleuze's anchoring of ethics in abundance and gratitude, while keeping open the possibility that others can gain more positive sustenance than you readily imagine from the experience of fundamental indebtedness.

I indeed am a Jamesleuzian. I have come to believe that this combination deepens the commitment to cultural pluralism that each thinker already evinces. Indeed, I also think that Derrida, while he does not touch as many chords in my being as James and Deleuze do, also makes a distinctive contribution to a culture of pluralism, pulling those ensnared in the experience of fundamental indebtedness toward appreciation of the case for pluralism.[13]

The tests of abundance

I construe James, Smith, Deleuze and Nietzsche, who disagree with each other along several dimensions, to be philosophers of abundance. One binds the idea of abundance to the soft voice of a limited God; the others link it to radical immanence. James is perhaps the most hesitant partisan of abundance on this list, not because of an experience of primordial debt, but because of the bouts of depression he periodically struggled with and against. James said he wanted to become more like Spinoza, in the latter's love of the abundance of being amidst suffering, but he often found it difficult to get up in the morning.

But what is 'abundance'? It is an experience of overflowing, joined to a love of the world in which we participate. It is the experience of vitality, of having more to draw upon in negotiating everyday life than it takes to protect your faith, secure your identity, make a living, rear your children, defend your creed, nourish your partner or secure your basic interests. The experience of abundance, for that reason, is marked by fragility and vulnerability. While it retains a certain capacity for resurgence after this or that setback, it can nonetheless be lost through ill health, the death of a loved one, political repression, a devastating war or other misfortunes. Its vitality is filled with contingency.

It is no coincidence that the greatest modern philosopher of abundance, Friedrich Nietzsche, also doubles as a prophet of the tragic. *He thinks abundance and the tragic character of existence together, belying those fools who equate a philosophy of immanence and abundance with a mood of 'optimism'.* Let us listen as Nietzsche enunciates each side of this sublime equation. First, abundance: 'What is astonishing about the religiosity of the ancient Greeks is the lavish abundance of gratitude that radiates from it. Only a very distinguished type of human being stands in that relation to nature and to life. Later, when the rabble came to rule in Greece, *fear* choked out religion and prepared the way for Christianity.'[14] This 'lavish abundance of gratitude' finds expression in a presumptive disposition of generosity to others. That is why pre-Platonic Greece, on Nietzsche's reading, could allow multiple theologies to contest each other nobly on the same territorial space. Note, even in this quotation, the ominous possibility hovering over existential gratitude for the abundance of being. It can be overtaken by fear. A culture of fear suffocates the energies of abundance. But abundance as existential gratitude can also be cultivated, up to a point. One way to prepare the soil for such cultivation is to come to terms affirmatively with a world that is neither predesigned for our dominion nor replete with the promise of eternal salvation.

Nietzsche calls for a 'spiritualization of enmity' between partisans of different fundamental faiths, meaning that they come to terms with each other by weaving reciprocal forbearance, hesitation and presumptive generosity into their relations. But the organised Christianity of his day was adamantly opposed to such diversity. It demanded cultural hegemony for itself; and it was hard on those who sought to render life more diverse. This experience led Nietzsche to suspect that those caught in the hope of transcendent salvation, or even in the aporias of impossible debts and obligations, too readily become weighed down by the burden of existence itself to respond affirmatively to such a call. Their experience of transcendence amidst the other burdens of life encouraged them to treat life itself as debt and to feel that debt weighing heavily upon their souls. Zarathustra says, 'Great indebtedness does not make men grateful, but vengeful, and if a little charity is not forgotten it turns into a gnawing worm ... But I am a giver of gifts. I like to give as a friend to friends.'[15] The element of paradox in this formulation is that some of those friends will be those who acknowledge a great indebtedness but who somehow, in ways opaque to Nietzsche, convert the experience of great indebtedness into presumptive generosity.

Nietzsche did not come to terms affirmatively enough with the positive possibilities lurking in spiritual sources he himself did not entertain. It is too bad that the work of the protestant Christian, William James, was not available to him as he addressed the Christian politics of his day; or that he did not have recourse to the work of Karl Jaspers, Hannah Arendt or Jacques Derrida. He might contest the tendency to ethical immobilisation discernible in the latter, but surely he would have acknowledged the nobility of Derrida's desire to open up a larger plurality of existential orientations in politics. He would have 'spiritualized' the contest between immanence and transcendence in this instance, and others too. Nietzsche and Derrida, my friends, would have become friends across an abyss of difference.

Should he have been more invitational, given his own philosophy of spiritualising enmity? Probably. However that may be, this philosopher of immanence makes a strong case for cultivating abundance in the self and pursuing generous relations with others across significant lines of difference, if and as they allow it. He contends that the affirmation of joy in life, amidst the abundant suffering life brings, opens a door to nobility in ethical life: 'Verily, I may have done this or that for sufferers; but always I seemed to have done better when I learned to feel better joys. As long as there have been men, man has felt too little joy: that alone our brothers is our original sin. And learning better how to feel joy, we learn best how not to hurt others or to plan hurts for them.'[16] Note Nietzsche's sense that life brings deep suffering with it. Nietzsche pursues gratitude for being amidst the suffering that life brings. He appreciates, again, that suffering may overwhelm gratitude. It may do so because, on the account of Nietzsche, there is nothing above human life to come to the rescue when things go radically astray. Nietzsche solicits gratitude for the abundance of life in a world without a higher design, purpose or meaning. He thinks that gratitude becomes profound when disconnected from other existential props. Perhaps we can adjust his thought to say that the experience of abundance is particularly vibrant in those who do not feel strong tremors of existential indebtedness coursing through their souls.

We have already signalled the tragic side of this philosophy of abundance. It consists, first, in acknowledging a certain potential for discordance between disparate forces that make up a world without transcendent purpose, second, in admitting that the resources ethical life can draw upon may or may not be sufficient to the need of them at a specific time, and, third, in a drive to affirm positively a world with these very traits. Such a world sets the condition in which the sweetness of life arises. To love life, on the Nietzschean reading, is to overcome existential resentment that the world is not designed with an intrinsic meaning.

You do indeed enter childhood with an obdurate feeling of lack: you desire to become what the other appears to be and you are not. Moreover, intense suffering in childhood and adulthood often brings with it uncertain feelings of guilt, shame or indebtedness. But Nietzsche, first, claims that these feelings *do not speak to something primordial or transcendent in need of recognition* and, second, that it is wise to draw upon the sweetness of life to attenuate or overcome these feelings of *primordial* guilt or indebtedness. Those who do not do so run the risk of becoming too resentful about life and mortality, seeking to punish others in turn for the will to revenge that inhabits them. This is not simply an individual issue, but also a cultural issue. For some cultural regimes are better equipped than others to curtail that fund of resentment and guilt from which the will to revenge emanates. This is the point of Nietzsche's invocation of Zeus at a key point in *The Genealogy of Morals*. Zeus comments on 'how mortals complain so loudly of the gods' whose actions bring pain to them. But they 'make themselves wretched through folly, even counter to fate,' says Zeus. Nietzsche now interprets this comment by Zeus:

> this Olympian spectator and judge is far from holding a grudge against them or thinking ill of them on that account: 'how foolish they are!', he thinks ... foolishness, not sin! Do you grasp that? ... In this way the gods served in those days to justify man to a certain extent even in his wickedness, they served as the originators of evil – in those days they took upon themselves, not the punishment but, what is nobler, the guilt.[17]

Immanence, abundance, democracy

The larger cultural context in which these existential struggles occur makes a significant difference to their tone and tenor. It is difficult, according to Nietzsche, to cultivate the abundance of life in a world governed by the God of Paul or Augustine. They concentrate primordial guilt on humanity, whereas the pagan gods *absorb a portion of guilt back into themselves* through the nobility of their competition and absence of omnipotence. This is noble, because it attenuates the tendency to transduct uncertain feelings of primordial guilt into a culture of revenge. We are speaking here of primordial guilt, not the feeling of guilt about this or that injury to others. You *might* lapse into a bleak feeling of guilt or deep indebtedness occasioned by the immense suffering of others, or yourself or a heavy faith that consumes you, or all of these together. But, as 'the Greeks' showed, human beings are not doomed by an unavoidable logic to live and act in such negational ways. It is, rather, one possible response to the travails of life among others, a tragic possibility to be fought and resisted if and as you can mobilise the energy to do so. The Nietzschean idea of 'keeping aloft' expresses such an idea. One way to start is by testing whether it is possible for *you* to live nobly without insisting that life comes pre-equipped with infinite debts and impossible obligations. For some can *affirm* the tragic character of being without becoming bleak, while others cannot. Let us listen to things Nietzsche, in his later work, says about the tragic character of existence, keeping the theme of abundance in mind as we proceed:

> This type of *artists' pessimism* is precisely the *opposite* of that religio-moral pessimism that suffers from the 'corruption' of man and the riddle of existence – and that by all means craves a solution, or at least a hope for a solution. The suffering, desperate, and self-mistrustful ... have at all times had need of entrancing *visions* to endure life ... The profundity of the tragic *artist* lies in this, that his aesthetic instinct surveys the more remote consequences ... that he affirms *the large scale economy* which justifies the terrible, the evil, the questionable – and more than merely justifies them.
>
> This pessimism of strength also ends in a *theodicy*, i.e., in an absolute affirmation of the world – but for the very reasons that formerly led one to deny it – and in this fashion to a conception of this world as the actually-achieved highest possible ideal.
>
> *I have been the first to discover the tragic* ... Even resignation is not a lesson of the tragic, but a misunderstanding of it! Yearning for nothingness is a *denial* of tragic wisdom, its opposite.
>
> The faith that a good meaning lies in evil means to abandon the struggle against it.[18]

In these enunciations Nietzsche challenges theodicies that link suffering and evil to a divine design *or* reduce it entirely to freely undertaken disobedience from divinely imposed laws; he construes tragic possibility to be wired into life; he suggests that attempts to redeem existential suffering through indebtedness to transcendence can undercut the struggle against other modes of suffering; he refuses resignation in the face of the tragic character of being; he encourages the fight against tragic binds as they arise; and he suggests that coming to terms with the co-existence between the tragic and the abundance of life helps prepare us to fight against these binds: 'The faith that a good meaning lies in evil means to abandon the struggle against it.'

Again, Nietzsche provides no guarantee that the resources of abundance will stand up against the pressures of life – including dominant cultural orientations, devastating historical events or private disasters. It would deny tragic possibility to say that. He does contend that tapping into a gratitude for being already simmering in you provides a noble way to dilute the weight of primordial indebtedness and the hidden resentment against life such an experience of being might foment.

But, how can Nietzsche's claim be *tested* against alternative orientations? Is there an *argument* that settles the issue between him and visions that link transcendence, debt and infinite obligation together? Both Nietzsche and James doubt that such a definitive argument is available. Though the nobility James pursues is not identical to that Nietzsche celebrates, and though the limited God James invokes departs from the radical immanence convened by Nietzsche, both think that the issue we are now addressing is resolved in part through *existential tests*. By trying a philosophy of abundance on for size, by experimenting with the thoughts, actions and exercises it solicits, by tapping the existential gratitude it commends, *you run the most basic tests to which it is susceptible*. Here Nietzsche and James touch the religions of the Book. The most radical test of abundance is performative. Those tests will not take with everybody, but they may take with some. That is life ... Everyone already realises this at some level, except a few priests and philosophers. The different philosophy/faiths we confess express thought-imbued sensibilities infused into the soft tissues of life. Almost everybody, moreover, is moved by a desire to confirm their faith by soliciting the consent of others to it. Otherwise, we would not be so eager to write, teach, preach, confess, or speak to each other. It is because these tests are existential and experimental that they affect different individuals and constituencies in different ways. It is because the effects are apt to vary that it is *noble* to cultivate, where possible, the spiritualisation of enmity with those who respond differently.

To gauge the cultural importance of such existential tests, it helps to recall the intense debates accompanying the death of Spinoza, the inveterate philosopher of immanence, joy and an ethic of cultivation who burst on to the scene in the seventeenth century to shock Christians, disturb Jews and rattle the chains of Cartesians. His death produced an intense public debate about his last days that continued off and on for decades. The debate about his death revolved around the question whether ethical life *can* be infused by an abundant gratitude for being or *must* be grounded in the infinite debt human beings owe to God.

Did Spinoza die in serenity? Or did he confess, on his deathbed, that he was a miserable atheist who had shunned the only redemption available to human beings? Some, such as Pierre Bayle, who opposed his doctrine, confirmed the testimony of Spinoza's friends that he died in serenity and confidence. Most concluded, however, that since it is impossible to be an 'atheist' all the way down, Spinoza must have acknowledged his faith in a personal God as the end approached. Doing so, he died a wretched death, regretting the course of his life. For example, 'Hector Gottfried Masius (1653–1709), German Court preacher ... poured scorn on Bayles' account of Spinoza's death, maintaining that there are no 'true theoretical atheists', men who are categorically convinced there is no God. But ... there are undoubtedly dangerous men, professed speculative doubters and mockers ... at the head of whom stands Spinoza.'[19] Spinoza, Masius insisted, died in acute distress, acknowledging the God he had 'mocked', admitting it was too late to avoid the fate awaiting him, in abject misery that he had been so prideful.

The public debate over Spinoza's death is revelatory, as debates over the deaths of Moses, Socrates, Jesus, Buddha and Deleuze have been. The debate reveals, first, the practical and existential dimensions of the issue. Existential tests are needed to ascertain to what extent abundance can be cultivated, whether its cultivation makes a positive difference to the conduct of life and which cultivators must presuppose transcendence as they proceed. The debate reveals, second, how the call toward a theo-philosophical faith is set in a larger cultural context of political hegemony, a politics that renders some experiments culturally obligatory, discourages others and issues dire warnings about others even before they are attempted. In this instance, an active minority in several European countries sought to run Spinozist experiments with life. A larger, hegemonic group, led by the Catholic Church, many Jewish temples, state authority, most philosophers of the day and much of what Spinoza called 'the multitude', authorised established experiments in pursuit of transcendence, including prayer, confession and subservience to the wisdom of priests. They made dire predictions about what would happen to those who fell away from that faith and these practices, predictions closely linked to the investments the parties had already made in their own faith and practices. Fear and the promise of joy after death were used to condemn experiments with immanence and the abundance of life. The political stakes were high. Was the cultural hegemony of monotheism to remain unchallenged? Or would a significant minority of adventurers experiment with the intensities of immanence, drawing courage from them to press for a pluralisation of public culture? For Spinoza was a pluralist.

The dominant cultural context helps to shape, as James puts it, the 'conception of the world', which 'arises in you somehow'. That faith, in turn, infuses the sensibility through which you later explore other philosophies and adopt practical tests appropriate to them. Nietzsche, the individualist, appreciated the weight of culture when he celebrated how the Greek gods, more than the God of monotheism, relieves a portion of primordial guilt from Greek life. If the task of individuals drawn to a philosophy of immanence is to experiment with themselves on its behalf, *our task in politics is to challenge the collective hegemony of creeds of transcendence so that the voices of immanence can assume a more active presence in public life, so that the depth grammar of public life itself becomes more actively pluralised.*

What kind of the experimental tests? You might read new books, adopt new friends, pursue new strategies of meditation, think new thoughts before going to bed to prime your dream life or participate in neuro-therapy. If we do not become our own guinea pigs to some extent we are simply the guinea pigs of experiments a hegemonic culture imposes upon us. Sure, their experiments will often backfire, but our own are nonetheless urgently needed. Faith abhors a vacuum. But the range of defensible faiths is much wider than admitted by those who most commonly assert this fact.

I run practical tests on behalf of gratitude for the abundance of being, set in a philosophy of radical immanence, punctuated by appreciation of the tragic character of being. In doing so I am informed by formulation of Nietzsche – the philosopher of radical immanence, abundance and the tragic, an enunciation that invites comparison to the one presented by James – the philosopher of abundance through transcendence: 'Out of damp and gloomy days, out of solitude, out of loveless words directed at us, conclusions grow up in us like fungus: one morning they are there, we know not how, and they gaze upon us. Woe to the thinker who is not the gardener but only the soil of the plants that grow up in him.'[20]

Radical democracy

Nietzsche was no democrat, for his experience told him that most people lacked sufficient abundance to pursue the noble virtues he commended. But most philosophers of abundance – in either its transcendent or immanent variations – espouse democratic sentiments that are more radical than those expressed by the majority of thinkers in their own day. I include Epicurus, Lucretius, Spinoza, James, Bergson, Deleuze, Foucault and Smith on that list, and many others as well. What vision of radical democracy could inspire such a gang under contemporary conditions? I am not sure. But I suspect that an appropriate vision includes at least three elements.[21] First, it solicits a regime of deep, multidimensional pluralism. Deep pluralism is a condition in which multiple faiths find public expression in the same territorial regime; each constituency brings pieces and chunks of its faith into the public realm when it is pertinent to do so;

and the constituencies together negotiate a positive ethos of engagement that enables them to produce general policies in the public realm. Second, it envisions a regime in which a majority assemblage composed of diverse types works to reduce inequalities of income, educational opportunity, job security, medical care, retirement prospects and housing possibilities, seeking a regime in which every citizen can participate with dignity in the common cultural economy. Third, it pursues a regime in which numerous lines of affinity and interdependence between human beings and nonhuman nature are acknowledged much more widely and actively than today, and in which the pursuit of pluralism and equality is infused with the drive to reconstitute historically dominant relations between the human animal and the rest of nature.[22]

The public hegemony of faith in transcendence for innumerable centuries has failed to draw humanity closer to such a condition. Maybe, then, it is time to incorporate other orientations more actively into the operational equations of public life. My sense is that radical democracy has the best chance to progress if and as a significant minority of citizens in a large variety of positions – including labour leaders, feminists, environmentalists the elderly, church goers, professors and the young – come to terms actively with the abundance of life, insinuate that faith into their church, school, governmental and media activities, and draw upon it to resist pressure from bellicose Unitarians who seek to 'restore' a fictive unity of faith, to protect inequality or to pretend that the earth provides an infinite amount of resources to use as we please.

One way in which this vision of radical democracy diverges from other such visions, perhaps, is in the conviction that deep, multidimensional pluralism and economic egalitarianism support each other more than they are at odds with one another. It is often argued that only when the pursuit of cultural diversity is relaxed can a national movement emerge to reduce economic inequality.[23] On the contrary, the activism and ethos of engagement needed to apply political pressure upon capitalist institutions to reduce inequality are the same as those needed to support deep, multidimensional pluralism: the micropolitics and macropolitics by which an ethos of deep pluralism is promoted is also that by which the drive to reduce economic inequality is fostered.

I have outlined elsewhere programmes to reduce economic inequality that are compatible with deep, multidimensional pluralism. They focus first and foremost *on the public infrastructure of consumption* in the domains of health care, transportation, public security, education, housing and retirement. The policies themselves make it possible for more citizens to make ends meet by rendering the dominant forms of consumption subsidised by the state more inclusive in character. They move from expensive state subsidy of exclusive goods, in which the extension of exclusive goods to more and more people increases the unit costs and intensifies strains on the environment, to extensive subsidies of inclusive goods. The state, for instance, currently subsidises medical care extensively; but it supports a mode of care that is high-tech in character, curative rather than preventative in emphasis, drug centred in treatment, controlled by private insurance companies and dependent upon the private fees of physicians. A change in the state-supported infrastructure of medical care could shift each of these priorities. The effect would be to make medical care available to more people at cheaper unit costs. And the large state expenditures to cover the adverse effects of the current system would also be reduced. It would become a priority of the state and the medical care system together, for instance, to reverse the current combination of fast food restaurants, overweight citizens, diabetes, high cholesterol, heart disease and the expensive curative treatment that now cripples the health of many, taxes the health care system and increases the medical costs of low-income citizens.

Such a change in state subsidised modes of consumption could be instituted in several zones of life. The cumulative effect would be to reconfigure capitalism by altering the state subsidies, infrastructural supports, and regulations in which it is set, include all citizens in the established economy and relieve the difficulties many now face in making ends meet.

But, it may be asked, on what *common basis* could citizens in such a diverse state unite behind such general programmes? Does it not require a unified national *consensus* to promote such an agenda? If so, does that not carry us back to pursuit of a unified nation grounded, say, in a common religious tradition? Not so. Historically, the pursuit of a unified nation is connected to authoritative drives to deprive this or that constituency of effective economic inclusion; proposed changes in the infrastructure of consumption are even rejected *because* degraded minorities would be included in it.

The drive to restructure the infrastructure of consumption requires the emergence of a significant minority of citizens in a large variety of subject positions who cultivate an abundance of life anchored in either immanence or transcendence, insinuate those energies into the every day politics of churches, media, schools and workplaces, and devote their political energies to the extension of diversity and the reduction of inequality alike. This preliminary assemblage, in turn, needs to forge alliances with others, who despite the initial expectations coded into our faiths, convert confessions of primordial debt, alterity, responsibility and obligation into the pursuit of deep pluralism and equality. For while 'we' exude confidence in our faith, we must also be open to the possibility that they are moved by inspirations exceeding the terms of our expectation. If 'they' pursue the same relation of agonistic respect from their side, we will take another step toward a culture of deep pluralism and economic egalitarianism.

Such engagements at the academic level simulate the process by which a majority assemblage composed of diverse constituencies could be forged more broadly. Rather than pursuit of a nation unified around a general faith or the shallow pluralism of secular proceduralism, such an assemblage contains the most promise today. If and as it lifts off, some will support its programmes out of dire need; some out of this or that material interest; some because they seek to meet moral responsibilities, obligations or inspiration flowing from a particular creed or philosophy that informs them; some because their loyalty to the assemblage on other grounds impels them to concede this issue in exchange for others dear to them; some because they believe the long-term effects of inequality increase crime levels, deplete the quality of democracy and damage future prospects for cultural diversity; some out of aesthetic considerations; and most out of a mixture of several of these concerns varying in shape and intensity from case to case and constituency to constituency. Further, some who participate will do so because the programmes resonate with elements in their own identities, interests or ethical sensibilities, while others will be linked to it in more attenuated ways.

The difficulties in forging such a majority assemblage are impressive. Indeed the odds are stacked against it. But we are interested in *possibilities* in relation to the contemporary *need* for them more than political probabilities unconnected to such a need. When the first equation is given priority the strategic promise of reducing inequality is enhanced if you approach it through the lens of multidimensional pluralism and a majority assemblage rather than that of national unity, shallow secularism or the revolutionary overturn of capitalism.[24] A majority assemblage in a culture of deep pluralism grows out of a series of positive resonances between local meetings, internet campaigns, television exposes, church organisation, film portrayals, celebrity testimonials, labour rank and file education and electoral campaigns by charismatic leaders; multidimensional diversity, inspirational leadership, militant action and media publicity of the private suffering and public expense generated by the current infrastructure of consumption – that is the positive resonance machine to put into motion today. Coming to terms more deeply and widely with the abundance of life over identity does not suffice to generate momentum for the radicalisation of democracy. It merely helps. Nor does it rule the carriers of transcendence out of such coalitions. It, rather, contests those among them who oppose pluralism and equality; and it refuses to give the others a monopoly over these ideals.

Notes

1 D. W. Smith, 'Deleuze and Derrida, immanence and transcendence', in P. Patton and J. Protevi (eds), *Between Deleuze and Derrida* (London: Continuum, 2003), p. 57.
2 In *Cinema II: The Time Image*, trans H. Tomlinson and R. Galeta (Minneapolis, MN: University of Minnesota Press, 1985), Deleuze discusses how a series of film directors seek to nurture 'belief in this world', meaning by that a world in which time is becoming and immanent forces elude our best efforts to know or master them.
3 Smith, 'Deleuze and Derrida, immanence and transcendence', pp. 62f.

4 W. James, *A Pluralistic Universe* (Lincoln: University of Nebraska Press, 1996), p. 311.
5 *Ibid.*, p. 45.
6 G. Deleuze, *Difference and Repetition*, trans. P. Patton (New York: Columbia University Press, 1994), p. 222.
7 When a theorist of immanence plays up the *torsion* between being and becoming, there are always some, perhaps disturbed by the becoming side of the equation, who *hear* only the latter side of the assertion. And who therefore misrepresent the position in the pretence of presenting it. That is to be expected. I was still surprised, though, to read the editors of a book on different methods and approaches to politics in which an essay of mine is included, summarise my position in the Introduction as one in which 'the world is in a state of constant and unpredictable flux'. That would be a world with no persisting political institutions, no new species surviving for thousands of years after their emergence, no book in which an essay on immanent naturalism is included, that is, no torsion between being and becoming. A position, hence, which one need not examine seriously. See I. Shapiro, R. M. Smith, and T. E. Masoud, *Problems and Methods in The Study of Politics* (Cambridge: Cambridge University Press, 2004), p. 11.
8 I discuss Bergson's image of time in chapter 4 of *Pluralism* (Durham: Duke University Press, 2005). A philosophy of radical immanence is also one of time as becoming, in which time is always out of joint with itself.
9 James, *A Pluralistic Universe*, p. 299.
10 D. Smith, 'Deleuze and the theory of immanent ideas', paper given at the Symposium on 'Experimenting With Intensities', Trent University, Peterborough, Ontario, 12–15 May 2004.
11 James, *A Pluralistic Universe*, p. 328
12 *Ibid.*, p. 328.
13 Derrida's interview in *Le Monde* on 8 August 2004, two months before his death, may express eloquently his lived relation to a philosophy of immanence. He speaks of how he had sought to accept death as a way of honouring life, and how he found himself less and less ready to accept it as death approached. This might be read as a nod of respect to Nietzsche's commendation to prepare to die at the right time to affirm the abundance of life, while finding himself inclined to a different course as time closed in. Deleuze, it seems, found himself taking the opposite course. One gets the sense that each giant would honour the existential imperative of the other, even as each was infused by a different faith in following his course. Is theirs a relation of agonistic respect with reference to the test of life in the face of death?
14 F. Nietzsche, *Beyond Good and Evil*, trans. M. Gowan (South Bend, Indiana: Gateway Editions, 1955), p. 58.
15 F. Nietzsche, *Thus Spoke Zarathustra*, trans. W. Kaufmann (New York: Vintage Book, 1966), p. 89
16 *Ibid.*, p. 88.
17 F. Nietzsche, *On The Genealogy of Morals*, trans. W. Kaufmann and R. J. Hollingdale (New York: Random House, 1967), p. 94.
18 F. Nietzsche, *The Will To Power*, trans. Walter Kaufmann (New York: Vintage Books, 1968), in order, §852 (pp. 450f), §1019 (pp. 526f); §1029 (pp. 531f) and §1019 (p. 527).
19 J. Israel, *Radical Enlightenment: Philosophy and the Making of Modernity 1650–1750* (Oxford: Oxford University Press, 2002), p. 300. Israel devotes an entire section to this question, evincing in this way his own appreciation of the intimate link between philosophical arguments and practical tests.

20 F. Nietzsche, *Daybreak: thoughts on the prejudices of morality*, trans. R. J. Hollingdale (Cambridge: Cambridge University Press, 1982), p. 171.
21 I omit for reasons of space a fourth element, the engagement by citizens in activist citizen networks which reach above the level of the state, speaking to global issues and striving to affect the practices of states, transnational corporations, and supranational institutions of governance alike. I discuss this dimension of chapter 7 of *Neuropolitics: Thinking, Culture, Speed* (Minneapolis, MN: University of Minnesota Press, 2002) and chapter 5 of *Pluralism* (Durham: Duke University Press, 2005).
22 An excellent place to start thinking about this third dimension is in Jane Bennett, *The Enchantment of Modern Life: Attachments, Crossings and Ethics* (Princeton, NJ: Princeton University Press, 2000).
23 In the last chapter of *Pluralism*, I contend that late-modern capitalism is neither a tightly defined structure of contradictions nor a self-sustaining system susceptible to governance through light state policies. It is potentially open to being twisted and turned into economic practices that reduce structural inequalities on several fronts significantly. The political leverage for these practices is difficult to establish, but that is less because the structure is closed and more because of the power of the corporate media and the willingness of many to give priority to conservative faiths over their own economic interests. The last item shows *why* pluralism and egalitarianism must be promoted together.
24 I first explored ways to reduce economic inequality in a mixed economy with Michael Best in *The Politicized Economy*, 2nd edition (Lexington: D. C. Heath, 1982). There we developed the distinction between exclusive modes of consumption and inclusive modes, supporting the latter in the domains of housing, travel, communication, insurance, and medical care. The dominant mode of consumption today takes the shape of exclusive goods. These themes are connected more closely to pluralism in chapter 3 of *The Ethos of Pluralization* (Minneapolis, MN: University of Minnesota Press, 1995), and 'Assembling the Left', *boundary 2* (Fall, 1999), 47–54. The latter essay appears in a Symposium on 'Left Conservatism', where, among other things, several participants challenge the idea that being on the Left and being a pluralist are contradictory.

15 • Ernesto Laclau

The future of radical democracy

THE EDITORS of this volume have asked me to write an afterword dealing with two precise subjects: the relation that the ontological categories of 'lack' and 'excess' have in my thought,[1] and the defining dimensions of radical democracy. I will deal successively with each issue.

Excess and lack

Let me say, to start with, that I do not see 'lack' and 'excess' as two opposite categories, so that asserting the priority of one would necessarily exclude the other, but as being two necessary moments of a unique ontological condition. It is because there is lack, conceived as deficient being, that excess becomes possible. An immanent fullness, without any internal rents, would make both lack and excess redundant. The crucial issue is the role assigned to *negativity*. A purely immanentist conception has necessarily to reduce any antagonistic moment within the social to the phenomenal expression of a deeper objectivity. Thus, antagonism and negativity would be purely apparential. Let us consider the classical problem of evil as posed in Christian theology. How to make compatible God's sovereignty and his being absolute goodness with the existence of evil in the world? The solution given by John Scotus Eriugena to this aporia was to conceive of evil as merely apparential: what looks evil to us is necessary, because it actually is a stage God has to go through in order to reach his absolute perfection. We have there – one thousand years before the *Phenomenology of Spirit*[2] – all the defining features of a radical immanentism. The 'cunning of reason' is pre-announced in the conception of a deeper objectivity revealing a meaning not accessible to the actual historical actors. What is decisive for our subject is that there is no room here for either lack or excess: there can be no deficient being for a view which reduces the latter to a necessary stage on the road to absolute fullness. But, for the same reason, there cannot be excess either.

If, on the contrary, evil is conceived as constitutive, as irreducible to anything different from itself, the terrain which made possible a monistic ontology necessarily collapses. That collapse does not leave us, however, with a mere multiplicity. The presence of evil threatens the good, whose being thus becomes *deficient being*. *Ergo*, the primary ontological terrain is not one of multiplicity but of *failed unicity*.

Let us abandon now the theological terrain and move to social ontology. We should here replace the notion of evil for that of social antagonism. The homology of both is shown by the fact that they confront us with an identical alternative: either antagonisms are the phenomenal appearance of a deeper objectivity (which would not, itself, be antagonistic), or antagonism is irreducible, in which case social objectivity cannot be fully constituted. This explains why antagonisms cannot be conceived as dialectical contradictions. For the latter, negativity is only present to be superseded by a higher form of objectivity. Hegel's Absolute Spirit and Marx's classless society, are the names of a fullness which makes it possible to detect the ultimate meaning of all previous stages and, thus, to transform negativity in the apparential form of a deeper objectivity. What happens if, instead, we avoid this reductionist operation and take antagonism at face value? In that case, as we have asserted earlier, what cannot be fully constituted is objectivity as such. As we have asserted several times, antagonism is not an objective relation but the limit of all objectivity.[3] This explains enough why for us deficient being and failed unicity constitute the primary ontological terrain. In other works, I have shown why that terrain presupposes the primacy of discourse and rhetoricity.[4] What I want to show here, however, to remain within the scope of this afterword, is how the two moments of lack and excess enter into the determination of social ontology.

The notion of failed unicity already presupposes a lack conceived of as absent fullness. Every identity is a threatened identity. That is why antagonism is ontologically primary. But an important consequence follows from this remark. If an identity was not threatened by an antagonistic relation, it would be what it is as a pure objective datum. Between what it ontically is and the ontological fact that it is, there would be no distance. It would be a mere positivity, closed in itself. Antagonism is what creates a gap between these two dimensions. This distance between fullness of being and actual being is what we call lack. Representation of that distance, however, requires not only the discursive presence of actual being but also of the fullness of being. But this creates an immediate problem, for fullness of being is that which is constitutively absent. The difficulty can be summarised in the following terms: the distance between full and actual being needs to be represented – which involves the two poles being somehow present in such representation – but one of the two cannot have a *direct* representation because it operates through its very absence. Actual beings are the only means of representation. In such conditions, representation of the fullness of being can only take place if there is an essential unevenness among actual beings – that is, if an ontic particularity becomes the body through which an incommensurable fullness 'positivises' itself. This means that one element assumes an ontological function, which far exceeds its ontic content. This is the moment of *excess*. As we see, we are not dealing with an excess which is opposed to lack, but with one which directly results from the latter. (This notion of excess is, obviously, very different from the one to be found in the work of Gilles Deleuze, for whom the passage through negativity, which is essential in our approach, is entirely absent.)

Let us give a couple of examples of this articulation of lack/excess. The first can be found in the hegemonic link. As I have argued in my work, there is hegemony whenever a certain particular symbol or actor, without entirely ceasing to be particular, assumes the function of representing the incommensurable universality of the community.[5] Our approach thus differs from those asserting that we can have direct access to such universality and that we can identify it with a precise ontic content. The notion of a 'universal class', identified by Hegel with bureaucracy and by Marx with the proletariat, are clear examples of a non-hegemonic type of universality. Hegemony belongs to a terrain in which universality and particularity mutually contaminate each other. Hegemony thus defines the essence of the political, which requires the permanent retreat of the communitarian fullness and its identification with successive particularistic contents (which, through such identification, cease to be merely particularistic).

A second example can be found in the Lacanian notion of object *a*. The Freudian Thing, the fullness associated with a primordial mother, is a retrospective illusion and, as such, constitutively absent. This is the moment of lack. This absent fullness is, however, invested in particular objects representing it, the objects *a*. This is the moment of excess, what we have earlier presented as the ontological transcendence of the ontic givenness. As I have argued in my work the hegemonic logic and the logic of the object *a* are identical.[6] Both reveal, in one case from the angle of political theory and in the other from that of psychoanalysis, something belonging to the very structure of objectivity. It is this radical unevenness that is at the root of the ontic/ontological distinction.

Radical democracy

As for the question of radical democracy, it confronts us with similar unevennesses, for radical democracy refers to a cluster of dimensions, which do not easily cohere with each other. The question of radical democracy is not a simple one for, to start with, we do not exactly know what it is about. Does it refer to a political *regime*, whose institutional dimensions would be clearly specifiable and distinguishable from other kinds of regime? Does it make allusion to a political *actor*, as when we conceive democracy as the government by the *people*? Or, rather, is it linked to a *plurality* of such actors, so that the radicalism of democracy would be extensively and not intensively conceived? It is a mistake to think

The future of radical democracy

that a square circle could be found that would bring these different alternatives together into a harmonious whole – which was what the classical notion of *politeia* attempted to do.

Let us start considering the conception of democracy as a political regime. This is the most usual approach and, at the same time, a source of countless misunderstandings. Democracy, conceived in this sense, would be a system of institutional rules – freedom of political organisation, universal suffrage, absence of discrimination towards particular sectors of the population and so on. This is a formal conception of democracy, in which it shades into a liberal system of institutional rules, whose democratic character is just given by their universal application. The purely formal character of the rules has been widely criticised, but it would be wrong to think that radicalism is absent from this institutionalist conception: the universalisation of the application of the rules (which does not necessarily follow from the rules themselves) requires the introduction of some extra postulates – for instance, freedom and equality for everybody. This kind of radicalism was very much in evidence in the campaigns for electoral reforms extending the franchise, during the nineteenth century. I want to insist on this point, which I see as crucial: it is entirely wrong to speak of liberal-democratic regimes as constituting an undifferentiated homogeneous whole. Liberal institutional arrangements are perfectly possible with only a limited kind of democratic participation. To speak of a liberal-democratic regime is not to refer to a coherent and self-defined object, but to the space of a tension. So, the internal democratisation of liberal institutions on the basis of an unlimited application of universal rules is a first possible meaning of radical democracy.

But it is not, of course, the only possible one. For what remains as valid from the critique to the purely formal conception of universality is that the latter is unable to constitute any democratic subjectivity. Democracy as a system of institutional rules is only possible if the idea of a democratic subjectivity – which always evokes the notion of a certain partiality within the communitarian order – is systematically ignored. However, even struggles such as the ones we have just evoked, for the extension of the electoral franchise, already involve a new sense of democracy, whose radicalism presupposes the constitution of an underdog as a political actor. This puts the argument in a new terrain: the moment of universality is still very much present, for those excluded claim rights that the community theoretically accepts as legitimate but denies them in practice. Universality in this case ceases to be abstract and is incarnated in a sector whose lack of possible representation within the communitarian order makes it the pure expression of that unachieved universality. Democracy, in this new sense of radicalism, is synonymous with the constitution of the 'people' – the masses – as a new historical actor. In this sense, radical democracy is always 'populist', providing that this term is deprived of the pejorative connotations usually associated with it.

Ernesto Laclau

Could these two meanings of radicalism – one liberal, the other populist – be linked in such a way that they logically require each other? Two seconds of reflection show us that the answer to the question should be negative. Nothing guarantees that the liberal forms are the only ones that make possible – through their universalisation/radicalisation – the constitution of the underdog as a historical actor. That is why a purely proceduralist conception of democracy is begging the whole question. Liberalism and democracy remained distinct political traditions in the European experience of most of the nineteenth century – liberalism being the main ideology of the establishment, while democracy was mostly associated with the ghost of mob-rule and hated Jacobinism – and it was only very slowly that some kind of precarious integration between both became possible. And, in most of the world, the democratic mobilisations of the masses took place under forms that were not only non-liberal but, frequently, even formally anti-liberal. However, it is not possible either to transform this distinction between liberal and populist democracy into a sharp dichotomy, for the collapse of liberal forms can lead, in some contexts to situations in which the defence of liberal principles becomes an integral part of the populist demands of the underdog. Under the Latin American military dictatorships of the period 1960–85, for instance, human rights did not function as established rules of the system, but as central demands in the democratic constitution of a 'people'.

We have now to move to a third way in which democratic radicalism should be understood. We have so far taken for granted that the democratic demands of the underdog tend, in spite of their plurality, to coalesce around a popular pole, which would give populist democracy its distinctive character. But this assumption is clearly excessive. Democratic demands have a variety of aims, and there is no guarantee that they will all move in the same direction. This is what makes some versions of the notion of 'democratic revolution' so simplistic, especially those which conceive it as a unifying horizon dominated by the expansion of the equalitarian logic to wider spheres of social relations. The crystallisation of a group of demands around a 'people' is perfectly compatible with the exclusion of many other demands from the equivalential chain. This leads to a third way in which radical democracy can be conceived, in which radicalisation is linked to *pluralism*. It is clear that populist democracy does not guarantee, by itself, the recognition of *all* democratic demands. To give just one example, the democratic populist movement of American farmers at the end of the nineteenth century, although highly radical in its opposition to dominant forms of economic power, had serious difficulties in accommodating the demands of blacks and women – let alone those of Asiatic immigrant workers. In a similar way, the populist regimes established in Africa after the decolonisation process increasingly reduced the discursive construction of the underdog as an emancipatory subject, to a vacuous entelechy whose *langue de bois* barely concealed its lack of democratic irradiation.

The future of radical democracy

So, radicalisation conceived as pluralism is very different from the other two forms that we had previously discussed. In the case of liberal democracy we found that radicalisation was identified with universalisation – that is, with a doing away with all differences and exceptions. In the case of populist democracy, this universality was attributed to a subject who was less than the community as a whole but who claims the right to be identified with the latter. But, in the case of radical pluralism, we have, on the contrary, that the very principle of universality is put into question. We are dealing with a differentiality which asserts itself as the only and irreducible universal principle. That this third sense of radical democracy underlies the discourse of vast sections of the population in the contemporary world, who assert democracy as the right to particularism, is only too obvious.

So where does this plurality of ways of radicalisation leave us as far as democracy is concerned? We can start approaching the question by stressing that the unilateralisation of any of the three meanings leads, in actual fact, to the collapse of democracy. A purely liberal democracy, in which the democratic element was restricted to the level of the regime, is perfectly compatible with all kinds of anti-democratic practices at the level of civil society. A purely populist democracy would rigidly identify the community (the *populus*) with a particular section within it (the *plebs*) and so would also make impossible any kind of democratic interaction. But the pure principle of pluralism and differentiality would not feature any better either: a society based only on this would lack any kind of common symbolic framework, and would not, actually, be a society at all.

So democratic functioning requires that all three senses of radicalism are active in actual political processes. However, this presents a problem: the three senses are not only different but, also, ultimately incompatible with each other. This, however, is less of a problem than it looks at first glance. That they are incompatible with each other only means that there is no square circle which could subsume them under a unified conceptual scheme. But it is precisely the impossibility of this subsumption that requires that the interaction between them is conceived as a *political* articulation and not as a *logical* mediation. *The undecidable character of this interaction, the impossibility of conceptually mastering the contingent forms in which it crystallises, is exactly what we call radical democracy.* Many consequences follow from this, among them that radical democracy is the first strictly political form of social organisation, because it is the first one in which the posing and the withdrawal of the social ground is entirely dependent on political interventions.

Notes

1 In this context, I believe that 'abundance' and 'excess' mean exactly the same, only I think that excess is clearer insofar as it refers to a going beyond the given (a kind of

negativity), while in 'abundance' this meaning of 'going beyond' seems to be missing.
2   G. W. F. Hegel, *Phenomenology of the Spirit*, trans. A. V. Miller (Oxford: Clarendon Press, 1977).
3   E. Laclau and C. Mouffe, *Hegemony and Socialist Strategy: Towards a Radical Democratic Politics*, 2nd edition (London: Verso, 2001).
4   J. Butler, E. Laclau and S. Žižek, *Contingency, Hegemony, Universality: Contemporary Dialogues on the Left* (London: Verso, 2000); and E. Laclau, 'Paul de Man and the politics of rhetoric', *Pretexts*, 7:2 (1998), 153–70.
5   E. Laclau, *Emancipation(s)* (London: Verso, 1996); and Butler, Laclau and Žižek, *Contingency, Hegemony, Universality*.
6   *Ibid.*

Index

Note: 'n.' after a page reference indicates the number of a note on that page

Abensour, M. 231
abundance 6, 245
    actants 137
    contestable 7
    cultural populism 158
    Deleuze 6
    different from lack 2, 6, 26, 32, 36, 68, 113
    immanence 8, 215
    ontological imaginary 2
    Patton, P. on 9
    radical difference 2, 6–7
    radical politics 2, 7, 200
    rhizome 6
    tragic 246, 247
    Widder, N. on 9
    see also Deleuze, G.; difference; immanence; micropolitics; rhizomatic politics
agency 134
    lack 156
agonistic respect 4
    Coles, R. on 5
    Mouffe, C. 4–5, 126
Amazonia 133, 145
    see also Latour, B.
antagonism 24, 107–9, 126–7
    Lefort, C. 25
    see also Laclau, E. and Mouffe, C.

Badiou, A. 8, 11, 22
    anarchic meta-politics 234n.15

    ethics 196
    Lacan, J. 197
    Truth-Event 74
    void 23
Balibar, E. 73
Barad, K. 137, 146n.14
Bataille, G. 207
Beck, U. 127
Bennett, J. 151, 153, 164
    advertisement, 161
    enchantment 160
    the nonhuman 10
Bergson, H. 241
Butler, J. 34, 36, 70, 79, 85n.56, 98

Cacciari, M. 131
capitalism 210–11
    becoming 211
    dislocation 223
    Laclau, E. 221, 222
    Marx, K. 221
    see also community; Marx, K.
class analysis 3, 212–13, 221, 224
Coles, R. 9
communitarianism 4
community 4, 104, 203, 208
    the disparate 208
    inessential commonality 11, 204, 206
    political economy 209
complexity theory 138
Connolly, W. E. 28, 56
    ethos of critical engagement 62

Index

identity\difference 12n.6
immanence and transcendence
    11–12
Laclau, E. 115
pluralisation 141
contestation 6, 14, 125, 248
Coole, D. 186
Copjec, J. 94, 96
Critchley, S. 11
    Badiou, A. 198
cultural studies
    Birmingham School 161
    Frankfurt School 154, 156
    hegemony 157
    popular culture 159
    see also media

deconstruction 26, 90, 97
    undecidability and hegemony 92
    see also Derrida, J.
Deleuze, G. 6, 9, 137, 243
    critique of lack 6
    critique of transcendence 58
    democratic politics 54
    differentiation 49n.38
    Hegel, G. W. F. 41–2
    immanence 240
    Lacan. J. 17, 43
    the left 57
    political theory 50
    power of opinion 63
    radical difference 7
    transcendental argument 242
    see also abundance; Deleuze, G. and Guattari, F.; immanence
Deleuze, G. and Guattari, F.
    becoming 60–1, 62, 64
    body without organs ('BwO') 46–7
    deterritorialisation 51, 54
    Laclau, E. and Mouffe C. 52
    Rawls, J. 51, 55
    rhizome 206
    Spinoza, B. 205
    see also Deleuze, G.; micropolitics; rhizomatic politics

democracy
    consumerism 190
    deliberative 124
    democratisation 227, 230, 232
    'moving democracy' 81
    two senses of democracy 53–4
    see also the political; radical democracy; representation
Derrida, J. 3, 10, 12, 204, 243
    decentring of structure 91
    différance 26
    hauntology 18
    immanence 254n.13
    transcendence 239
    see also deconstruction; difference; transcendence
desire 20–1, 30n.10, 37, 187
    Deleuze 26, 44
    feminine 39
    see also Lacan, J.
difference 1
    abundance 2, 35
    class analysis 3
    discourse 105
    lack 2, 34
    litter 241
    ontology 18
    radical 3, 29n.2, 33, 43
    versions of radical democracy 2
    see also Deleuze, G.; Derrida, J.
discourse 1, 7, 97
    difference 105
    empty signifier 104, 105
    Lacan, J. 5
    orientational metaphors 179
    see also hegemony; Laclau, E.
disjunctive synthesis 35, 42
Dworkin, R. 124
Dyrberg, T. 11

Evil 256–7
exclusion 103, 109, 112, 115
    inclusion 116

fantasy 21, 24, 189

[264]

Index

see also Lacan, J.
federalism 131
Fiske, J. 158, 161
French revolution 11, 175

Gasché, R. 88, 91, 99
Gauchet, M. 128
Gibson-Graham, J. K. 212–13
Giddens, A. 127
Glynos, J. 192
Goodin, R. 116

Habermas, J. 124, 142
Hall, S. 157, 161
Hardt, M. and Negri, A. 11
   capitalism 209–10
   multitude 159, 161, 210, 225
Hart, W. 79
Heidegger, M. 8, 19
Hegel, G. W. F. 9, 228, 256
   Deleuze 41
   Heideggerianisation 19
hegemony 103, 223
   deconstruction 92
   logic of articulation 87
   political logic 88
   representation 106
   see also discourse; Laclau, E.; Laclau, E. and Mouffe, C.; lack
heterogeneity 112
   capitalism 212
   lack 113
   radical democracy 114
human rights 58–60, 128

Ideology 24
immanence 8, 204–5, 240, 242, 243
   immanentism 207, 229, 256
   materialism 136
   Nietzsche, F. 244–5
   political economy 209, 229
   politics of pure immanence 54
   Spinoza, B. 204, 249
   transcendence 239, 206–8, 242
   see also abundance; Deleuze, G.
Industrial Areas Foundation 145

Irigaray, L. 40–1

James, W. 11, 240–1, 242
Johnson, S. 138
   organised complexity 147n.18
Judgment 79–80, 82

Kojève, A. 8, 19, 37

Lacan, J. 5, 9, 10, 11, 37
   Deleuze, G. 17
   desire 187
   Freud, S. 20, 39
   jouissance 189, 191
   lack, 186, 195, 258
   limit of signification 5
   the Other 21
   Phallic Law 39, 43
   the real 188
   see also desire; fantasy; lack
lack 5, 17–21
   absence within presence 21
   consumerism 191
   contestable 7
   difference 2, 5
   different from abundance 2, 26, 32, 35, 113
   excess 256, 258
   failed unicity 257
   hegemony 2, 6, 157
   heterogeneity 113
   immanence 22
   ontological imaginary 2
   radical democracy 5
   Stavrakakis, Y. 5
   transcendence 8
   see also hegemony; Lacan, J.; Laclau, E.; negativity; transcendence
Laclau, E. 9–10
   abundance and lack 12, 89, 92, 93, 99
   affect and rhetoric 95
   as bricoleur 86, 88
   critique of Žižek, S. 96, 193, 195
   decision 93
   deconstruction 88, 93
   empty signifier 104

Index

formalism 98
hegemony 86, 95, 96
Lacan, J. 89, 94
negativity 185
see also discourse; hegemony; Laclau, E. and Mouffe, C.
Laclau, E. and Mouffe, C. 8
  antagonism 107–9
  capitalism 210–11
  deconstruction 90
  hegemony 157
  impossibility of society 24
  Marxist theory 88, 90–1
  see also discourse; hegemony; Laclau, E.; Mouffe C.
Latour, B. 10, 133, 137
  actant 134
  cosmos 142
  democratic action 143
  in parliament with things 144
  see also Amazonia; Bennett, J.
Lefort, C.
  democratic revolution 189
  empty place of power 11, 25
the Left
  Deleuze, G. 57
  nostalgia 193
  radical right 168
  see also radical democracy
Levinas, E. 231
liberalism 4, 124, 129, 260
  radical democracy 4

Marchart, O. 8
Marrati, P. 61
Marx, K. 2, 11, 209, 219
  capitalism 220–1, 223
  coalition 229
  'disco-Marxism' 222
  Hegel, G. F. W. 224, 227
  Lumpenproletariat 113
  ontology 224
  popular sovereignty 228
  see also capitalism; Marx, K. and Engel, F.; radical democracy

Marx, K. and Engel, F.
  Communist Manifesto 220, 222
  the liberal state 2
  see also Marx, K.
materialism 136
media 154
  Foucault, M. 162–3
  television 158
  see also cultural studies
Mengue, P. 52, 54–6, 58, 61
Merleau-Ponty, M. 215
  abundance 76
  depth 77
McGuigan, J. 160
micropolitics 45–6
  Deleuzian concept 54, 56
  institutions 55
  see also Deleuze, G. and Guattari, F.
Mouffe, C. 8
  agonistic conception of public sphere 10
  left politics 167
  moralisation of politics 232
  see also Laclau E. and Mouffe, C.; the political
MoveOn.org 145

Nancy, J. L. 229
  critique of immanence 206–7
  transcendence 207
  see also transcendence
negativity 19, 37, 185
  affirmation 186
  cultural codes 180
  immanence 256
  irresolvability of negation 20
  Laclau E., and Mouffe, C. 31n.22
  modernity 187
  productive 21
  see also heterogeneity; lack
Nietzsche, F.
  abundance 244, 248
  critique of lack 247
  democracy 250
  Derrida, J. 245

[266]

see also immanence
Norval, A. 9–10

ontology
  democratic theory 135
  Marx, K. 224
  the ontic 18, 27
  return to 18
  unstable 28
  'weak ontology' 31n.29
orientational metaphors 169–70
  French revolution 175, 176
  political frontiers 179
  see also discourse

Panagia, D. 140
Patton, P. 9
pluralisation 4
  see also Connolly, W. E.
the political 3, 92, 126
  democracy 167
  ethics 230
  friend/enemy 129
  morality 124
  naming 224
  negativity 187
  orientational metaphors 169
  right/left 177
  Žižek, S. 190
  see also difference; Mouffe, C.; radical democracy
poststructuralism 12n.1, 158
public sphere 180

radical democracy
  agential capacities 134
  agonistic pluralism 126
  citizenship 130
  classical democratic theory 1
  communitarianism 4
  community 203–4
  deep pluralism 250–1
  difference 2, 3, 152
  liberalism 4, 151
  liberty and equality 168
  Marx, K. (and Marxism) 2, 3, 150

negativity 192
New Left 149–50
non-human members 143
the people 152
political economy 213–14, 251–2
populism 259, 260
poststructuralism 2
socialism 151
strategy 180
'to-come' 3
see also democracy; difference
Rancière, J. 73, 231
  democracy 139
  demos 140
  Habermas, J. 142
  'post-democracy' 190
Rawls, J. 125
  functions of political philosophy 51
  political economy 218n.37
  reflexive equilibrium 80
representation 106
  heterogeneity 111
rhizomatic politics 54, 206
  see also Deleuze, G. and Guattari, F.
right-wing populism 124
  the Left 174
  orientational metaphors 172
  Western European politics 171
Rorty, R. 125
Rousseau, J. J. 203

Sartre, J. P. 20
Smith, D. 239–40, 242
Stallybrass, P. 113
state 225–6, 252
Staten, H. 101n.36, 110
Stavrakakis, Y. 11
Simons, J. 10
social movements 80
Spinoza, B.
  death 248–9
  philosophy of immanence 204–5
  see also immanence
subjectivity 20, 94
  'big bang' 76
  Deleuze, G. 44

generative powers 78
Lacan, J. 38
subject-as-lack 25, 70
see also Lacan, J.

Thoburn, N. 52
Thomassen, L. 10
Tønder, L. 11
transcendence 207–8, 239, 242
Deleuze, G. 58, 216n.16
James, W. 240
Lacan, J. 217n.24
lack 21
see also Derrida, J.; lack; Nancy, J. L.

utopia 188

Warren, M. 135–6
White, S. K. 31n.29
'weak ontology' 225

Widder, N. 9
lack 12n.3
Laclau, E. 112

Žižek, S. 8, 9, 11, 96, 99, 150, 233
act 75
antagonism 108
Badiou, A. 74
Butler, J. 70
capitalism 74
Christianity 72–3
fantasy 189
Kant, I. 70
Lacanian theory of politics 23
Laclau, E. and Mouffe, C. 25
radical democracy 194
theorist of lack 71
see also Lacan, J.; lack